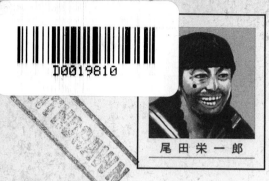

尾田栄一郎

Buzzzzz!!
Three p.m. I turn off my alarm clock.
I open the curtains, make coffee, head for my desk.
I put my coffee mug in its usual place, open my idea book,
sharpen my pencils, slowly lean back...
ZZZ...
Falling back to sleep is bliss.
YAY! (Get to work!)

–Eiichiro Oda, 2002

Eiichiro Oda began his manga career at the age of 17, when his one-shot cowboy manga **Wanted!** won second place in the coveted Tezuka manga awards. Oda went on to work as an assistant to some of the biggest manga artists in the industry, including Nobuhiro Watsuki, before winning the Hop Step Award for new artists. His pirate adventure **One Piece**, which debuted in **Weekly Shonen Jump** in 1997, quickly became one of the most popular manga in Japan.

ONE PIECE VOL. 26
SKYPIEA PART 3

SHONEN JUMP Manga Edition

STORY AND ART BY EIICHIRO ODA

English Adaptation/Lance Caselman
Translation/JN Productions
Touch-up Art & Lettering/Elena Diaz
Design/Fawn Lau
Supervising Editor/Yuki Murashige
Editor/Alexis Kirsch

ONE PIECE © 1997 by Eiichiro Oda. All rights reserved.
First published in Japan in 1997 by SHUEISHA Inc., Tokyo.
English translation rights arranged by SHUEISHA Inc.

The rights of the author(s) of the work(s) in this publication to be
so identified have been asserted in accordance with the Copyright,
Designs and Patents Act 1988. A CIP catalogue record for this book is
available from the British Library.

Printed in the U.S.A.

Published by VIZ Media, LLC
P.O. Box 77010
San Francisco, CA 94107

10 9 8 7 6 5 4 3
First printing, January 2010
Third printing, June 2011

www.viz.com

THE WORLD'S
MOST POPULAR MANGA
www.shonenjump.com

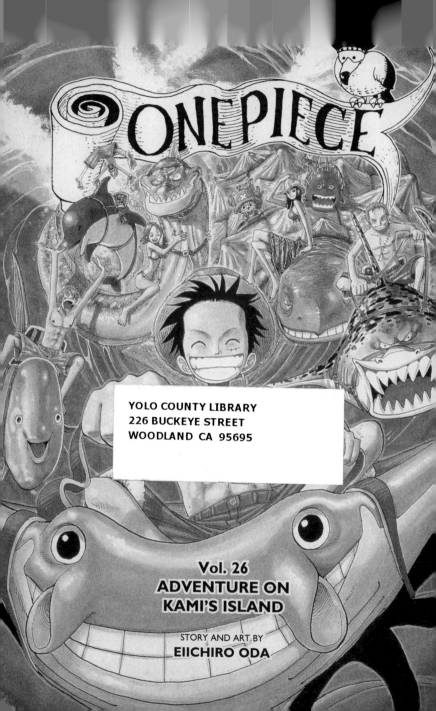

ONE PIECE

Vol. 26
ADVENTURE ON
KAMI'S ISLAND

STORY AND ART BY
EIICHIRO ODA

Boundlessly optimistic and able to stretch like rubber, he is determined to become King of the Pirates.

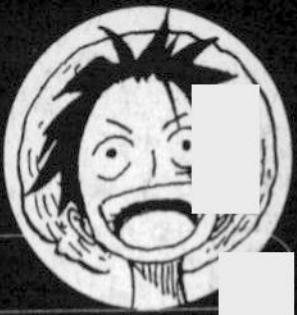

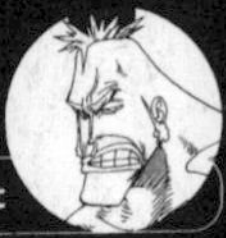

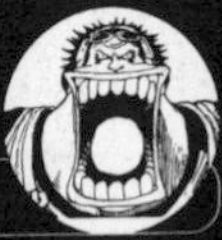

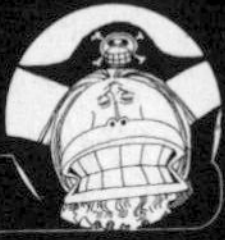

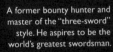

Monkey D. Luffy

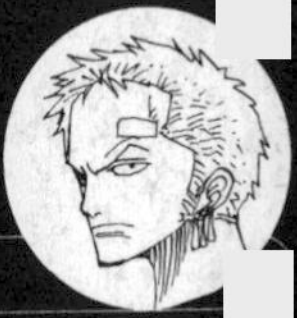

A former bounty hunter and master of the "three-sword" style. He aspires to be the world's greatest swordsman.

Roronoa Zolo

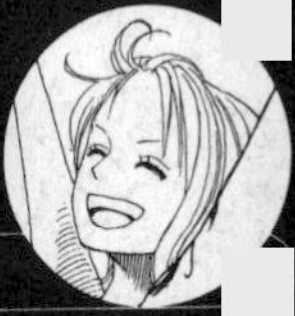

A thief who specializes in robbing pirates. Nami hates pirates, but Luffy convinced her to be his navigator.

Nami

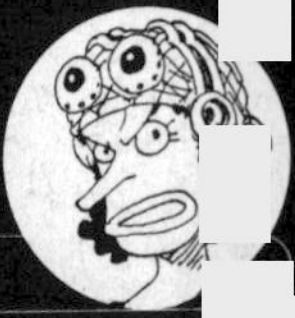

A village boy with a talent for telling tall tales. His father, Yasopp, is a member of Shanks's crew.

Usopp

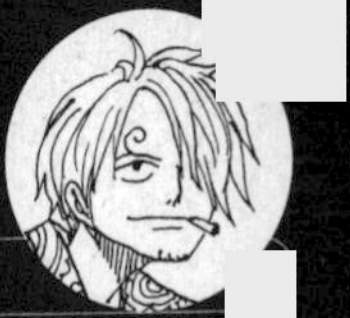

The big-hearted cook (and ladies' man) whose dream is to find the legendary sea, the "All Blue."

Sanji

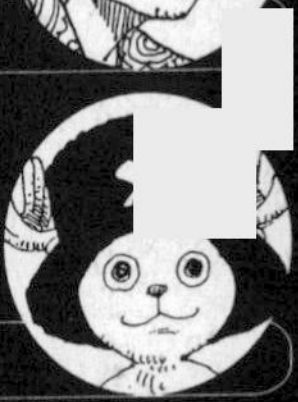

A blue-nosed man-reindeer and the ship's doctor.

Tony Tony Chopper

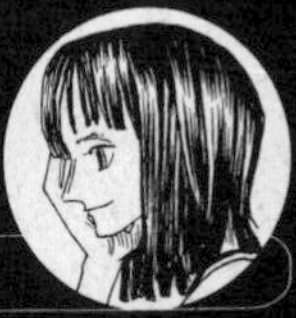

A mysterious woman in search of the Poneglyff on which true history is recorded.

Nico Robin

The Monkey Mountain Allied Force

Pirates who helped Luffy and his crew get to Sky Island.

Mont Blanc Cricket

Masira

Shoujou

THE STORY OF ONE PIECE

Volume 26

Monkey D. Luffy started out as just a kid with a dream—to become the greatest pirate in history! Stirred by the tales of pirate "Red-Haired" Shanks, Luffy vowed to become a pirate himself. That was before the enchanted Devil Fruit gave Luffy the power to stretch like rubber, at the cost of being unable to swim—a serious handicap for an aspiring sea dog. Undeterred, Luffy set out to sea and recruited some crewmates—master swordsman Zolo; treasure-hunting thief Nami; lying sharpshooter Usopp; the high-kicking chef Sanji; Chopper, the walkin' talkin' reindeer doctor; and the mysterious archaeologist Robin.

Having defeated Sir Crocodile and restored peace to the Kingdom of Alabasta, Luffy and crew bid Princess Vivi a tearful farewell and set sail once more upon the Grand Line. When the Log Pose suddenly points straight up, Nico Robin relates the legend of an island in the sky and Luffy becomes determined to go there. They sail to Jaya and seek out a dreamer named Mont Blanc Cricket, who tells them of a mysterious ocean current that can carry a ship up to the sky. With the help of the Monkey Mountain Allied Force, they make preparations. But when Cricket's gold is stolen, Luffy goes to get it back, and in the process settles the score with Bellamy the Hyena.

Running late, the Straw Hat pirates set sail for the Knock Up Stream. But Marshall Teech, the leader of the Blackbeard Pirates who wants to become one of the Seven Warlords of the Sea, is waiting for them. Just as Teech issues his challenge, the Knock Up Stream hurls the *Merry Go* skyward. What adventures await our heroes in the mysterious land of Skypiea?!

Blackbeard Pirates

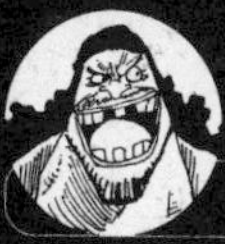

Captain

Marshall D. Teech

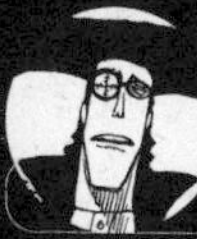

"Supersonic" – Sharpshooter

Van Ogre

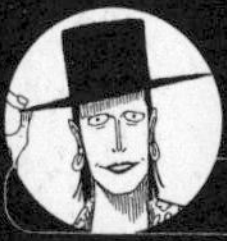

Lafitte

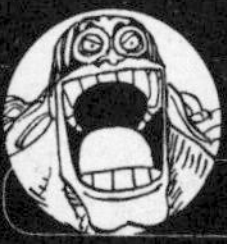

"Champ" – Helmsman

Jesus Burgess

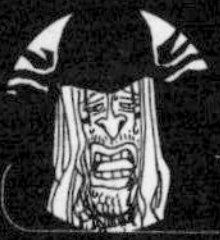

"The Grim Reaper" – Ship's Doctor

Doc Q

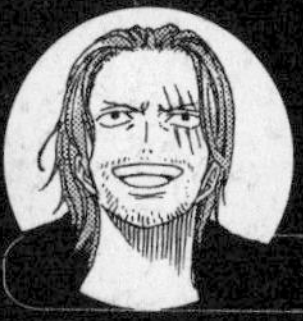

A pirate that Luffy idolizes. Shanks gave Luffy his trademark straw hat.

"Red-Haired" Shanks

Vol. 26
Adventure on Kami's Island

CONTENTS

Chapter 237:
HIGH IN THE SKY

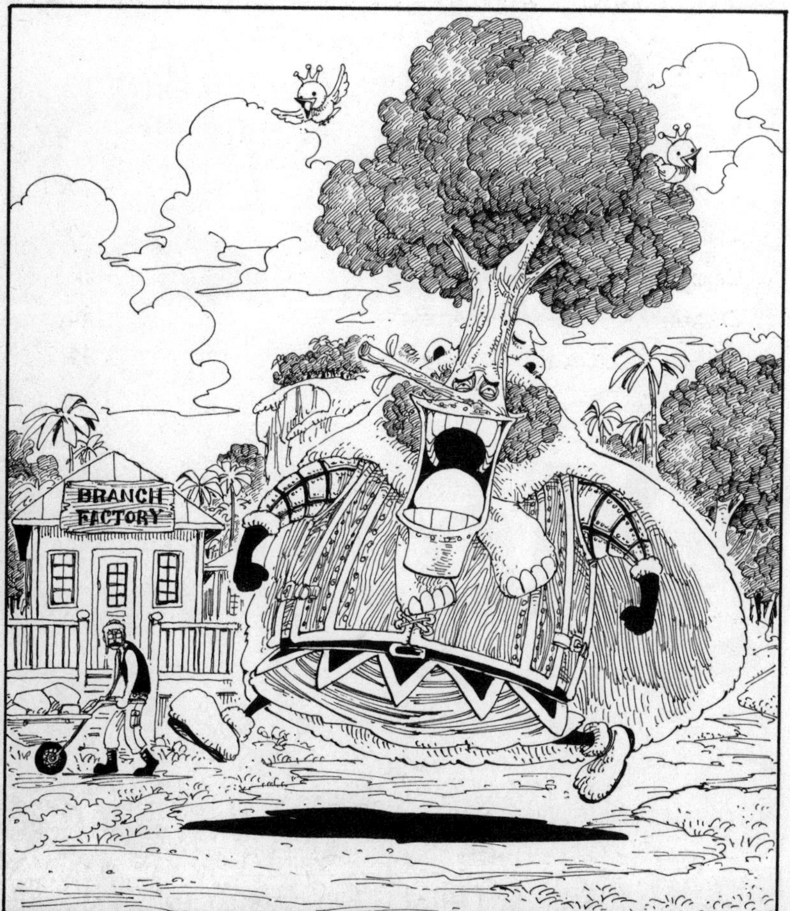

BRANCH FACTORY

WAPOL'S OMNIVOROUS RAMPAGE, VOL. 2:
"I EAT TREES"

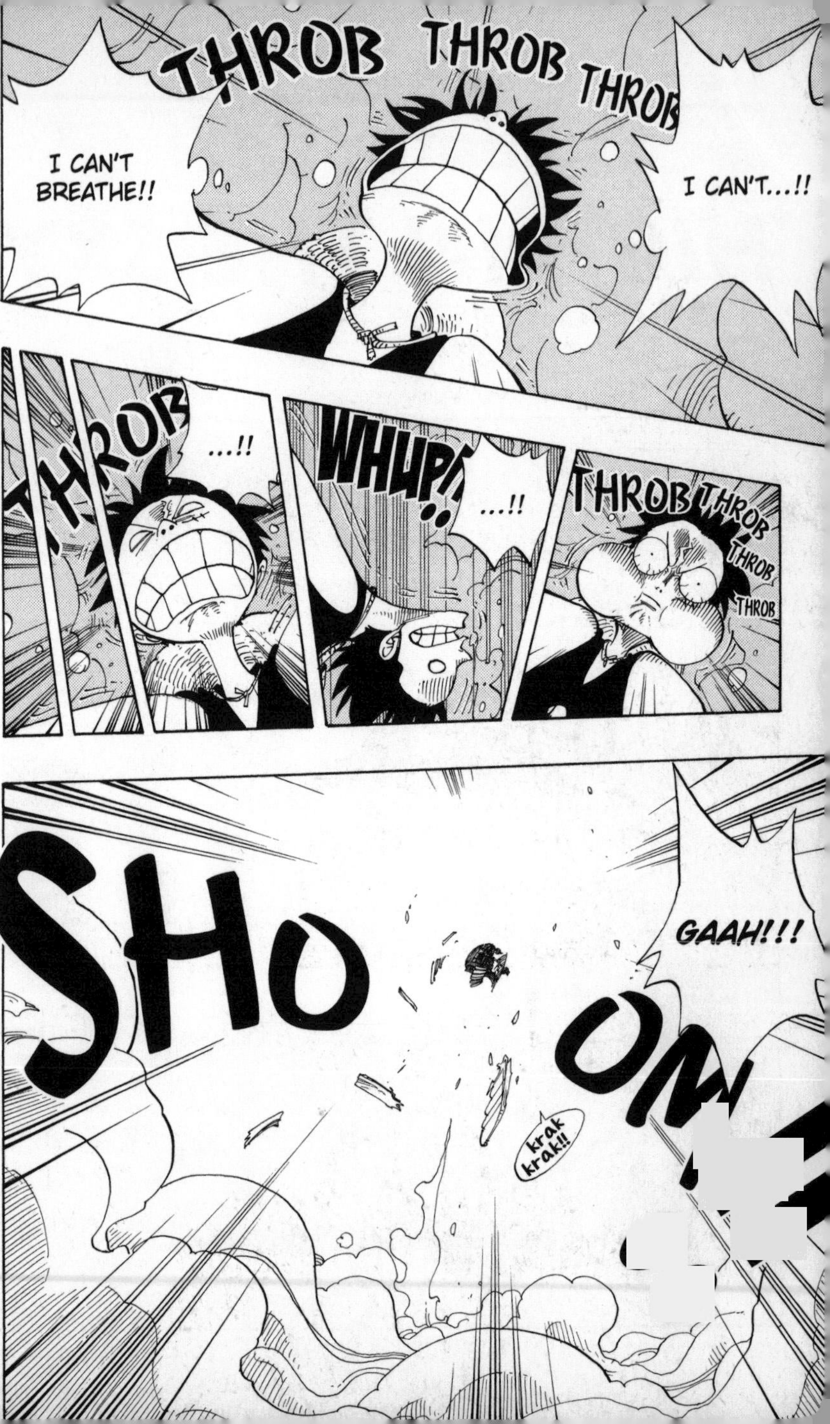
THROB THROB THROB
I CAN'T...!!
I CAN'T BREATHE!!
THROB THROB THROB THROB
...!!
WHUP!!
...!!
THROB
GAAH!!!
SHO
OM
krak krak!!

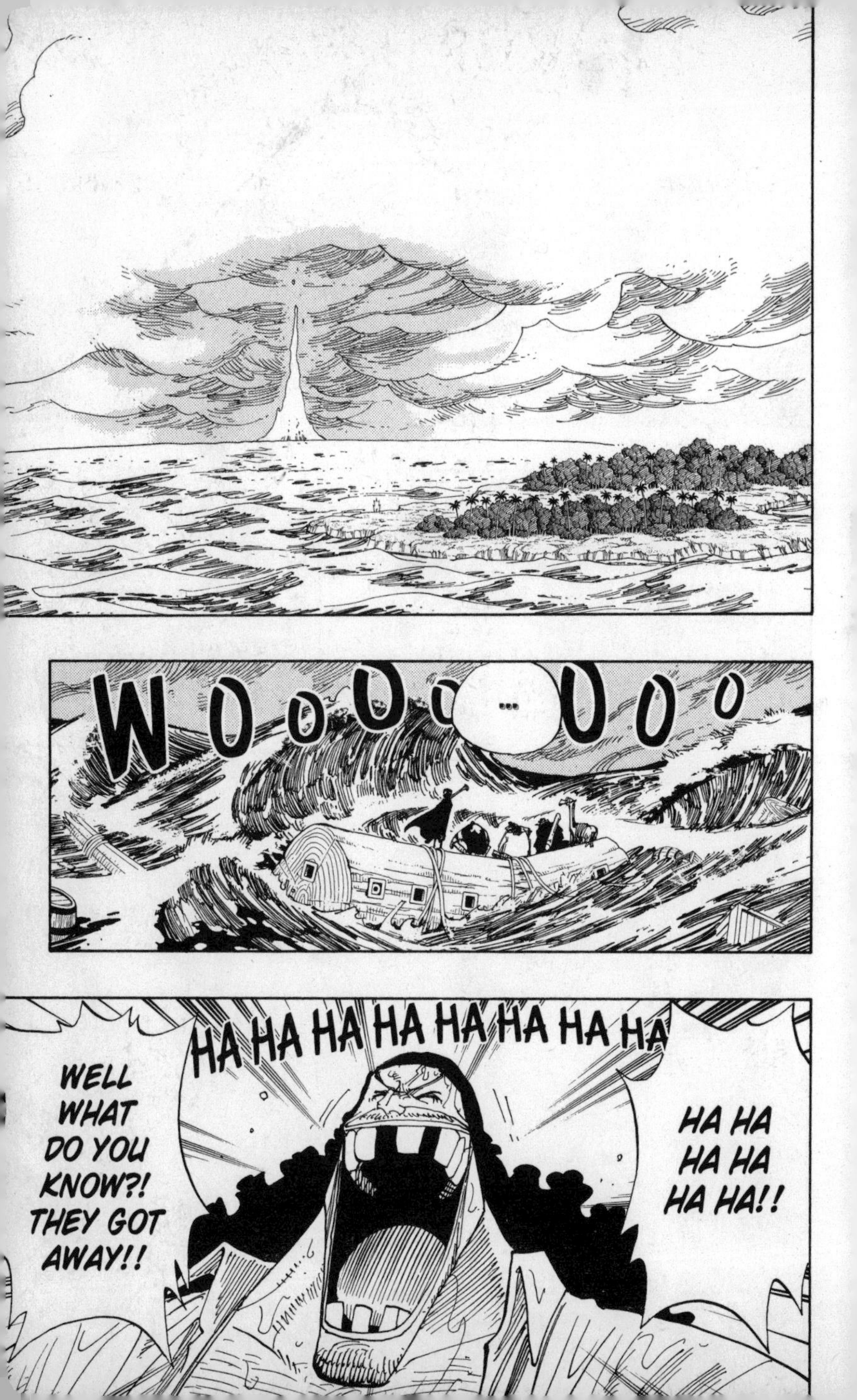
WOOOOOOOO
...
HA HA HA HA HA HA HA HA
HA HA HA HA HA HA!!
WELL WHAT DO YOU KNOW?! THEY GOT AWAY!!

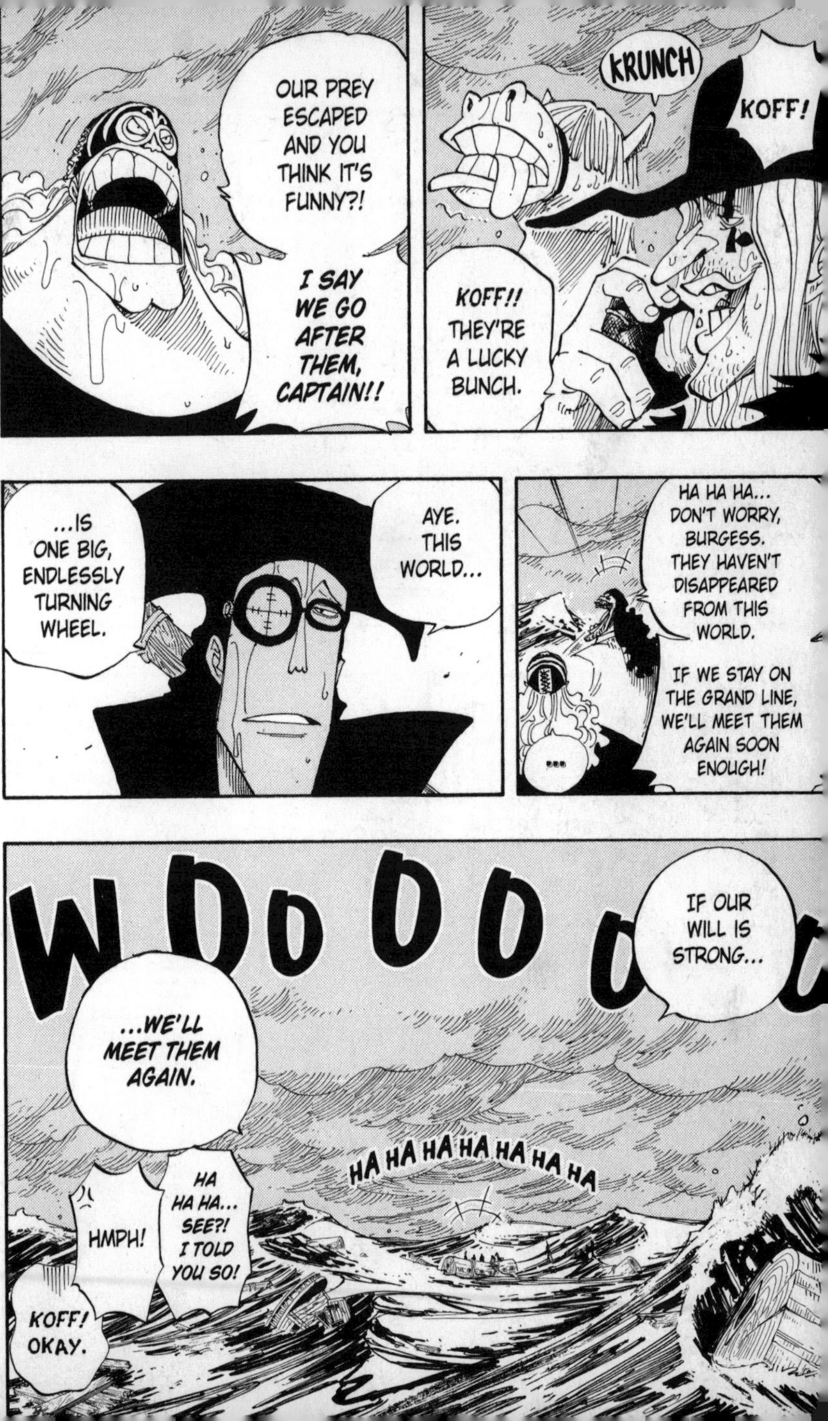
KRUNCH
KOFF!
KOFF!! THEY'RE A LUCKY BUNCH.
OUR PREY ESCAPED AND YOU THINK IT'S FUNNY?!
I SAY WE GO AFTER THEM, CAPTAIN!!
HA HA HA... DON'T WORRY, BURGESS. THEY HAVEN'T DISAPPEARED FROM THIS WORLD.
IF WE STAY ON THE GRAND LINE, WE'LL MEET THEM AGAIN SOON ENOUGH!
...
AYE. THIS WORLD...
...IS ONE BIG, ENDLESSLY TURNING WHEEL.
WOOOOOO
IF OUR WILL IS STRONG...
...WE'LL MEET THEM AGAIN.
HA HA HA HA HA HA HA HA
HA HA HA... SEE?! I TOLD YOU SO!
HMPH!
KOFF! OKAY.

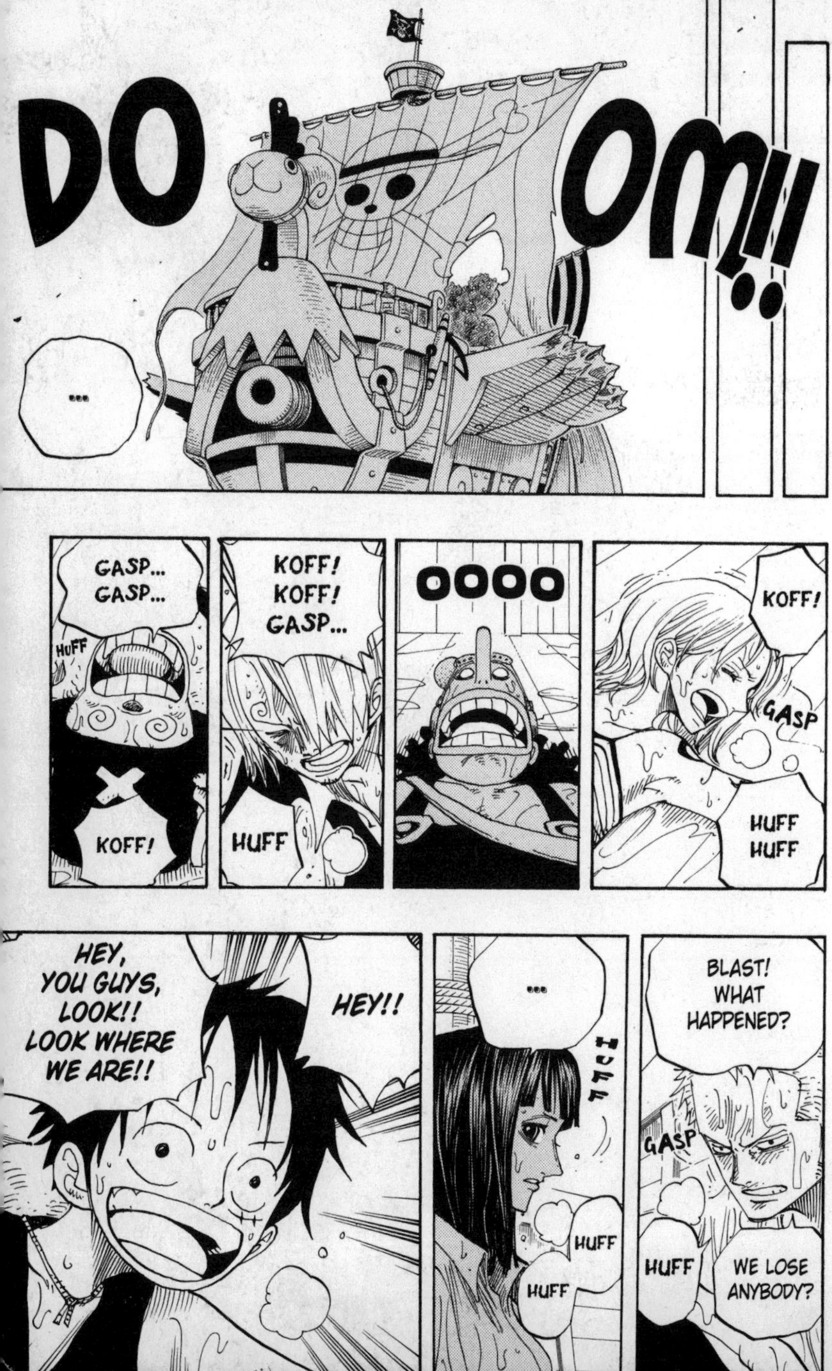
DOOOM!!
...
KOFF!
GASP
HUFF HUFF
OOOO
KOFF! KOFF! GASP...
HUFF
GASP... GASP...
HUFF
KOFF!
BLAST! WHAT HAPPENED?
GASP
WE LOSE ANYBODY?
HUFF
...
HUFF
HUFF
HUFF
HEY!!
HEY, YOU GUYS, LOOK!! LOOK WHERE WE ARE!!

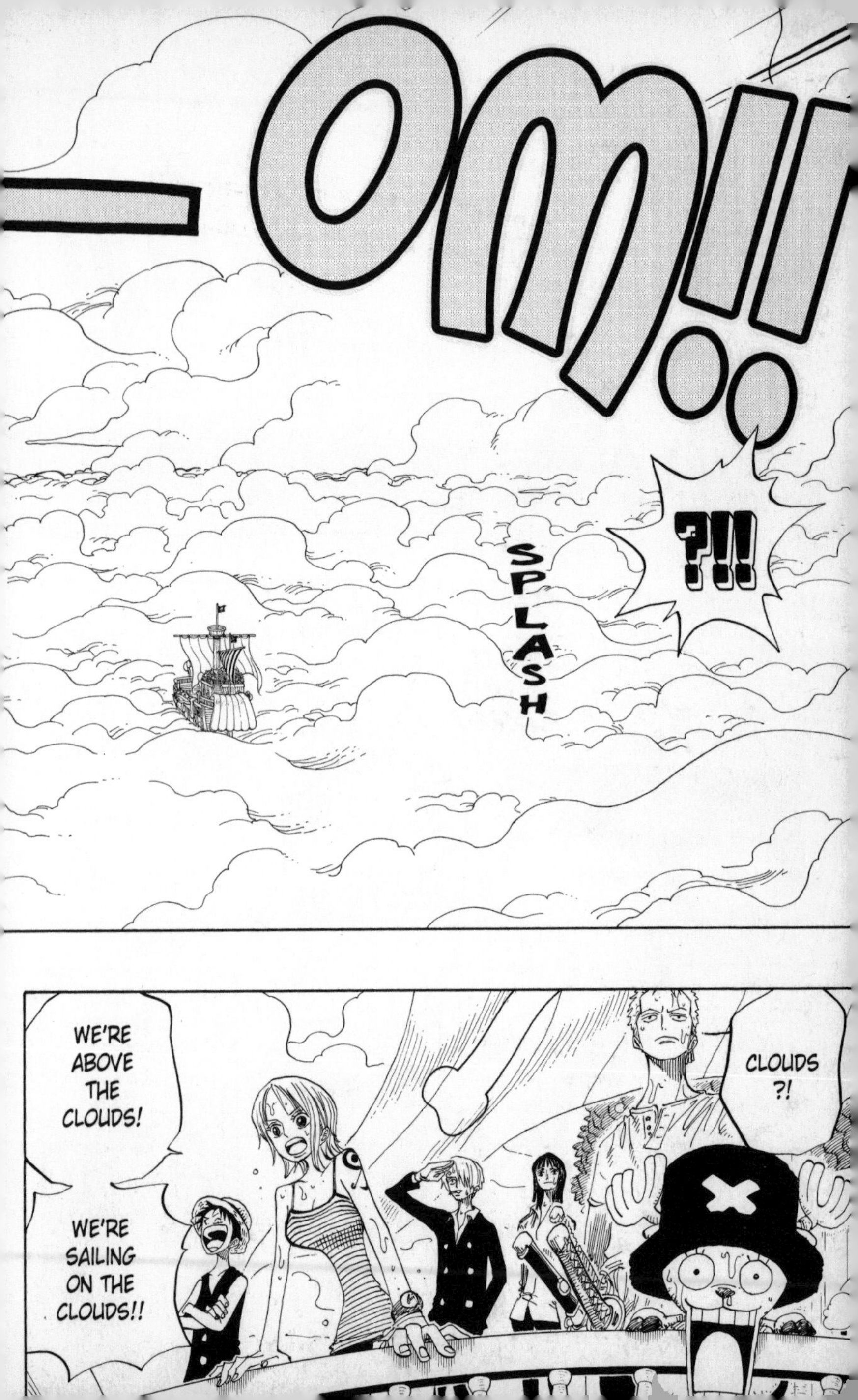
-OM!!
?!!
SPLASH
CLOUDS ?!
WE'RE ABOVE THE CLOUDS!
WE'RE SAILING ON THE CLOUDS!!

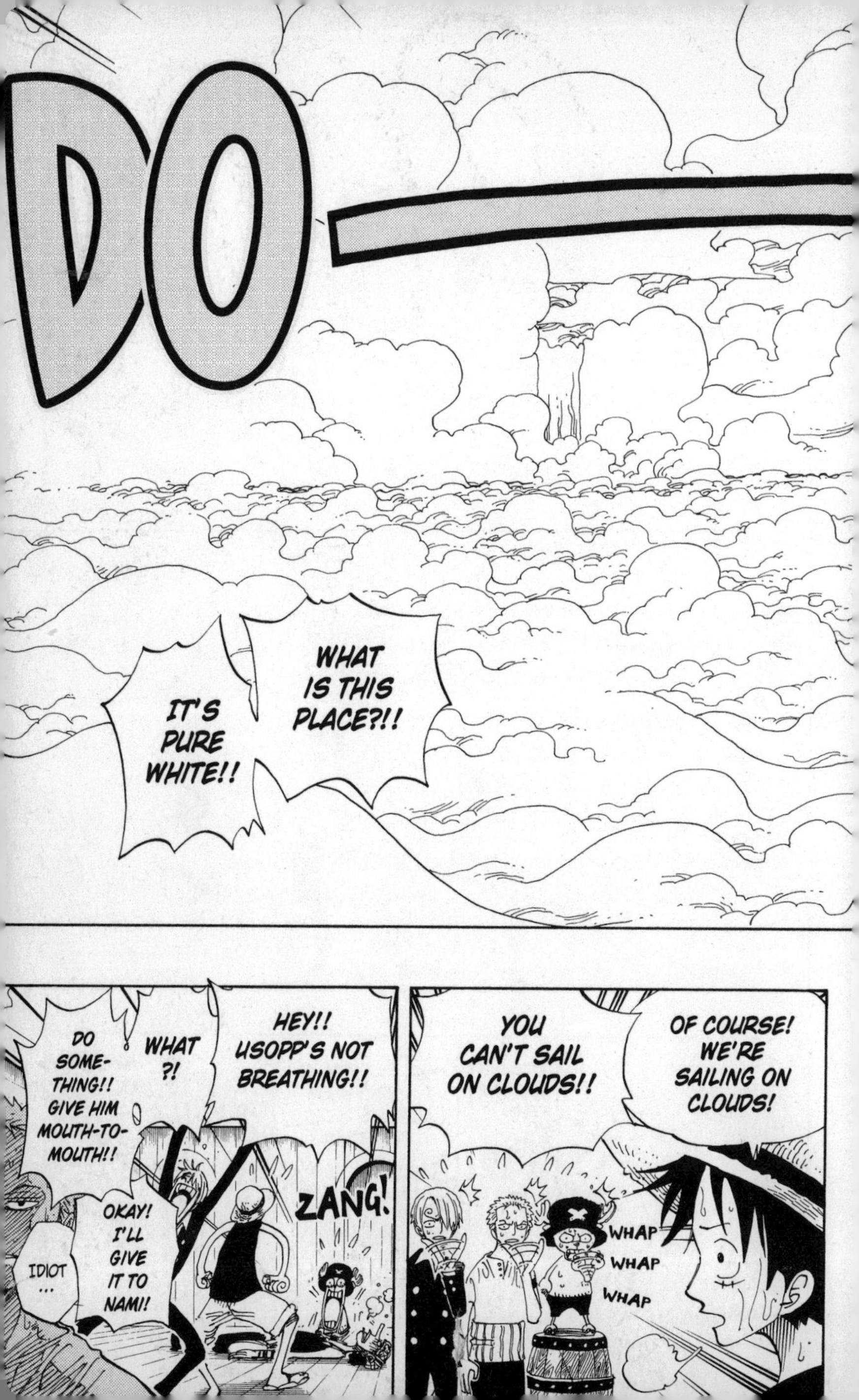
DO—
WHAT IS THIS PLACE?!!
IT'S PURE WHITE!!
OF COURSE! WE'RE SAILING ON CLOUDS!
YOU CAN'T SAIL ON CLOUDS!!
WHAP
WHAP
WHAP
HEY!! USOPP'S NOT BREATHING!!
WHAT ?!
DO SOME-THING!! GIVE HIM MOUTH-TO-MOUTH!!
ZANG!
OKAY! I'LL GIVE IT TO NAMI!
IDIOT ...

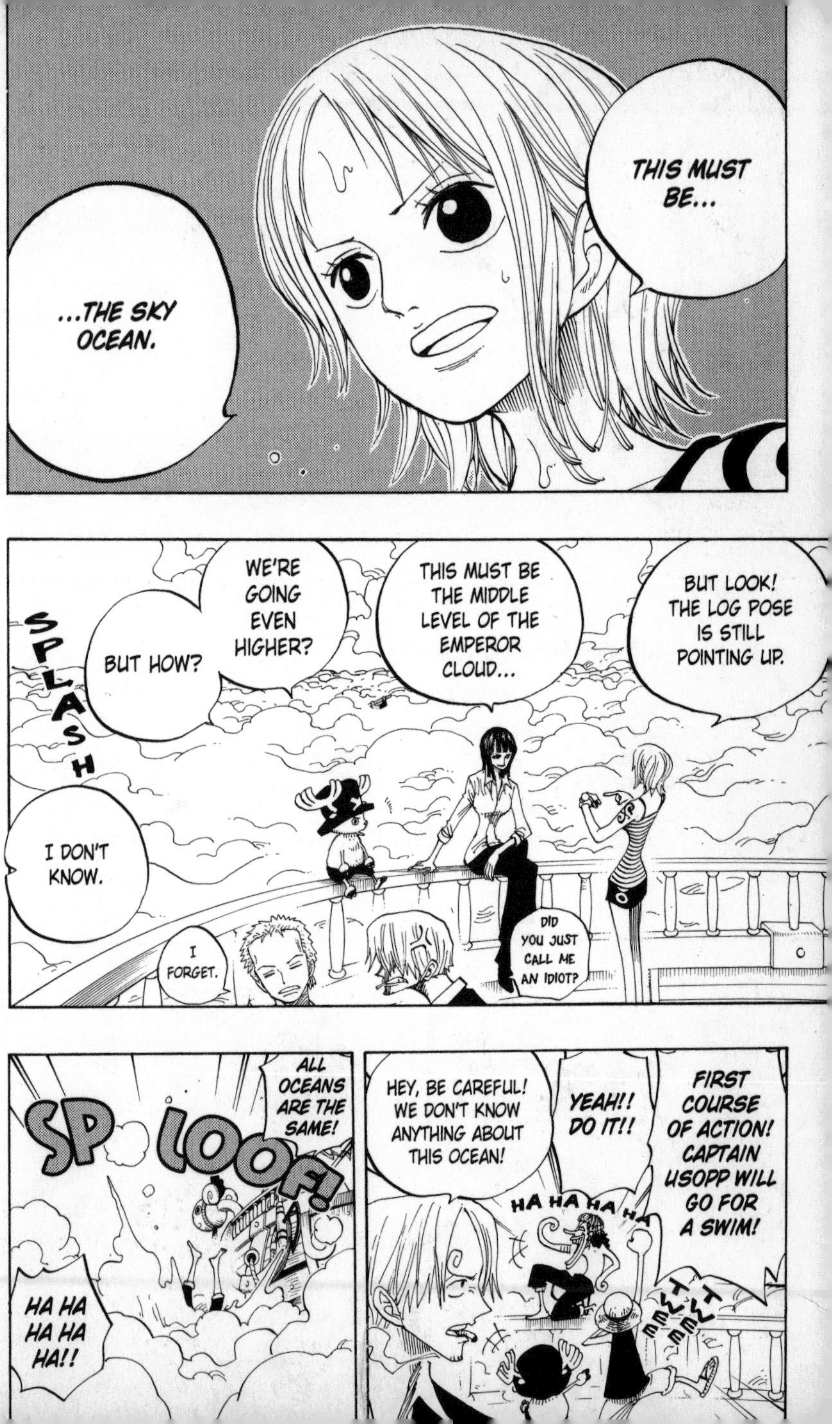
THIS MUST BE...
...THE SKY OCEAN.
BUT LOOK! THE LOG POSE IS STILL POINTING UP.
THIS MUST BE THE MIDDLE LEVEL OF THE EMPEROR CLOUD...
WE'RE GOING EVEN HIGHER?
BUT HOW?
SPLASH
I DON'T KNOW.
DID YOU JUST CALL ME AN IDIOT?
I FORGET.
FIRST COURSE OF ACTION! CAPTAIN USOPP WILL GO FOR A SWIM!
YEAH!! DO IT!!
HEY, BE CAREFUL! WE DON'T KNOW ANYTHING ABOUT THIS OCEAN!
HA HA HA HA HA
TWEET TWEET
ALL OCEANS ARE THE SAME!
SPLOOF!
HA HA HA HA HA!!

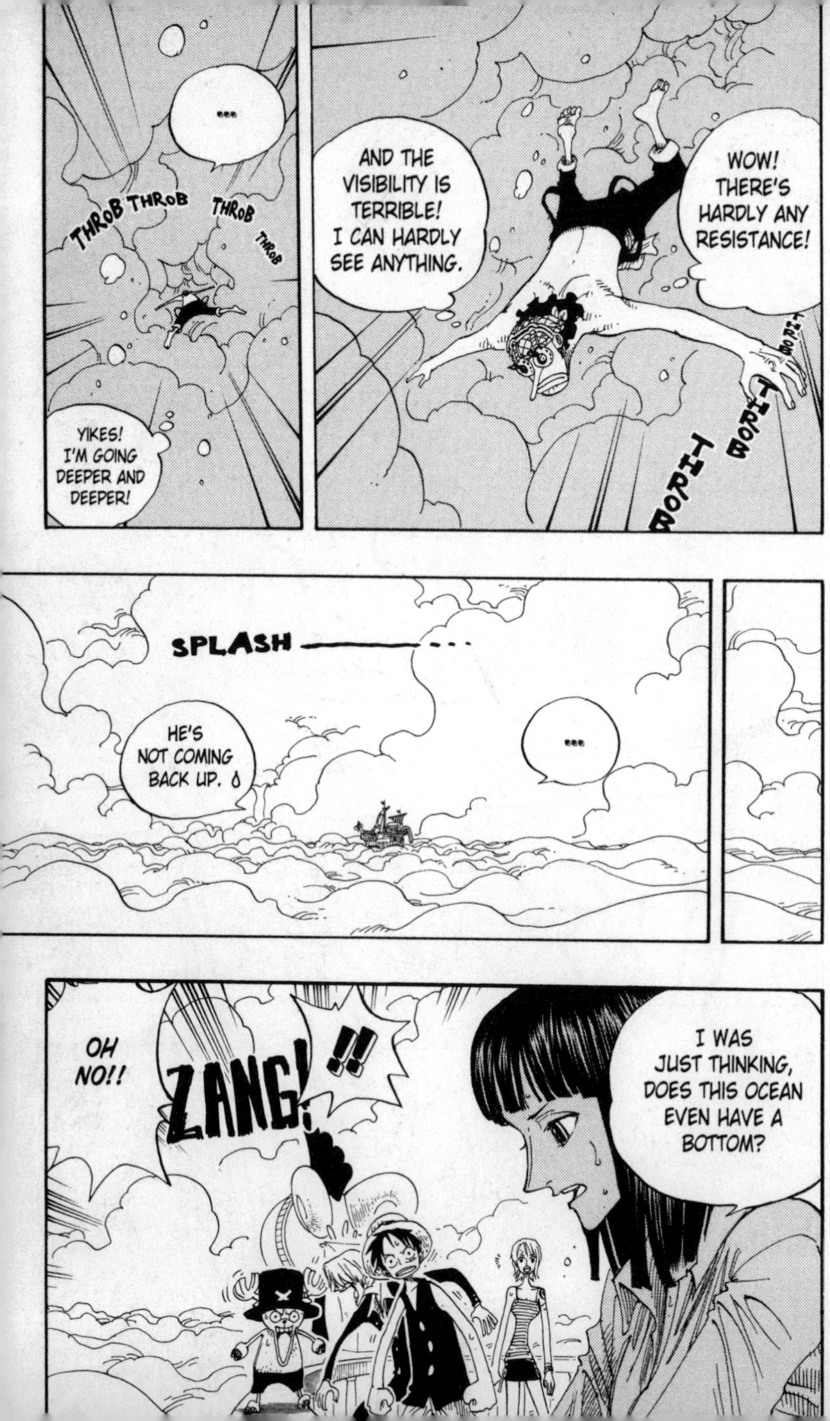
WOW! THERE'S HARDLY ANY RESISTANCE!
AND THE VISIBILITY IS TERRIBLE! I CAN HARDLY SEE ANYTHING.
THROB THROB THROB
...
THROB THROB THROB THROB
YIKES! I'M GOING DEEPER AND DEEPER!
SPLASH
...
HE'S NOT COMING BACK UP.
I WAS JUST THINKING, DOES THIS OCEAN EVEN HAVE A BOTTOM?
ZANG!!
OH NO!!

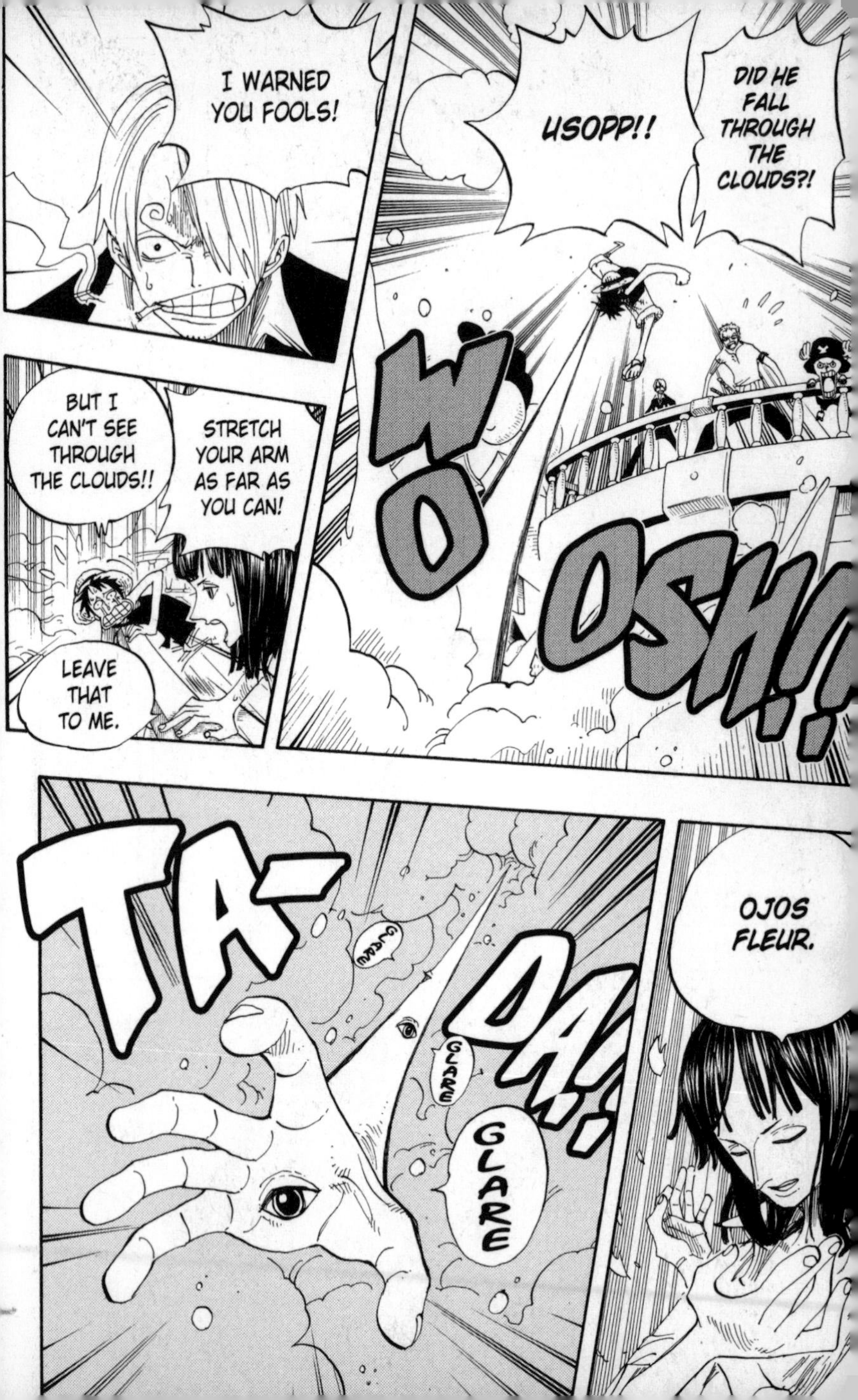
DID HE FALL THROUGH THE CLOUDS?!
USOPP!!
WOOSH!!
I WARNED YOU FOOLS!
STRETCH YOUR ARM AS FAR AS YOU CAN!
BUT I CAN'T SEE THROUGH THE CLOUDS!!
LEAVE THAT TO ME.
OJOS FLEUR.
TA-DA!!
GLARE
GLARE
GLARE

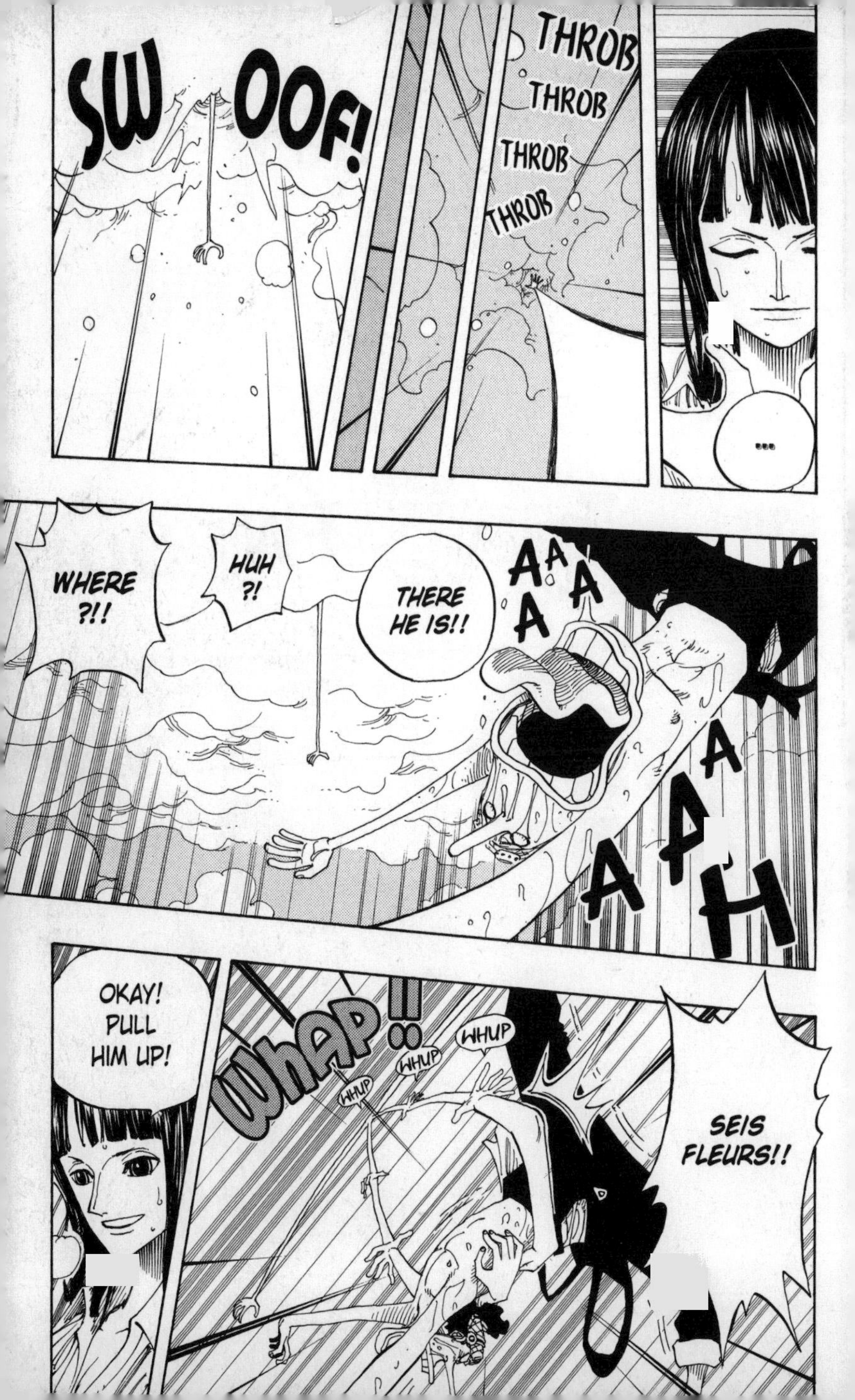
...
THROB
THROB
THROB
THROB
SWOOF!
AAAA
AAAAH
THERE HE IS!!
HUH?!
WHERE?!!
SEIS FLEURS!!
WHUP
WHUP
WHUP
WHAP!!
OKAY! PULL HIM UP!

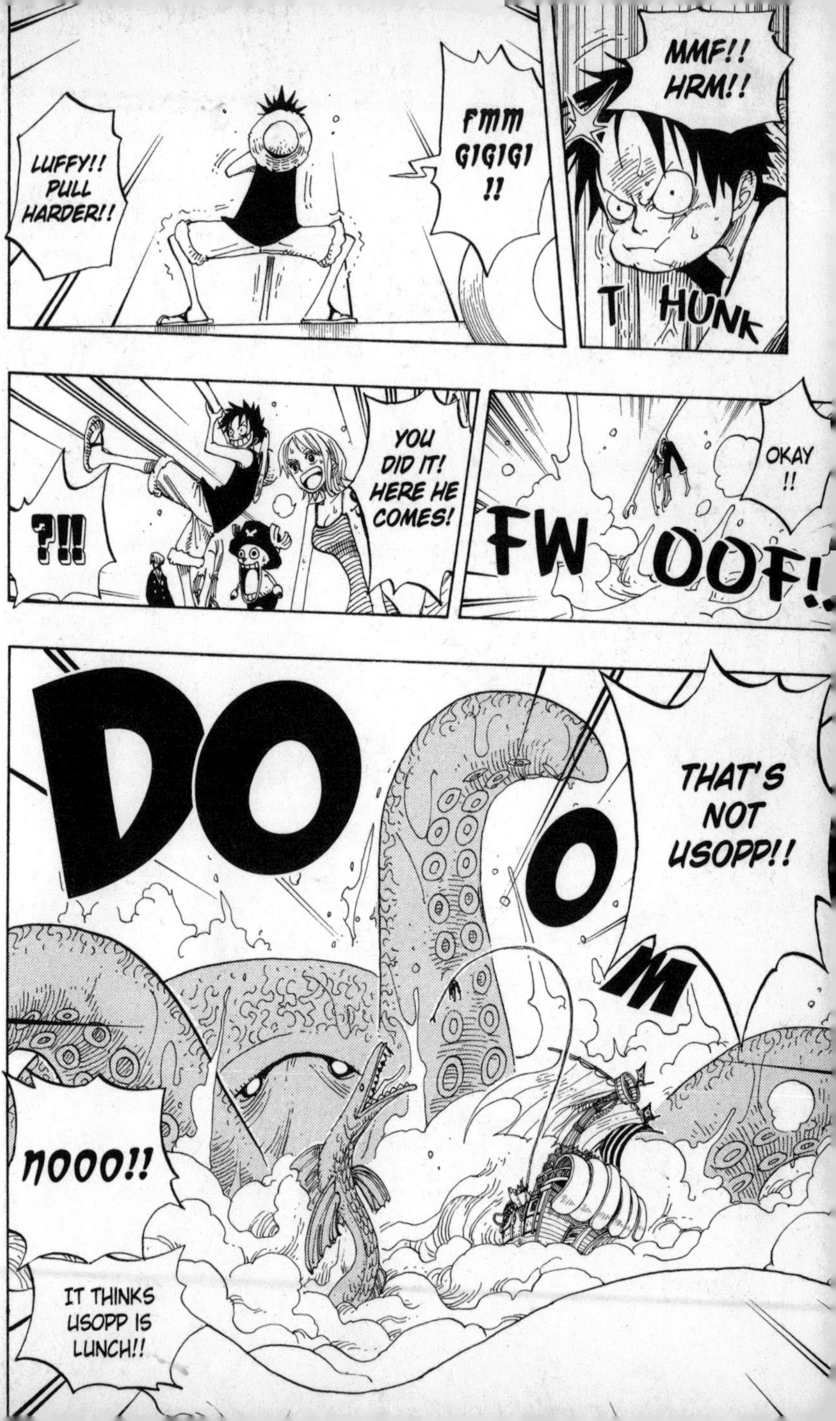
MMF!! HRM!!
THUNK
FMM GIGIGI !!
LUFFY!! PULL HARDER!!
OKAY !!
FWOOF!!
YOU DID IT! HERE HE COMES!
?!!
THAT'S NOT USOPP!!
DOOM
NOOO!!
IT THINKS USOPP IS LUNCH!!

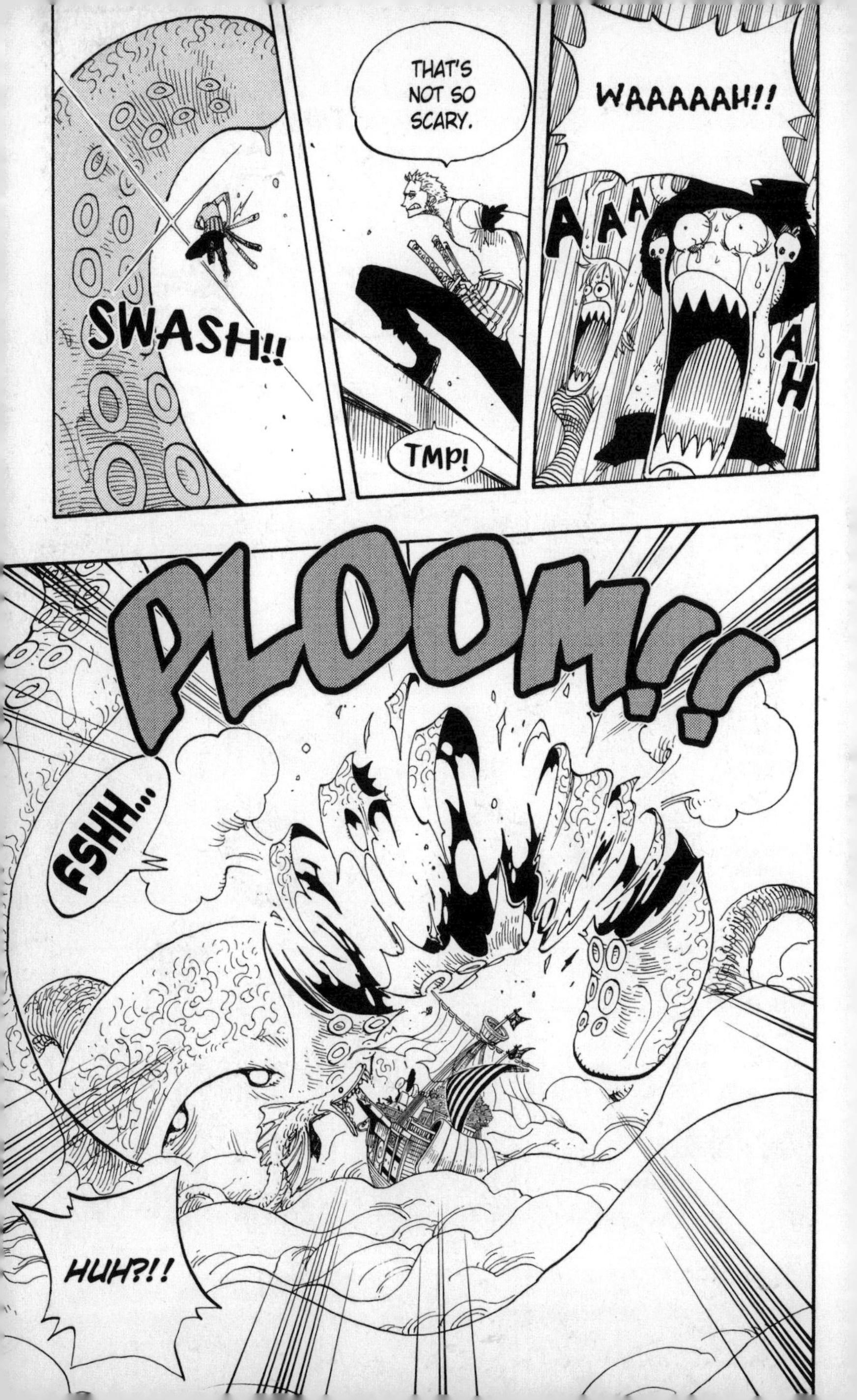
WAAAAAH!!
AAA
AH
THAT'S NOT SO SCARY.
TMP!
SWASH!!
PLOOM!!
FSHH...
HUH?!!

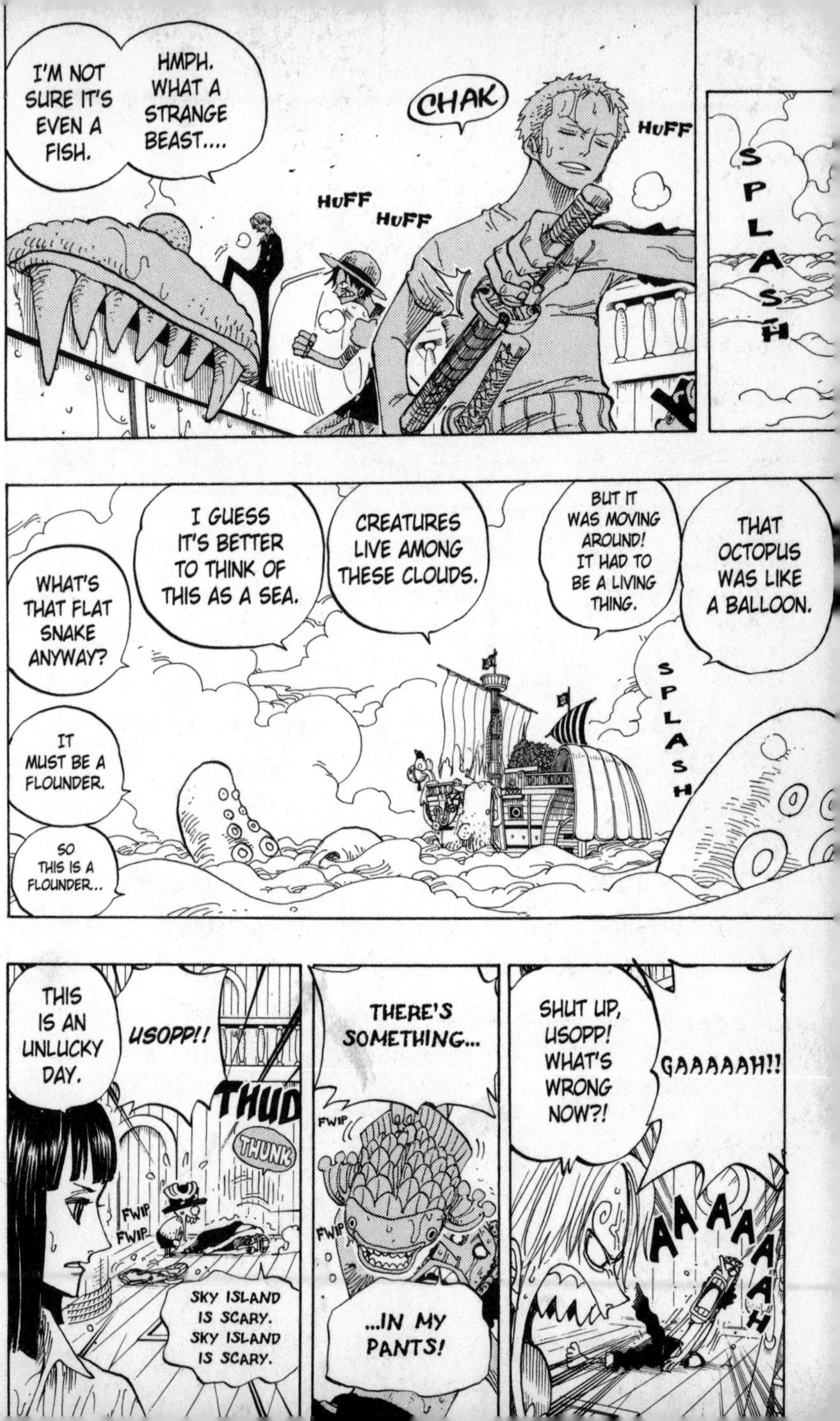
SPLASH
CHAK
HUFF
HMPH. WHAT A STRANGE BEAST....
I'M NOT SURE IT'S EVEN A FISH.
HUFF
HUFF
THAT OCTOPUS WAS LIKE A BALLOON.
BUT IT WAS MOVING AROUND! IT HAD TO BE A LIVING THING.
SPLASH
CREATURES LIVE AMONG THESE CLOUDS.
I GUESS IT'S BETTER TO THINK OF THIS AS A SEA.
WHAT'S THAT FLAT SNAKE ANYWAY?
IT MUST BE A FLOUNDER.
SO THIS IS A FLOUNDER...
SHUT UP, USOPP! WHAT'S WRONG NOW?!
GAAAAAH!!
AAAAAAH
THERE'S SOMETHING...
FWIP
FWIP
...IN MY PANTS!
USOPP!!
THIS IS AN UNLUCKY DAY.
THUD
THUNK
FWIP
FWIP
SKY ISLAND IS SCARY. SKY ISLAND IS SCARY.

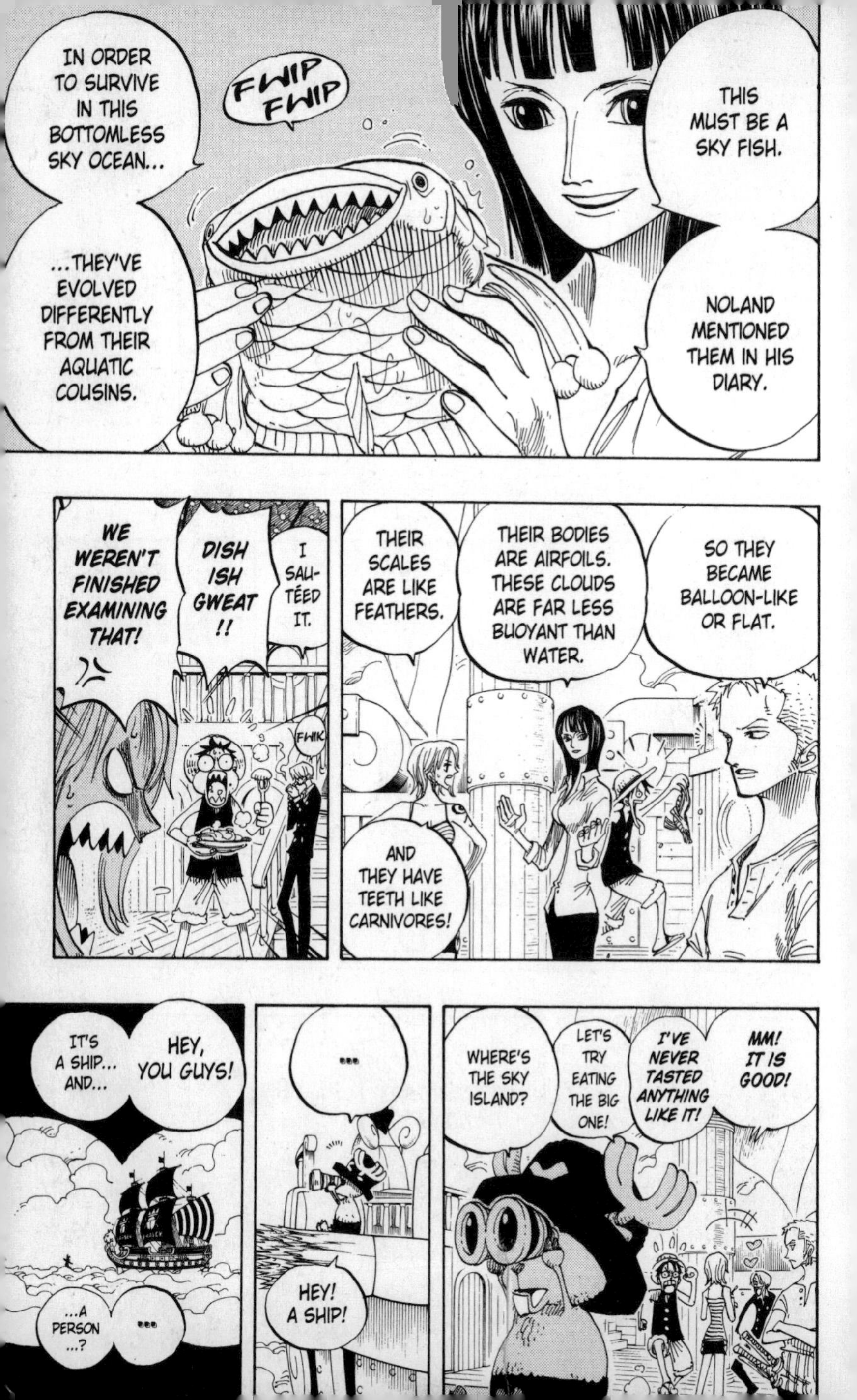
THIS MUST BE A SKY FISH.
NOLAND MENTIONED THEM IN HIS DIARY.
FWIP FWIP
IN ORDER TO SURVIVE IN THIS BOTTOMLESS SKY OCEAN...
...THEY'VE EVOLVED DIFFERENTLY FROM THEIR AQUATIC COUSINS.
SO THEY BECAME BALLOON-LIKE OR FLAT.
THEIR BODIES ARE AIRFOILS. THESE CLOUDS ARE FAR LESS BUOYANT THAN WATER.
THEIR SCALES ARE LIKE FEATHERS.
AND THEY HAVE TEETH LIKE CARNIVORES!
I SAUTÉED IT.
DISH ISH GWEAT!!
FWIK
WE WEREN'T FINISHED EXAMINING THAT!
MM! IT IS GOOD!
I'VE NEVER TASTED ANYTHING LIKE IT!
LET'S TRY EATING THE BIG ONE!
WHERE'S THE SKY ISLAND?
...
HEY! A SHIP!
HEY, YOU GUYS!
IT'S A SHIP... AND...
...
...A PERSON ...?

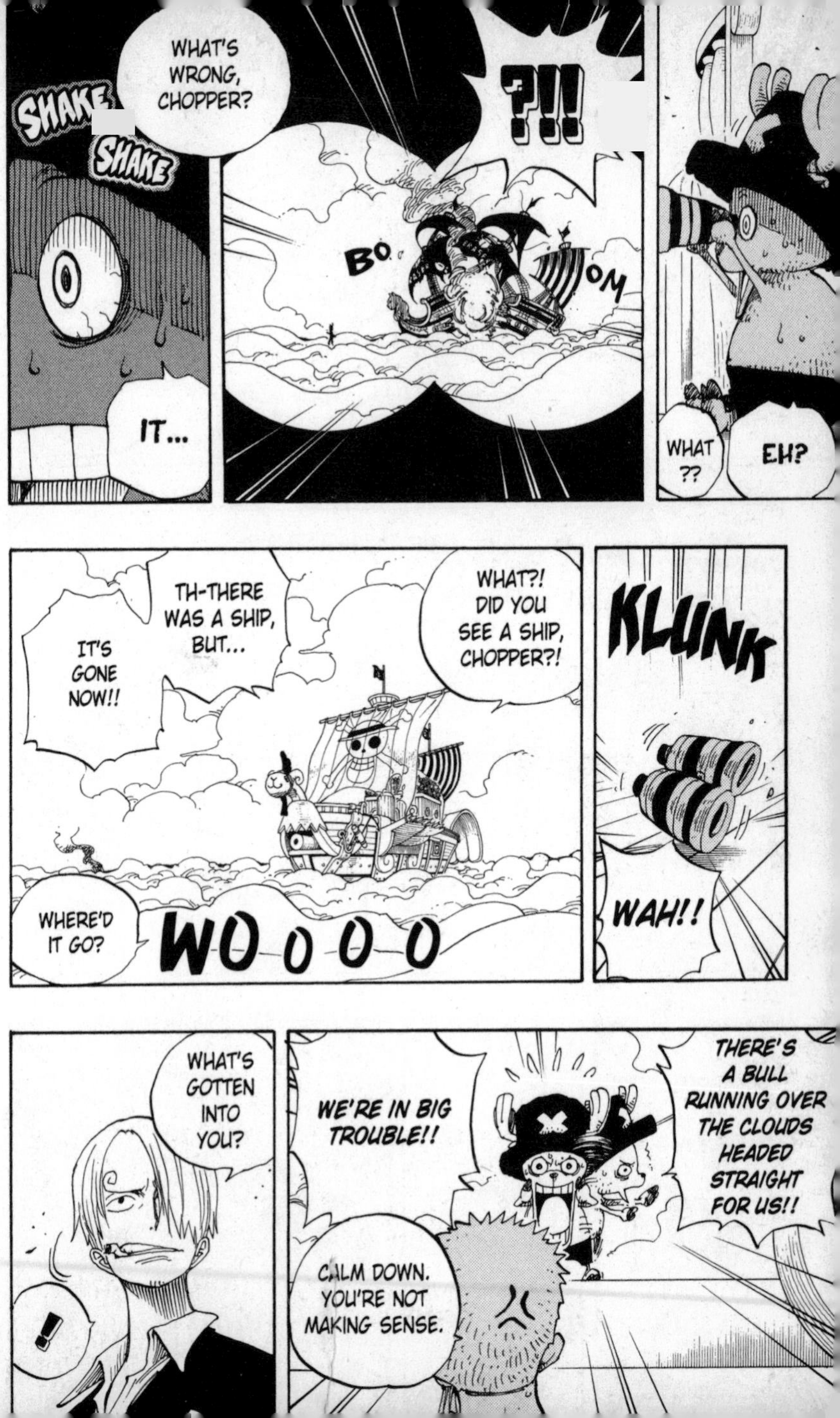
EH?
WHAT ??
?!!
BO
OM
WHAT'S WRONG, CHOPPER?
SHAKE
SHAKE
IT...
KLUNK
WAH!!
WHAT?! DID YOU SEE A SHIP, CHOPPER?!
TH-THERE WAS A SHIP, BUT...
IT'S GONE NOW!!
WHERE'D IT GO?
WOOOO
THERE'S A BULL RUNNING OVER THE CLOUDS HEADED STRAIGHT FOR US!!
WE'RE IN BIG TROUBLE!!
CALM DOWN. YOU'RE NOT MAKING SENSE.
WHAT'S GOTTEN INTO YOU?
!

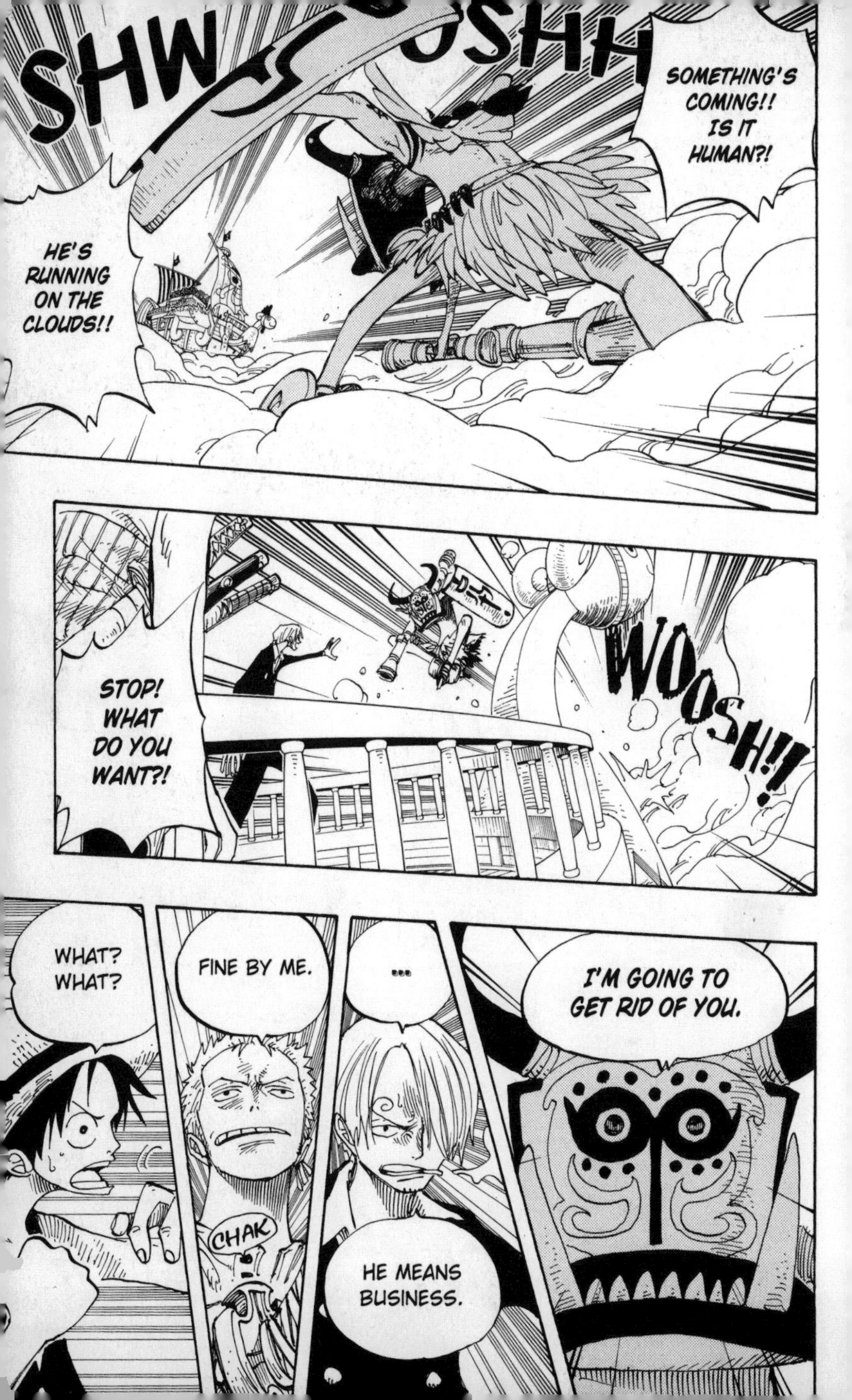
SOMETHING'S COMING!! IS IT HUMAN?!
SHW OSHH
HE'S RUNNING ON THE CLOUDS!!
WOOSH!!
STOP! WHAT DO YOU WANT?!
I'M GOING TO GET RID OF YOU.
...
HE MEANS BUSINESS.
FINE BY ME.
CHAK
WHAT? WHAT?

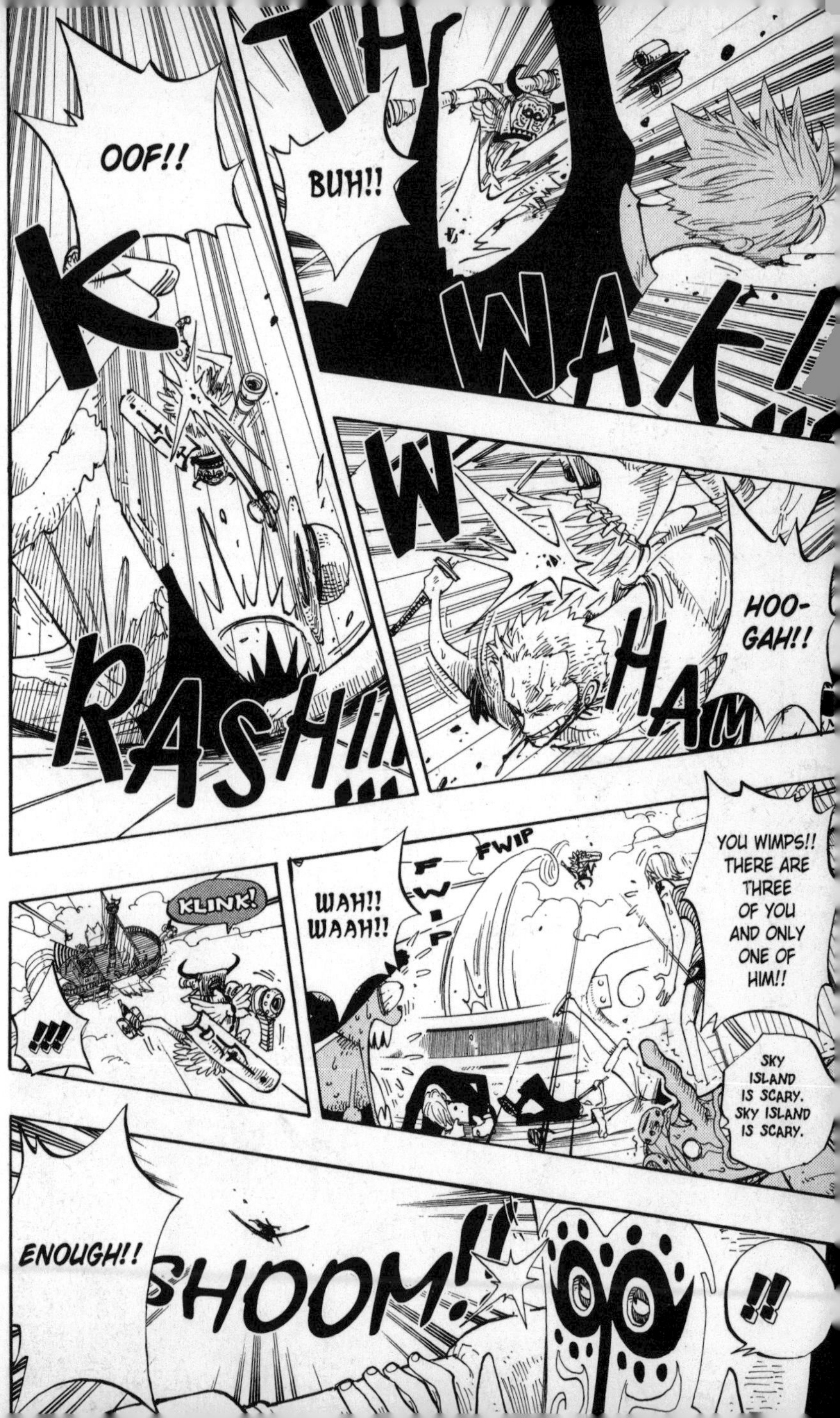
BUH!!
THWAK!!
HOO-GAH!!
WHAM
OOF!!
KRASH!!!
YOU WIMPS!! THERE ARE THREE OF YOU AND ONLY ONE OF HIM!!
FWIP
F-W-I-P
WAH!! WAAH!!
SKY ISLAND IS SCARY. SKY ISLAND IS SCARY.
KLINK!
!!!
!!
SHOOM!!
ENOUGH!!

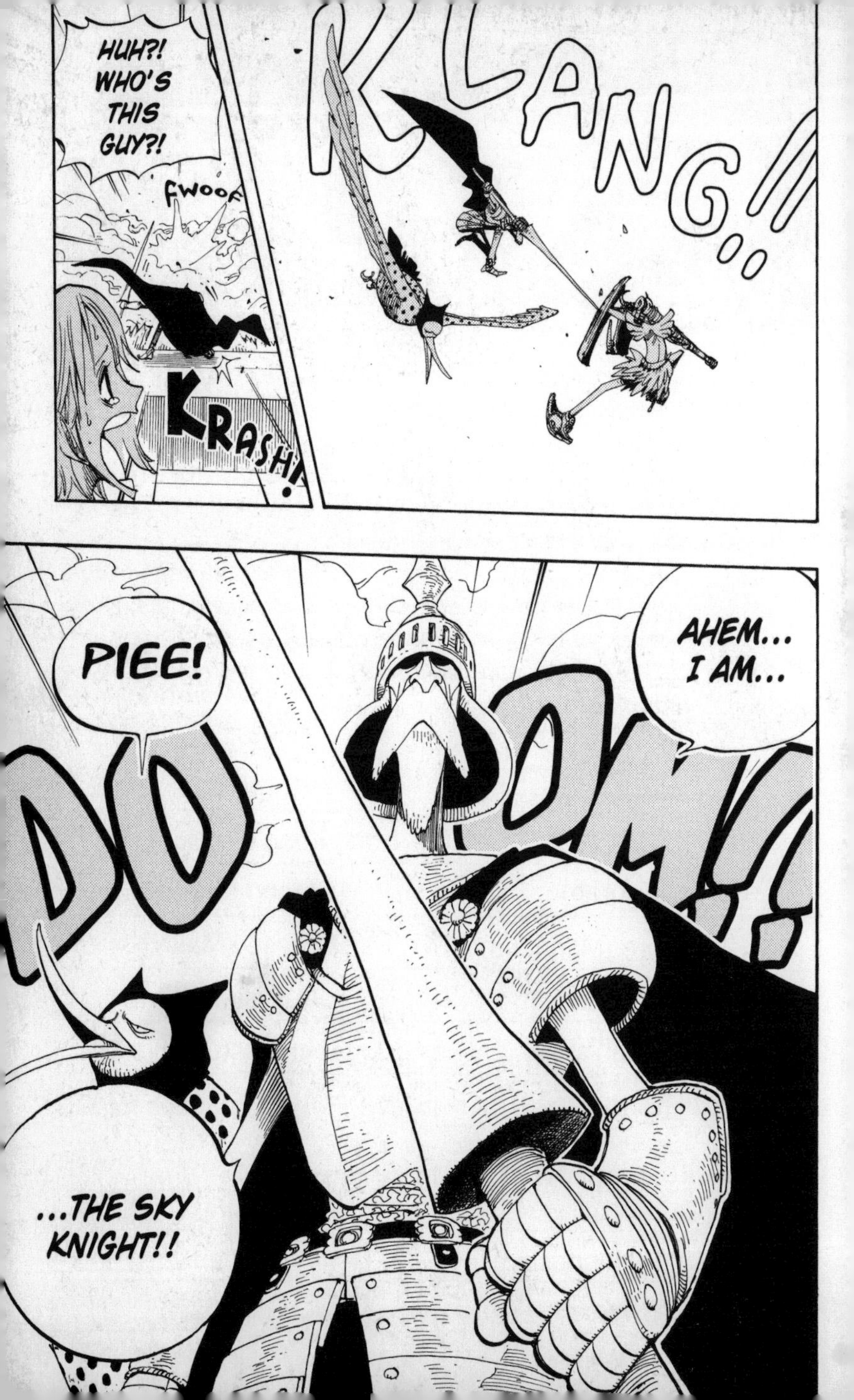
KLANG!!
HUH?! WHO'S THIS GUY?!
FWOOF
KRASH!
AHEM... I AM...
DOOM
PIEE!
...THE SKY KNIGHT!!

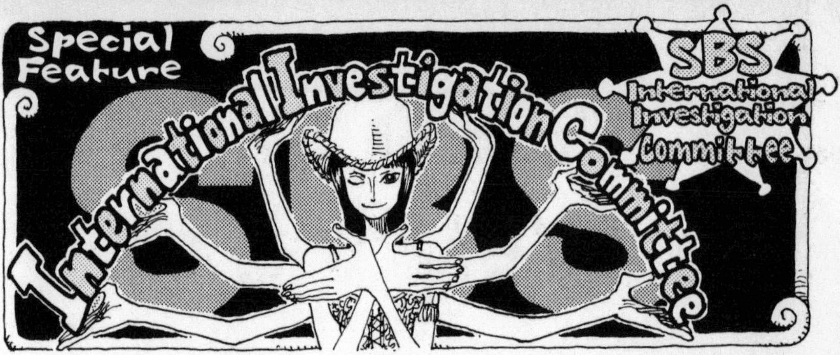
Special Feature
International Investigation Committee
SBS
International Investigation Committee

O: (Oda): In a previous volume's SBS Question Corner, I mentioned that we get quite a few One Piece questions from overseas. And I, the author, knew only a few of the countries it was sold in. So in this volume, with the help of the international department staff at Shueisha, I checked into it. Thank you very much. The following chart shows the countries that were selling One Piece comics as of October 2002. But you definitely won't be able to get any foreign editions in Japan.

Country	Country
Taiwan (Mandarin)	Hong Kong (Cantonese)
Korea (Korean)	Thailand (Thai)
Singapore (Mandarin)	Malaysia (Malay)
France (French)	Italy (Italian)
Spain (Spanish)	Germany (German)
Brazil (Portuguese)	*Eleven countries total.*

The four countries listed below are scheduled to begin selling One Piece after 2003.

Country	Country
Indonesia (Indonesian)	Denmark (Danish)
Sweden (Swedish)	Mexico (Spanish)

Amazing, huh?

Chapter 238:
HEAVEN'S GATE

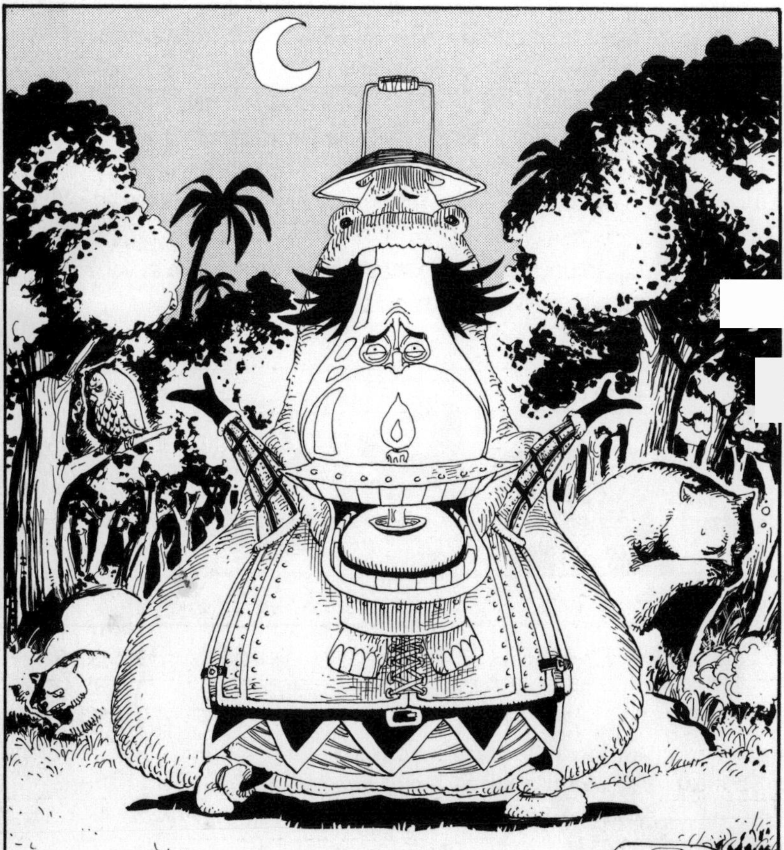

WAPOL'S OMNIVOROUS RAMPAGE, VOL. 3:
"I EAT LAMPS"

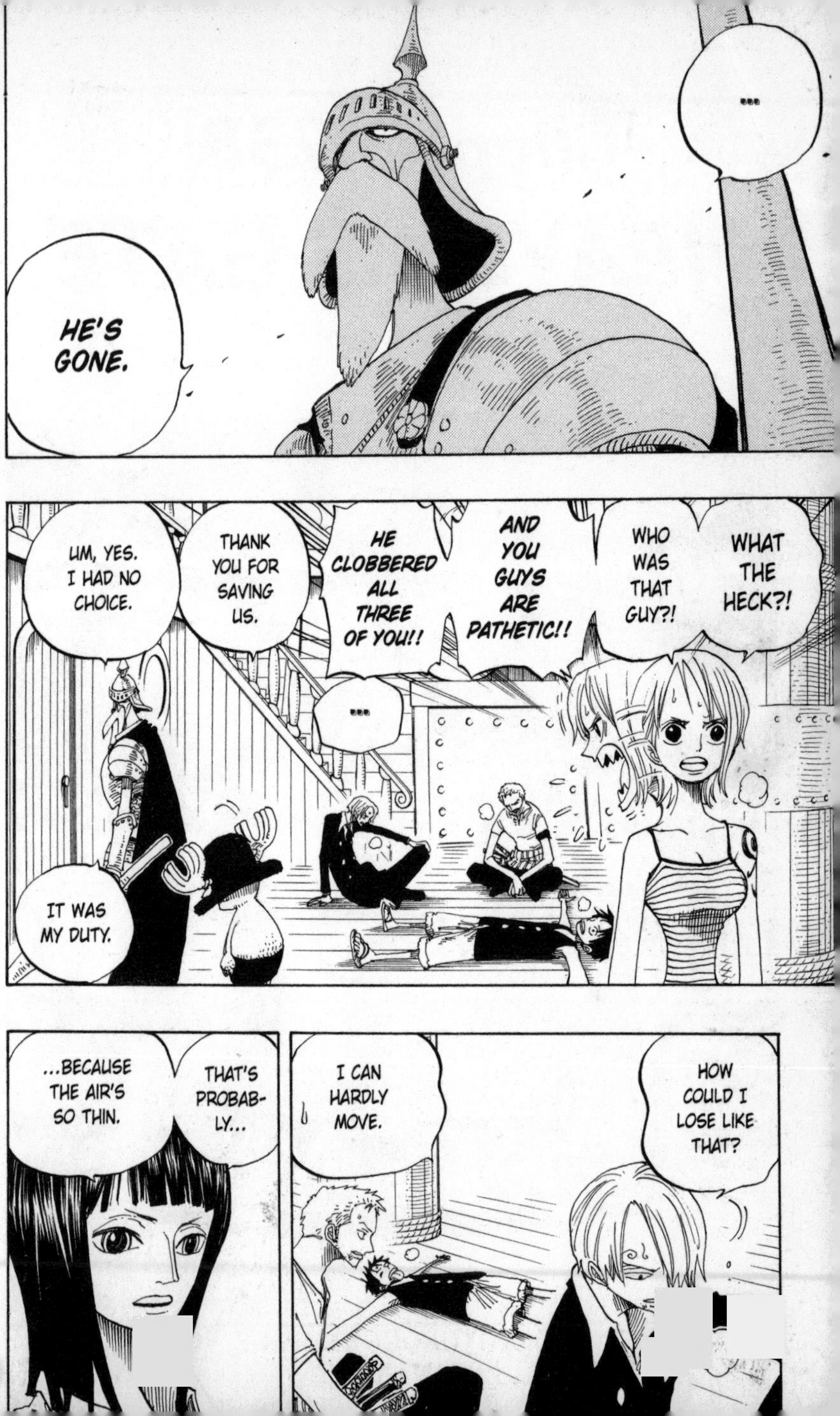
...
HE'S GONE.
WHAT THE HECK?!
WHO WAS THAT GUY?!
AND YOU GUYS ARE PATHETIC!!
HE CLOBBERED ALL THREE OF YOU!!
THANK YOU FOR SAVING US.
UM, YES. I HAD NO CHOICE.
...
IT WAS MY DUTY.
HOW COULD I LOSE LIKE THAT?
I CAN HARDLY MOVE.
THAT'S PROBAB-LY...
...BECAUSE THE AIR'S SO THIN.

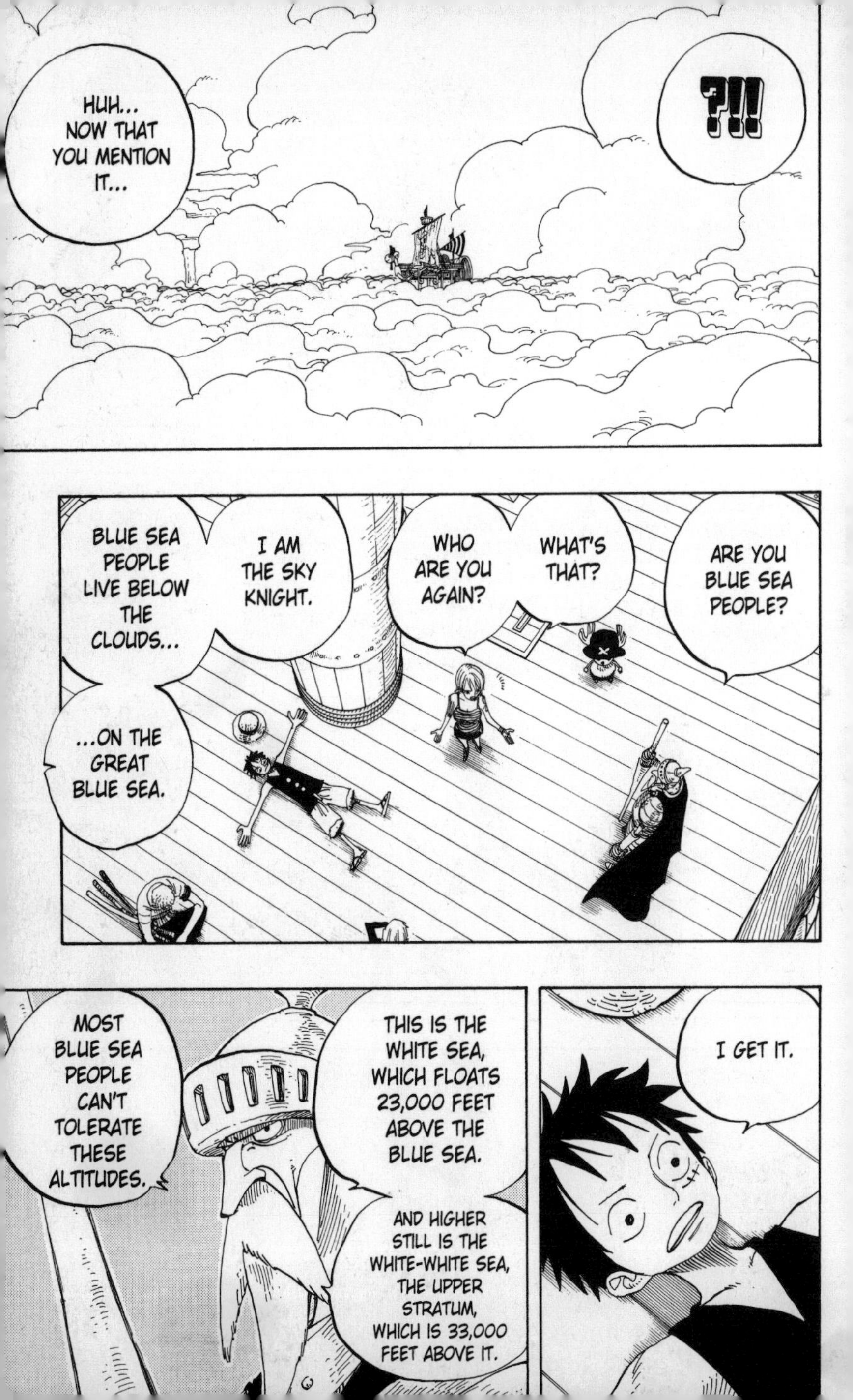
?!!
HUH... NOW THAT YOU MENTION IT...
ARE YOU BLUE SEA PEOPLE?
WHAT'S THAT?
WHO ARE YOU AGAIN?
I AM THE SKY KNIGHT.
BLUE SEA PEOPLE LIVE BELOW THE CLOUDS...
...ON THE GREAT BLUE SEA.
I GET IT.
THIS IS THE WHITE SEA, WHICH FLOATS 23,000 FEET ABOVE THE BLUE SEA.
AND HIGHER STILL IS THE WHITE-WHITE SEA, THE UPPER STRATUM, WHICH IS 33,000 FEET ABOVE IT.
MOST BLUE SEA PEOPLE CAN'T TOLERATE THESE ALTITUDES.

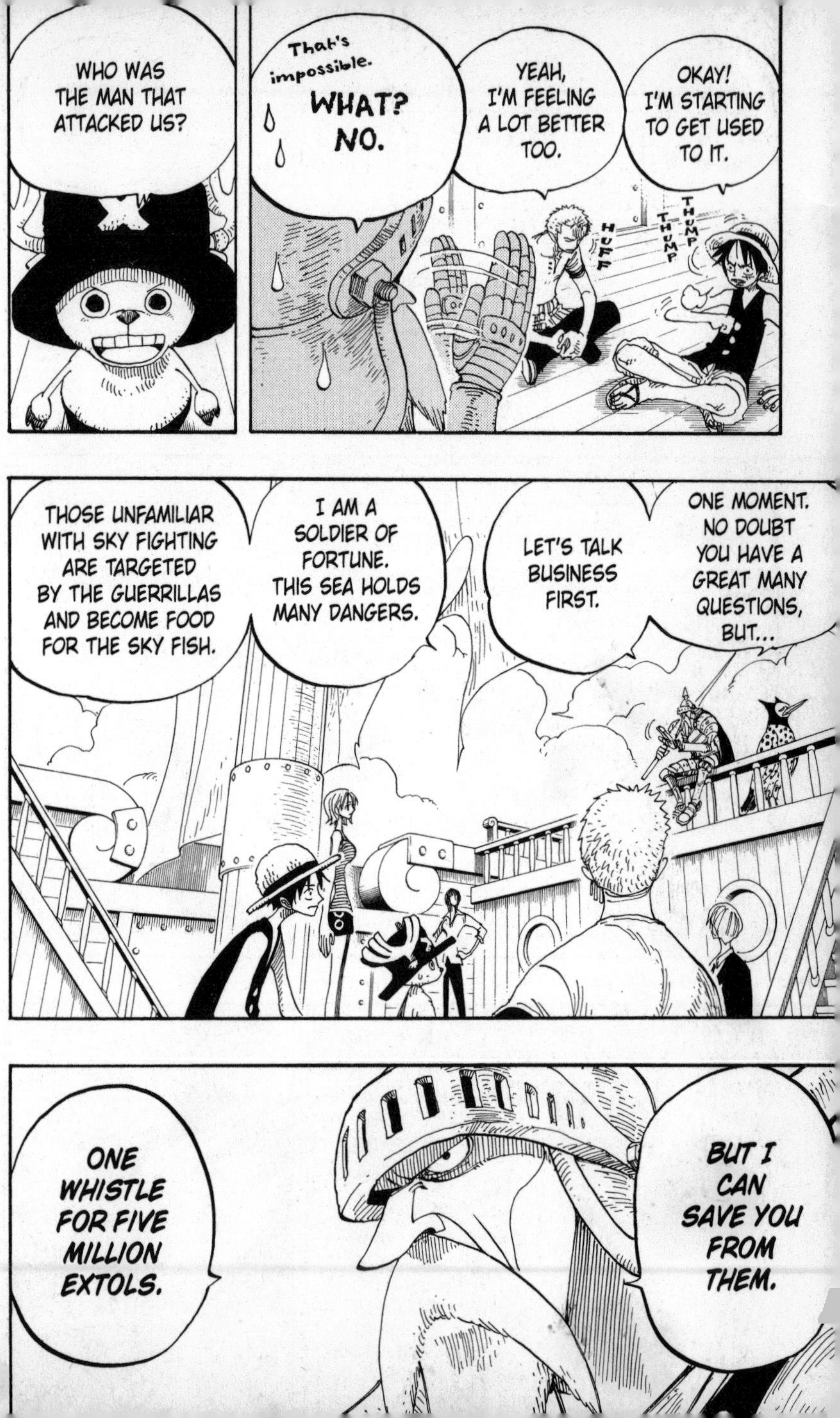
OKAY! I'M STARTING TO GET USED TO IT.
THUMP THUMP
YEAH, I'M FEELING A LOT BETTER TOO.
HUFF
That's impossible.
WHAT? NO.
WHO WAS THE MAN THAT ATTACKED US?
ONE MOMENT. NO DOUBT YOU HAVE A GREAT MANY QUESTIONS, BUT...
LET'S TALK BUSINESS FIRST.
I AM A SOLDIER OF FORTUNE. THIS SEA HOLDS MANY DANGERS.
THOSE UNFAMILIAR WITH SKY FIGHTING ARE TARGETED BY THE GUERRILLAS AND BECOME FOOD FOR THE SKY FISH.
BUT I CAN SAVE YOU FROM THEM.
ONE WHISTLE FOR FIVE MILLION EXTOLS.

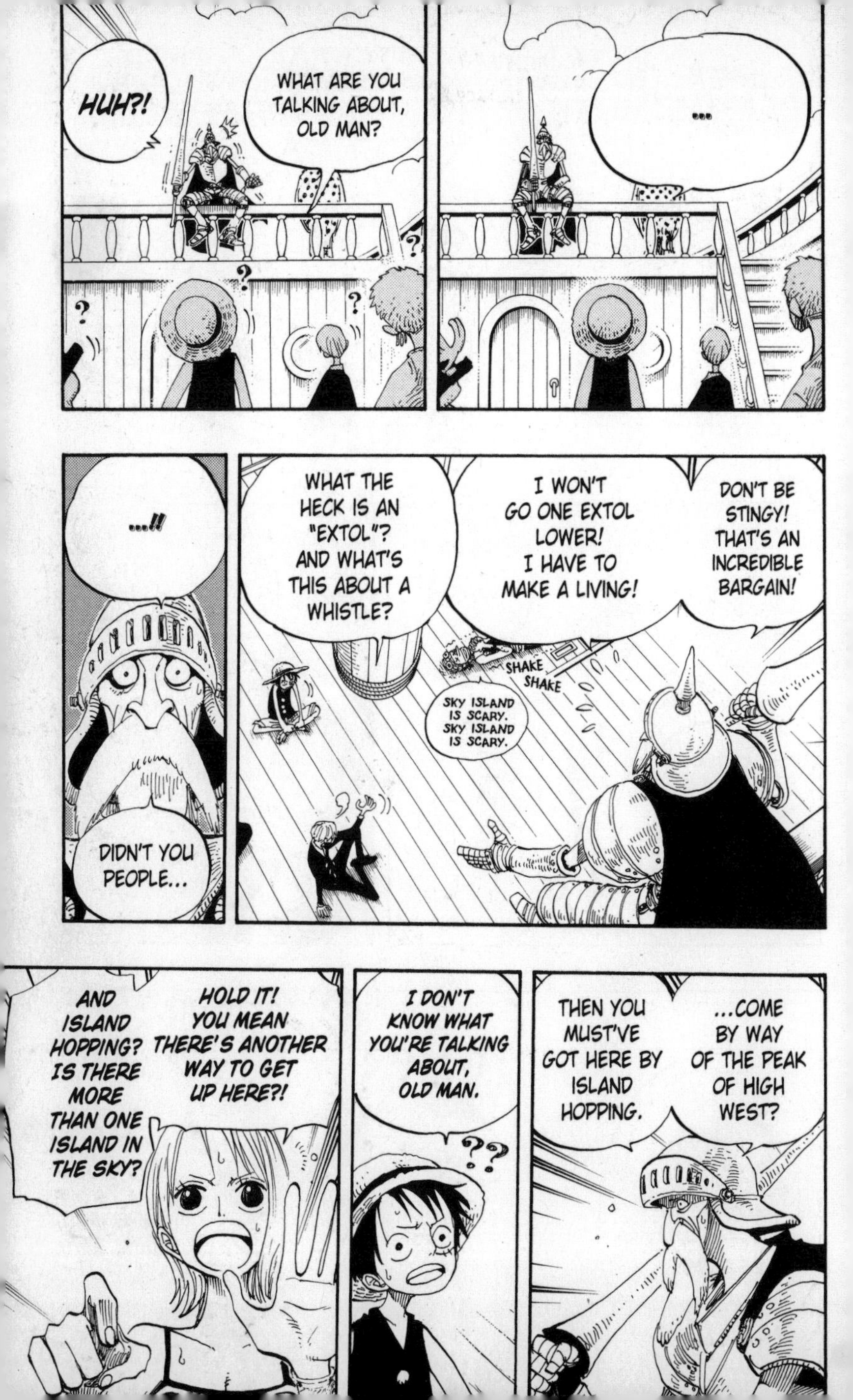
...
WHAT ARE YOU TALKING ABOUT, OLD MAN?
HUH?!
DON'T BE STINGY! THAT'S AN INCREDIBLE BARGAIN!
I WON'T GO ONE EXTOL LOWER! I HAVE TO MAKE A LIVING!
WHAT THE HECK IS AN "EXTOL"? AND WHAT'S THIS ABOUT A WHISTLE?
SHAKE SHAKE
SKY ISLAND IS SCARY. SKY ISLAND IS SCARY.
...!!
DIDN'T YOU PEOPLE...
...COME BY WAY OF THE PEAK OF HIGH WEST?
THEN YOU MUST'VE GOT HERE BY ISLAND HOPPING.
I DON'T KNOW WHAT YOU'RE TALKING ABOUT, OLD MAN.
HOLD IT! YOU MEAN THERE'S ANOTHER WAY TO GET UP HERE?!
AND ISLAND HOPPING? IS THERE MORE THAN ONE ISLAND IN THE SKY?

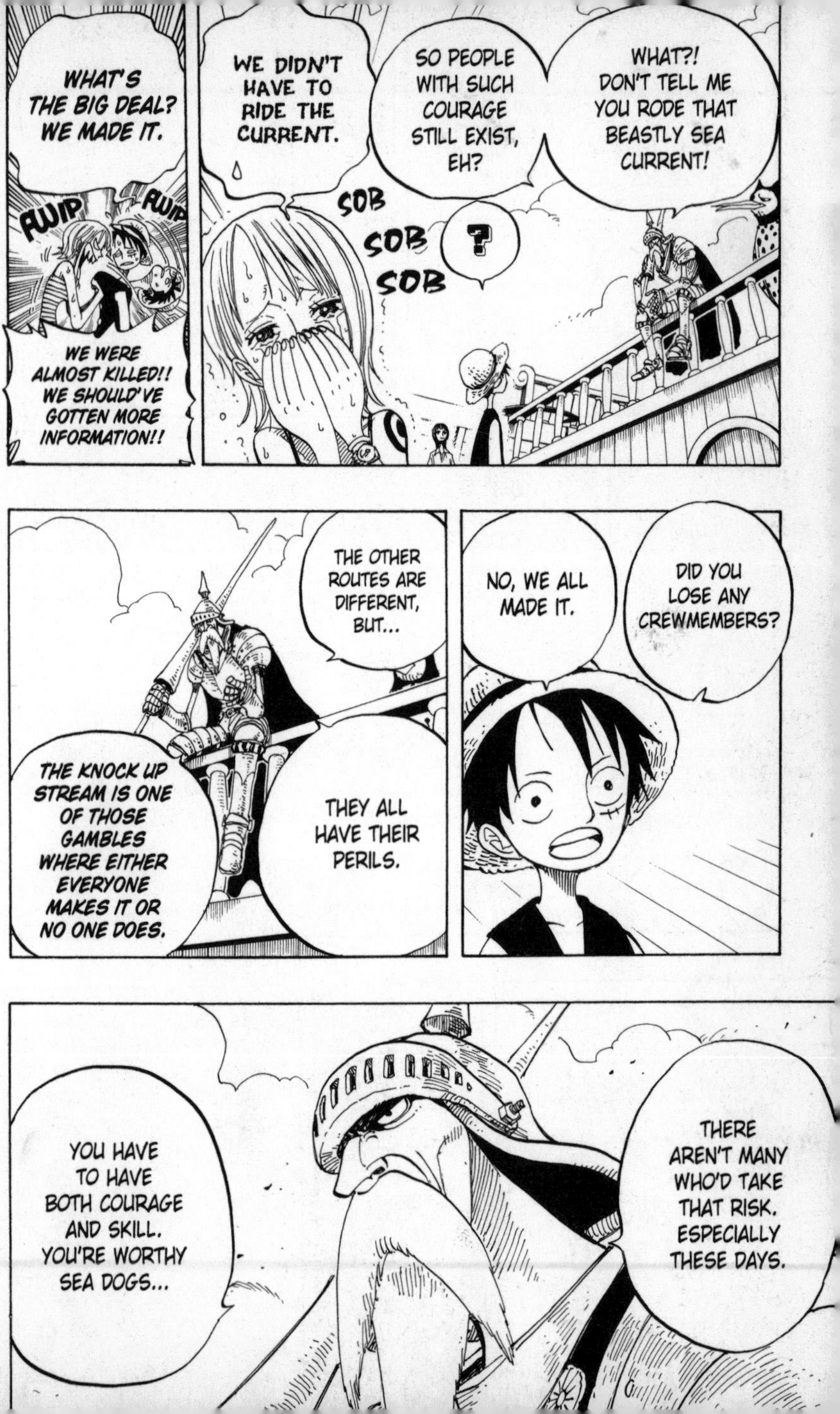
WHAT?! DON'T TELL ME YOU RODE THAT BEASTLY SEA CURRENT!
SO PEOPLE WITH SUCH COURAGE STILL EXIST, EH?
?
WE DIDN'T HAVE TO RIDE THE CURRENT.
SOB SOB SOB
WHAT'S THE BIG DEAL? WE MADE IT.
FWIP FWIP
WE WERE ALMOST KILLED!! WE SHOULD'VE GOTTEN MORE INFORMATION!!
DID YOU LOSE ANY CREWMEMBERS?
NO, WE ALL MADE IT.
THE OTHER ROUTES ARE DIFFERENT, BUT...
THEY ALL HAVE THEIR PERILS.
THE KNOCK UP STREAM IS ONE OF THOSE GAMBLES WHERE EITHER EVERYONE MAKES IT OR NO ONE DOES.
THERE AREN'T MANY WHO'D TAKE THAT RISK. ESPECIALLY THESE DAYS.
YOU HAVE TO HAVE BOTH COURAGE AND SKILL. YOU'RE WORTHY SEA DOGS...

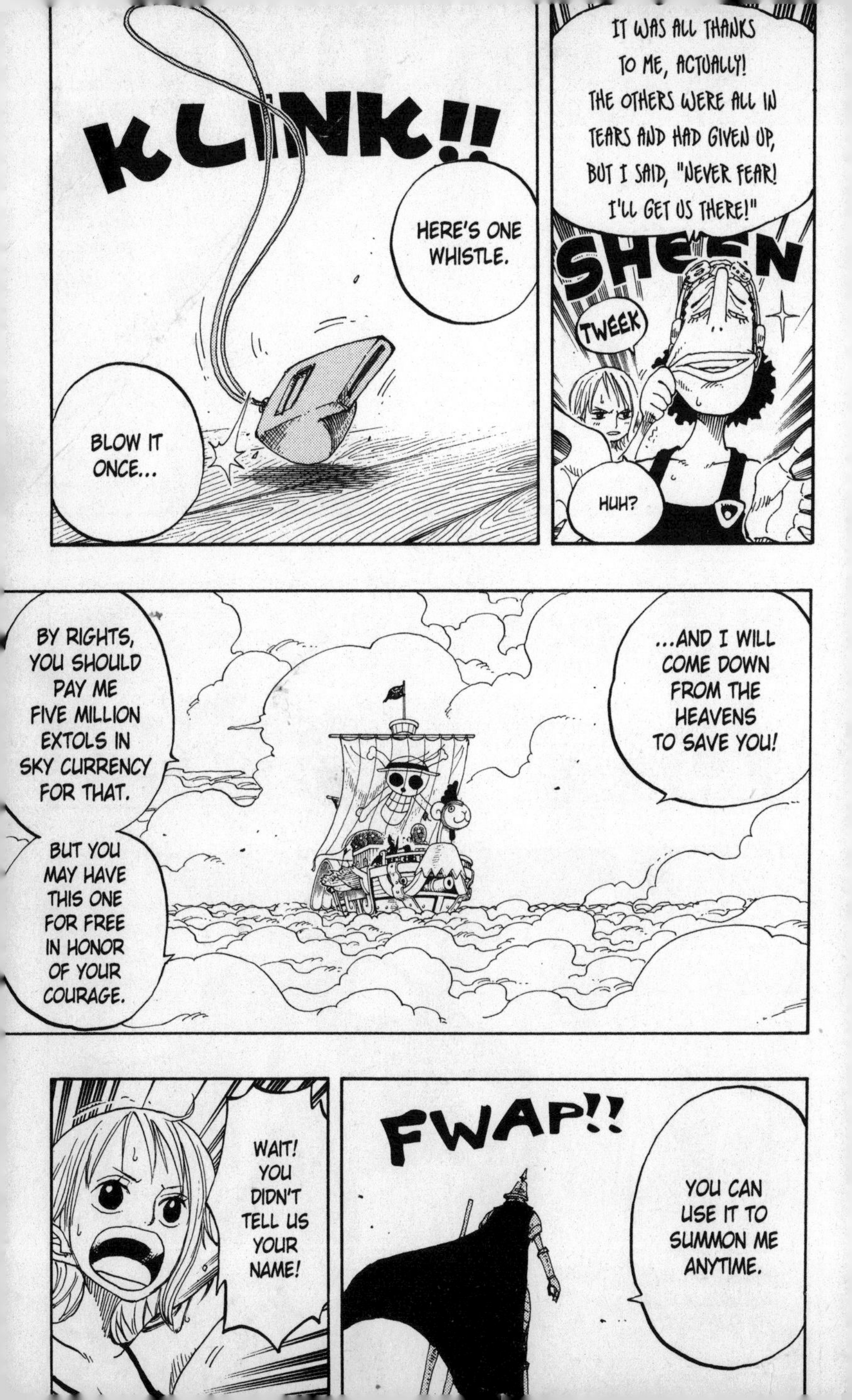
IT WAS ALL THANKS TO ME, ACTUALLY! THE OTHERS WERE ALL IN TEARS AND HAD GIVEN UP, BUT I SAID, "NEVER FEAR! I'LL GET US THERE!"
SHEEN
TWEEK
HUH?
KLINK!!
HERE'S ONE WHISTLE.
BLOW IT ONCE...
...AND I WILL COME DOWN FROM THE HEAVENS TO SAVE YOU!
BY RIGHTS, YOU SHOULD PAY ME FIVE MILLION EXTOLS IN SKY CURRENCY FOR THAT.
BUT YOU MAY HAVE THIS ONE FOR FREE IN HONOR OF YOUR COURAGE.
FWAP!!
YOU CAN USE IT TO SUMMON ME ANYTIME.
WAIT! YOU DIDN'T TELL US YOUR NAME!

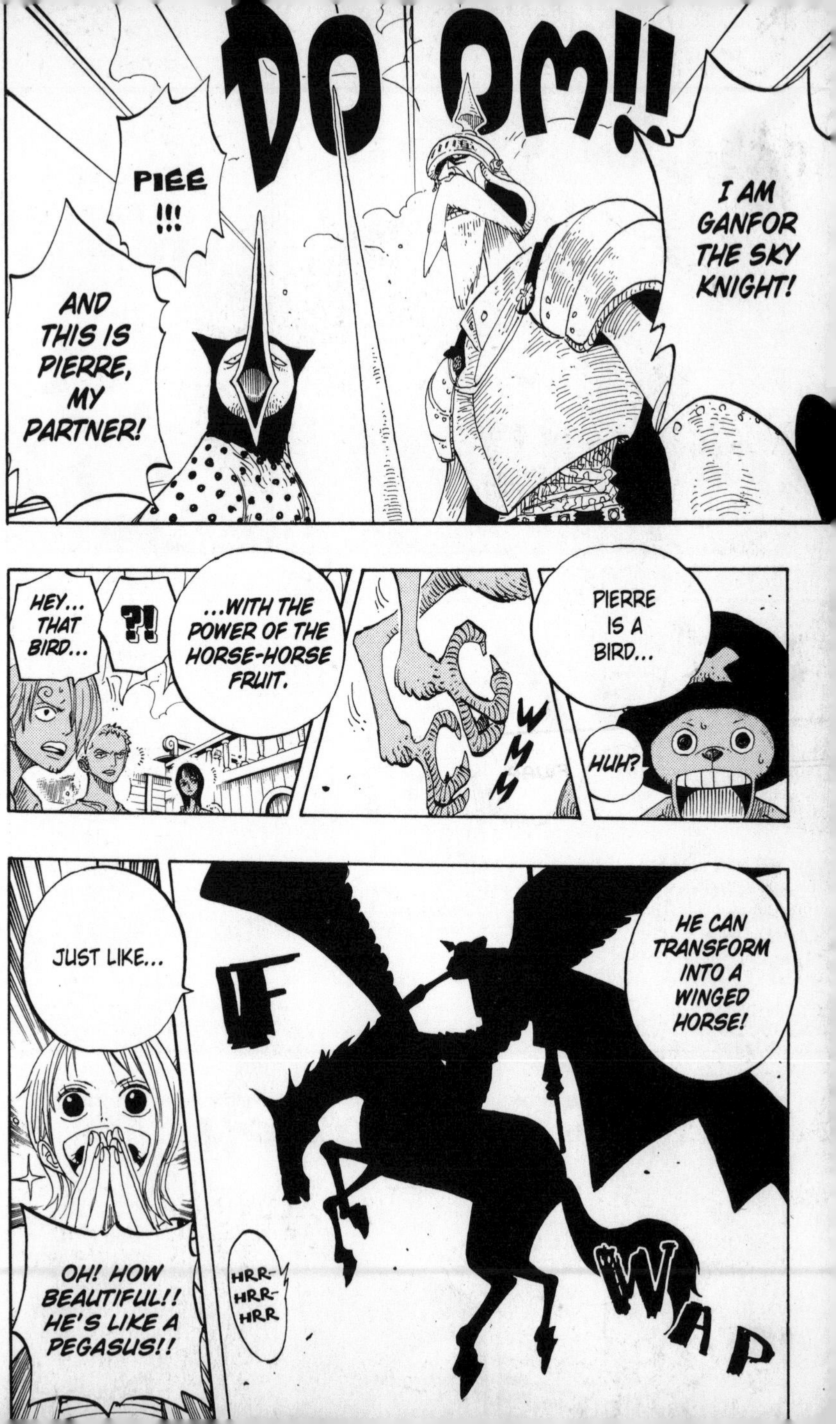
DO OM!!
I AM GANFOR THE SKY KNIGHT!
PIEE !!!
AND THIS IS PIERRE, MY PARTNER!
PIERRE IS A BIRD...
HUH?
WMMM
...WITH THE POWER OF THE HORSE-HORSE FRUIT.
?!
HEY... THAT BIRD...
HE CAN TRANSFORM INTO A WINGED HORSE!
F
WAP
HRR-HRR-HRR
JUST LIKE...
OH! HOW BEAUTIFUL!! HE'S LIKE A PEGASUS!!

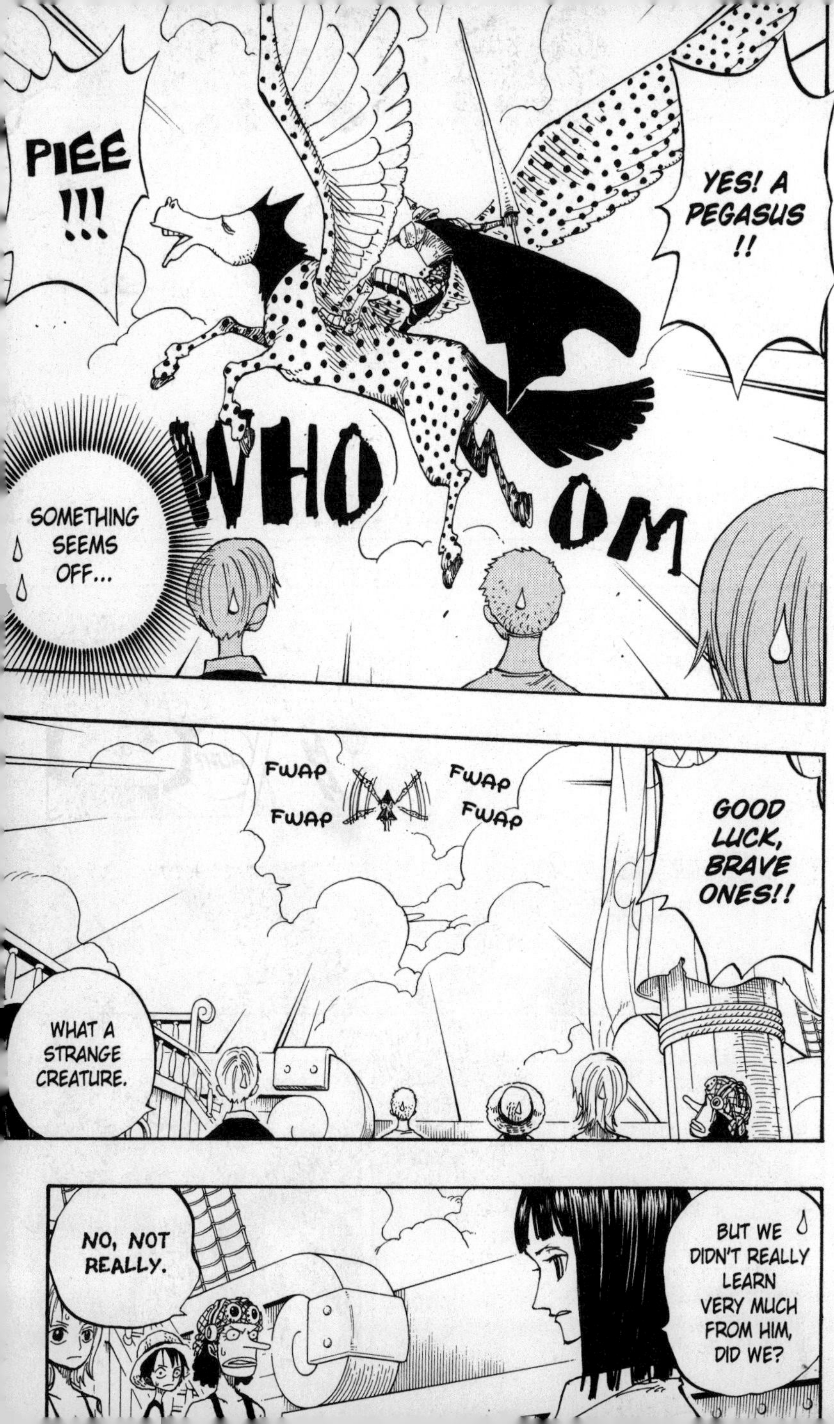
YES! A PEGASUS !!
PIEE !!!
WHOOM
SOMETHING SEEMS OFF...
GOOD LUCK, BRAVE ONES!!
FWAP
FWAP
FWAP
FWAP
WHAT A STRANGE CREATURE.
BUT WE DIDN'T REALLY LEARN VERY MUCH FROM HIM, DID WE?
NO, NOT REALLY.

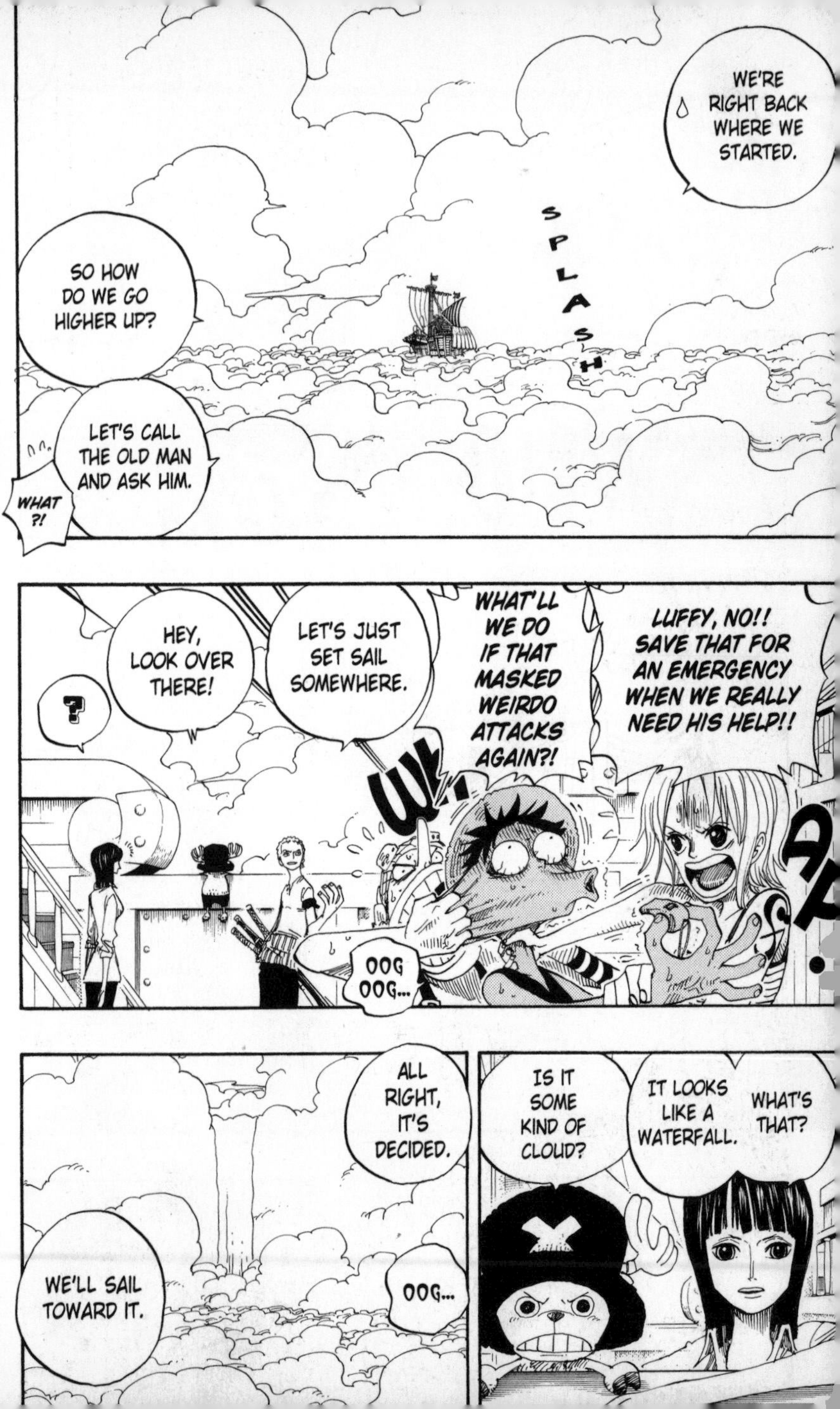
WE'RE RIGHT BACK WHERE WE STARTED.
SPLASH
SO HOW DO WE GO HIGHER UP?
LET'S CALL THE OLD MAN AND ASK HIM.
WHAT ?!
LUFFY, NO!! SAVE THAT FOR AN EMERGENCY WHEN WE REALLY NEED HIS HELP!!
WHAT'LL WE DO IF THAT MASKED WEIRDO ATTACKS AGAIN?!
UH!
LET'S JUST SET SAIL SOMEWHERE.
HEY, LOOK OVER THERE!
?
OOG OOG...
WHAT'S THAT?
IT LOOKS LIKE A WATERFALL.
IS IT SOME KIND OF CLOUD?
ALL RIGHT, IT'S DECIDED.
OOG...
WE'LL SAIL TOWARD IT.

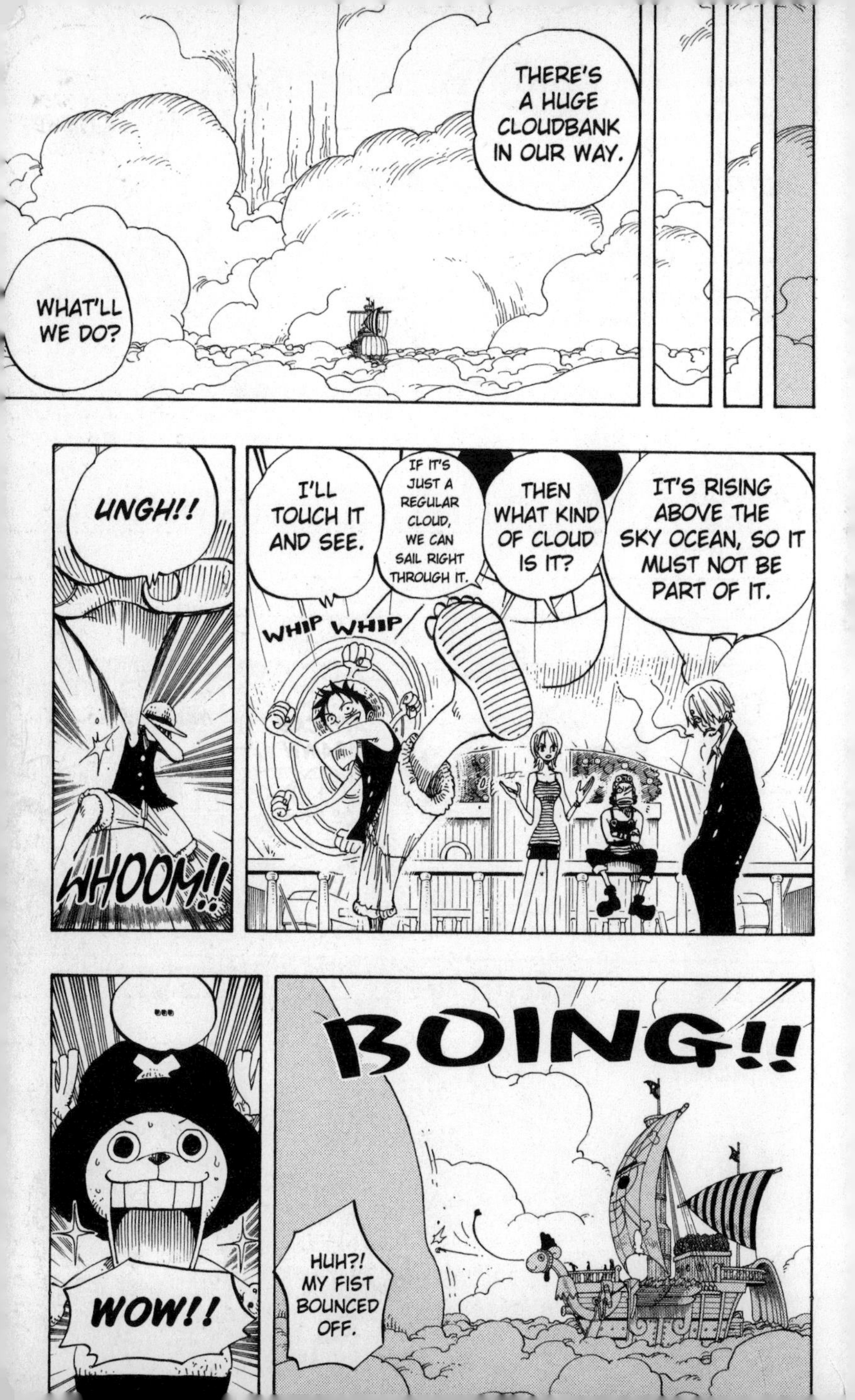
THERE'S A HUGE CLOUDBANK IN OUR WAY.
WHAT'LL WE DO?
IT'S RISING ABOVE THE SKY OCEAN, SO IT MUST NOT BE PART OF IT.
THEN WHAT KIND OF CLOUD IS IT?
IF IT'S JUST A REGULAR CLOUD, WE CAN SAIL RIGHT THROUGH IT.
I'LL TOUCH IT AND SEE.
WHIP WHIP
UNGH!!
WHOOM!!
BOING!!
HUH?! MY FIST BOUNCED OFF.
...
WOW!!

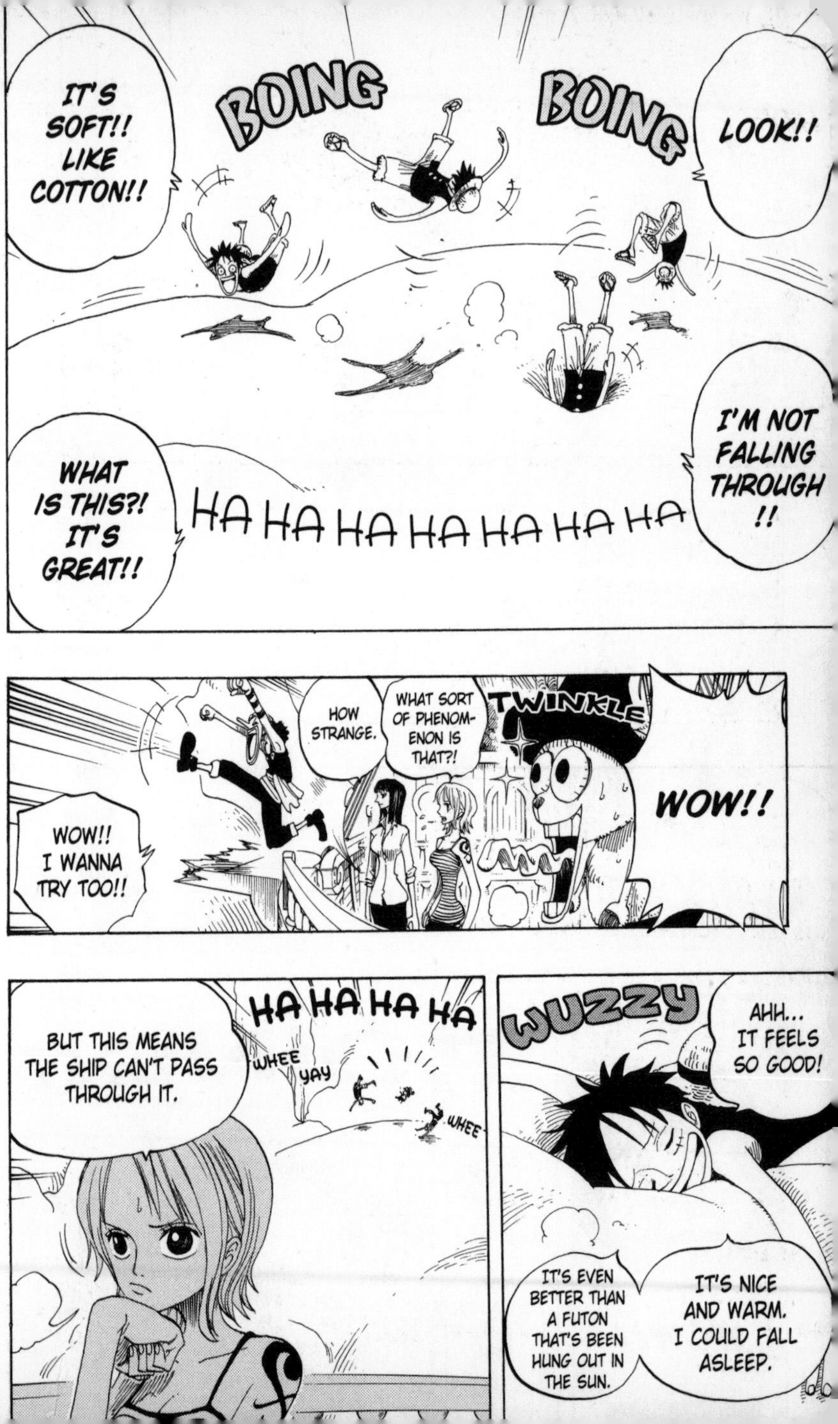
LOOK!!
BOING
BOING
IT'S SOFT!! LIKE COTTON!!
I'M NOT FALLING THROUGH!!
HA HA HA HA HA HA HA
WHAT IS THIS?! IT'S GREAT!!
WOW!!
TWINKLE
WHAT SORT OF PHENOM-ENON IS THAT?!
HOW STRANGE.
WOW!! I WANNA TRY TOO!!
WUZZY
AHH... IT FEELS SO GOOD!
IT'S NICE AND WARM. I COULD FALL ASLEEP.
IT'S EVEN BETTER THAN A FUTON THAT'S BEEN HUNG OUT IN THE SUN.
HA HA HA HA
WHEE
YAY
WHEE
BUT THIS MEANS THE SHIP CAN'T PASS THROUGH IT.

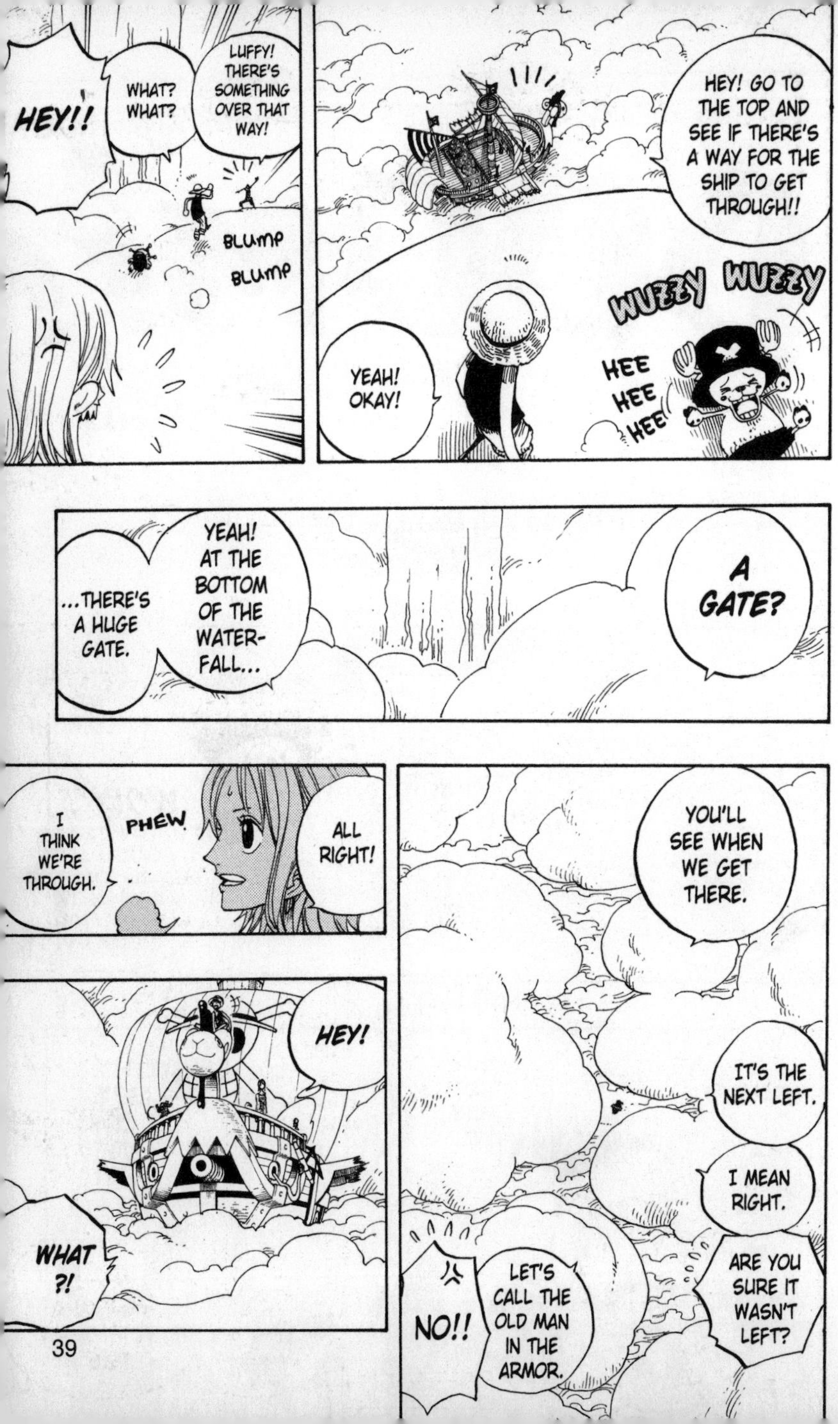
HEY! GO TO THE TOP AND SEE IF THERE'S A WAY FOR THE SHIP TO GET THROUGH!!
YEAH! OKAY!
WUZZY WUZZY
HEE HEE HEE
LUFFY! THERE'S SOMETHING OVER THAT WAY!
WHAT? WHAT?
HEY!!
BLUMP
BLUMP
A GATE?
YEAH! AT THE BOTTOM OF THE WATER-FALL...
...THERE'S A HUGE GATE.
YOU'LL SEE WHEN WE GET THERE.
IT'S THE NEXT LEFT.
I MEAN RIGHT.
ARE YOU SURE IT WASN'T LEFT?
LET'S CALL THE OLD MAN IN THE ARMOR.
NO!!
ALL RIGHT!
PHEW
I THINK WE'RE THROUGH.
HEY!
WHAT?!

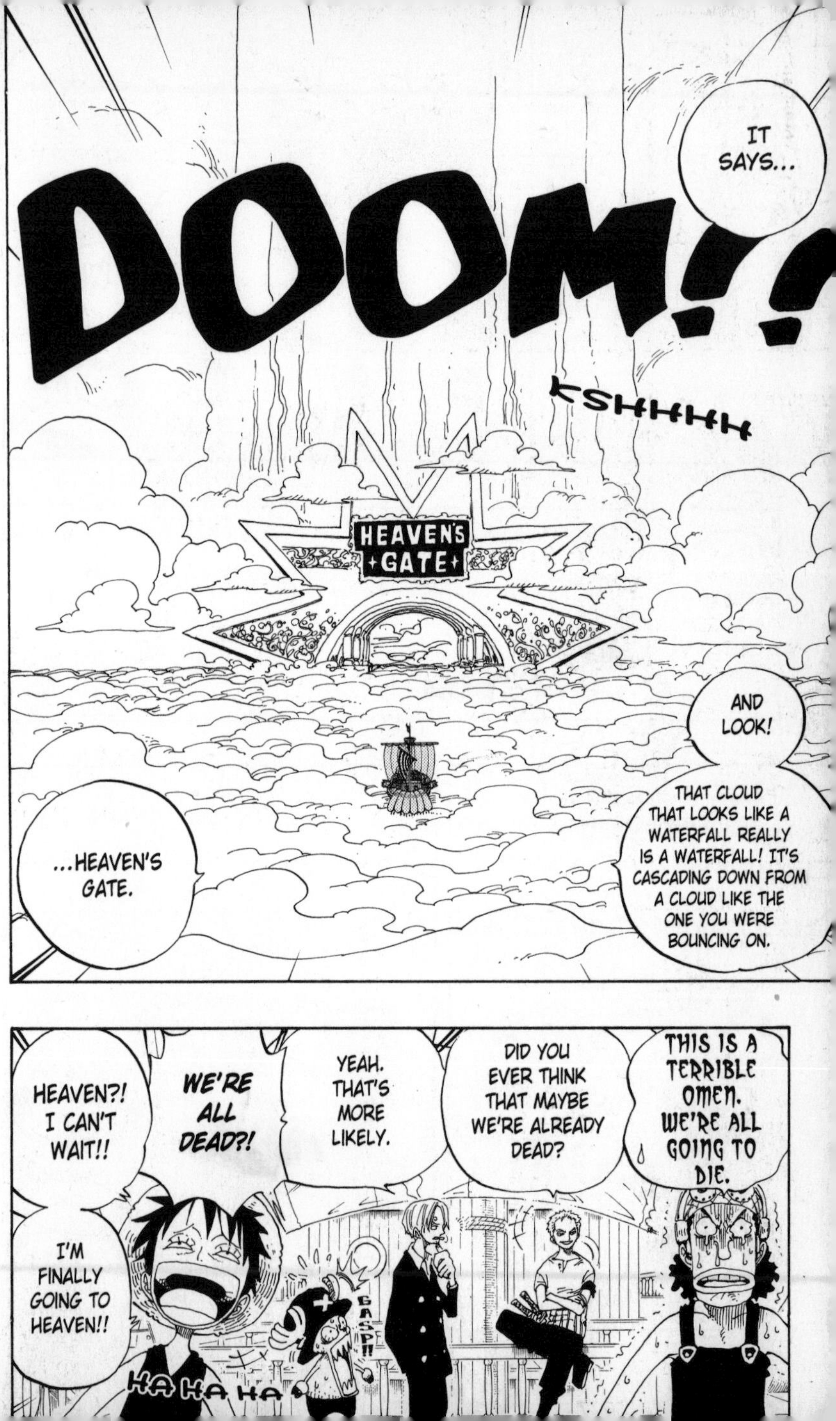
IT SAYS...
DOOM!?
KSHHHH
HEAVEN'S GATE
AND LOOK!
THAT CLOUD THAT LOOKS LIKE A WATERFALL REALLY IS A WATERFALL! IT'S CASCADING DOWN FROM A CLOUD LIKE THE ONE YOU WERE BOUNCING ON.
...HEAVEN'S GATE.
THIS IS A TERRIBLE OMEN. WE'RE ALL GOING TO DIE.
DID YOU EVER THINK THAT MAYBE WE'RE ALREADY DEAD?
YEAH. THAT'S MORE LIKELY.
WE'RE ALL DEAD?!
HEAVEN?! I CAN'T WAIT!!
I'M FINALLY GOING TO HEAVEN!!
GASP!!
HA HA HA

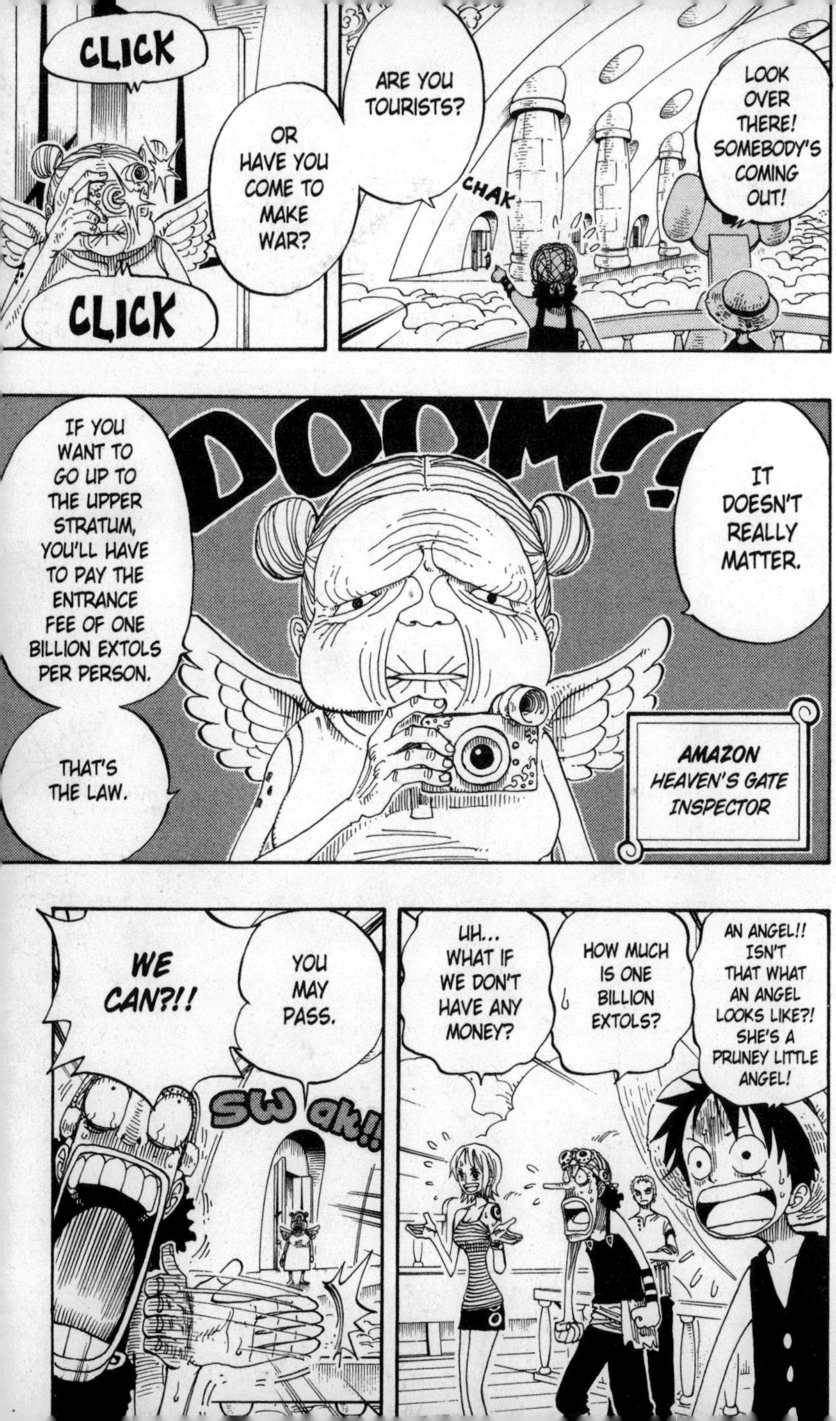
LOOK OVER THERE! SOMEBODY'S COMING OUT!
CHAK
ARE YOU TOURISTS?
OR HAVE YOU COME TO MAKE WAR?
CLICK
CLICK
DOOM!?
IT DOESN'T REALLY MATTER.
AMAZON HEAVEN'S GATE INSPECTOR
IF YOU WANT TO GO UP TO THE UPPER STRATUM, YOU'LL HAVE TO PAY THE ENTRANCE FEE OF ONE BILLION EXTOLS PER PERSON.
THAT'S THE LAW.
AN ANGEL!! ISN'T THAT WHAT AN ANGEL LOOKS LIKE?! SHE'S A PRUNEY LITTLE ANGEL!
HOW MUCH IS ONE BILLION EXTOLS?
UH... WHAT IF WE DON'T HAVE ANY MONEY?
YOU MAY PASS.
WE CAN?!!
SWAK!!

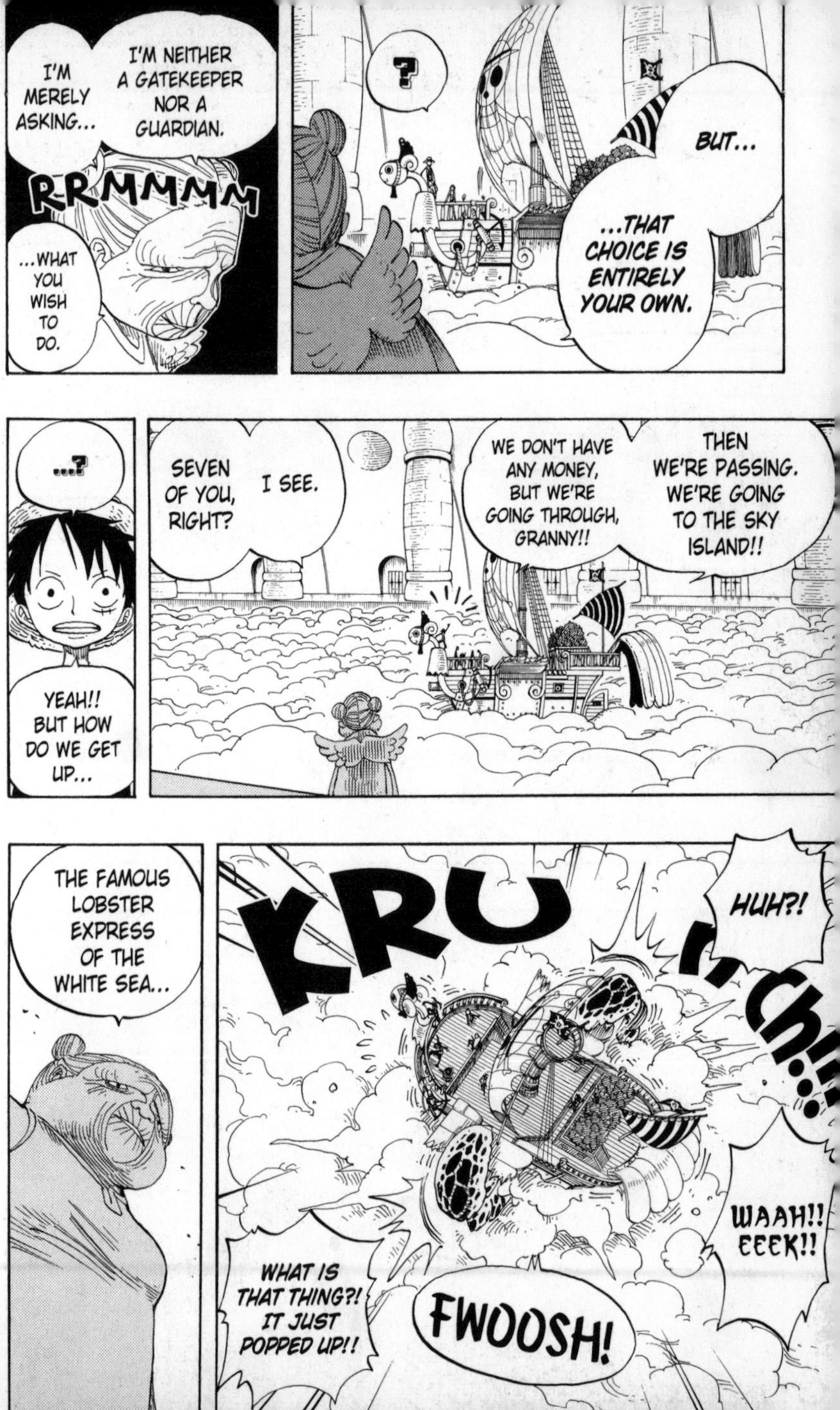
?
BUT...
...THAT CHOICE IS ENTIRELY YOUR OWN.
I'M NEITHER A GATEKEEPER NOR A GUARDIAN.
I'M MERELY ASKING...
RRMMMM
...WHAT YOU WISH TO DO.
THEN WE'RE PASSING. WE'RE GOING TO THE SKY ISLAND!!
WE DON'T HAVE ANY MONEY, BUT WE'RE GOING THROUGH, GRANNY!!
I SEE.
SEVEN OF YOU, RIGHT?
...?
YEAH!! BUT HOW DO WE GET UP...
KRU
CH!!!
HUH?!
WAAH!! EEEK!!
FWOOSH!
WHAT IS THAT THING?! IT JUST POPPED UP!!
THE FAMOUS LOBSTER EXPRESS OF THE WHITE SEA...

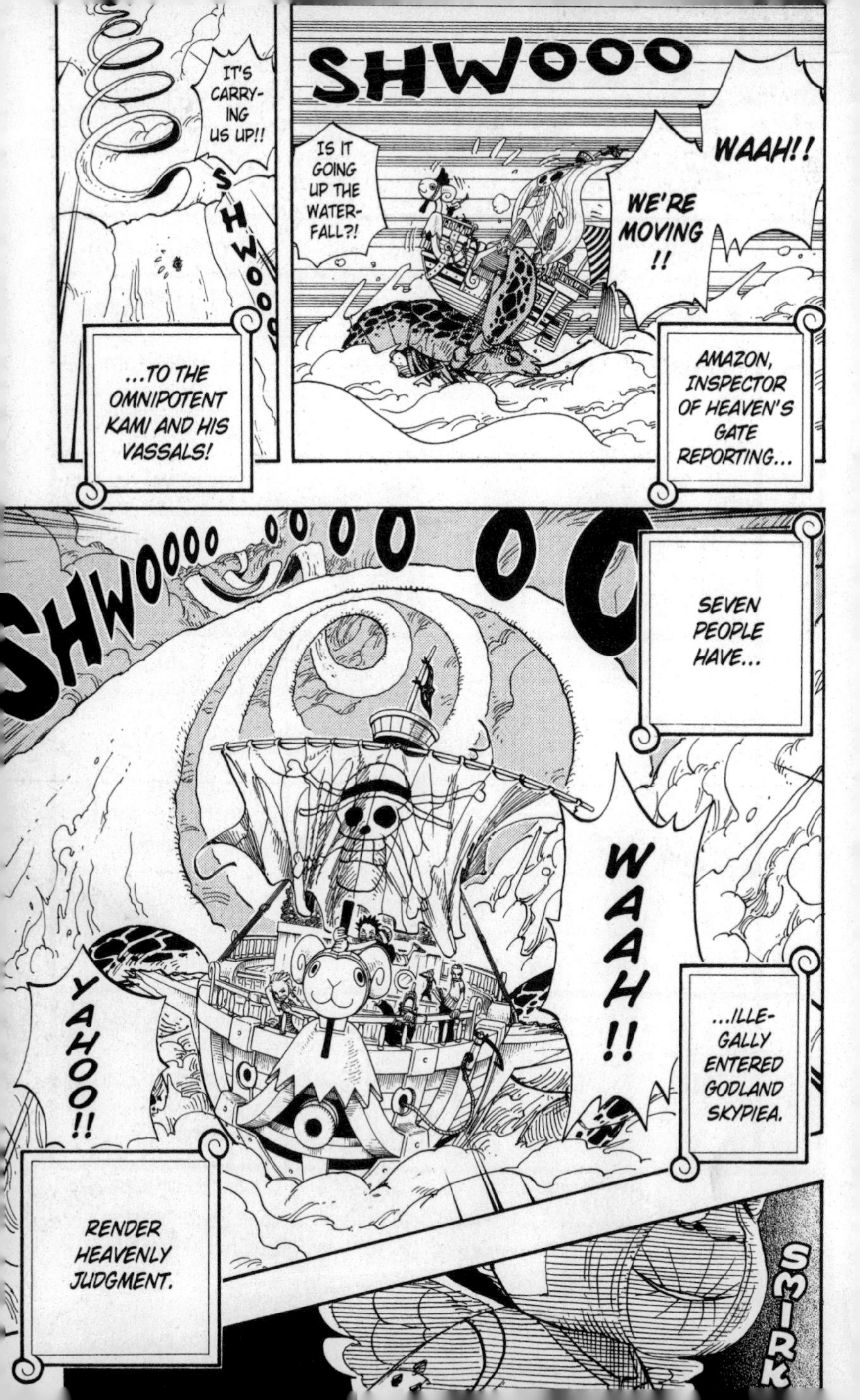
SHWOOO
WAAH!!
WE'RE MOVING!!
IS IT GOING UP THE WATERFALL?!
AMAZON, INSPECTOR OF HEAVEN'S GATE REPORTING...
IT'S CARRYING US UP!!
SHWOOO
...TO THE OMNIPOTENT KAMI AND HIS VASSALS!
SHWOOOO O O O O
SEVEN PEOPLE HAVE...
WAAH!!
...ILLEGALLY ENTERED GODLAND SKYPIEA.
YAHOO!!
SMIRK
RENDER HEAVENLY JUDGMENT.

Special Feature
International Investigation Committee
SBS International Investigation Committee

Q: Here is a list of how the main characters' names are pronounced in different countries.
Some of them are very different.

	Japanese	Written	Pronunciation
Korea	モンキー・D・ルフィ	몽키・D・루피	Monkee D. Lufee
	ロロノア・ゾロ	로로노아・조로	Lolonoa Zolo
	ナミ	나미	Nami
	ウソップ	우솝	Usopu
	サンジ	상디	Sandee
	チョッパー	쵸파	Choppaa
China	ルフィ	魯夫	Lufu
	ゾロ	索隆	Solon
	ナミ	娜美	Namei
	ウソップ	騙人布	Bienzanbu
	サンジ	香吉士	Shanjisu
	チョッパー	喬巴	Chaopaa
Brazil	モンキー・D・ルフィ	MONKEY D.RUFFY	Monkee Do Hafee
	ロロノア・ゾロ	RORONOA ZORO	Hohonoa Zolo
	ナミ	NAMI	Nami

Continued on page 62 ⬅

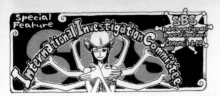

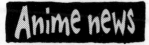

Anime news

Q: The *One Piece* anime is already being shown in Taiwan, Hong Kong, Indonesia, Singapore, Italy, and Greece.

Luffy and the gang speak in the language of each of those countries. I wish I could see it sometime.

Chapter 239:
ANGEL BEACH

WAPOL'S OMNIVOROUS RAMPAGE, VOL. 4:
"I EAT BENCHES"

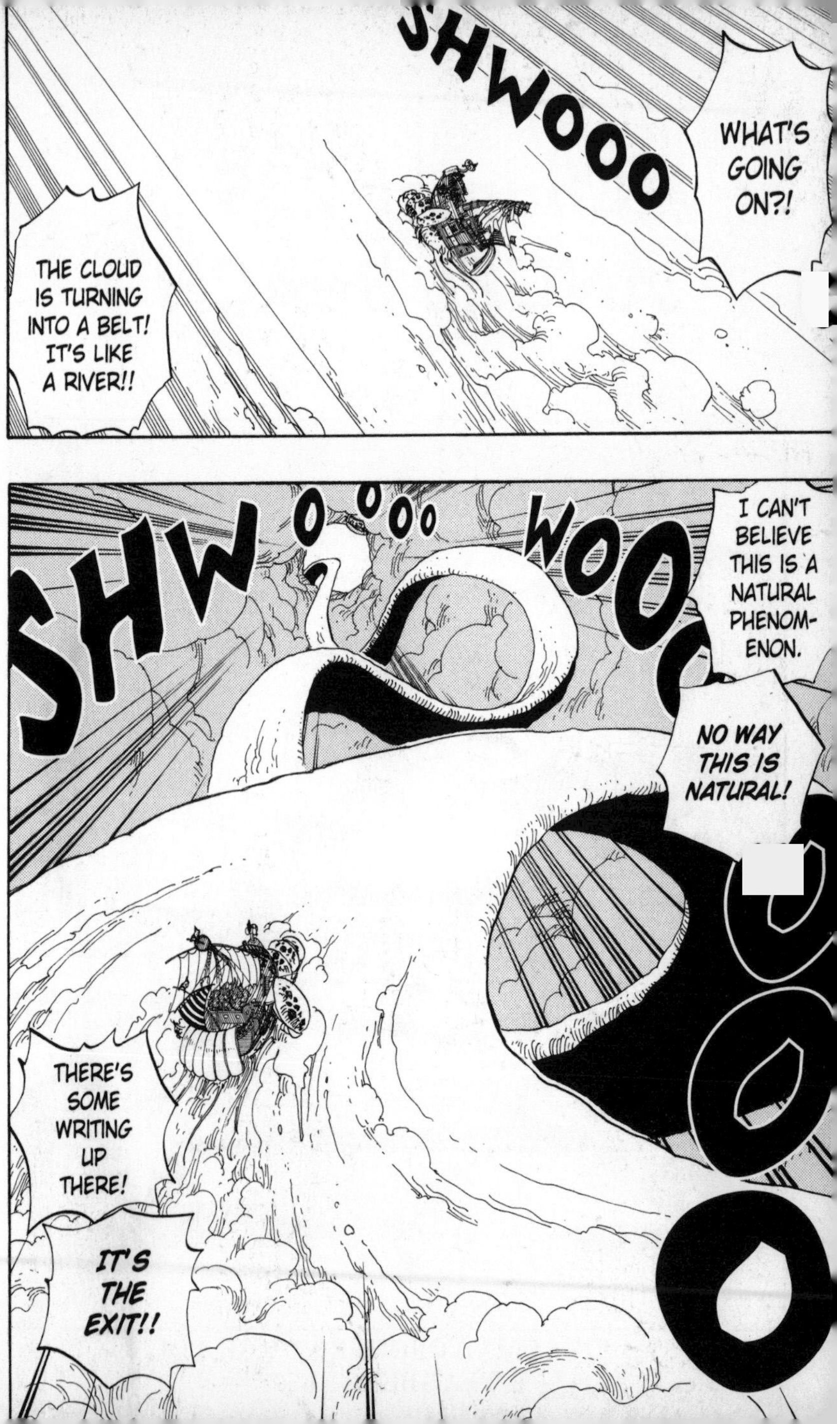
SHWOOO
WHAT'S GOING ON?!
THE CLOUD IS TURNING INTO A BELT! IT'S LIKE A RIVER!!
I CAN'T BELIEVE THIS IS A NATURAL PHENOM-ENON.
NO WAY THIS IS NATURAL!
SHWOOOO WOOOOOO
THERE'S SOME WRITING UP THERE!
IT'S THE EXIT!!

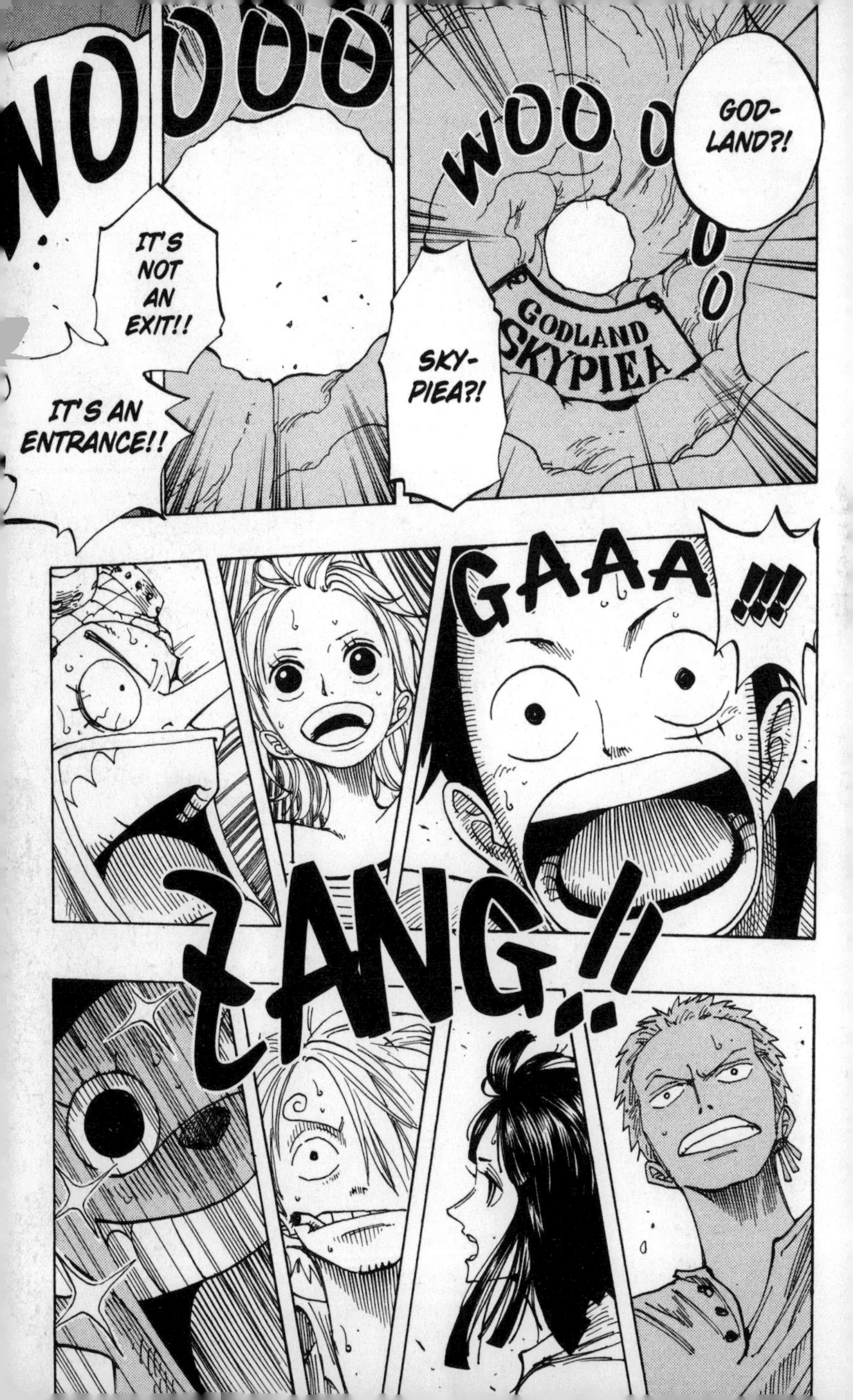
GOD-LAND?!
WOO O O O O
GODLAND SKYPIEA
SKY-PIEA?!
WOOOOO
IT'S NOT AN EXIT!!
IT'S AN ENTRANCE!!
GAAA!!!
ZANG!!

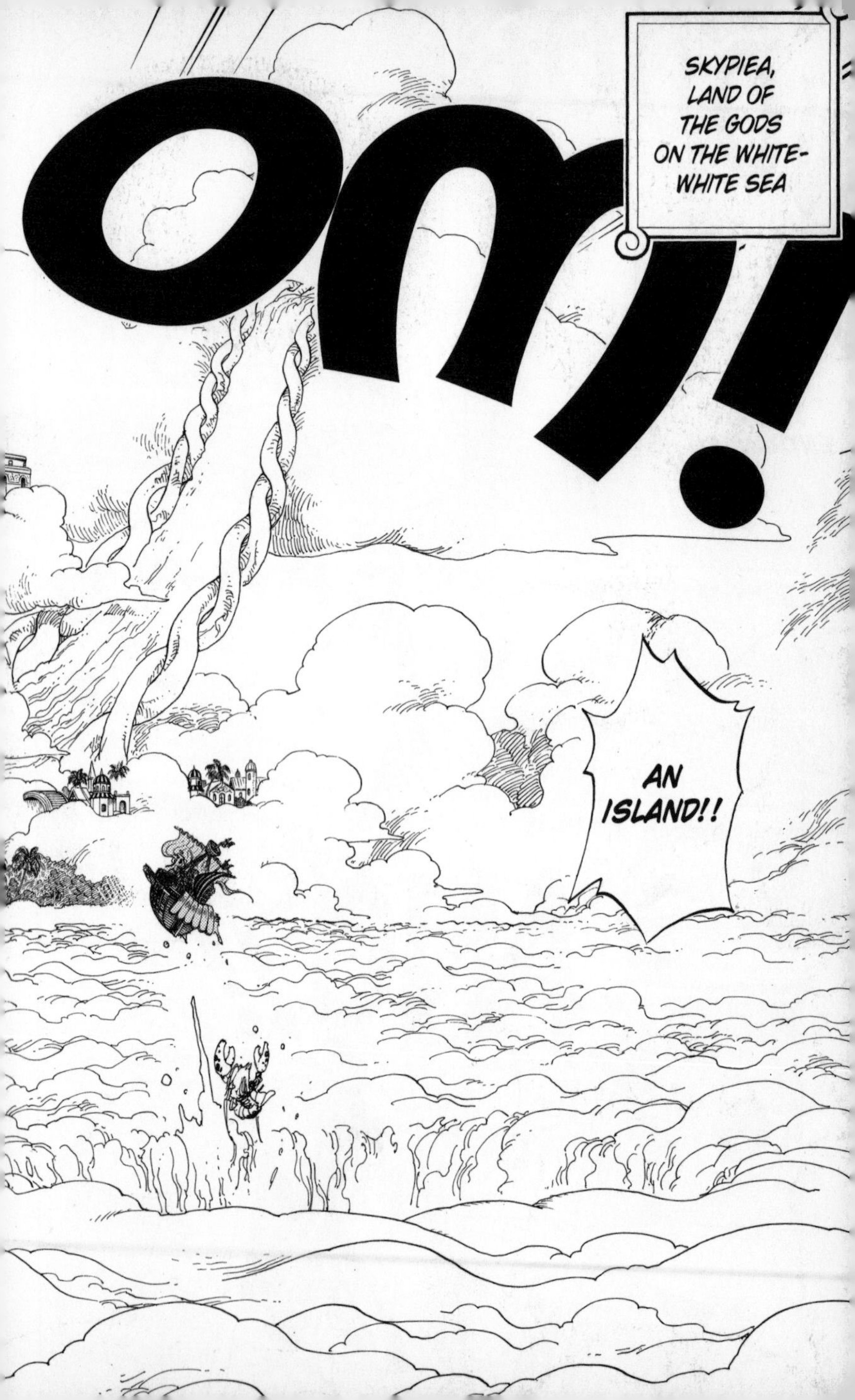
SKYPIEA, LAND OF THE GODS ON THE WHITE-WHITE SEA
OM!!
AN ISLAND!!

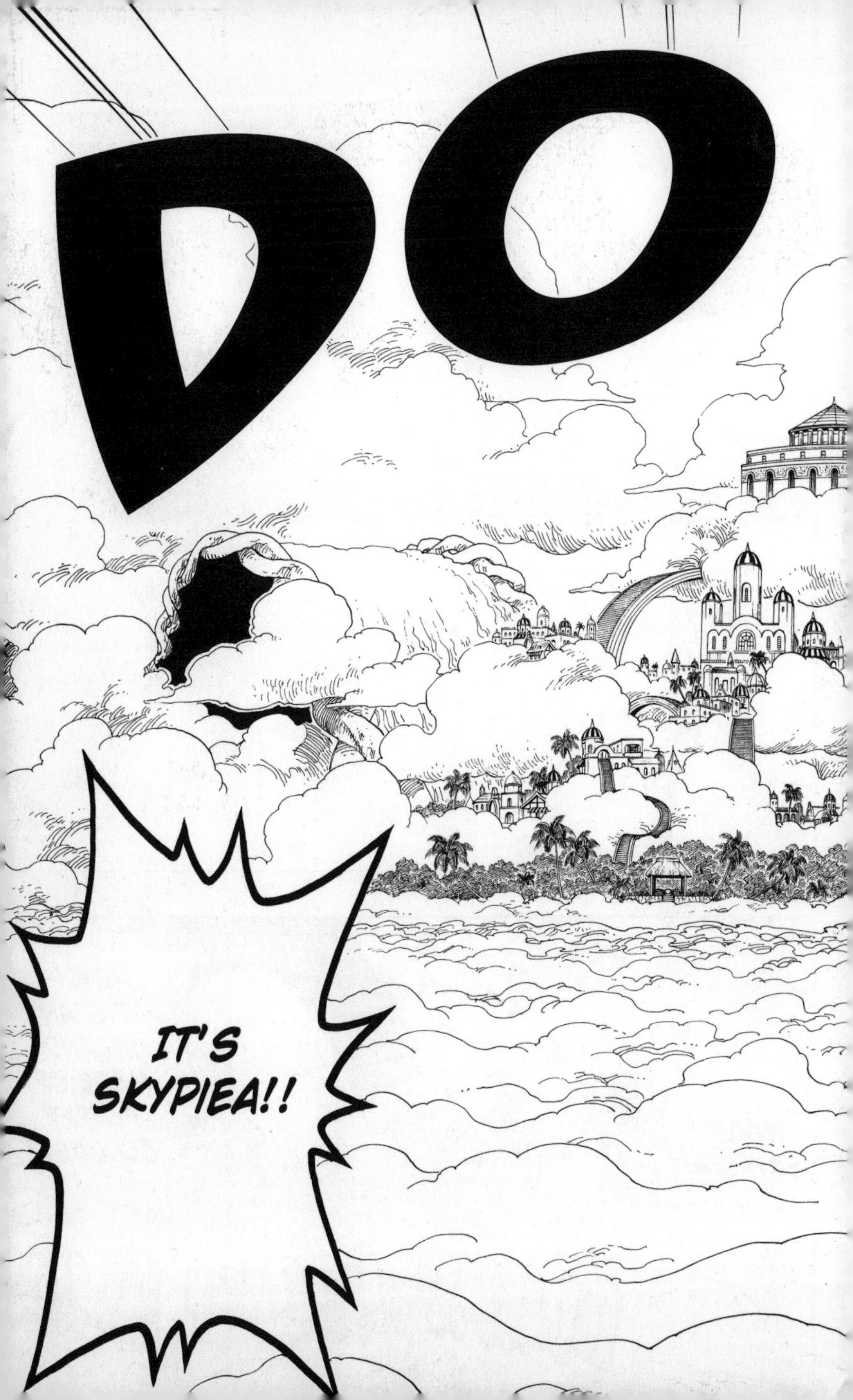
DO
IT'S SKYPIEA!!

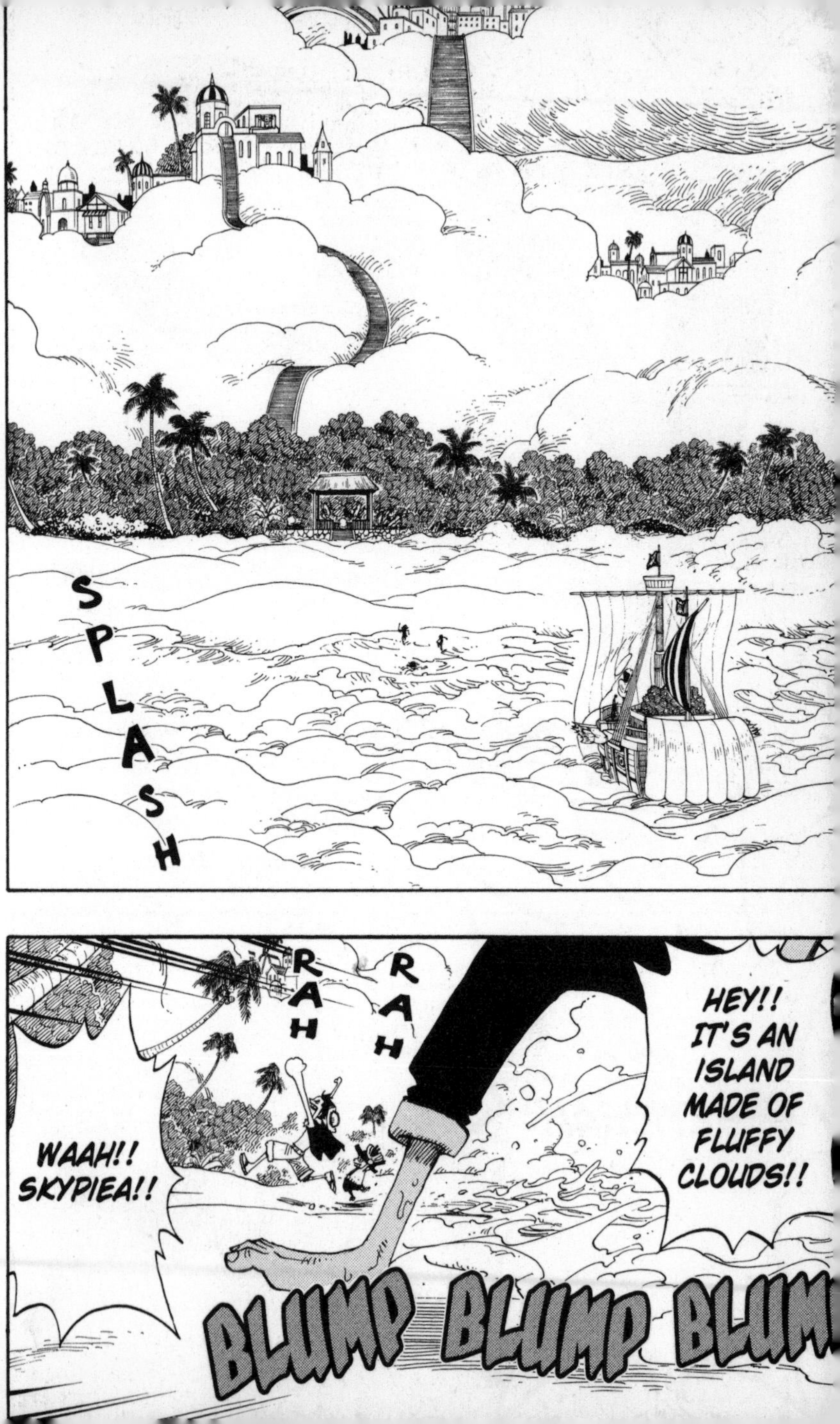
SPLASH
HEY!! IT'S AN ISLAND MADE OF FLUFFY CLOUDS!!
RAH RAH
RAH RAH
WAAH!! SKYPIEA!!
BLUMP BLUMP BLUM

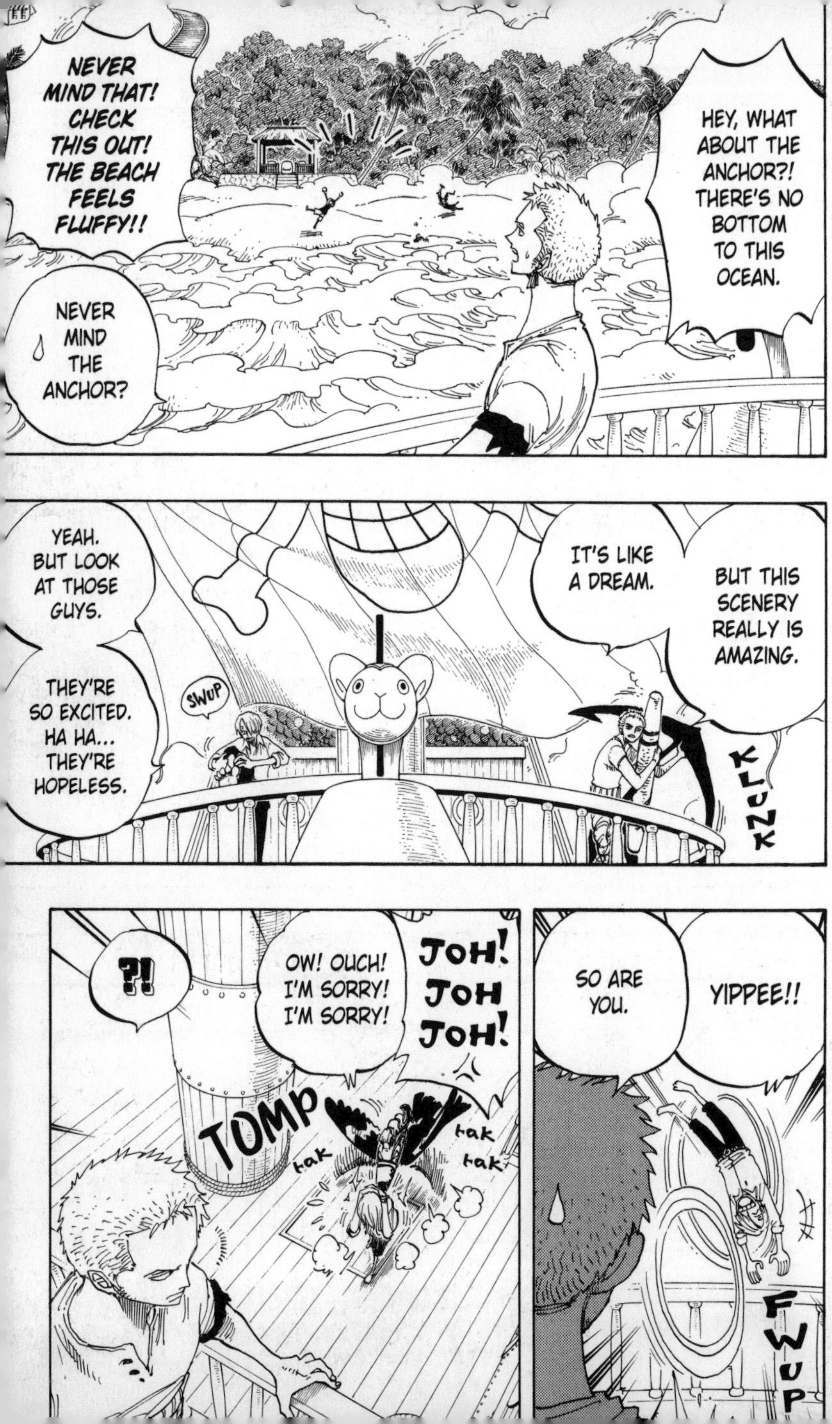
HEY, WHAT ABOUT THE ANCHOR?! THERE'S NO BOTTOM TO THIS OCEAN.
NEVER MIND THAT! CHECK THIS OUT! THE BEACH FEELS FLUFFY!!
NEVER MIND THE ANCHOR?
BUT THIS SCENERY REALLY IS AMAZING.
IT'S LIKE A DREAM.
KLUNK
SWUP
YEAH. BUT LOOK AT THOSE GUYS.
THEY'RE SO EXCITED. HA HA... THEY'RE HOPELESS.
YIPPEE!!
SO ARE YOU.
FWUP
JOH! JOH JOH!
OW! OUCH! I'M SORRY! I'M SORRY!
?!
TOMP
tak
tak
tak

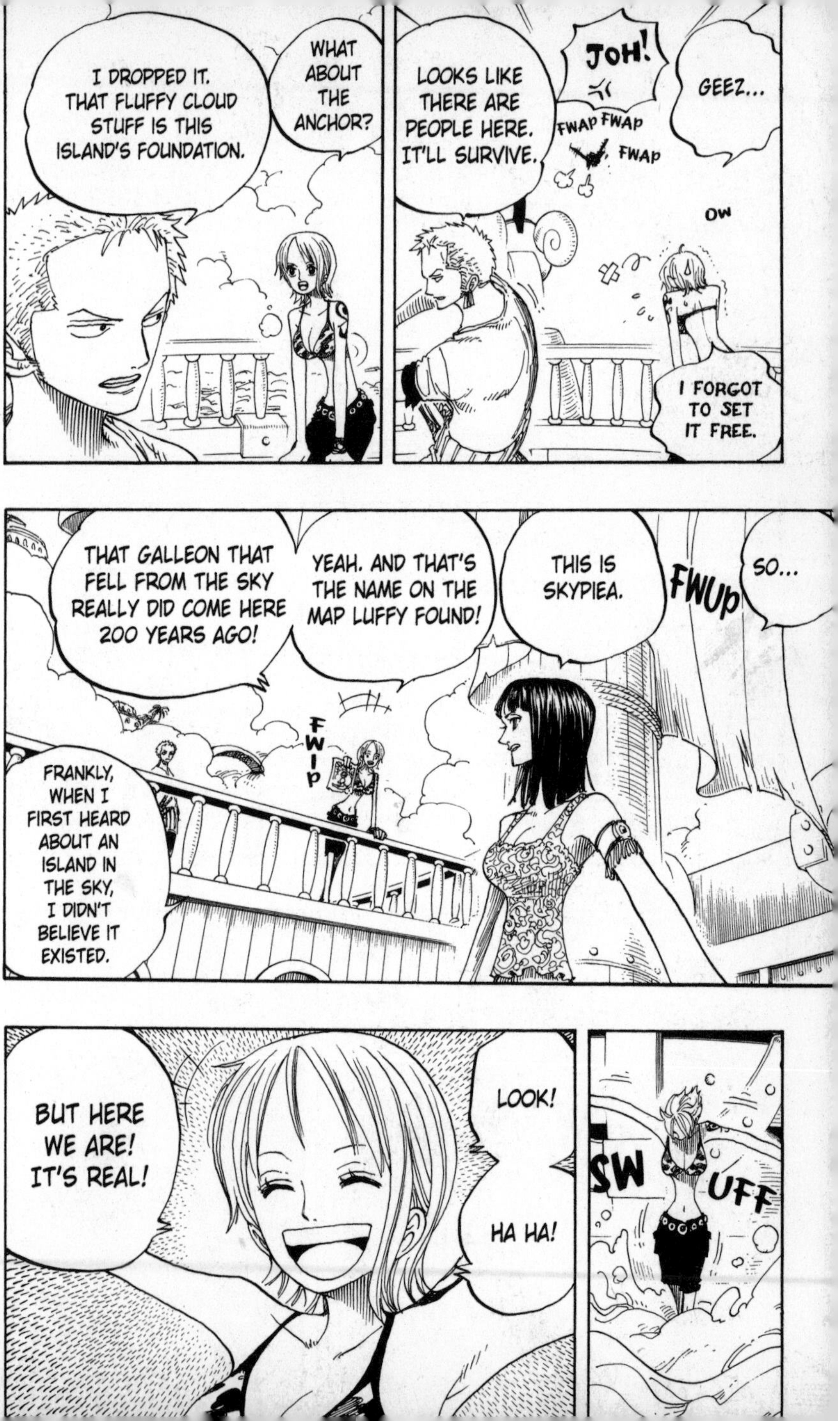
GEEZ...
JOH!
FWAP FWAP
FWAP
LOOKS LIKE THERE ARE PEOPLE HERE. IT'LL SURVIVE.
OW
I FORGOT TO SET IT FREE.
WHAT ABOUT THE ANCHOR?
I DROPPED IT. THAT FLUFFY CLOUD STUFF IS THIS ISLAND'S FOUNDATION.
SO...
FWUP
THIS IS SKYPIEA.
YEAH. AND THAT'S THE NAME ON THE MAP LUFFY FOUND!
THAT GALLEON THAT FELL FROM THE SKY REALLY DID COME HERE 200 YEARS AGO!
FWIP
FRANKLY, WHEN I FIRST HEARD ABOUT AN ISLAND IN THE SKY, I DIDN'T BELIEVE IT EXISTED.
SW
UFF
LOOK!
HA HA!
BUT HERE WE ARE! IT'S REAL!

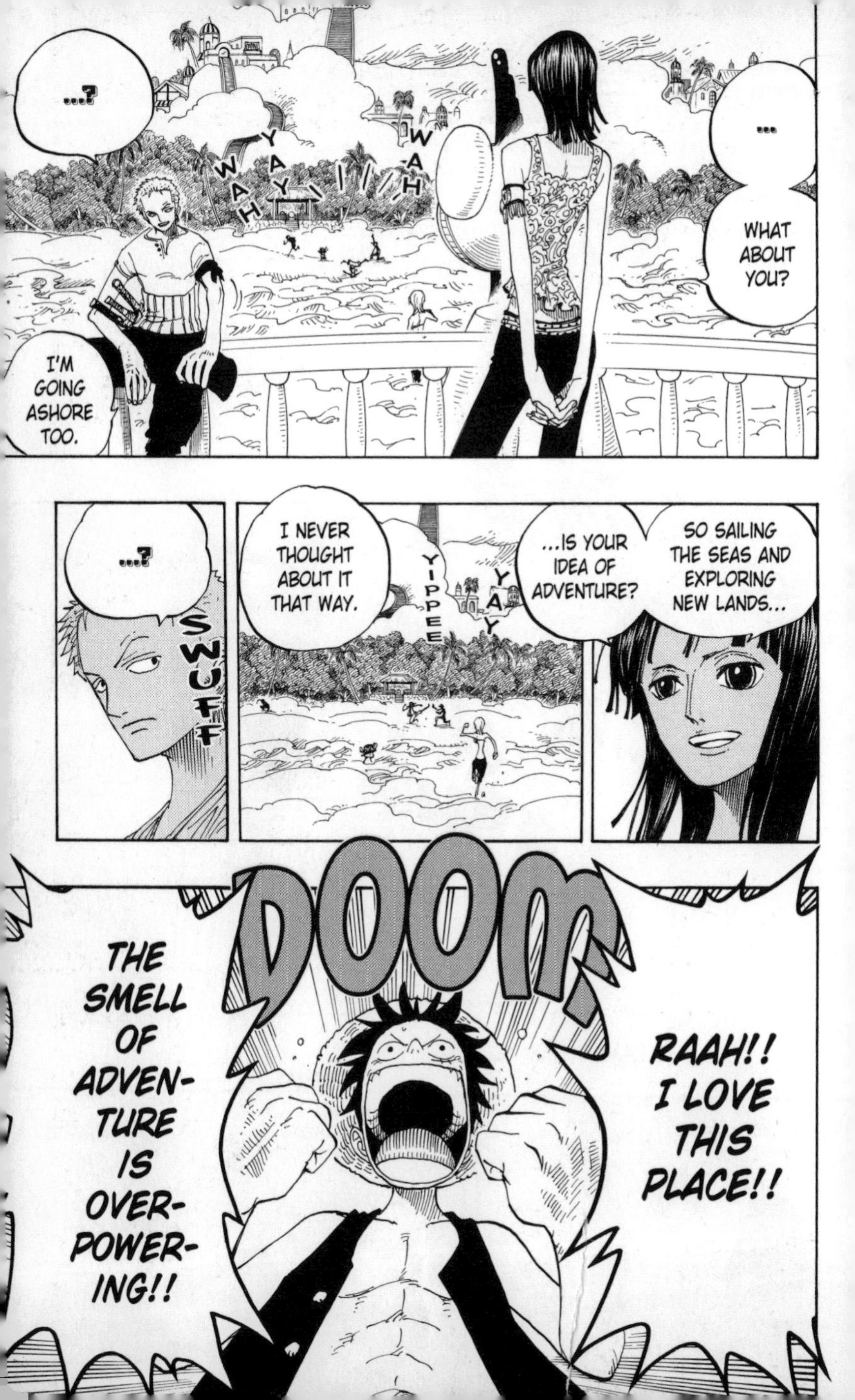
...
WHAT ABOUT YOU?
WAH
WAH
YAY
...?
I'M GOING ASHORE TOO.
SO SAILING THE SEAS AND EXPLORING NEW LANDS...
...IS YOUR IDEA OF ADVENTURE?
YAY
YIPPEE
I NEVER THOUGHT ABOUT IT THAT WAY.
...?
SWUFF
RAAH!! I LOVE THIS PLACE!!
DOOM
THE SMELL OF ADVENTURE IS OVERPOWERING!!

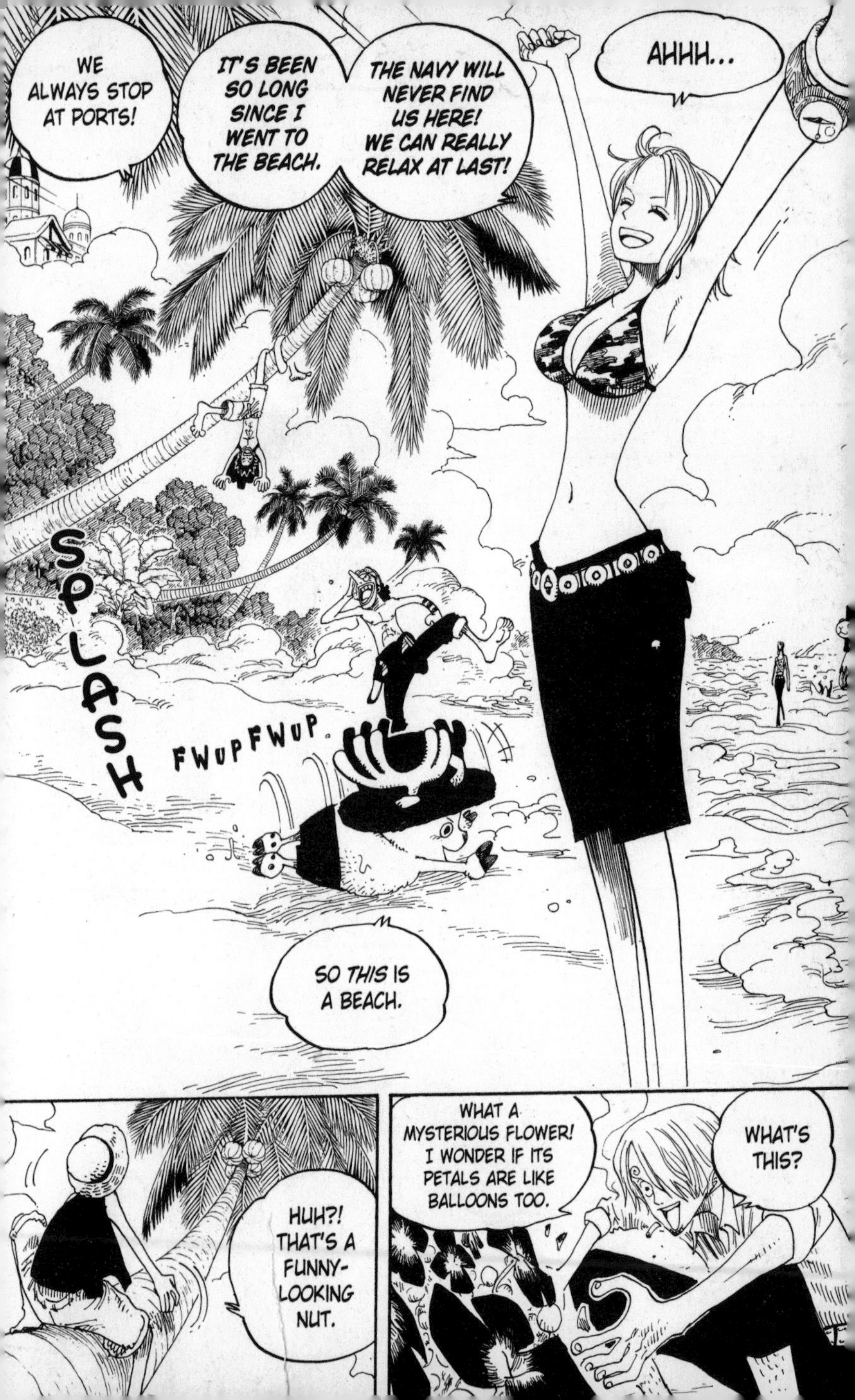
AHHH...
THE NAVY WILL NEVER FIND US HERE! WE CAN REALLY RELAX AT LAST!
IT'S BEEN SO LONG SINCE I WENT TO THE BEACH.
WE ALWAYS STOP AT PORTS!
FWUPFWUP
SPLASH
SO THIS IS A BEACH.
WHAT'S THIS?
WHAT A MYSTERIOUS FLOWER! I WONDER IF ITS PETALS ARE LIKE BALLOONS TOO.
HUH?! THAT'S A FUNNY-LOOKING NUT.

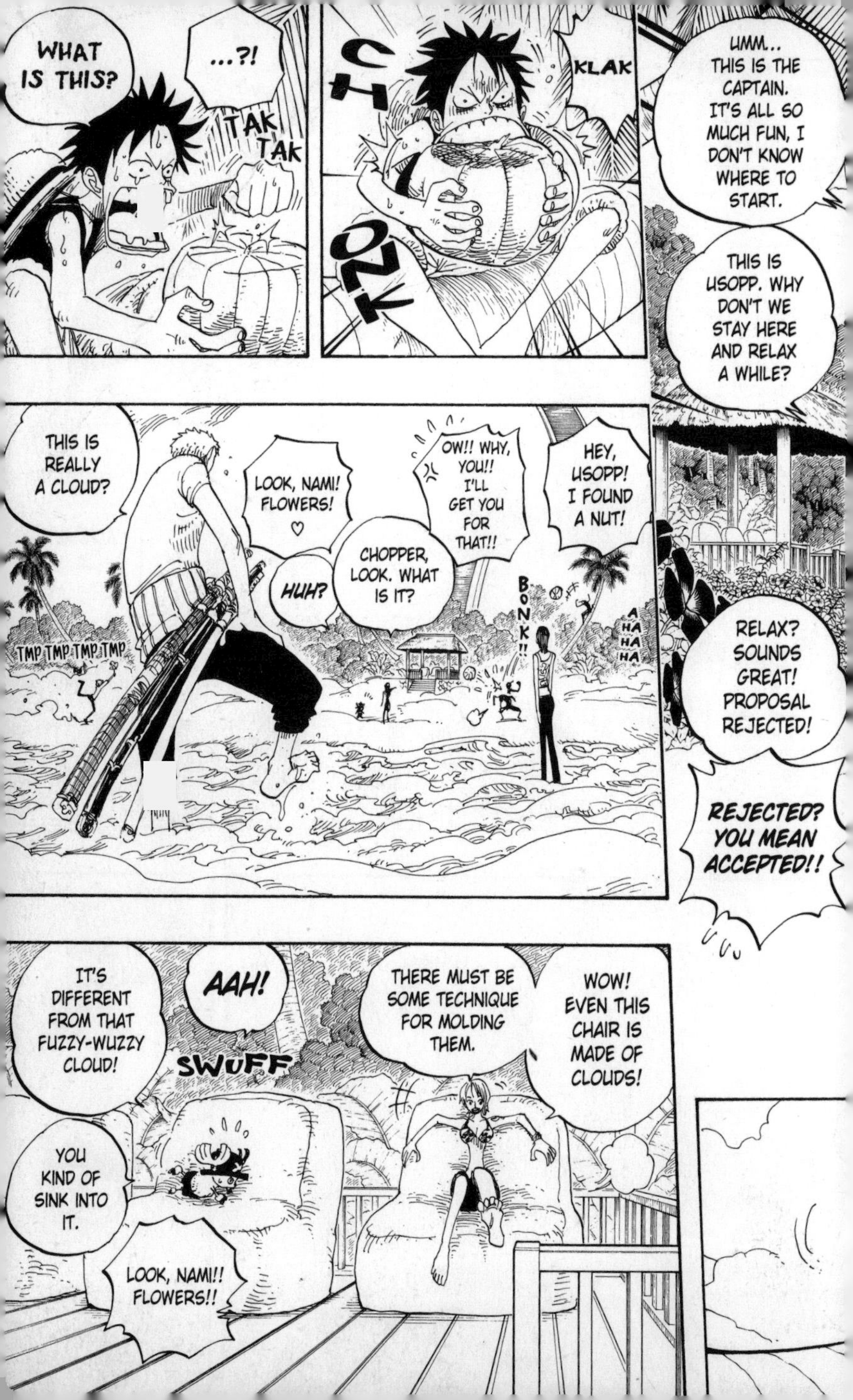
UMM... THIS IS THE CAPTAIN. IT'S ALL SO MUCH FUN, I DON'T KNOW WHERE TO START.
THIS IS USOPP. WHY DON'T WE STAY HERE AND RELAX A WHILE?
RELAX? SOUNDS GREAT! PROPOSAL REJECTED!
REJECTED? YOU MEAN ACCEPTED!!
KLAK
CH
ONK
...?!
TAK TAK
WHAT IS THIS?
HEY, USOPP! I FOUND A NUT!
OW!! WHY, YOU!! I'LL GET YOU FOR THAT!!
BONK!!
AHAHAHAHA
LOOK, NAMI! FLOWERS! ♡
CHOPPER, LOOK. WHAT IS IT?
HUH?
THIS IS REALLY A CLOUD?
TMP TMP TMP TMP
WOW! EVEN THIS CHAIR IS MADE OF CLOUDS!
THERE MUST BE SOME TECHNIQUE FOR MOLDING THEM.
AAH!
SWUFF
IT'S DIFFERENT FROM THAT FUZZY-WUZZY CLOUD!
YOU KIND OF SINK INTO IT.
LOOK, NAMI!! FLOWERS!!

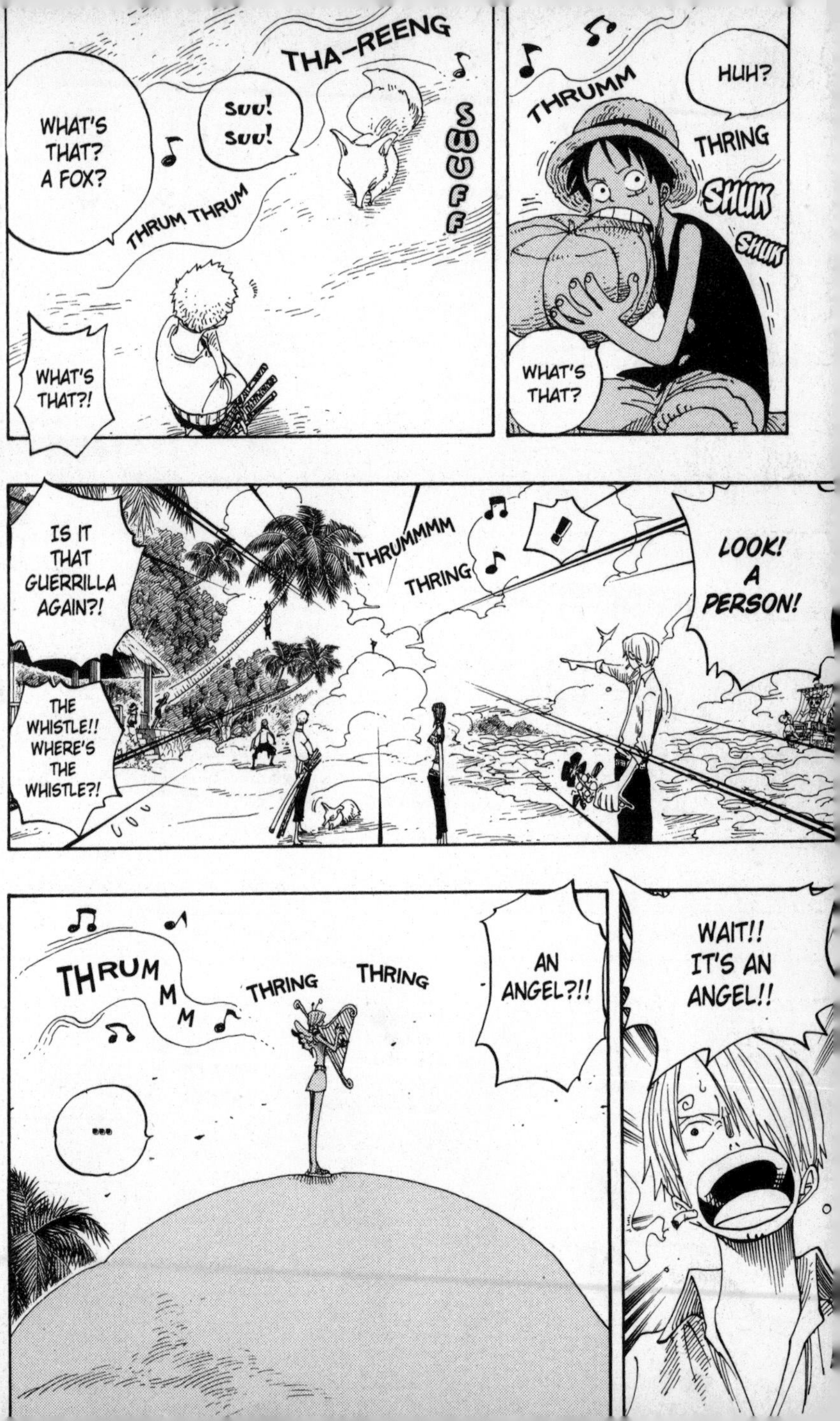
THRUMM
HUH?
THRING
SHUK
SHUK
WHAT'S THAT?
THA-REENG
SUU! SUU!
WHAT'S THAT? A FOX?
SWUFF
THRUM THRUM
WHAT'S THAT?!
LOOK! A PERSON!
!
THRUMMMM
THRING
IS IT THAT GUERRILLA AGAIN?!
THE WHISTLE!! WHERE'S THE WHISTLE?!
WAIT!! IT'S AN ANGEL!!
AN ANGEL?!!
THRING
THRING
THRUMMM
...

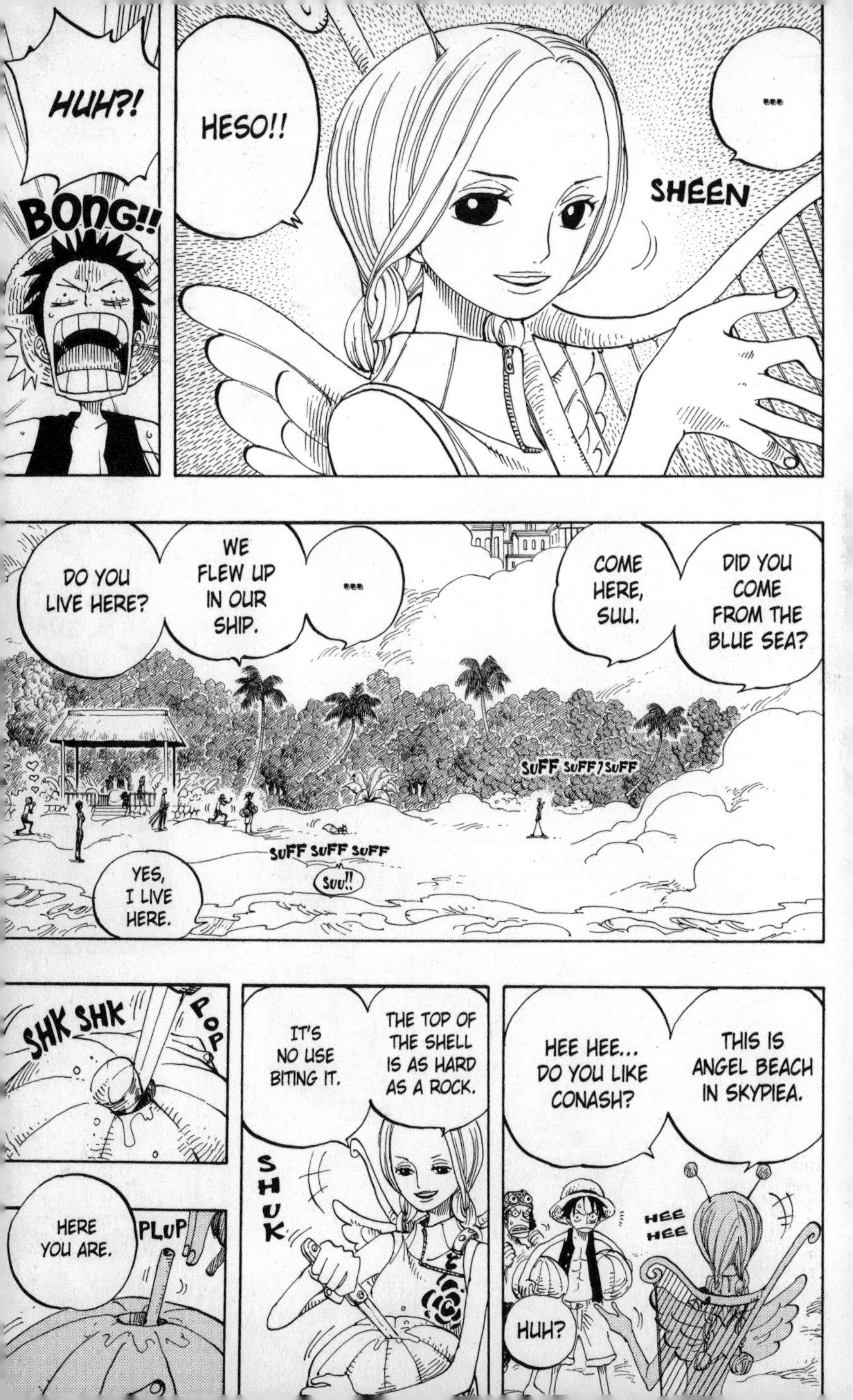
...
SHEEN
HESO!!
HUH?!
BONG!!
DID YOU COME FROM THE BLUE SEA?
COME HERE, SUU.
...
WE FLEW UP IN OUR SHIP.
DO YOU LIVE HERE?
SUFF SUFF SUFF
SUFF SUFF SUFF
SUU!!
YES, I LIVE HERE.
THIS IS ANGEL BEACH IN SKYPIEA.
HEE HEE... DO YOU LIKE CONASH?
HEE HEE
HUH?
THE TOP OF THE SHELL IS AS HARD AS A ROCK.
IT'S NO USE BITING IT.
SHUK
POP
SHK SHK
PLUP
HERE YOU ARE.

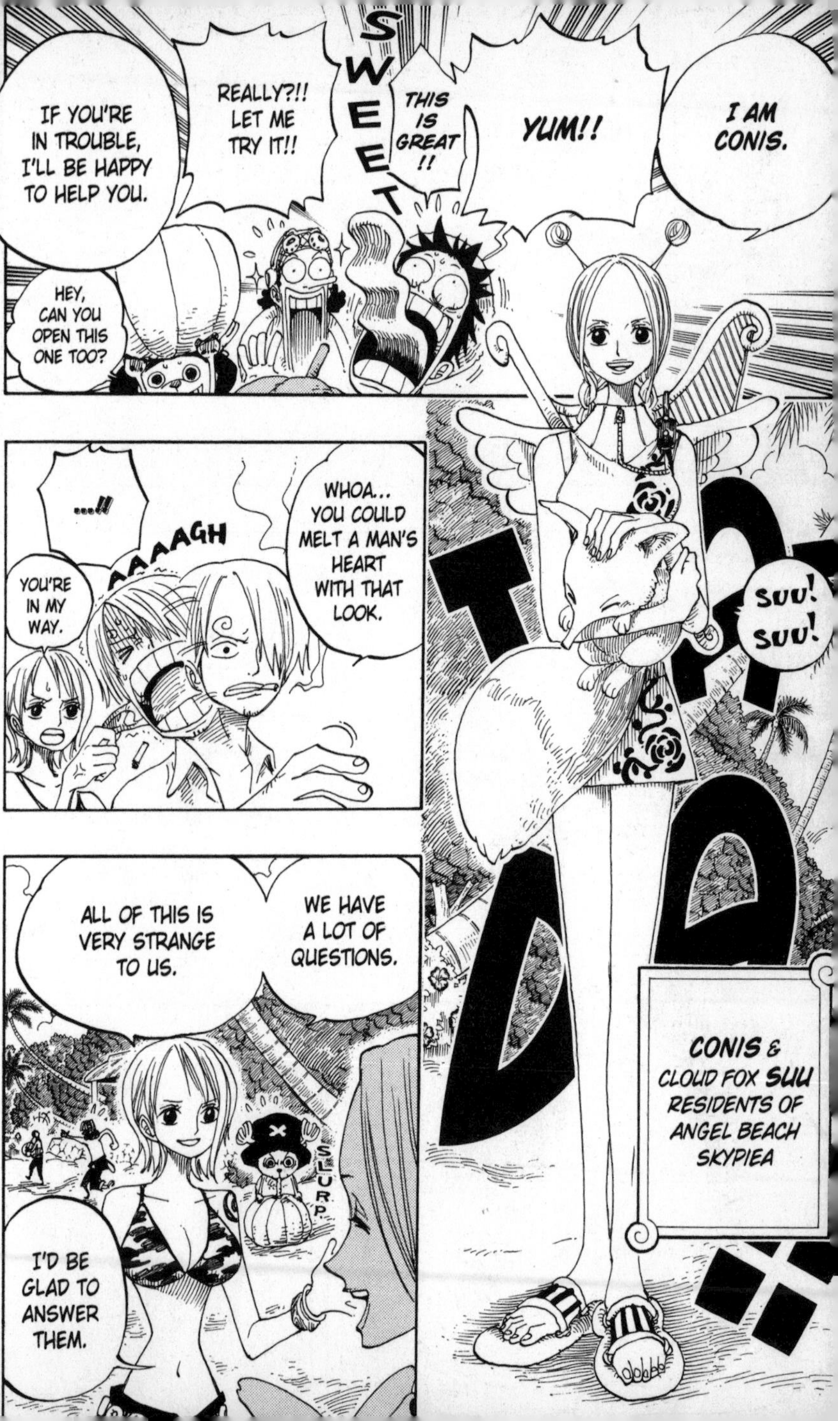
I AM CONIS.
YUM!!
THIS IS GREAT!!
SWEET
REALLY?!! LET ME TRY IT!!
IF YOU'RE IN TROUBLE, I'LL BE HAPPY TO HELP YOU.
HEY, CAN YOU OPEN THIS ONE TOO?
SUU! SUU!
CONIS & CLOUD FOX SUU RESIDENTS OF ANGEL BEACH SKYPIEA
WHOA... YOU COULD MELT A MAN'S HEART WITH THAT LOOK.
...!!
AAAAGH
YOU'RE IN MY WAY.
WE HAVE A LOT OF QUESTIONS.
ALL OF THIS IS VERY STRANGE TO US.
SLURP
I'D BE GLAD TO ANSWER THEM.

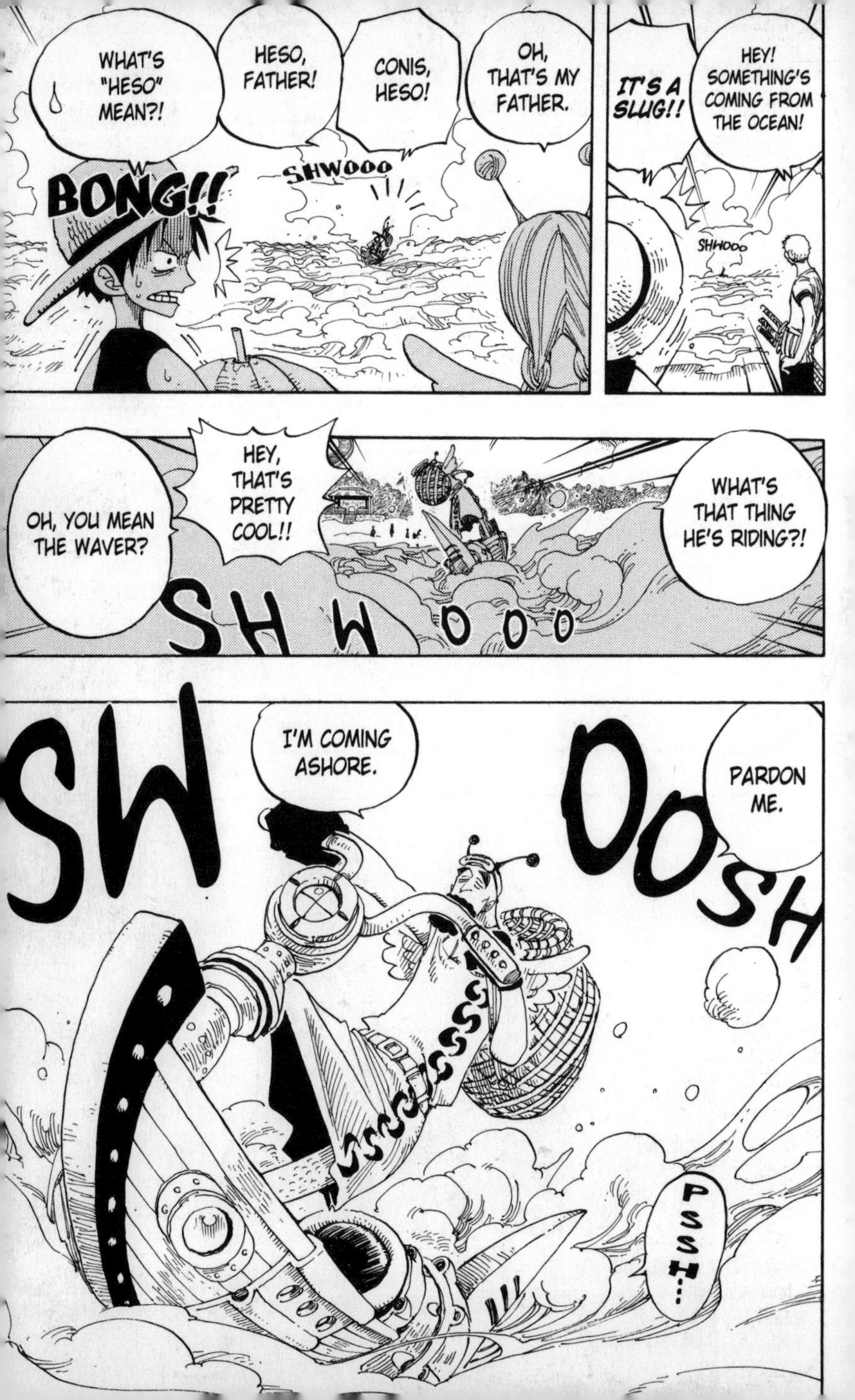
HEY! SOMETHING'S COMING FROM THE OCEAN!
IT'S A SLUG!!
SHWOOO
OH, THAT'S MY FATHER.
CONIS, HESO!
HESO, FATHER!
WHAT'S "HESO" MEAN?!
BONG!!
SHWOOO
WHAT'S THAT THING HE'S RIDING?!
HEY, THAT'S PRETTY COOL!!
OH, YOU MEAN THE WAVER?
SHWOOO
PARDON ME.
I'M COMING ASHORE.
SHWOOSH
PSSH...

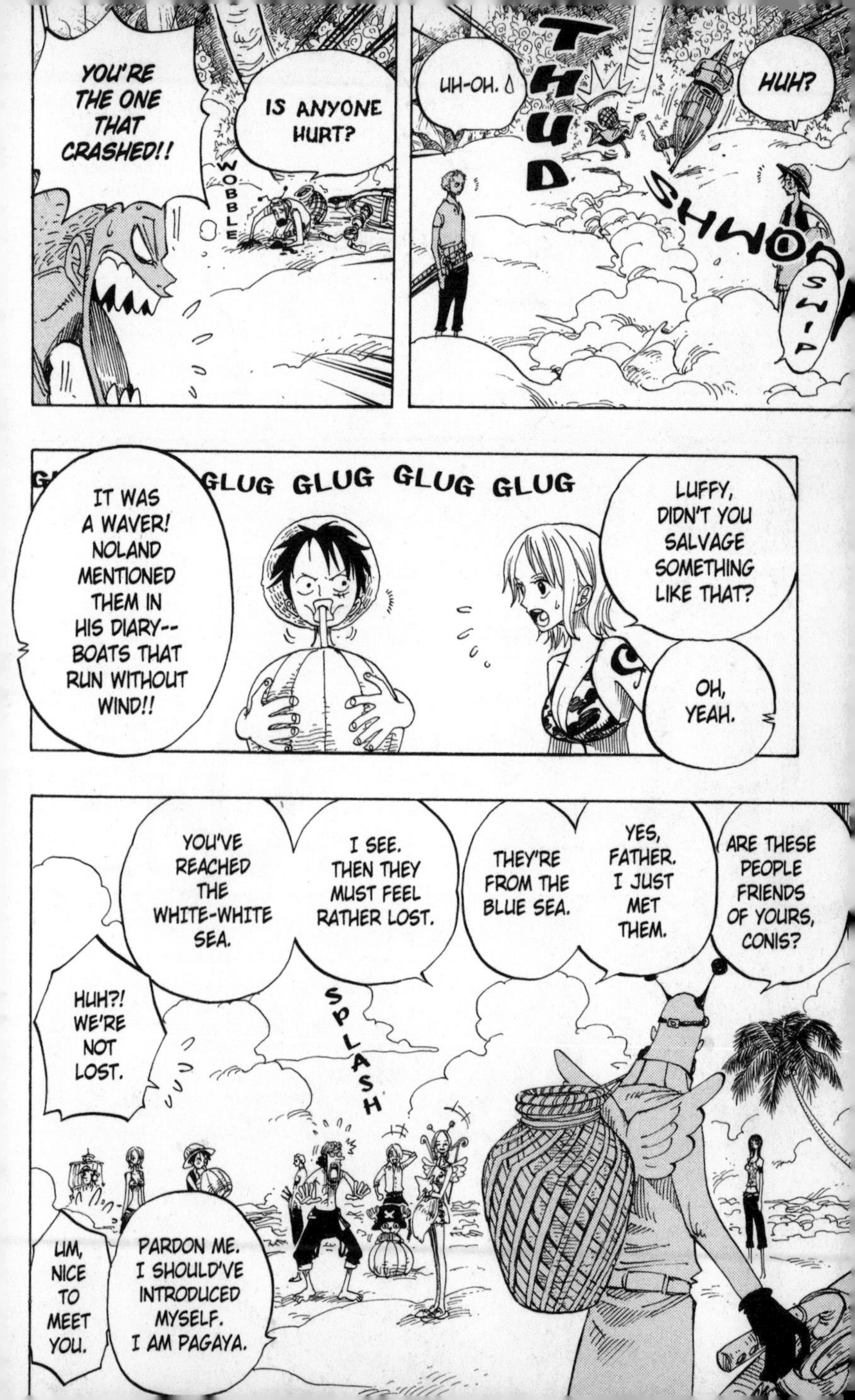
HUH?
UH-OH.
THUD
SHWOOP
SWIP
IS ANYONE HURT?
WOBBLE
YOU'RE THE ONE THAT CRASHED!!
LUFFY, DIDN'T YOU SALVAGE SOMETHING LIKE THAT?
OH, YEAH.
GLUG GLUG GLUG GLUG
IT WAS A WAVER! NOLAND MENTIONED THEM IN HIS DIARY-- BOATS THAT RUN WITHOUT WIND!!
ARE THESE PEOPLE FRIENDS OF YOURS, CONIS?
YES, FATHER. I JUST MET THEM.
THEY'RE FROM THE BLUE SEA.
I SEE. THEN THEY MUST FEEL RATHER LOST.
YOU'VE REACHED THE WHITE-WHITE SEA.
HUH?! WE'RE NOT LOST.
SPLASH
PARDON ME. I SHOULD'VE INTRODUCED MYSELF. I AM PAGAYA.
UM, NICE TO MEET YOU.

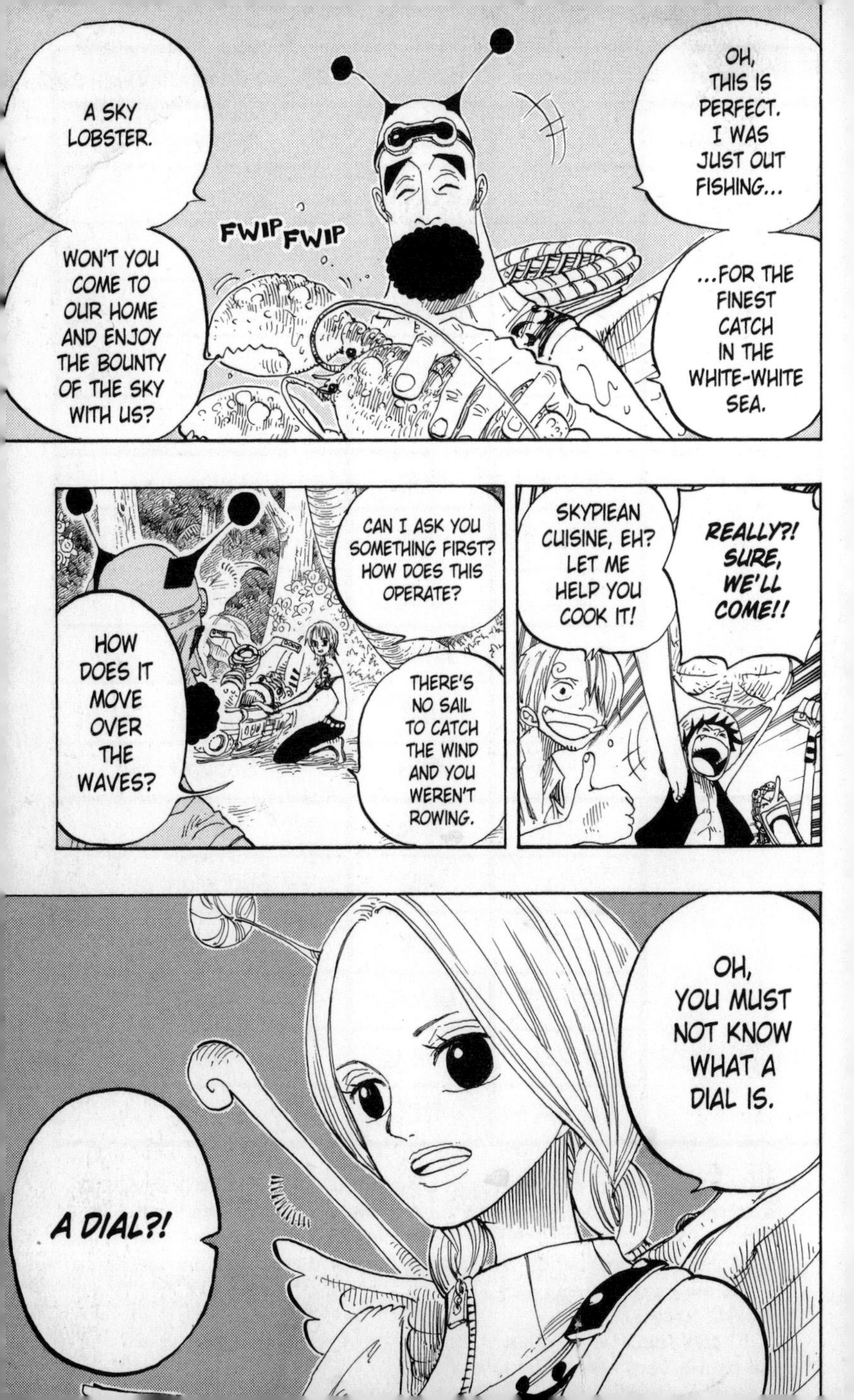

OH, THIS IS PERFECT. I WAS JUST OUT FISHING...
...FOR THE FINEST CATCH IN THE WHITE-WHITE SEA.
FWIP FWIP
A SKY LOBSTER.
WON'T YOU COME TO OUR HOME AND ENJOY THE BOUNTY OF THE SKY WITH US?
REALLY?! SURE, WE'LL COME!!
SKYPIEAN CUISINE, EH? LET ME HELP YOU COOK IT!
CAN I ASK YOU SOMETHING FIRST? HOW DOES THIS OPERATE?
THERE'S NO SAIL TO CATCH THE WIND AND YOU WEREN'T ROWING.
HOW DOES IT MOVE OVER THE WAVES?
OH, YOU MUST NOT KNOW WHAT A DIAL IS.
A DIAL?!

Country	Japanese	Written	Pronunciation
Germany	ルフィ	Ruffy	Luffy
	ゾロ	Zorro	Zolo
	ナミ	Nami	Nami
	ウソップ	Lysop	Lysop
	サンジ	Sanji	Sanji
	チョッパー	Chopper	Chopper
Hong Kong	ルフィ	路飛	Luffy
	ゾロ	卓洛	Cholo
	ナミ	奈美	Noimei
	ウソップ	烏索普	Usopo
	サンジ	山治	Sanji
	チョッパー	索柏	Soppa
Singapore	ルフィ	魯夫	Lufu
	ゾロ	索隆	Suoholon
	ナミ	娜美	Namei
	ウソップ	騙人布	Pyanlenbu
	サンジ	香吉士	Shanjishi
	チョッパー	乔巴	Ciaoppa

O: Although written differently in other countries, the pronunciation is often very similar, so we listed the more exotic ones here. Nico Robin isn't listed because she hasn't debuted yet in these countries. That's only natural since they started later than Japan did. Which reminds me, sometimes I get fan mail from abroad that *I CAN'T READ*. (GONG)

But I can feel the sentiment contained in the words, and that makes me very happy. Thank you.

Chapter 240:

DIAL POWER

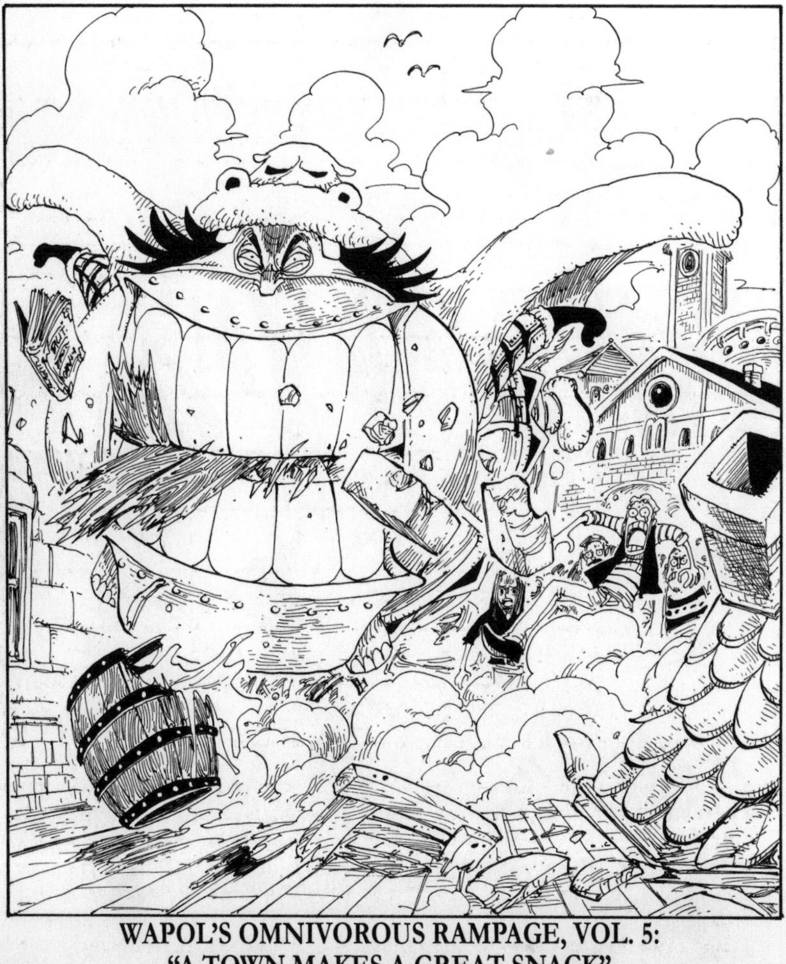

WAPOL'S OMNIVOROUS RAMPAGE, VOL. 5:
"A TOWN MAKES A GREAT SNACK"

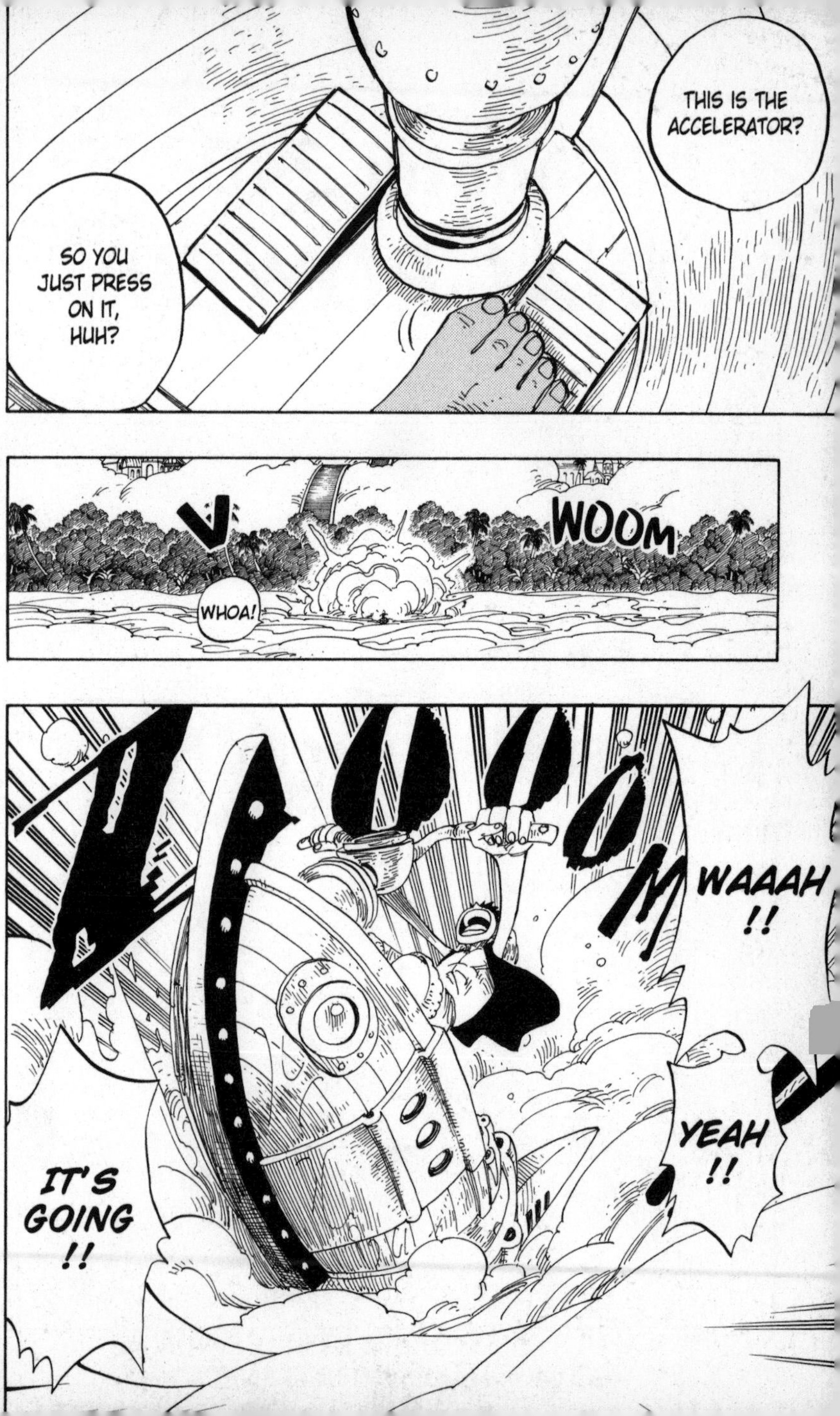
THIS IS THE ACCELERATOR?
SO YOU JUST PRESS ON IT, HUH?
WOOM
WHOA!
WAAAH !!
YEAH !!
IT'S GOING !!

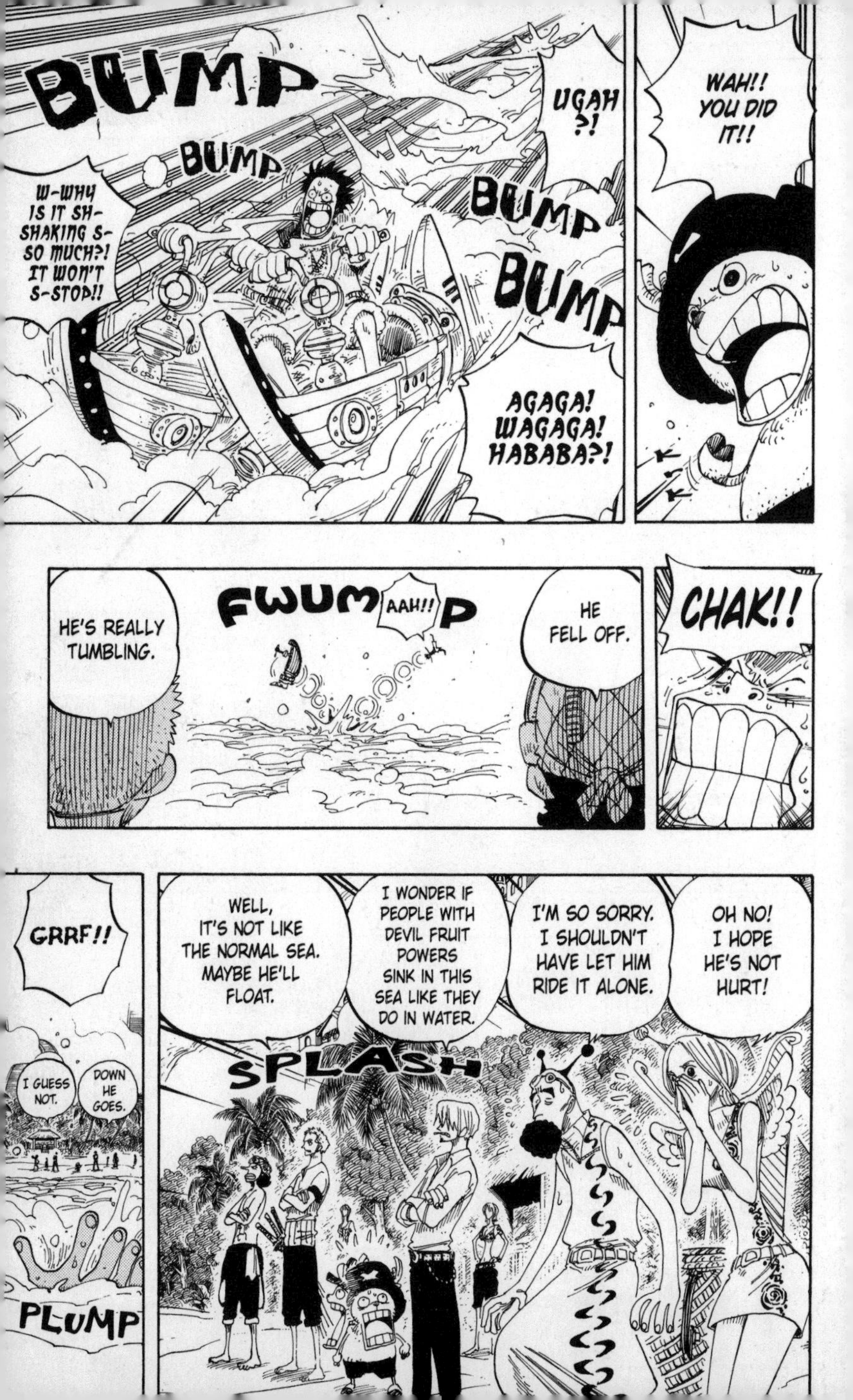
WAH!! YOU DID IT!!
UGAH ?!
BUMP
BUMP
W-WHY IS IT SH-SHAKING S-SO MUCH?! IT WON'T S-STOP!!
BUMP
BUMP
AGAGA! WAGAGA! HABABA?!
CHAK!!
HE FELL OFF.
FWUMP
AAH!!
HE'S REALLY TUMBLING.
OH NO! I HOPE HE'S NOT HURT!
I'M SO SORRY. I SHOULDN'T HAVE LET HIM RIDE IT ALONE.
I WONDER IF PEOPLE WITH DEVIL FRUIT POWERS SINK IN THIS SEA LIKE THEY DO IN WATER.
WELL, IT'S NOT LIKE THE NORMAL SEA. MAYBE HE'LL FLOAT.
SPLASH
GRRF!!
DOWN HE GOES.
I GUESS NOT.
PLUMP

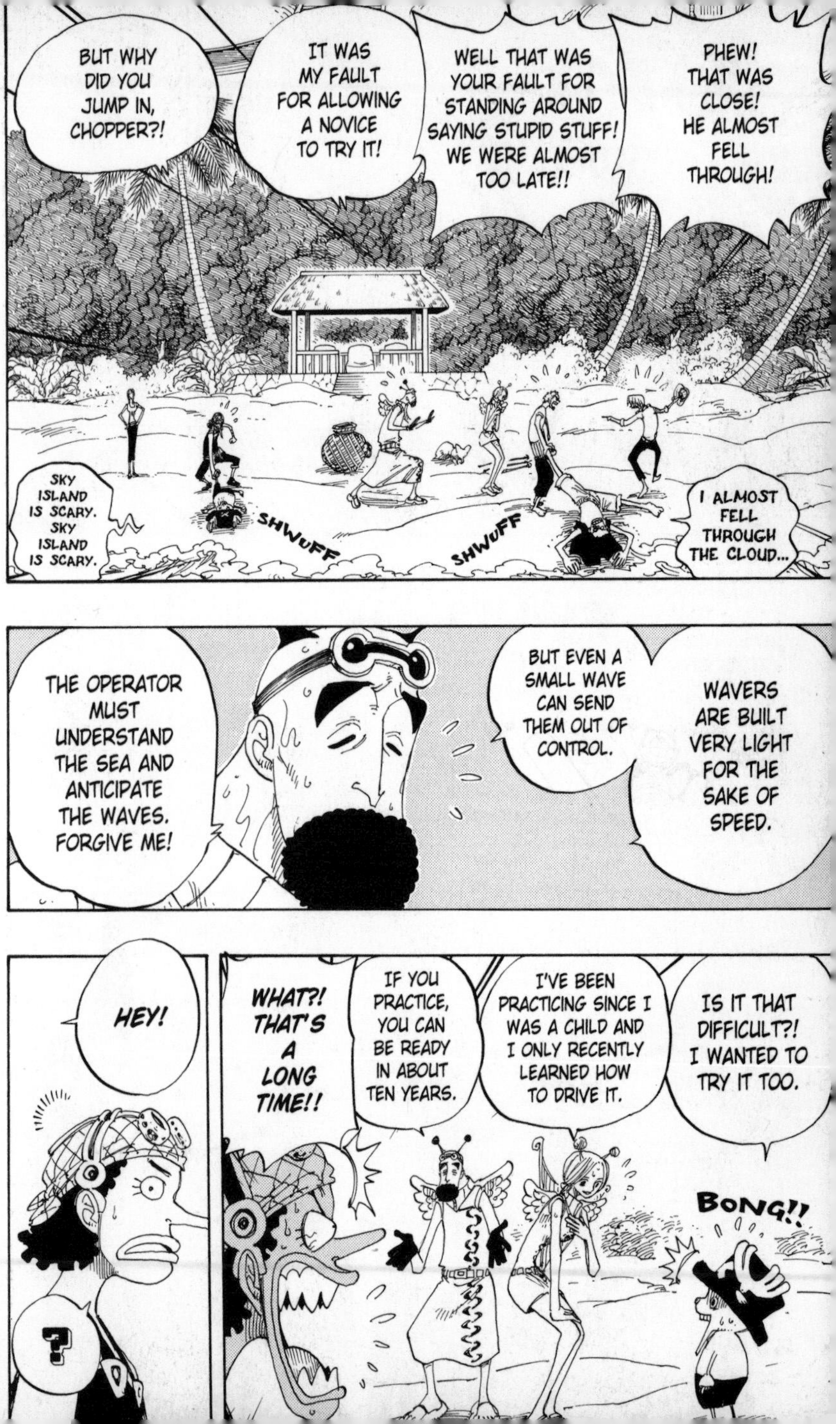
PHEW! THAT WAS CLOSE! HE ALMOST FELL THROUGH!
WELL THAT WAS YOUR FAULT FOR STANDING AROUND SAYING STUPID STUFF! WE WERE ALMOST TOO LATE!!
IT WAS MY FAULT FOR ALLOWING A NOVICE TO TRY IT!
BUT WHY DID YOU JUMP IN, CHOPPER?!
I ALMOST FELL THROUGH THE CLOUD...
SHWUFF
SHWUFF
SKY ISLAND IS SCARY. SKY ISLAND IS SCARY.
WAVERS ARE BUILT VERY LIGHT FOR THE SAKE OF SPEED.
BUT EVEN A SMALL WAVE CAN SEND THEM OUT OF CONTROL.
THE OPERATOR MUST UNDERSTAND THE SEA AND ANTICIPATE THE WAVES. FORGIVE ME!
IS IT THAT DIFFICULT?! I WANTED TO TRY IT TOO.
BONG!!
I'VE BEEN PRACTICING SINCE I WAS A CHILD AND I ONLY RECENTLY LEARNED HOW TO DRIVE IT.
IF YOU PRACTICE, YOU CAN BE READY IN ABOUT TEN YEARS.
WHAT?! THAT'S A LONG TIME!!
HEY!
?

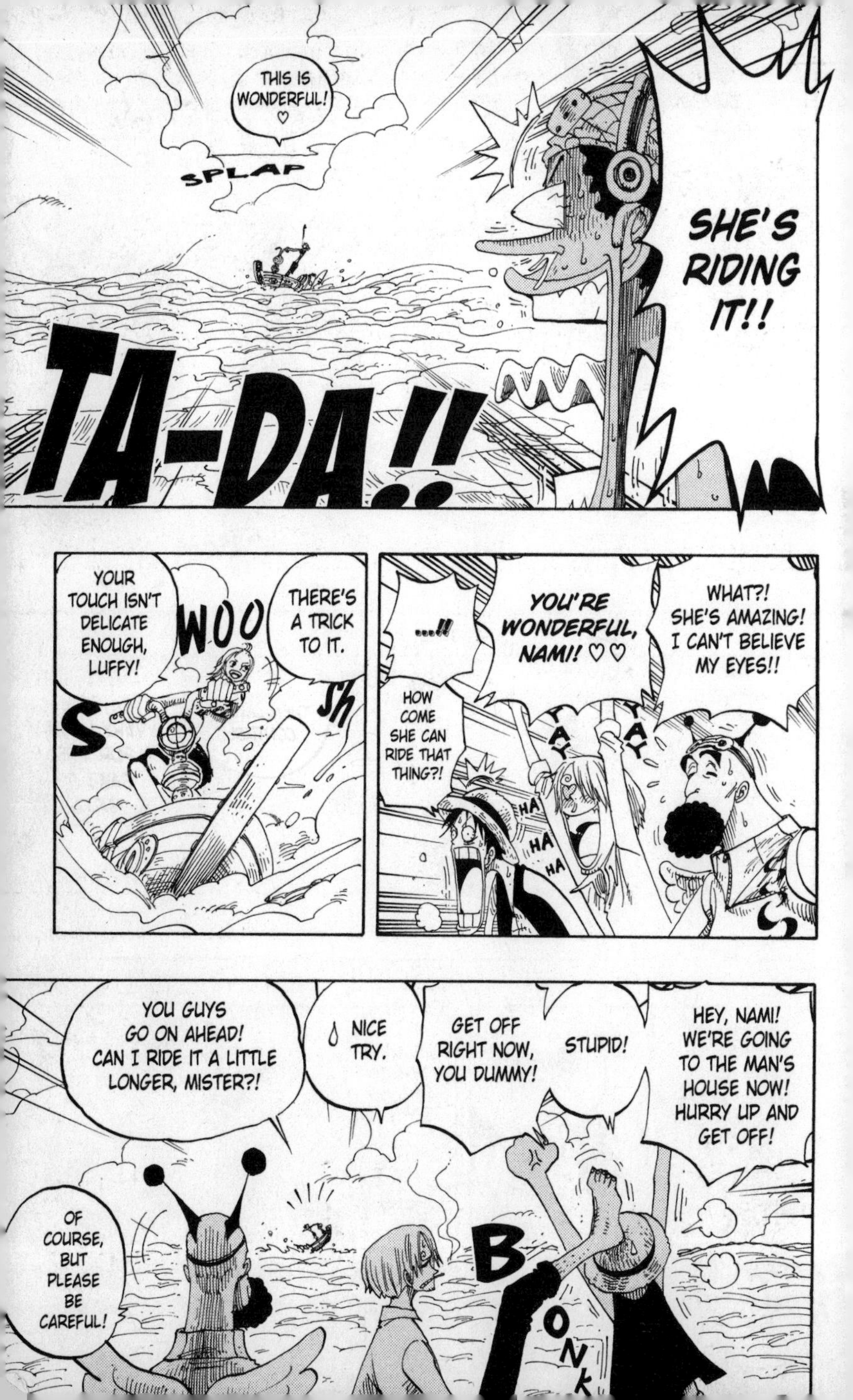
SHE'S RIDING IT!!
THIS IS WONDERFUL! ♡
SPLAP
TA-DA!!
WHAT?! SHE'S AMAZING! I CAN'T BELIEVE MY EYES!!
YOU'RE WONDERFUL, NAMI! ♡♡
...!!
YAY
YAY
HOW COME SHE CAN RIDE THAT THING?!
HA HA HA
THERE'S A TRICK TO IT.
WOO
YOUR TOUCH ISN'T DELICATE ENOUGH, LUFFY!
Sh
S
HEY, NAMI! WE'RE GOING TO THE MAN'S HOUSE NOW! HURRY UP AND GET OFF!
STUPID!
GET OFF RIGHT NOW, YOU DUMMY!
NICE TRY.
YOU GUYS GO ON AHEAD! CAN I RIDE IT A LITTLE LONGER, MISTER?!
OF COURSE, BUT PLEASE BE CAREFUL!
BONK

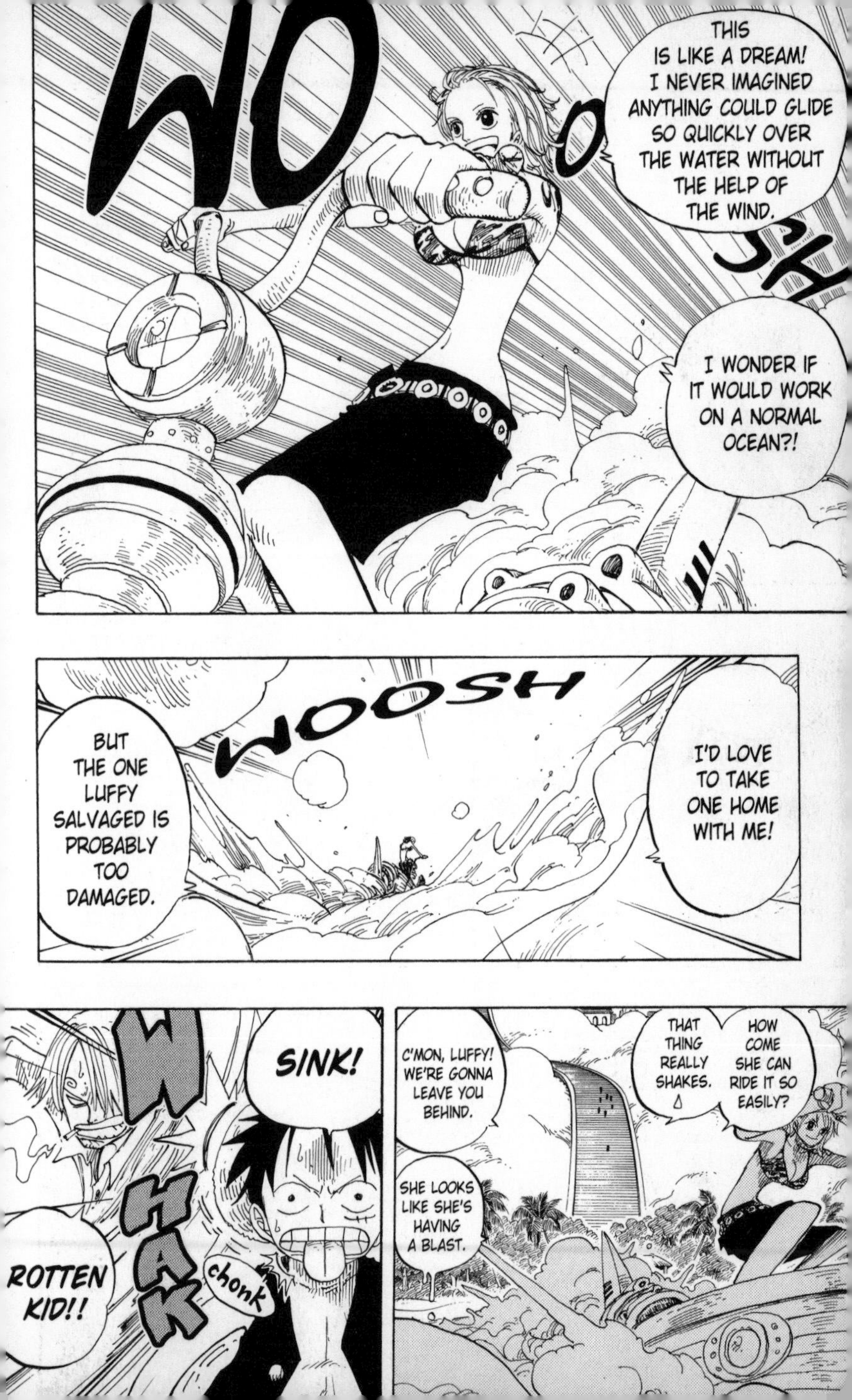
WO
O
SH
THIS IS LIKE A DREAM! I NEVER IMAGINED ANYTHING COULD GLIDE SO QUICKLY OVER THE WATER WITHOUT THE HELP OF THE WIND.
I WONDER IF IT WOULD WORK ON A NORMAL OCEAN?!
I'D LOVE TO TAKE ONE HOME WITH ME!
WOOSH
BUT THE ONE LUFFY SALVAGED IS PROBABLY TOO DAMAGED.
HOW COME SHE CAN RIDE IT SO EASILY?
THAT THING REALLY SHAKES.
C'MON, LUFFY! WE'RE GONNA LEAVE YOU BEHIND.
SHE LOOKS LIKE SHE'S HAVING A BLAST.
SINK!
WHAK
chonk
ROTTEN KID!!

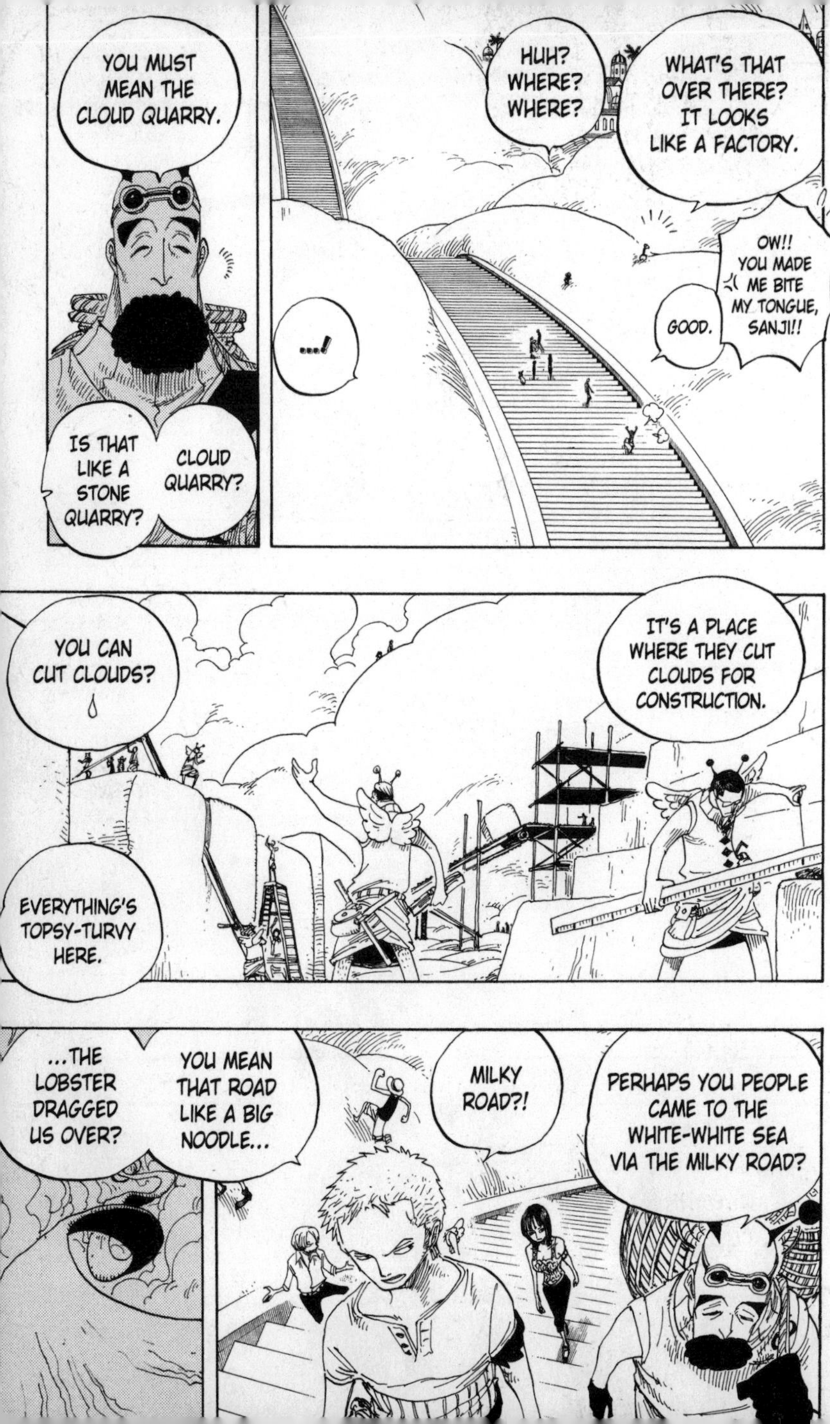
WHAT'S THAT OVER THERE? IT LOOKS LIKE A FACTORY.
HUH? WHERE? WHERE?
OW!! YOU MADE ME BITE MY TONGUE, SANJI!!
GOOD.
...!
YOU MUST MEAN THE CLOUD QUARRY.
CLOUD QUARRY?
IS THAT LIKE A STONE QUARRY?
IT'S A PLACE WHERE THEY CUT CLOUDS FOR CONSTRUCTION.
YOU CAN CUT CLOUDS?
EVERYTHING'S TOPSY-TURVY HERE.
PERHAPS YOU PEOPLE CAME TO THE WHITE-WHITE SEA VIA THE MILKY ROAD?
MILKY ROAD?!
YOU MEAN THAT ROAD LIKE A BIG NOODLE...
...THE LOBSTER DRAGGED US OVER?

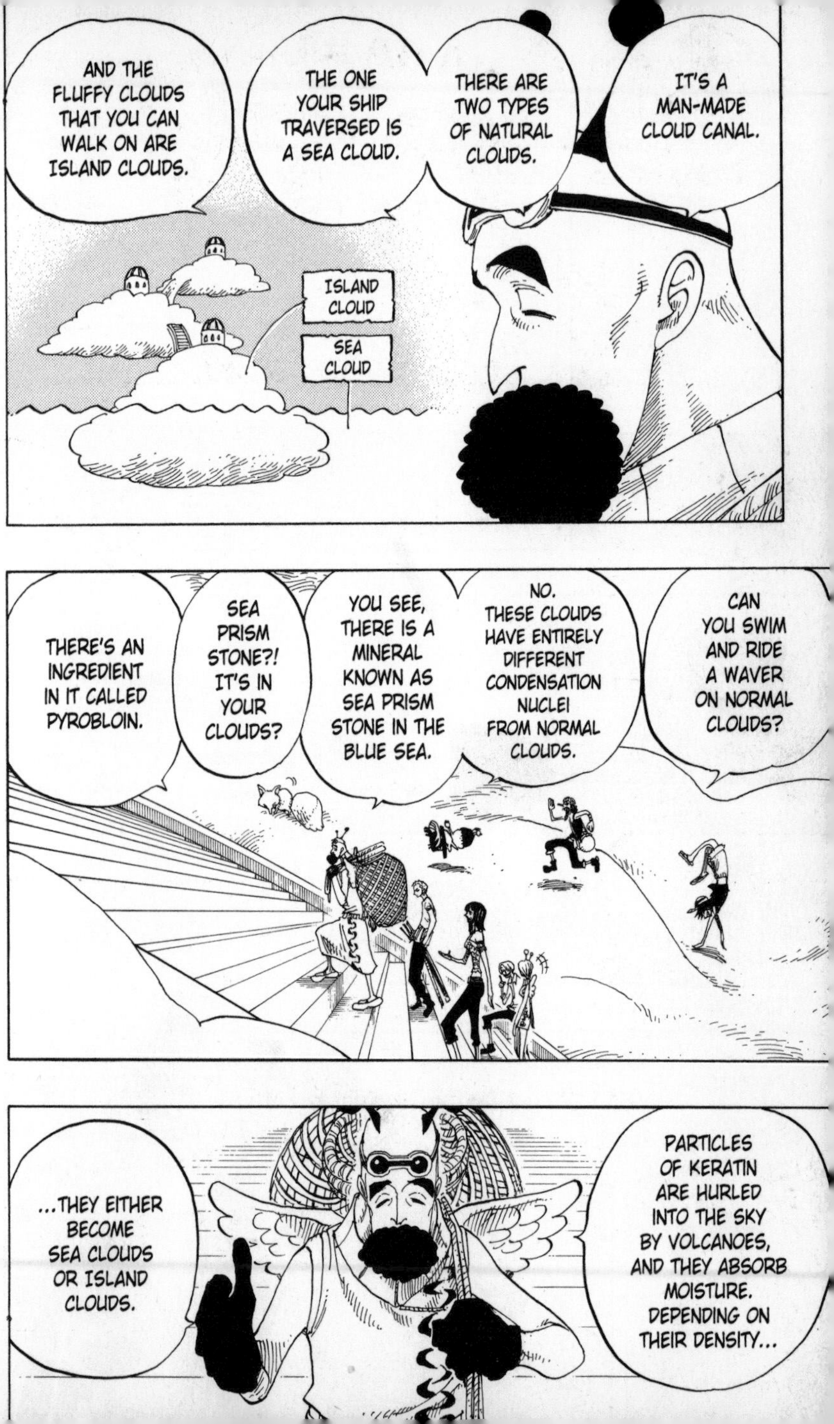
IT'S A MAN-MADE CLOUD CANAL.
THERE ARE TWO TYPES OF NATURAL CLOUDS.
THE ONE YOUR SHIP TRAVERSED IS A SEA CLOUD.
AND THE FLUFFY CLOUDS THAT YOU CAN WALK ON ARE ISLAND CLOUDS.
ISLAND CLOUD
SEA CLOUD
CAN YOU SWIM AND RIDE A WAVER ON NORMAL CLOUDS?
NO. THESE CLOUDS HAVE ENTIRELY DIFFERENT CONDENSATION NUCLEI FROM NORMAL CLOUDS.
YOU SEE, THERE IS A MINERAL KNOWN AS SEA PRISM STONE IN THE BLUE SEA.
SEA PRISM STONE?! IT'S IN YOUR CLOUDS?
THERE'S AN INGREDIENT IN IT CALLED PYROBLOIN.
PARTICLES OF KERATIN ARE HURLED INTO THE SKY BY VOLCANOES, AND THEY ABSORB MOISTURE. DEPENDING ON THEIR DENSITY...
...THEY EITHER BECOME SEA CLOUDS OR ISLAND CLOUDS.

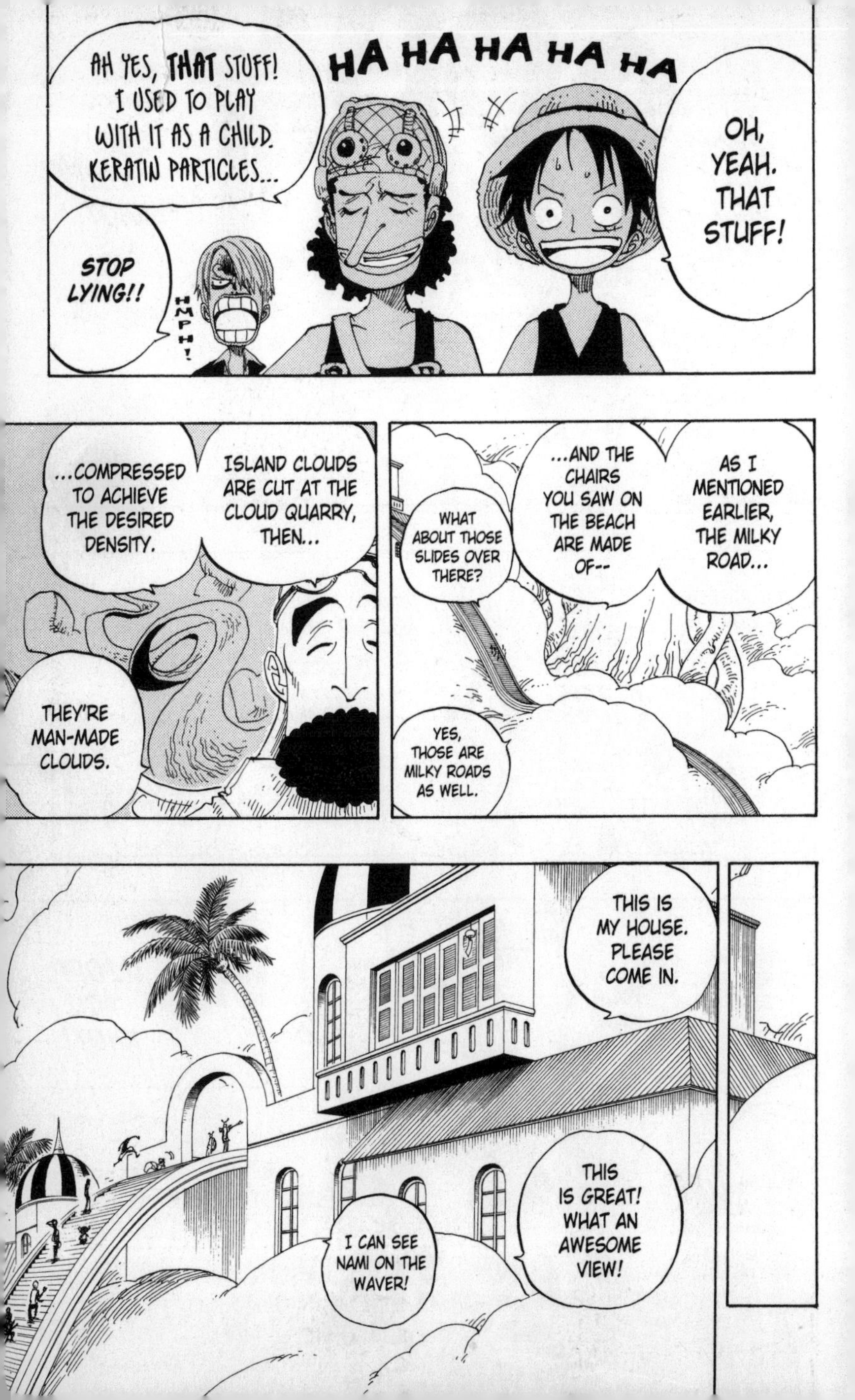
OH, YEAH. THAT STUFF!
HA HA HA HA HA
AH YES, **THAT** STUFF! I USED TO PLAY WITH IT AS A CHILD. KERATIN PARTICLES...
STOP LYING!!
HMPH!
AS I MENTIONED EARLIER, THE MILKY ROAD...
...AND THE CHAIRS YOU SAW ON THE BEACH ARE MADE OF--
WHAT ABOUT THOSE SLIDES OVER THERE?
YES, THOSE ARE MILKY ROADS AS WELL.
ISLAND CLOUDS ARE CUT AT THE CLOUD QUARRY, THEN...
...COMPRESSED TO ACHIEVE THE DESIRED DENSITY.
THEY'RE MAN-MADE CLOUDS.
THIS IS MY HOUSE. PLEASE COME IN.
THIS IS GREAT! WHAT AN AWESOME VIEW!
I CAN SEE NAMI ON THE WAVER!

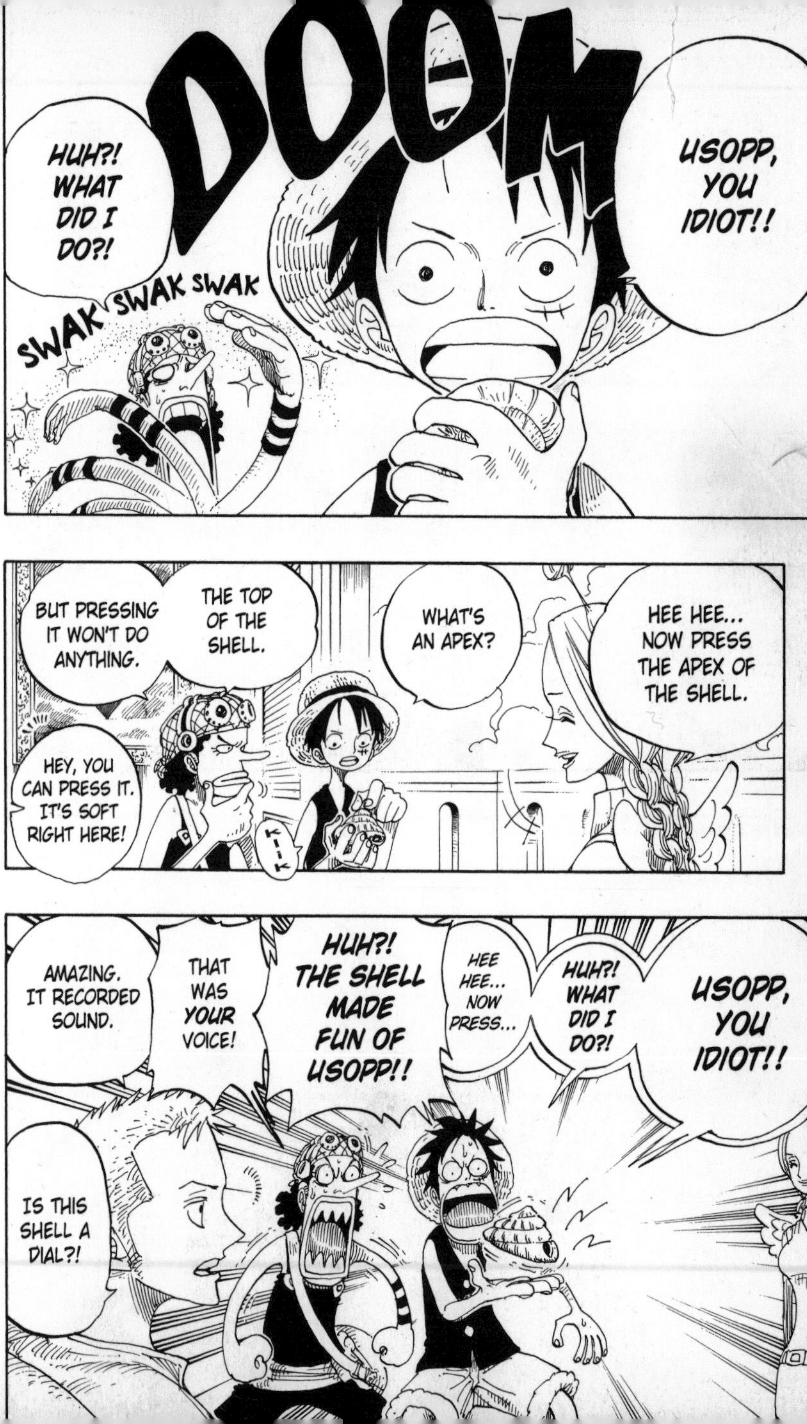
USOPP, YOU IDIOT!!
DOOM
HUH?! WHAT DID I DO?!
SWAK SWAK SWAK
HEE HEE... NOW PRESS THE APEX OF THE SHELL.
WHAT'S AN APEX?
THE TOP OF THE SHELL.
BUT PRESSING IT WON'T DO ANYTHING.
KLIK
HEY, YOU CAN PRESS IT. IT'S SOFT RIGHT HERE!
USOPP, YOU IDIOT!!
HUH?! WHAT DID I DO?!
HEE HEE... NOW PRESS...
HUH?! THE SHELL MADE FUN OF USOPP!!
THAT WAS YOUR VOICE!
AMAZING. IT RECORDED SOUND.
IS THIS SHELL A DIAL?!

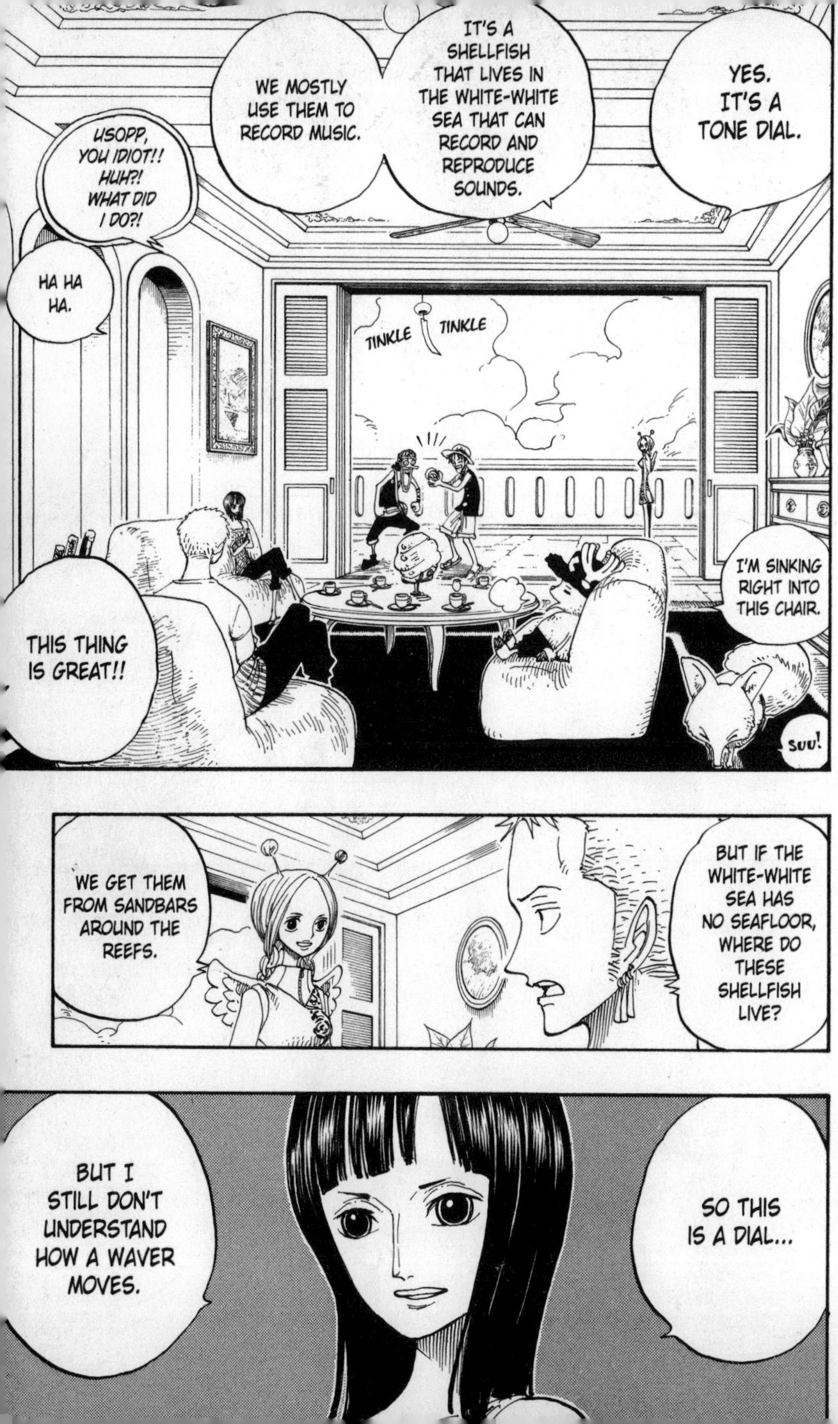
YES. IT'S A TONE DIAL.
IT'S A SHELLFISH THAT LIVES IN THE WHITE-WHITE SEA THAT CAN RECORD AND REPRODUCE SOUNDS.
WE MOSTLY USE THEM TO RECORD MUSIC.
USOPP, YOU IDIOT!! HUH?! WHAT DID I DO?!
HA HA HA.
TINKLE TINKLE
I'M SINKING RIGHT INTO THIS CHAIR.
SUU!
THIS THING IS GREAT!!
BUT IF THE WHITE-WHITE SEA HAS NO SEAFLOOR, WHERE DO THESE SHELLFISH LIVE?
WE GET THEM FROM SANDBARS AROUND THE REEFS.
SO THIS IS A DIAL...
BUT I STILL DON'T UNDERSTAND HOW A WAVER MOVES.

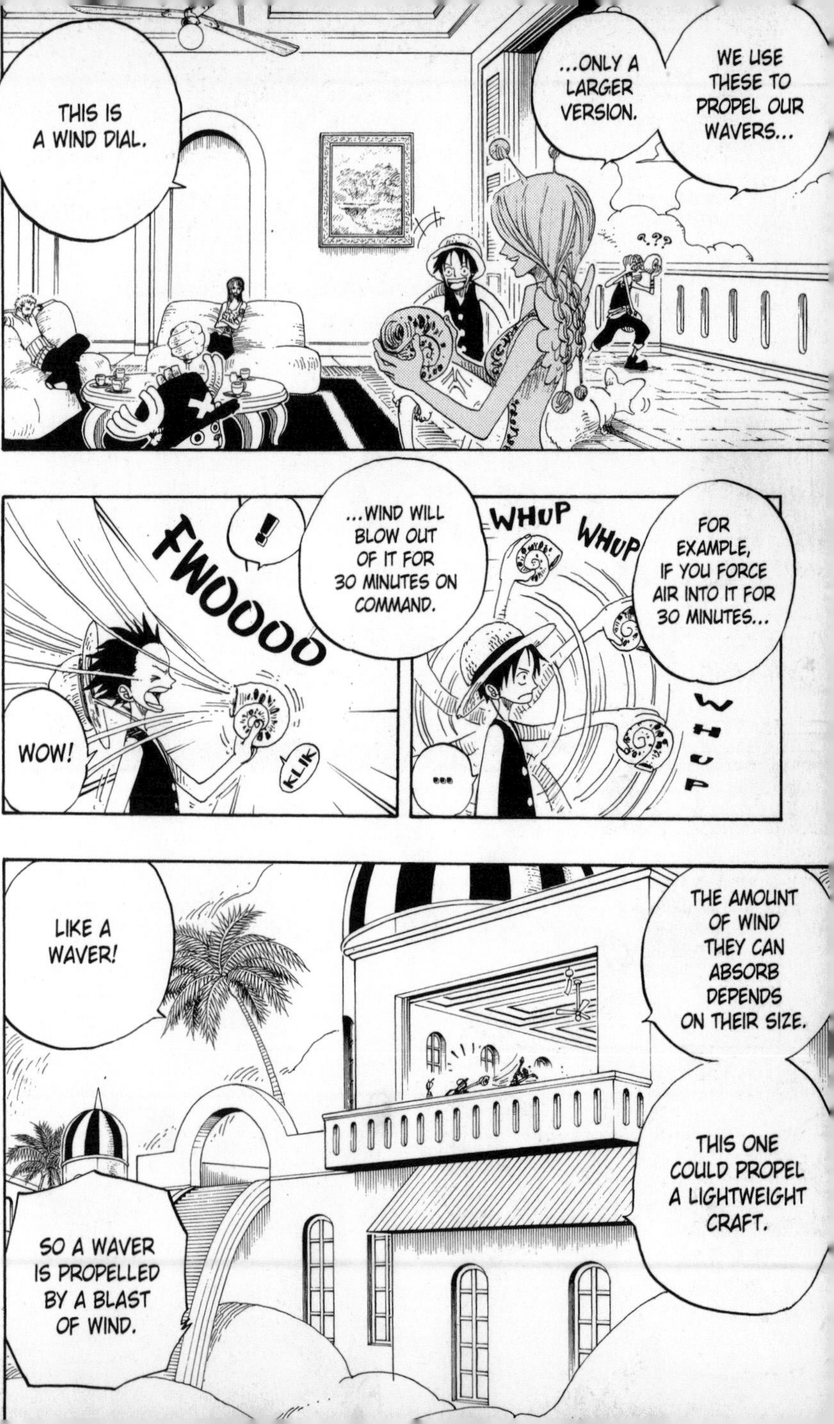
WE USE THESE TO PROPEL OUR WAVERS...
...ONLY A LARGER VERSION.
?.??
THIS IS A WIND DIAL.
WHUP WHUP
FOR EXAMPLE, IF YOU FORCE AIR INTO IT FOR 30 MINUTES...
WHUP
...
...WIND WILL BLOW OUT OF IT FOR 30 MINUTES ON COMMAND.
!
FWOOOOO
KLIK
WOW!
THE AMOUNT OF WIND THEY CAN ABSORB DEPENDS ON THEIR SIZE.
THIS ONE COULD PROPEL A LIGHTWEIGHT CRAFT.
LIKE A WAVER!
SO A WAVER IS PROPELLED BY A BLAST OF WIND.

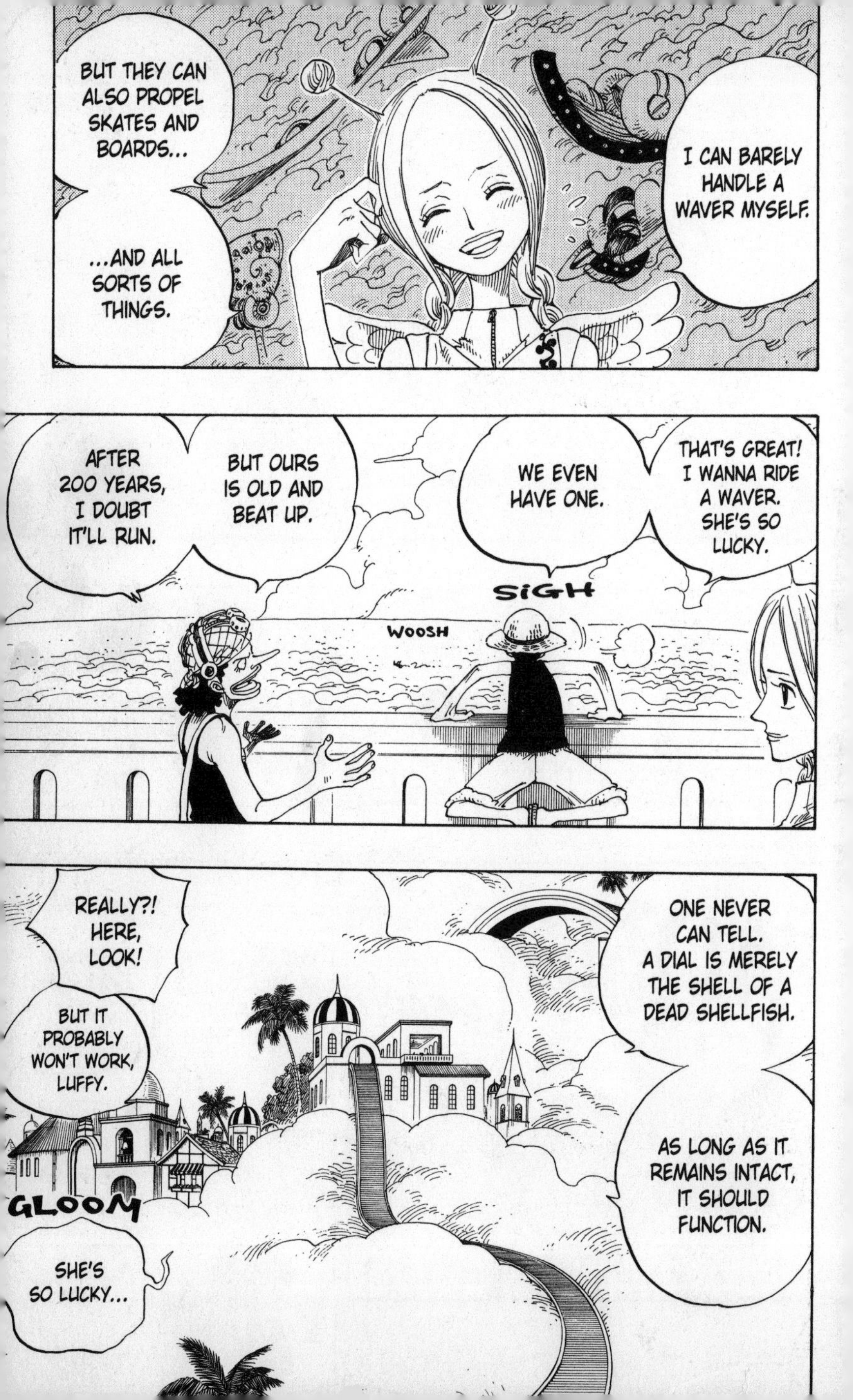
BUT THEY CAN ALSO PROPEL SKATES AND BOARDS...
...AND ALL SORTS OF THINGS.
I CAN BARELY HANDLE A WAVER MYSELF.
THAT'S GREAT! I WANNA RIDE A WAVER. SHE'S SO LUCKY.
WE EVEN HAVE ONE.
SIGH
WOOSH
BUT OURS IS OLD AND BEAT UP.
AFTER 200 YEARS, I DOUBT IT'LL RUN.
ONE NEVER CAN TELL. A DIAL IS MERELY THE SHELL OF A DEAD SHELLFISH.
AS LONG AS IT REMAINS INTACT, IT SHOULD FUNCTION.
REALLY?! HERE, LOOK!
BUT IT PROBABLY WON'T WORK, LUFFY.
GLOOM
SHE'S SO LUCKY...

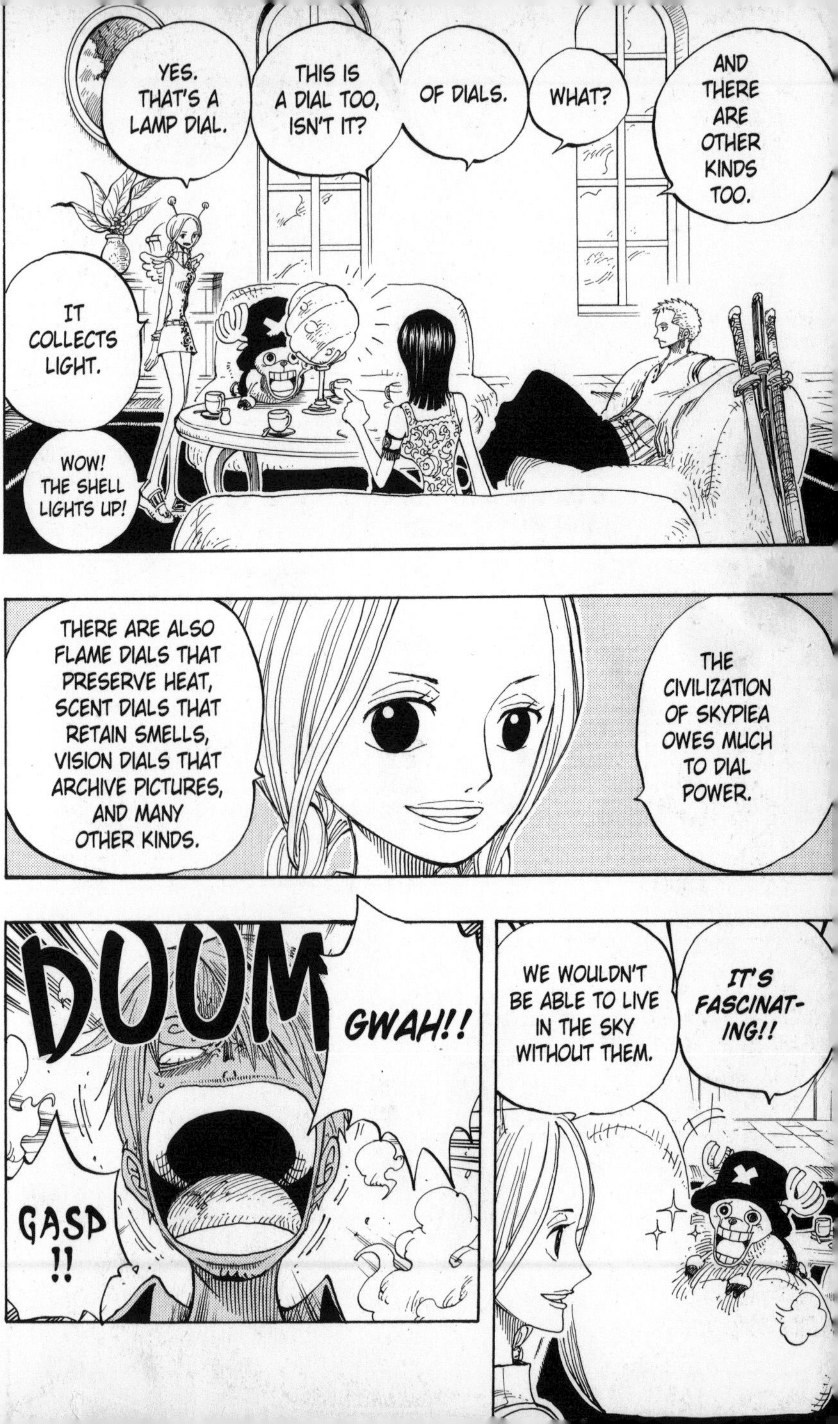
AND THERE ARE OTHER KINDS TOO.
WHAT?
OF DIALS.
THIS IS A DIAL TOO, ISN'T IT?
YES. THAT'S A LAMP DIAL.
IT COLLECTS LIGHT.
WOW! THE SHELL LIGHTS UP!
THE CIVILIZATION OF SKYPIEA OWES MUCH TO DIAL POWER.
THERE ARE ALSO FLAME DIALS THAT PRESERVE HEAT, SCENT DIALS THAT RETAIN SMELLS, VISION DIALS THAT ARCHIVE PICTURES, AND MANY OTHER KINDS.
IT'S FASCINAT-ING!!
WE WOULDN'T BE ABLE TO LIVE IN THE SKY WITHOUT THEM.
GWAH!!
DOOM
GASP !!

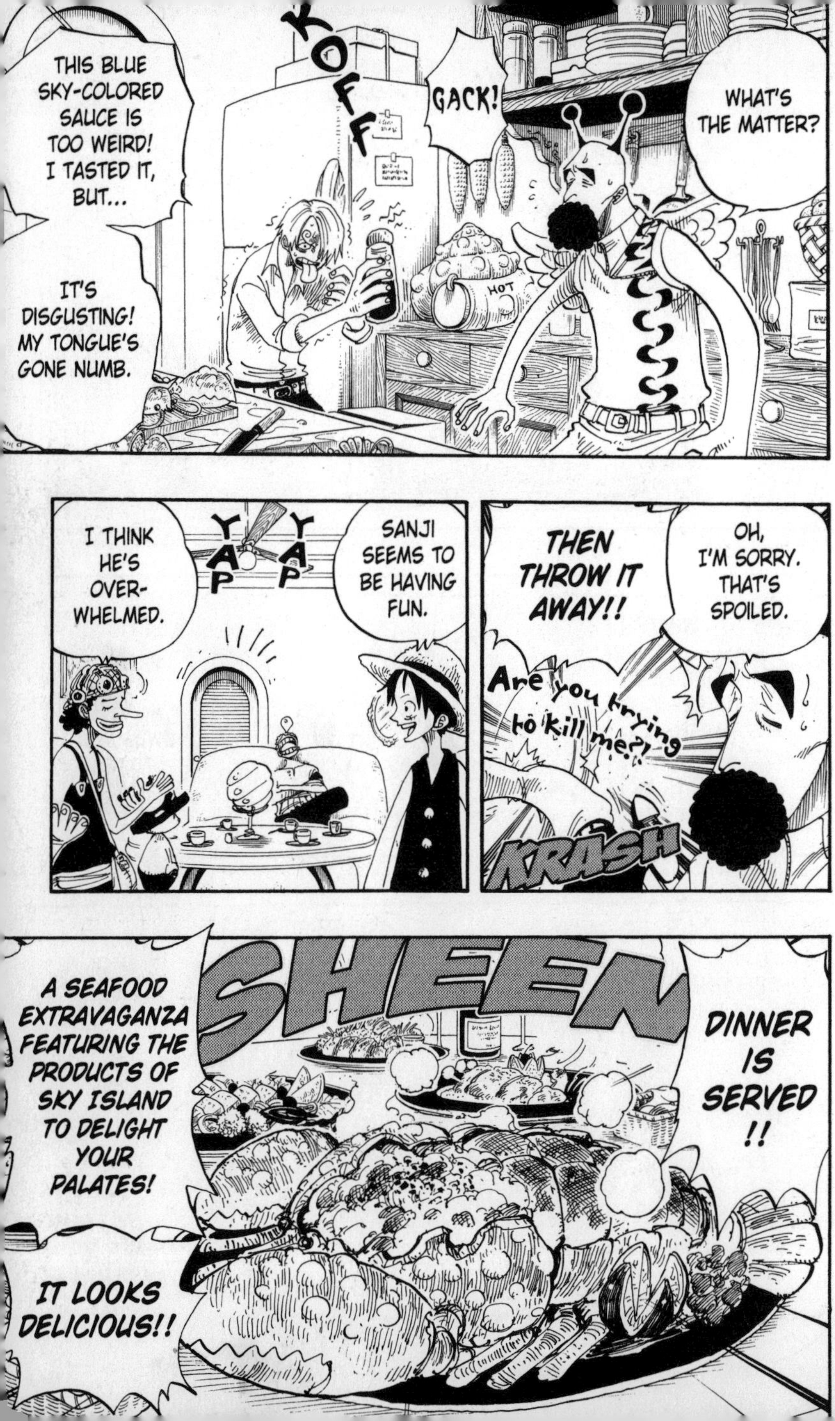
WHAT'S THE MATTER?
GACK!
KOFF KOFF
HOT
THIS BLUE SKY-COLORED SAUCE IS TOO WEIRD! I TASTED IT, BUT...
IT'S DISGUSTING! MY TONGUE'S GONE NUMB.
OH, I'M SORRY. THAT'S SPOILED.
THEN THROW IT AWAY!!
Are you trying to kill me?!
KRASH
SANJI SEEMS TO BE HAVING FUN.
YAP YAP
I THINK HE'S OVER-WHELMED.
DINNER IS SERVED!!
SHEEN
A SEAFOOD EXTRAVAGANZA FEATURING THE PRODUCTS OF SKY ISLAND TO DELIGHT YOUR PALATES!
IT LOOKS DELICIOUS!!

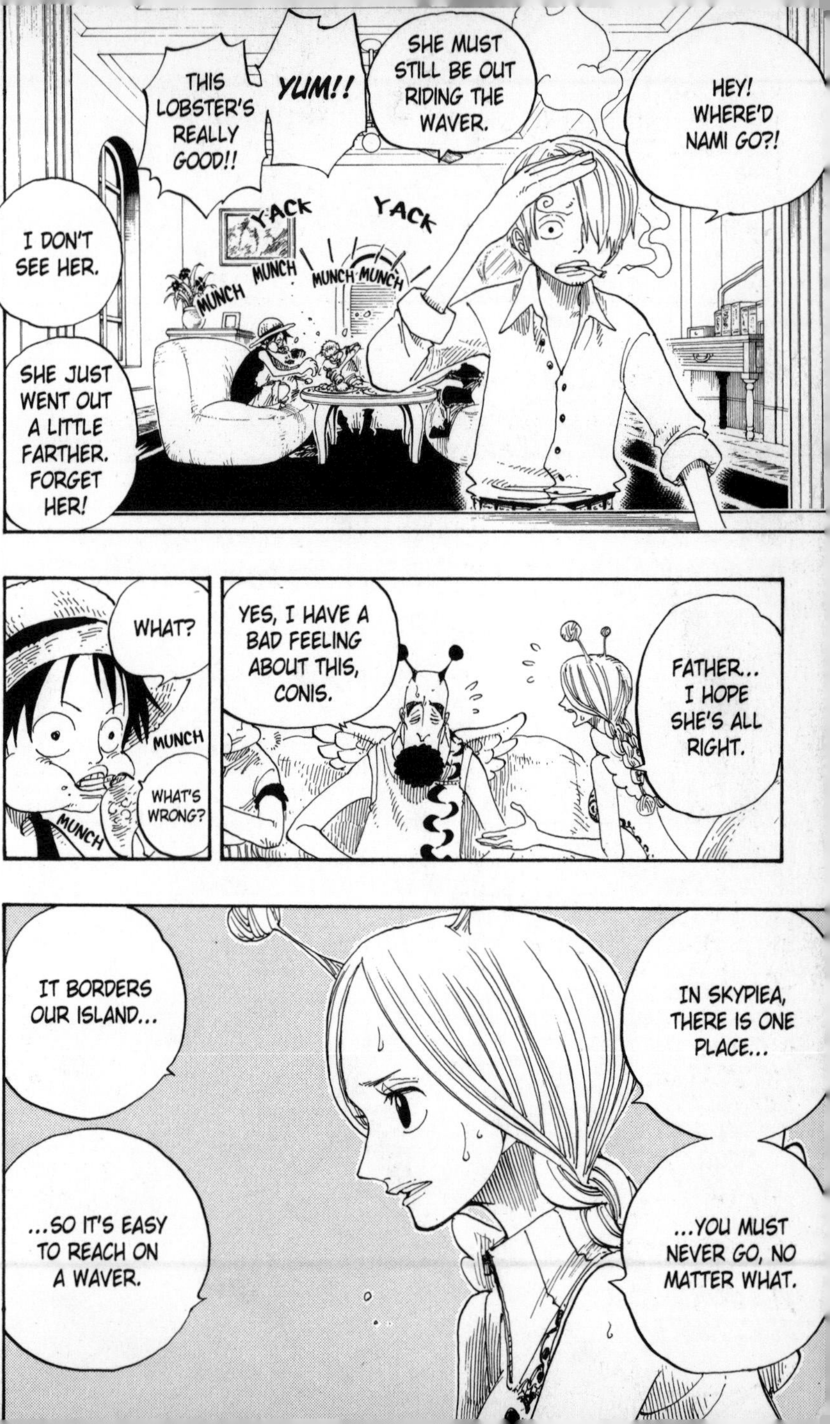
HEY! WHERE'D NAMI GO?!
SHE MUST STILL BE OUT RIDING THE WAVER.
YUM!!
THIS LOBSTER'S REALLY GOOD!!
YACK
YACK
MUNCH MUNCH
MUNCH
MUNCH
I DON'T SEE HER.
SHE JUST WENT OUT A LITTLE FARTHER. FORGET HER!
FATHER... I HOPE SHE'S ALL RIGHT.
YES, I HAVE A BAD FEELING ABOUT THIS, CONIS.
WHAT?
MUNCH
WHAT'S WRONG?
MUNCH
IN SKYPIEA, THERE IS ONE PLACE...
IT BORDERS OUR ISLAND...
...YOU MUST NEVER GO, NO MATTER WHAT.
...SO IT'S EASY TO REACH ON A WAVER.

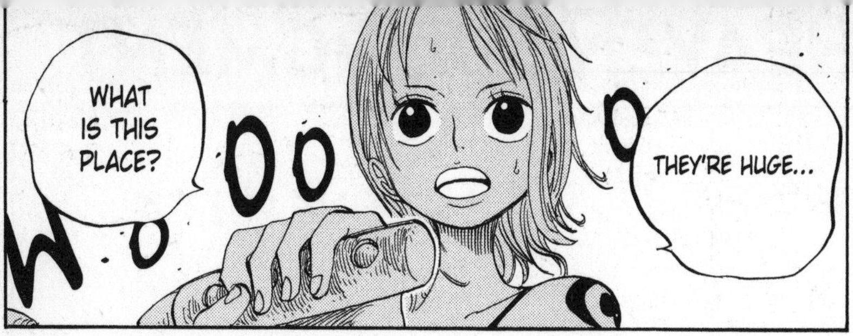
THEY'RE HUGE...
WHAT IS THIS PLACE?
WOOOO

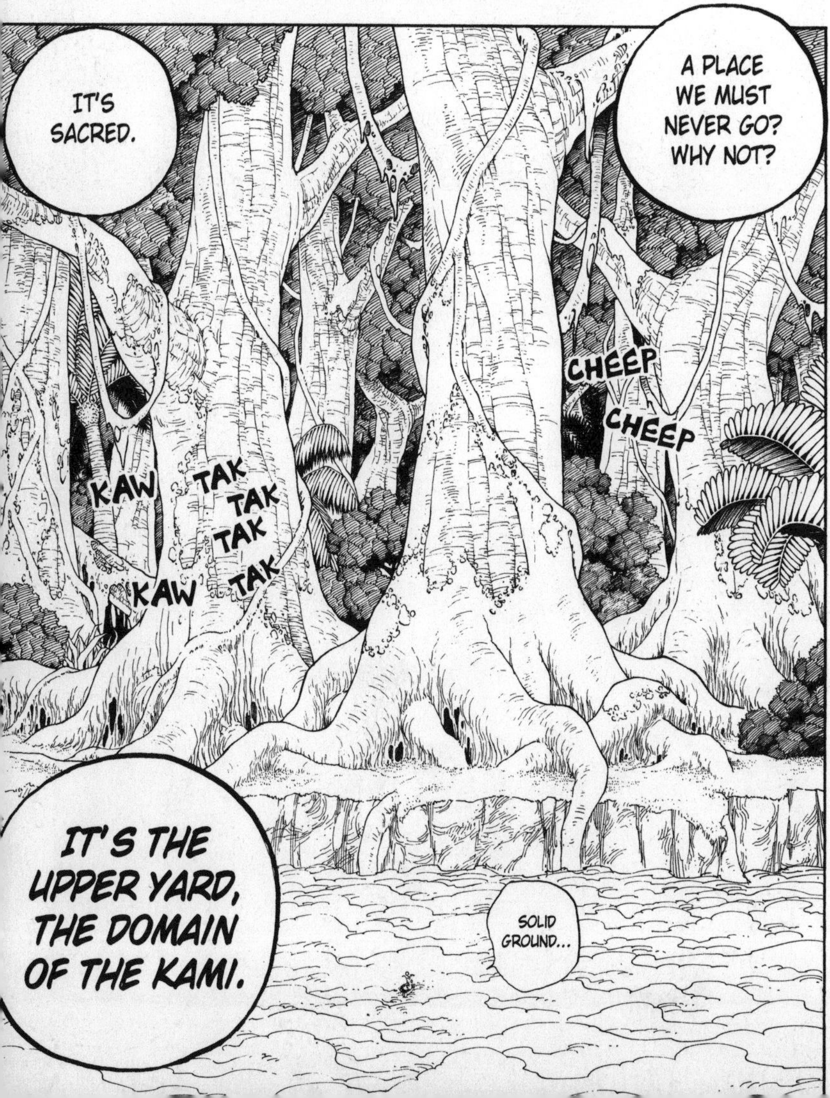
A PLACE WE MUST NEVER GO? WHY NOT?
IT'S SACRED.
CHEEP
CHEEP
TAK TAK TAK TAK
KAW
KAW
SOLID GROUND...
IT'S THE UPPER YARD, THE DOMAIN OF THE KAMI.

HEAVEN'S JUDGMENT

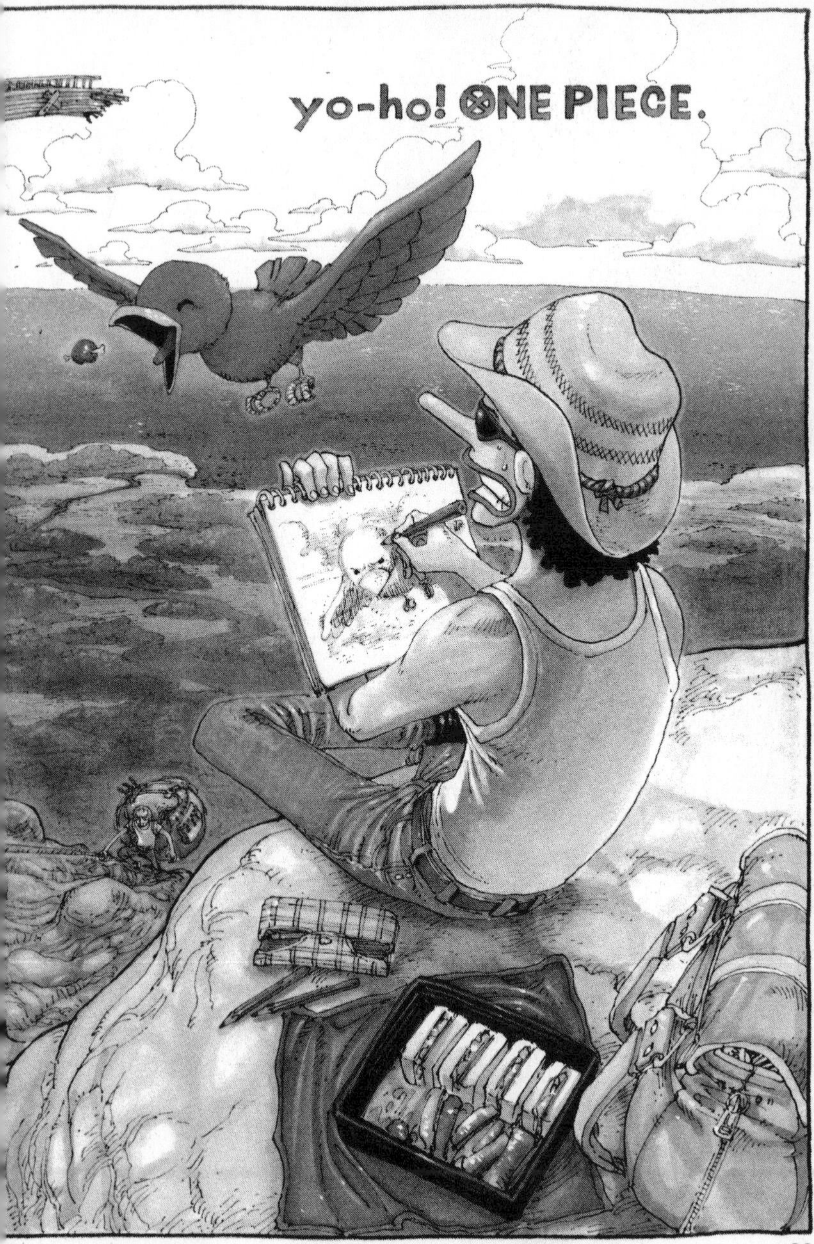
yo-ho! ONE PIECE.

Chapter 241:

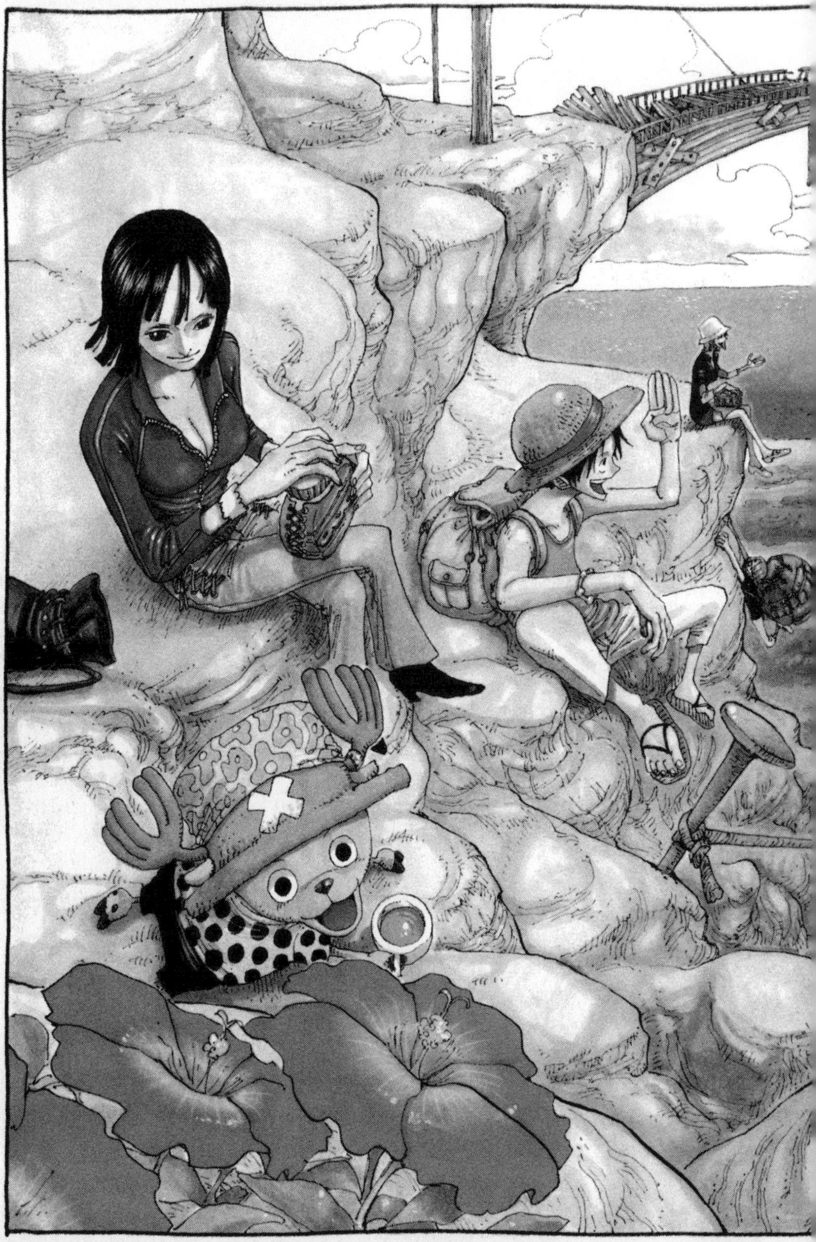

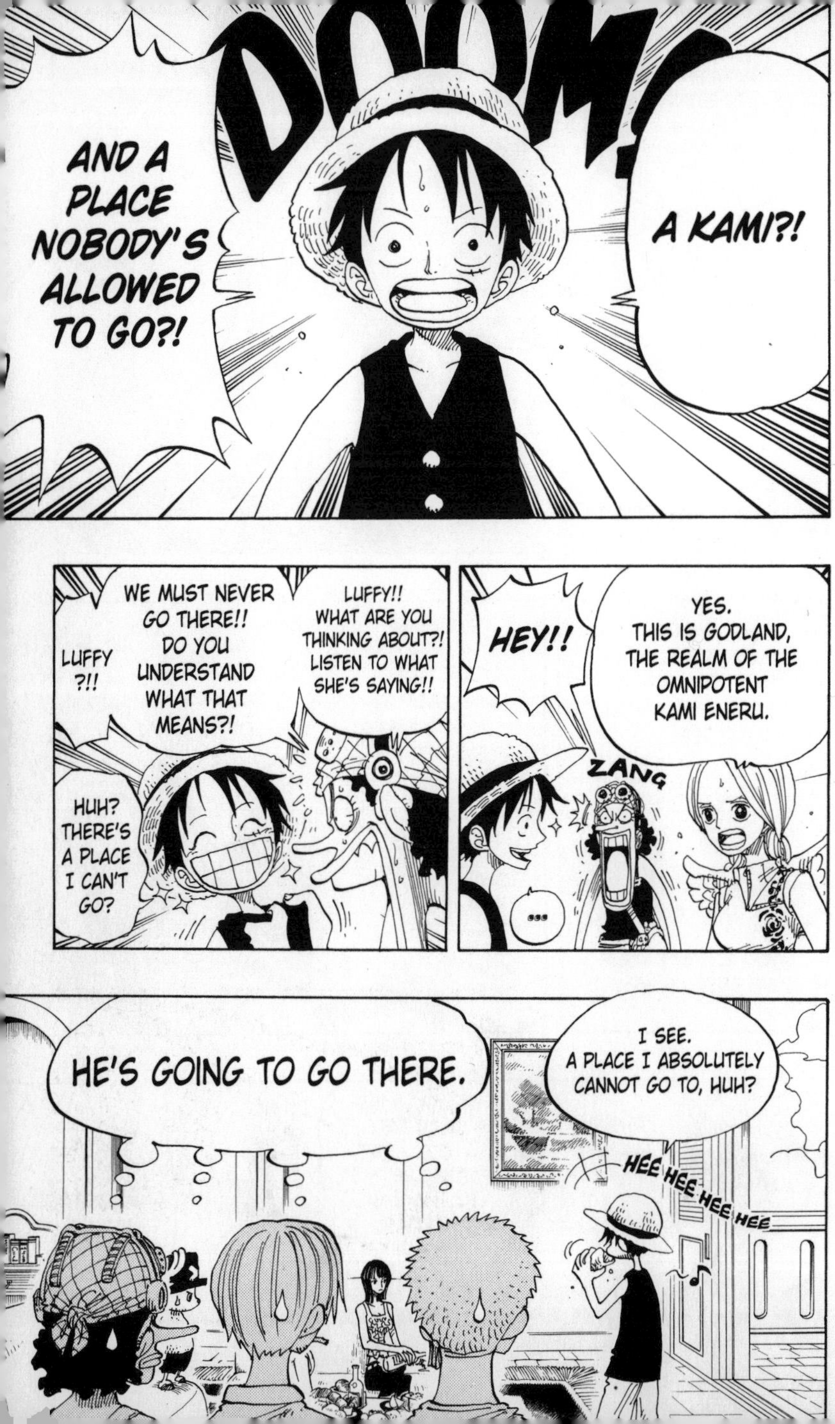
DOOM!
A KAMI?!
AND A PLACE NOBODY'S ALLOWED TO GO?!
YES. THIS IS GODLAND, THE REALM OF THE OMNIPOTENT KAMI ENERU.
HEY!!
ZANG
...
LUFFY!! WHAT ARE YOU THINKING ABOUT?! LISTEN TO WHAT SHE'S SAYING!!
WE MUST NEVER GO THERE!! DO YOU UNDERSTAND WHAT THAT MEANS?!
LUFFY ?!!
HUH? THERE'S A PLACE I CAN'T GO?
I SEE. A PLACE I ABSOLUTELY CANNOT GO TO, HUH?
HEE HEE HEE HEE
HE'S GOING TO GO THERE.

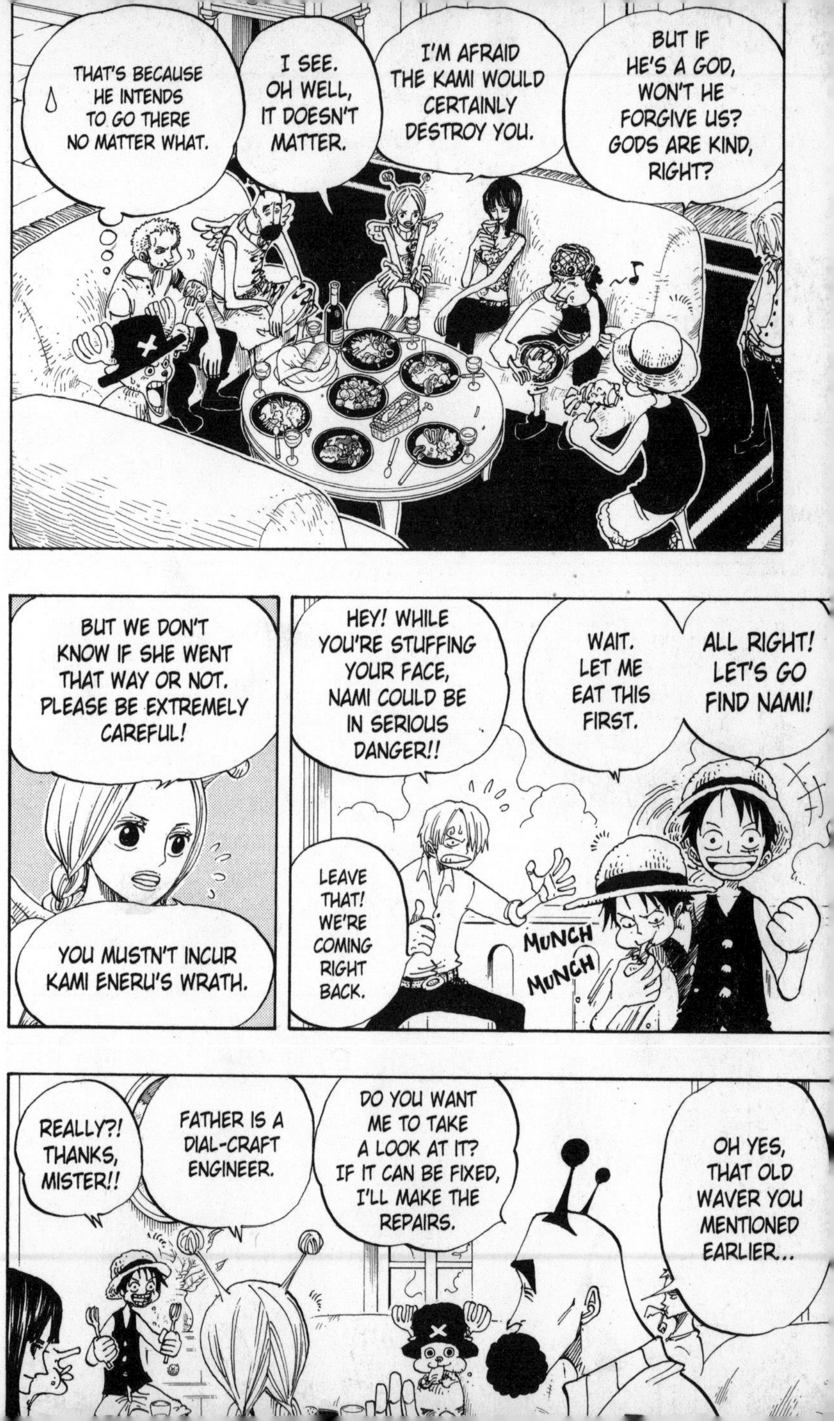
BUT IF HE'S A GOD, WON'T HE FORGIVE US? GODS ARE KIND, RIGHT?
I'M AFRAID THE KAMI WOULD CERTAINLY DESTROY YOU.
I SEE. OH WELL, IT DOESN'T MATTER.
THAT'S BECAUSE HE INTENDS TO GO THERE NO MATTER WHAT.
ALL RIGHT! LET'S GO FIND NAMI!
WAIT. LET ME EAT THIS FIRST.
HEY! WHILE YOU'RE STUFFING YOUR FACE, NAMI COULD BE IN SERIOUS DANGER!!
LEAVE THAT! WE'RE COMING RIGHT BACK.
MUNCH
MUNCH
BUT WE DON'T KNOW IF SHE WENT THAT WAY OR NOT. PLEASE BE EXTREMELY CAREFUL!
YOU MUSTN'T INCUR KAMI ENERU'S WRATH.
OH YES, THAT OLD WAVER YOU MENTIONED EARLIER...
DO YOU WANT ME TO TAKE A LOOK AT IT? IF IT CAN BE FIXED, I'LL MAKE THE REPAIRS.
FATHER IS A DIAL-CRAFT ENGINEER.
REALLY?! THANKS, MISTER!!

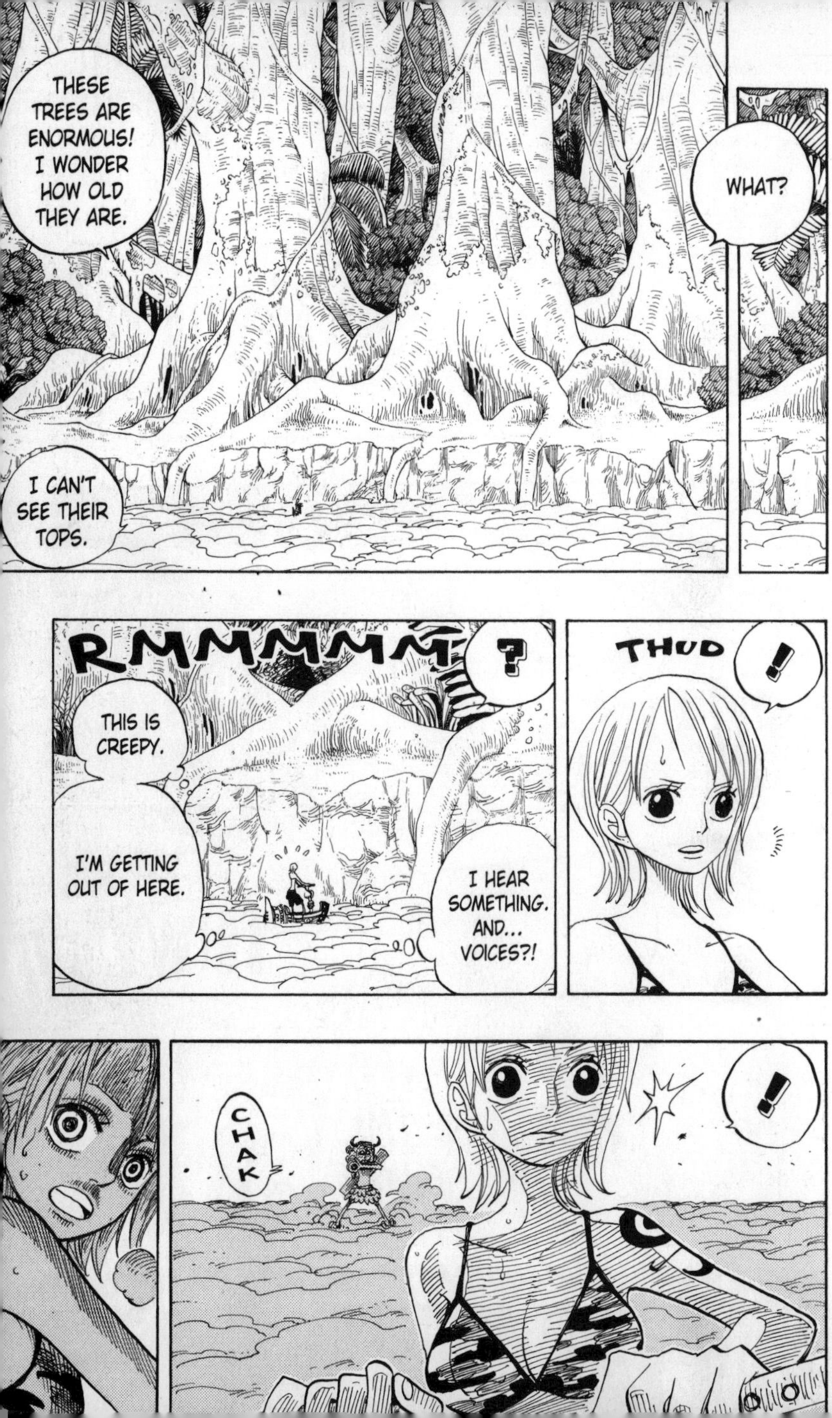
WHAT?
THESE TREES ARE ENORMOUS! I WONDER HOW OLD THEY ARE.
I CAN'T SEE THEIR TOPS.
THUD
!
THIS IS CREEPY.
I'M GETTING OUT OF HERE.
RMMMMMM
?
I HEAR SOMETHING. AND... VOICES?!
!
CHAK

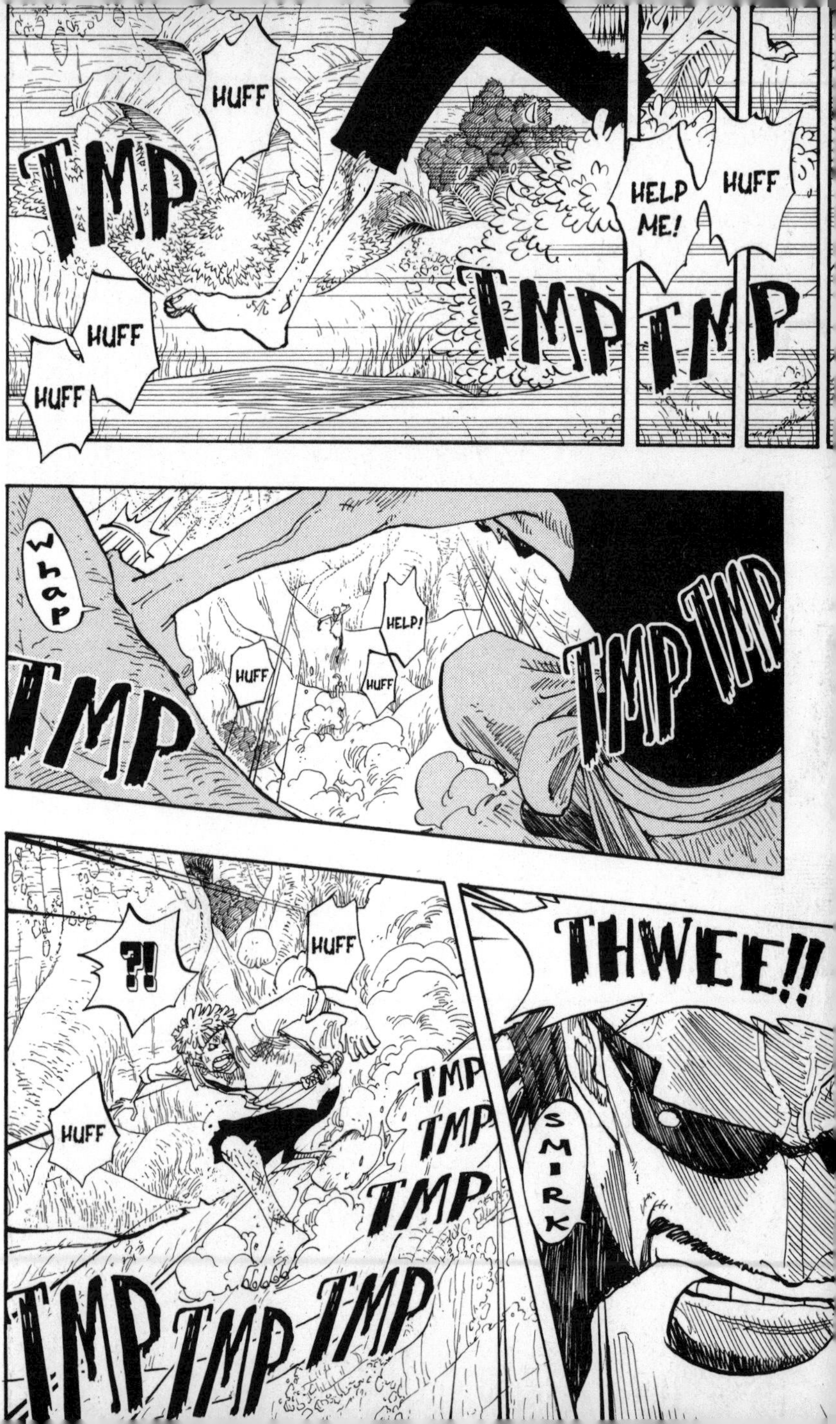
HUFF
HELP ME!
TMP
TMP
TMP
HUFF
TMP
HUFF
HUFF
TMP TMP
HELP!
HUFF
HUFF
Whap
TMP
THWEE!!
SMIRK
HUFF
?!
TMP
TMP
TMP
HUFF
TMP TMP TMP TMP

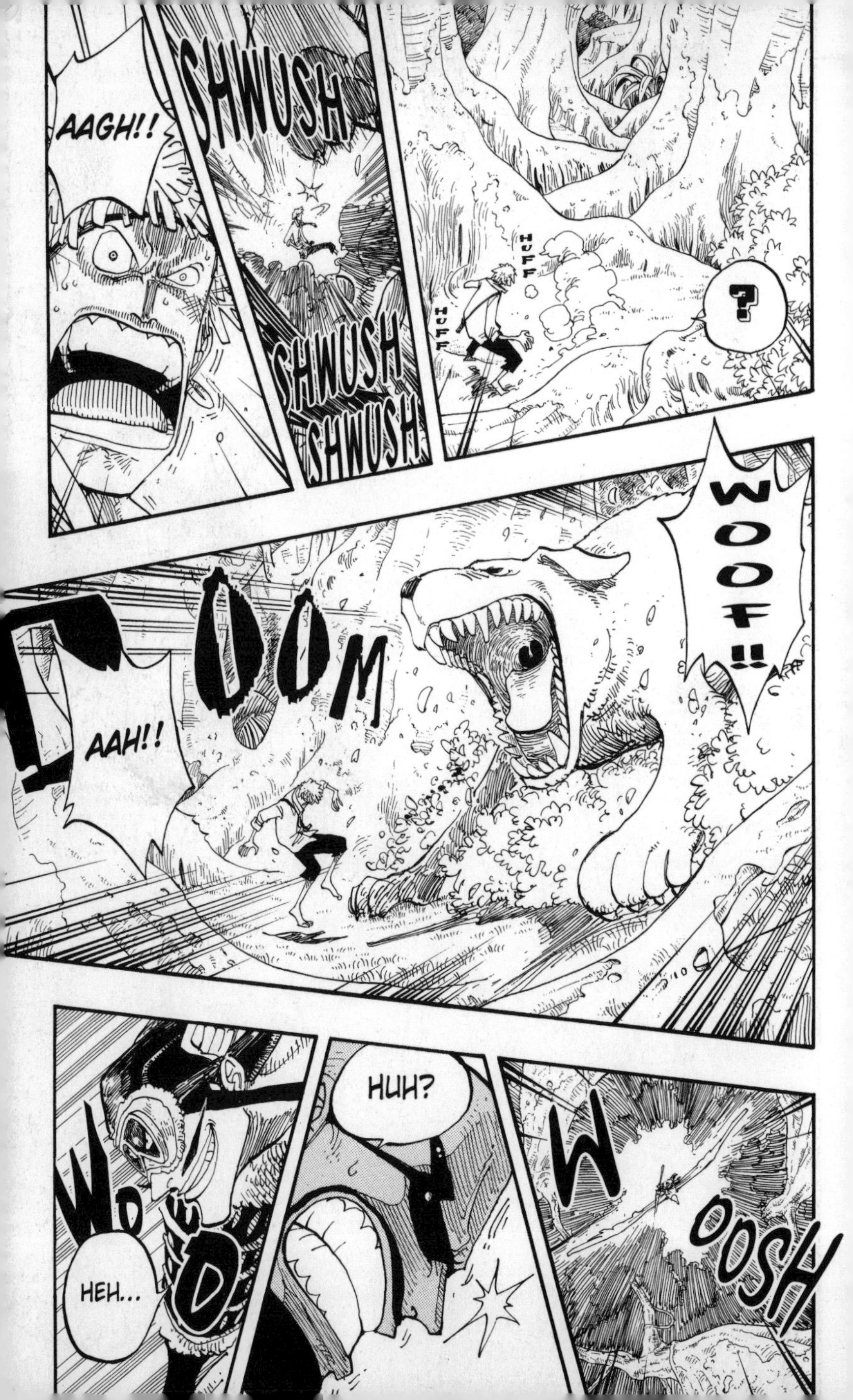
HUFF
HUFF
?
SHWUSH
SHWUSH
SHWUSH
AAGH!!
WOOF!!
DOOM
AAH!!
WOOSH
HUH?
HEH...

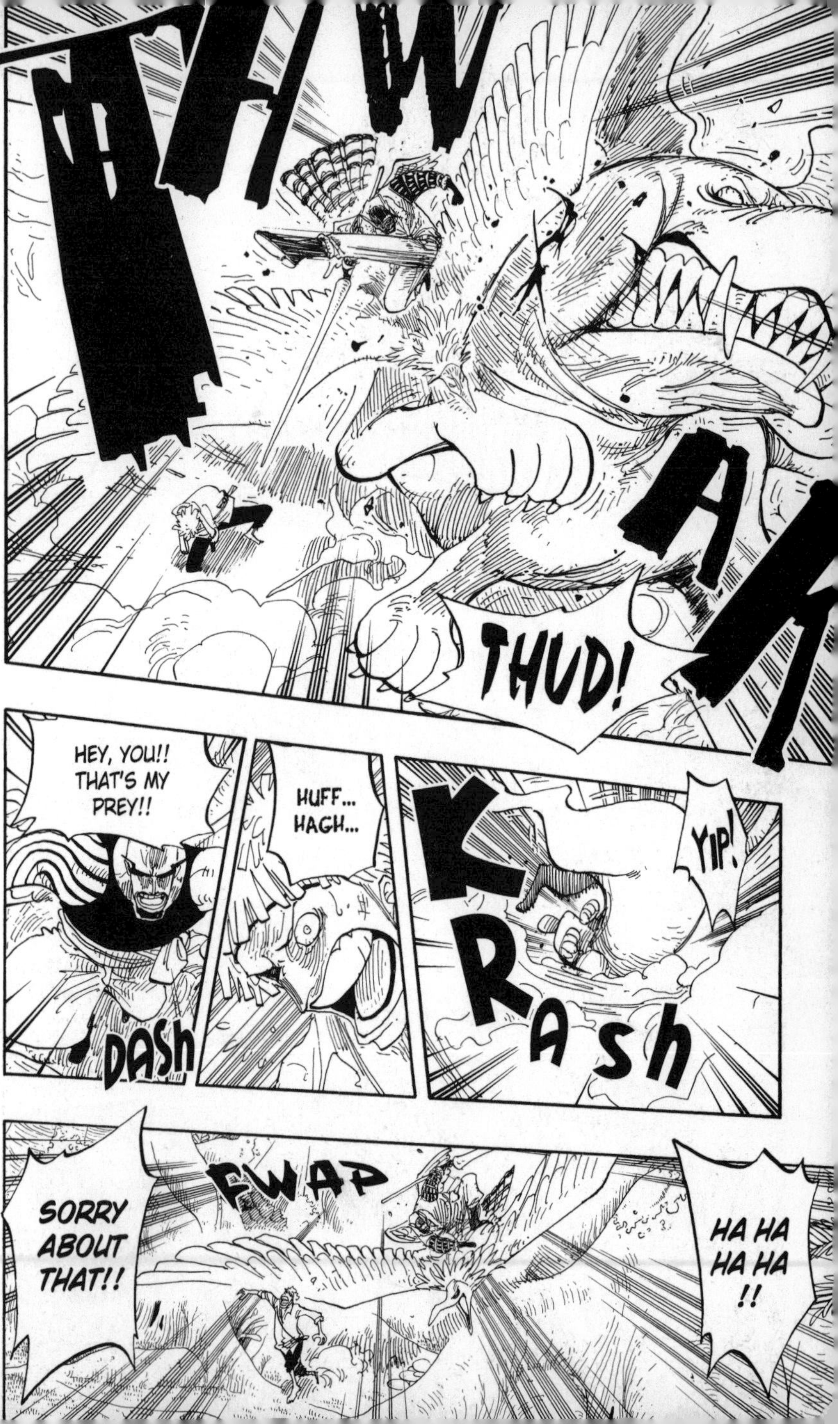
THWAK
THUD!
YIP!
KRASH
HUFF... HAGH...
HEY, YOU!! THAT'S MY PREY!!
DASH
HA HA HA HA !!
FWAP
SORRY ABOUT THAT!!

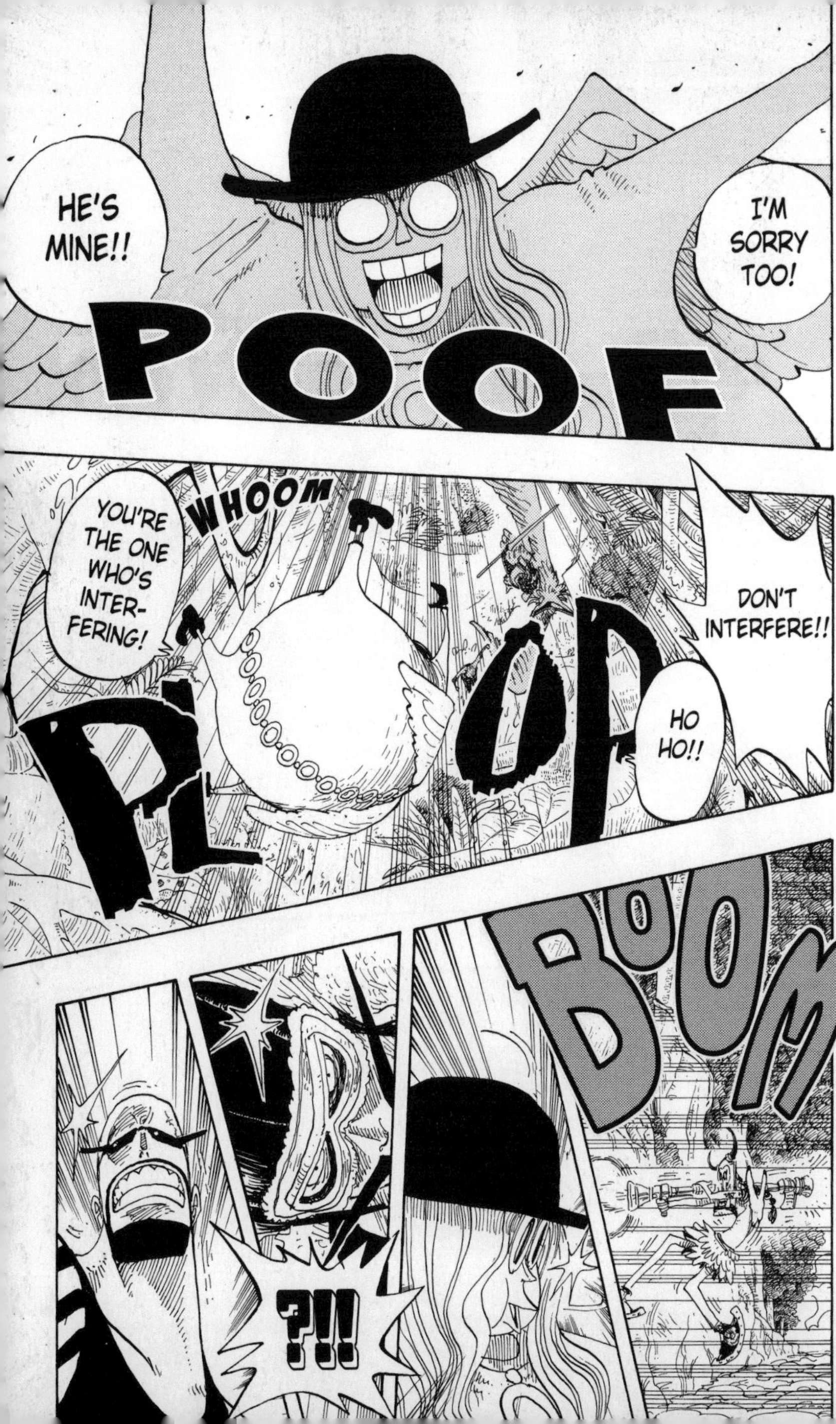
I'M SORRY TOO!
HE'S MINE!!
POOF
DON'T INTERFERE!!
HO HO!!
WHOOM
YOU'RE THE ONE WHO'S INTER-FERING!
PLOP
BOOM
?!!

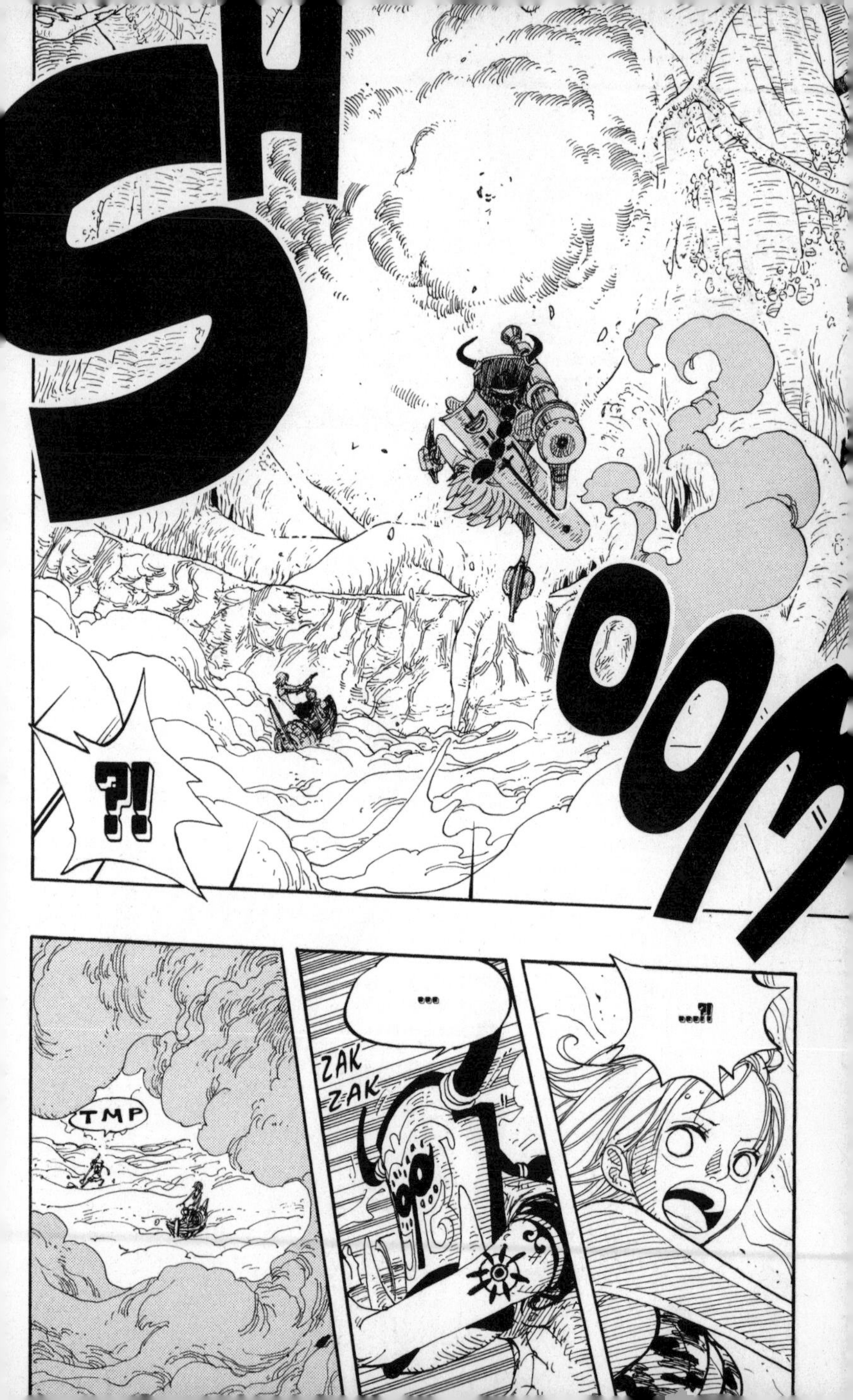
SHOOM
?!
...?!
...
ZAK
ZAK
TMP

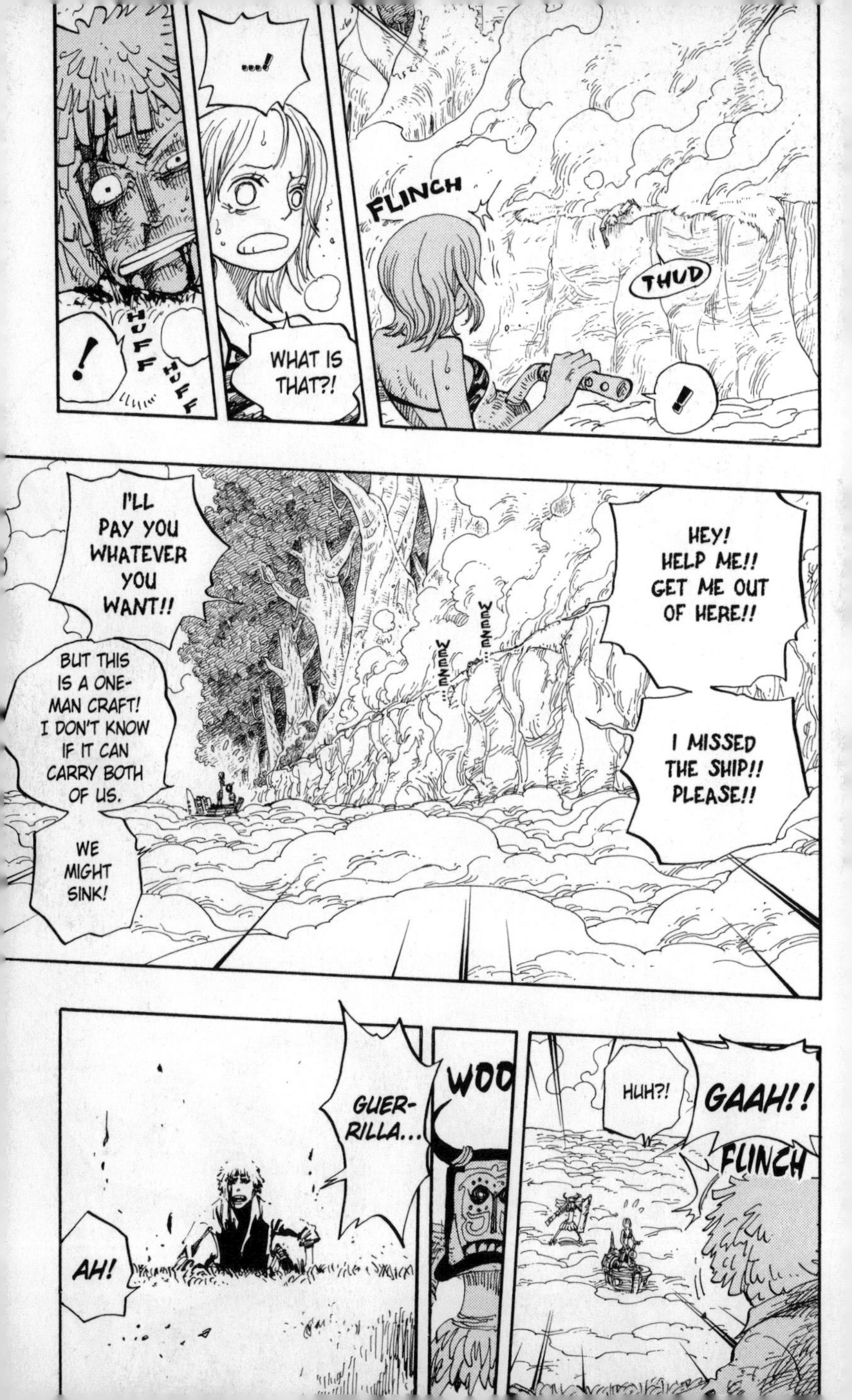
THUD
FLINCH
!
...!
WHAT IS THAT?!
HUFF HUFF
!
HEY! HELP ME!! GET ME OUT OF HERE!!
I MISSED THE SHIP!! PLEASE!!
WEEZE...
WEEZE...
I'LL PAY YOU WHATEVER YOU WANT!!
BUT THIS IS A ONE-MAN CRAFT! I DON'T KNOW IF IT CAN CARRY BOTH OF US.
WE MIGHT SINK!
HUH?!
GAAH!!
FLINCH
WOO
GUER-RILLA...
AH!

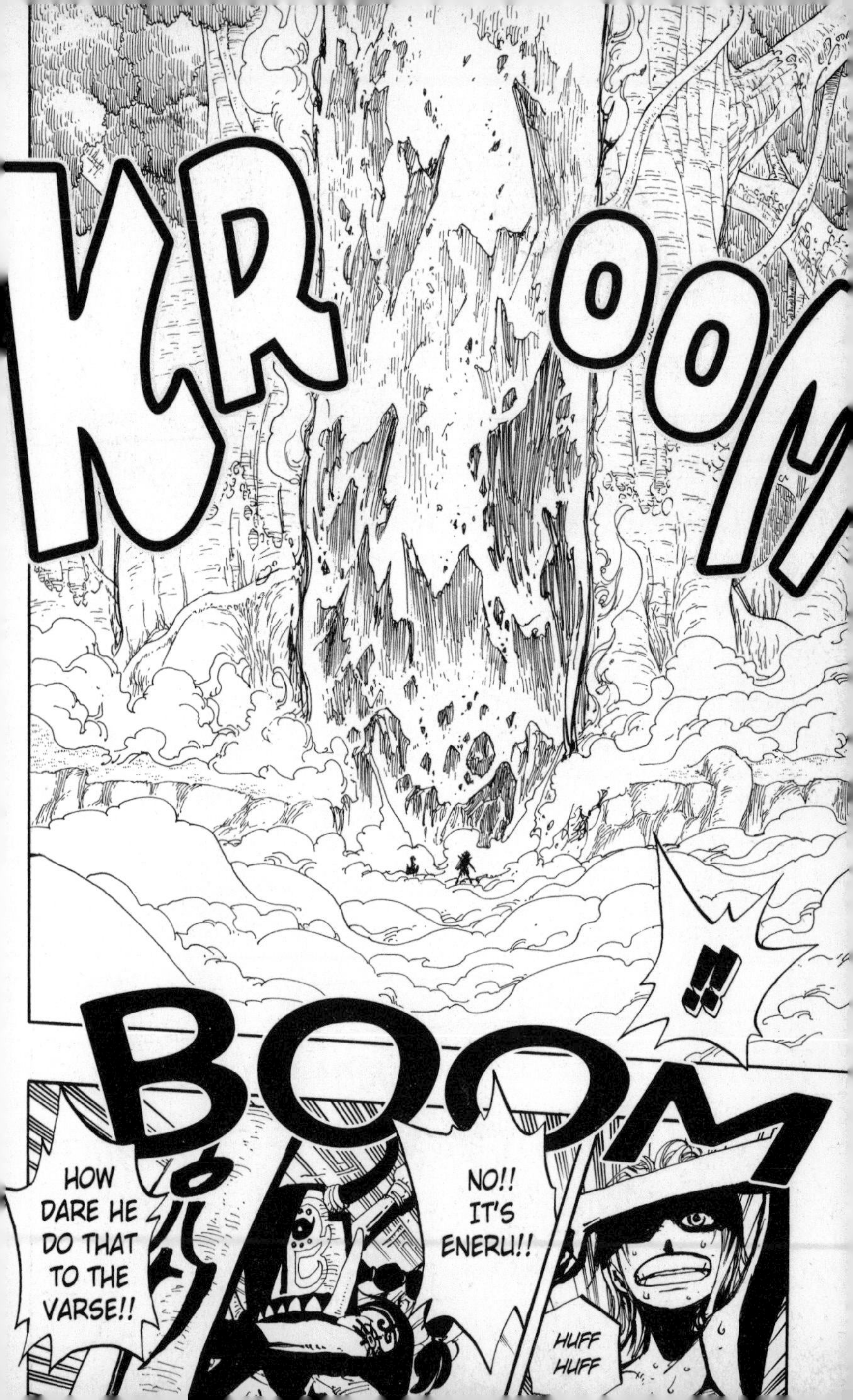

KROOM
!!
BOOM
NO!! IT'S ENERU!!
HUFF HUFF
HOW DARE HE DO THAT TO THE VARSE!!

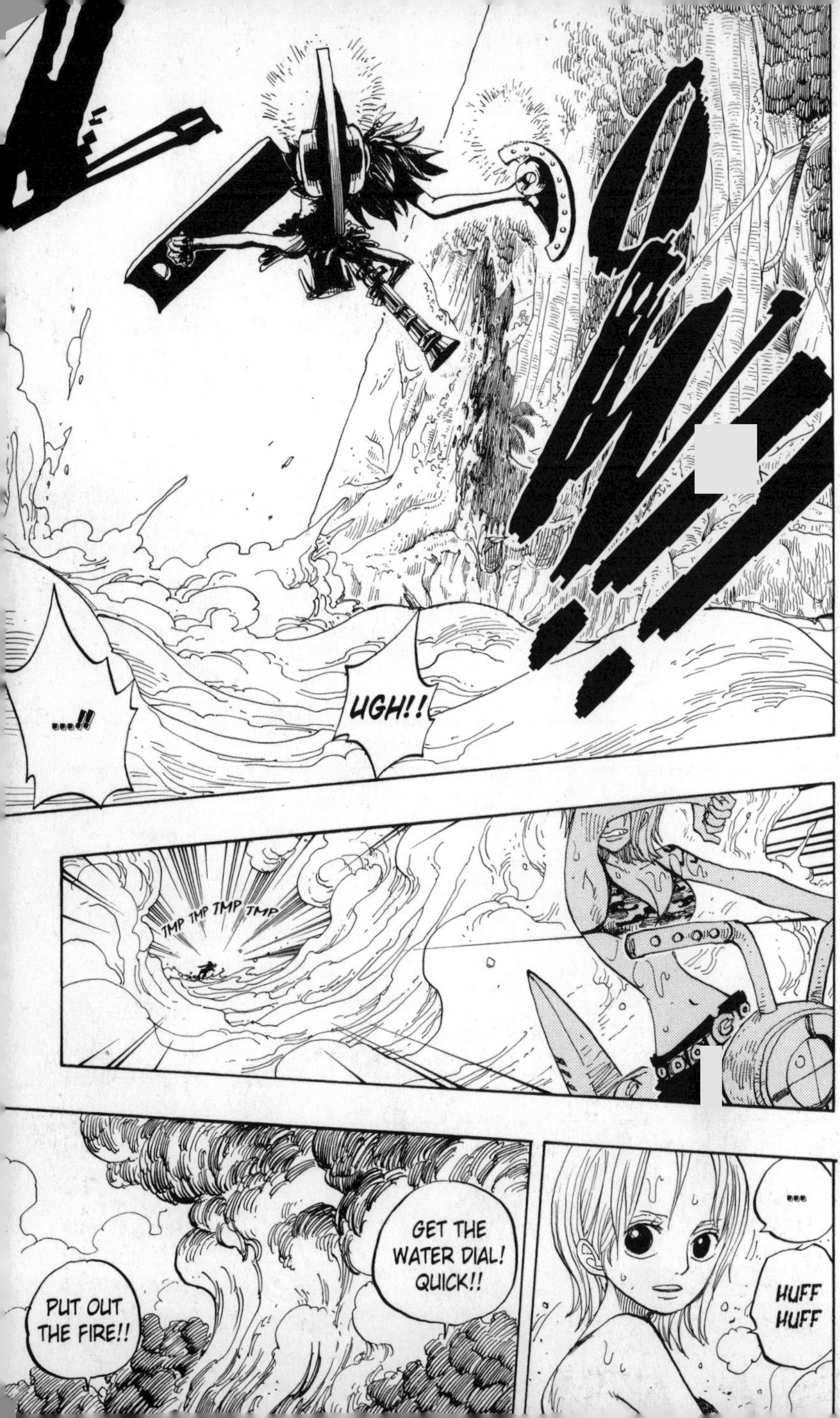
UGH!!
...!!
TMP TMP TMP TMP
...
HUFF HUFF
GET THE WATER DIAL! QUICK!!
PUT OUT THE FIRE!!

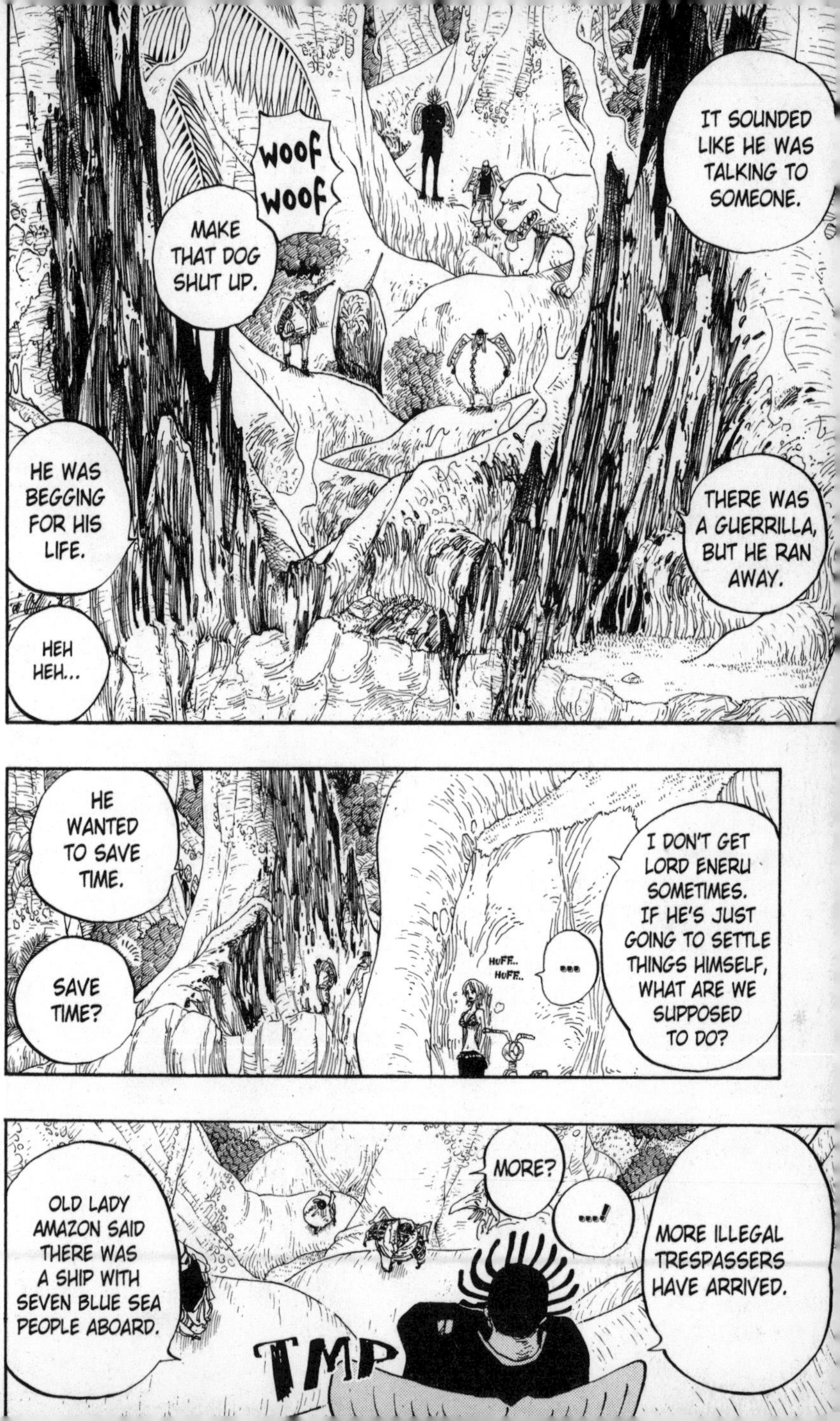
IT SOUNDED LIKE HE WAS TALKING TO SOMEONE.
WOOF WOOF
MAKE THAT DOG SHUT UP.
THERE WAS A GUERRILLA, BUT HE RAN AWAY.
HE WAS BEGGING FOR HIS LIFE.
HEH HEH...
I DON'T GET LORD ENERU SOMETIMES. IF HE'S JUST GOING TO SETTLE THINGS HIMSELF, WHAT ARE WE SUPPOSED TO DO?
...
HUFF.. HUFF..
HE WANTED TO SAVE TIME.
SAVE TIME?
MORE ILLEGAL TRESPASSERS HAVE ARRIVED.
MORE?
...!
OLD LADY AMAZON SAID THERE WAS A SHIP WITH SEVEN BLUE SEA PEOPLE ABOARD.
TMP

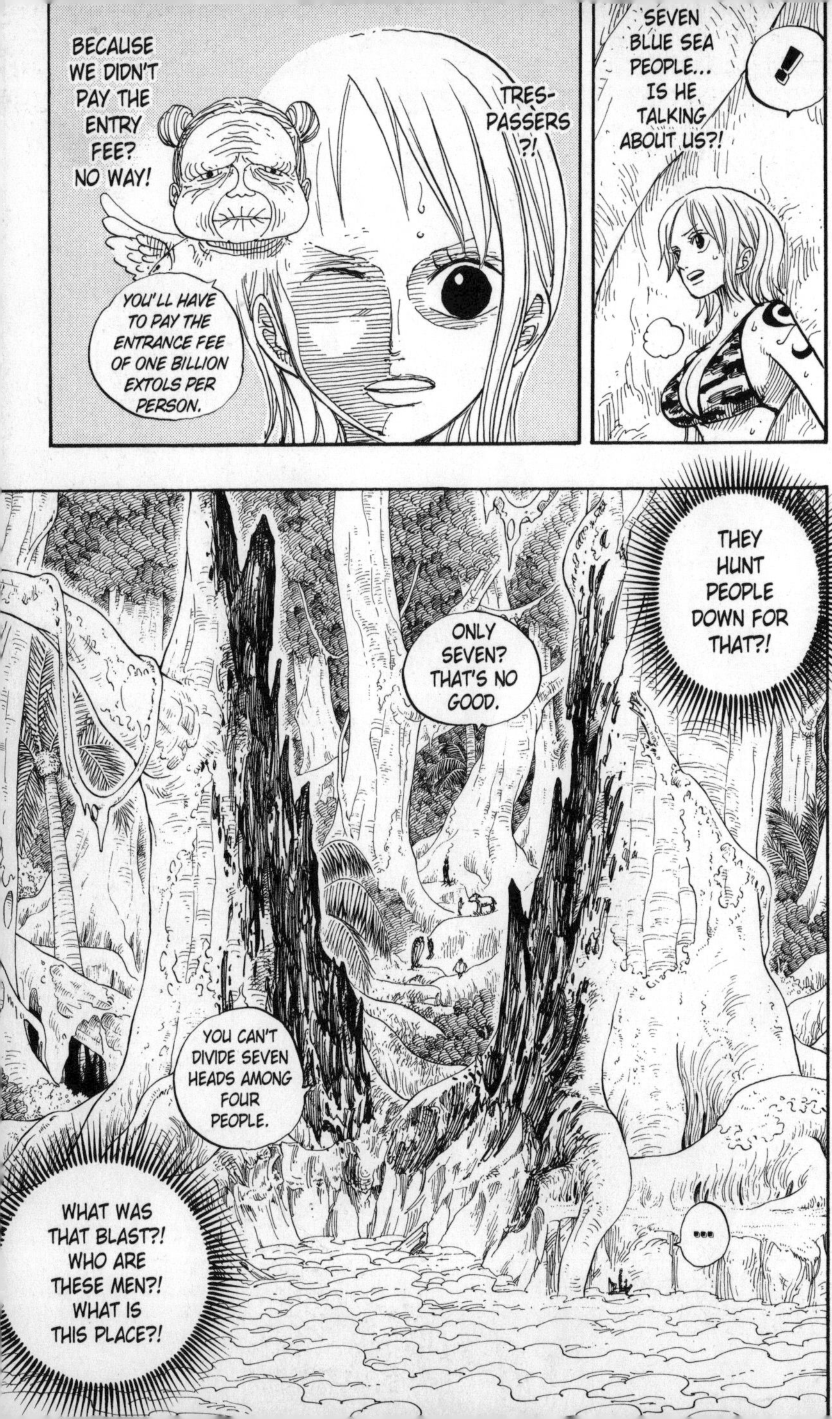
SEVEN BLUE SEA PEOPLE... IS HE TALKING ABOUT US?!
!
TRES-PASSERS?!
BECAUSE WE DIDN'T PAY THE ENTRY FEE? NO WAY!
YOU'LL HAVE TO PAY THE ENTRANCE FEE OF ONE BILLION EXTOLS PER PERSON.
THEY HUNT PEOPLE DOWN FOR THAT?!
ONLY SEVEN? THAT'S NO GOOD.
YOU CAN'T DIVIDE SEVEN HEADS AMONG FOUR PEOPLE.
...
WHAT WAS THAT BLAST?! WHO ARE THESE MEN?! WHAT IS THIS PLACE?!

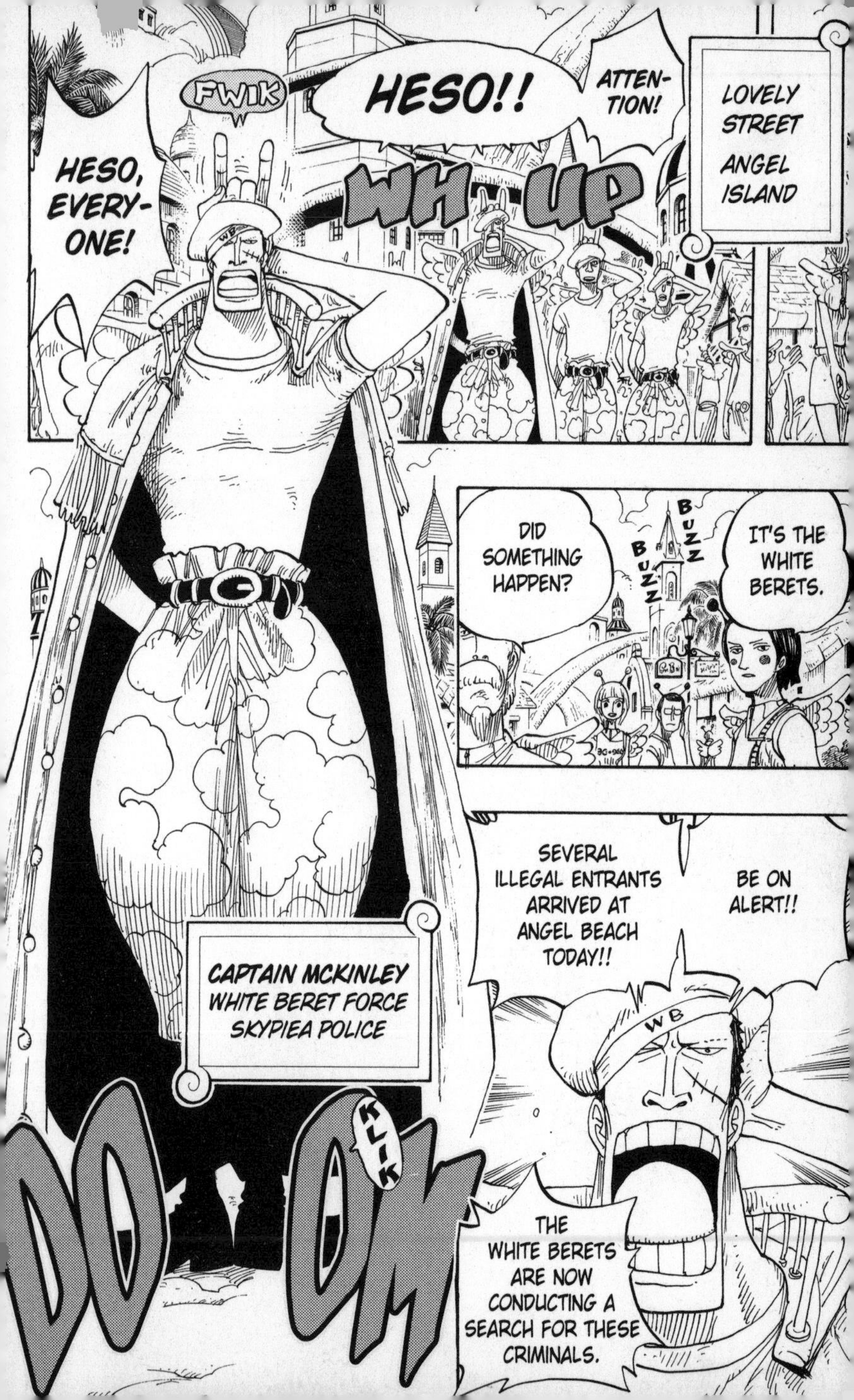
LOVELY STREET
ANGEL ISLAND
ATTEN-TION!
HESO!!
WH UP
FWIK
HESO, EVERY-ONE!
IT'S THE WHITE BERETS.
BUZZ
BUZZ
DID SOMETHING HAPPEN?
BE ON ALERT!!
SEVERAL ILLEGAL ENTRANTS ARRIVED AT ANGEL BEACH TODAY!!
THE WHITE BERETS ARE NOW CONDUCTING A SEARCH FOR THESE CRIMINALS.
CAPTAIN MCKINLEY
WHITE BERET FORCE
SKYPIEA POLICE
KLIK
DOOM

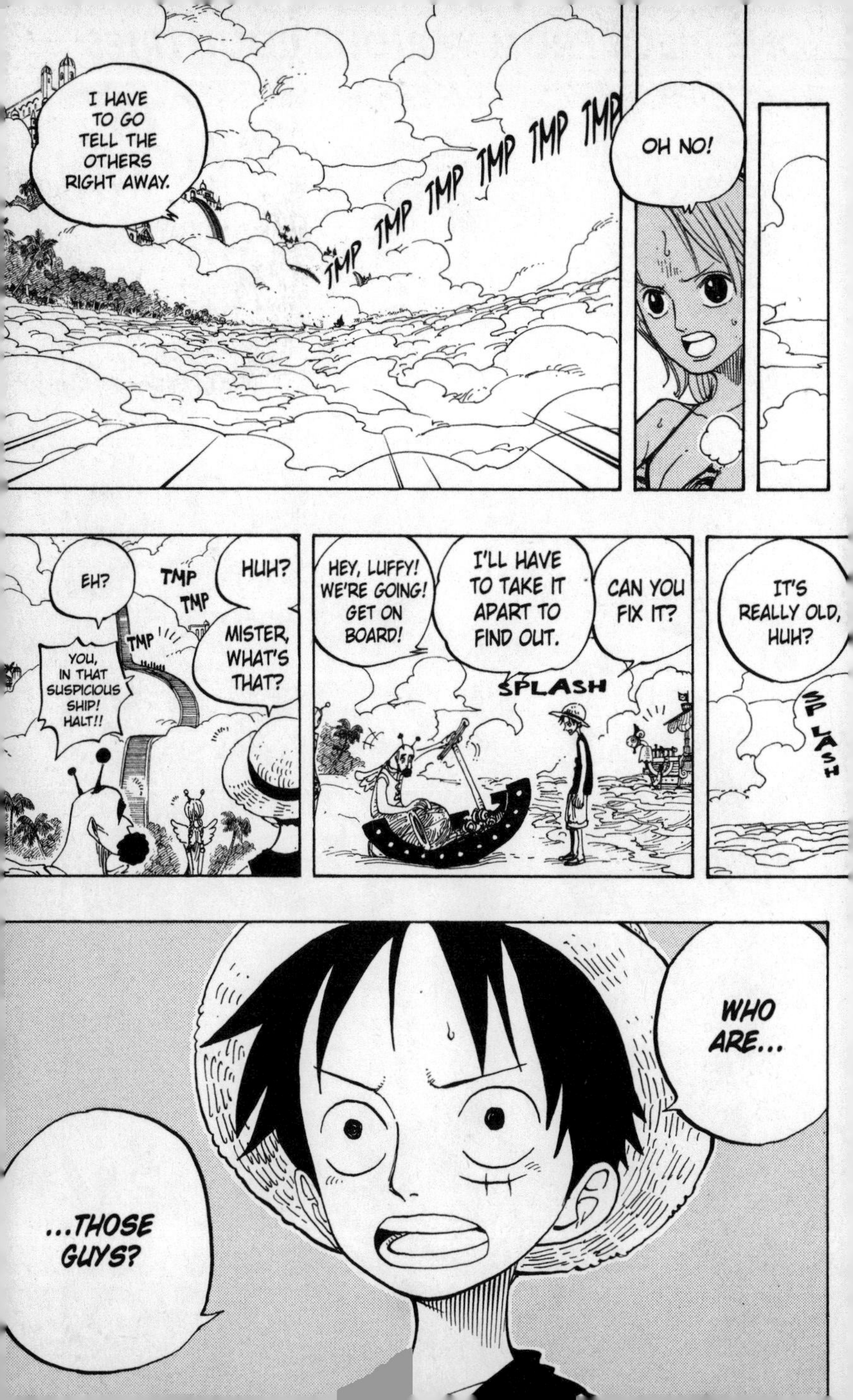
OH NO!
TMP TMP TMP TMP TMP TMP TMP
I HAVE TO GO TELL THE OTHERS RIGHT AWAY.
IT'S REALLY OLD, HUH?
SPLASH
CAN YOU FIX IT?
I'LL HAVE TO TAKE IT APART TO FIND OUT.
HEY, LUFFY! WE'RE GOING! GET ON BOARD!
SPLASH
HUH?
MISTER, WHAT'S THAT?
TMP
TMP
TMP
EH?
YOU, IN THAT SUSPICIOUS SHIP! HALT!!
WHO ARE...
...THOSE GUYS?

ONE PIECE FROM VARIOUS COUNTRIES

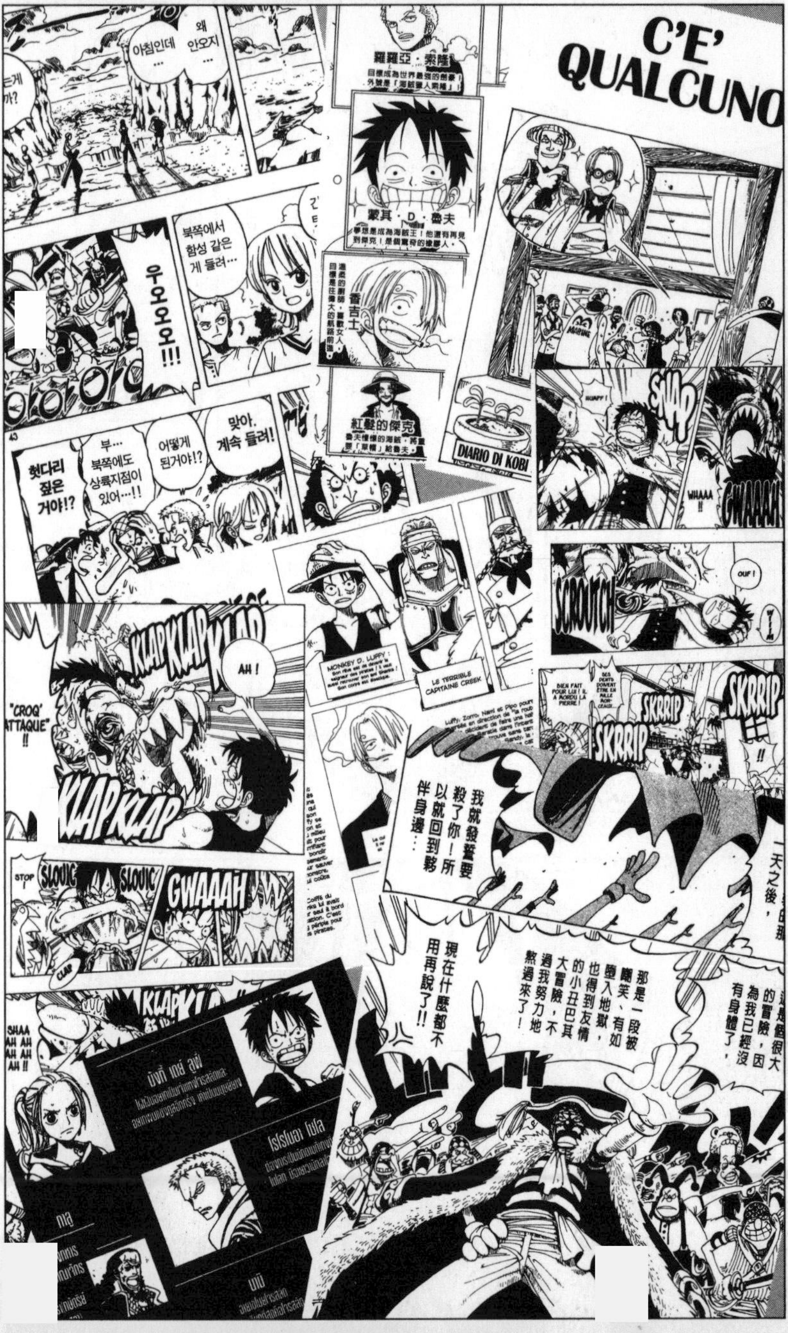
C'E' QUALCUNO
羅羅亞・索隆
目標成為世界最強的劍豪！外號是「海賊獵人索隆」
왜 안오지…
아침인데…
蒙其・D・魯夫
香吉士
북쪽에서 함성 같은 게 들려…
우오오오!!!
紅髮的傑克
DIARIO DI KOBI
SNAP
WHAAA !!
GWAAAH
맞아, 계속 들려!
어떻게 된거야!?
부… 북쪽에도 상륙지점이 있어…!!
헛다리 짚은 거야!?
OUF !
SCROUTCH
MONKEY D. LUFFY
LE TERRIBLE CAPITAINE CREEK
KLAP KLAP KLAP
AH !
"CROQ' ATTAQUE" !!
KLAP KLAP
BIEN FAIT POUR LUI ! IL A MORDU LA PIERRE !
SES DENTS DOIVENT ÊTRE EN MILLE MORCEAUX...
SKRRIP
SKRRIP
SKRRIP
我就發誓要殺了你！所以就回到夥伴身邊…
一天之後，
STOP !
SLOUIC
SLOUIC
GWAAAH
CLAP
那是一段被嘲笑、有如墮入地獄的小丑巴其大冒險，不過我努力地熬過來了！
現在什麼都不用再說了!!
SHAA AH AH AH AH !!

Chapter 242: CLASS-2 CRIMINALS

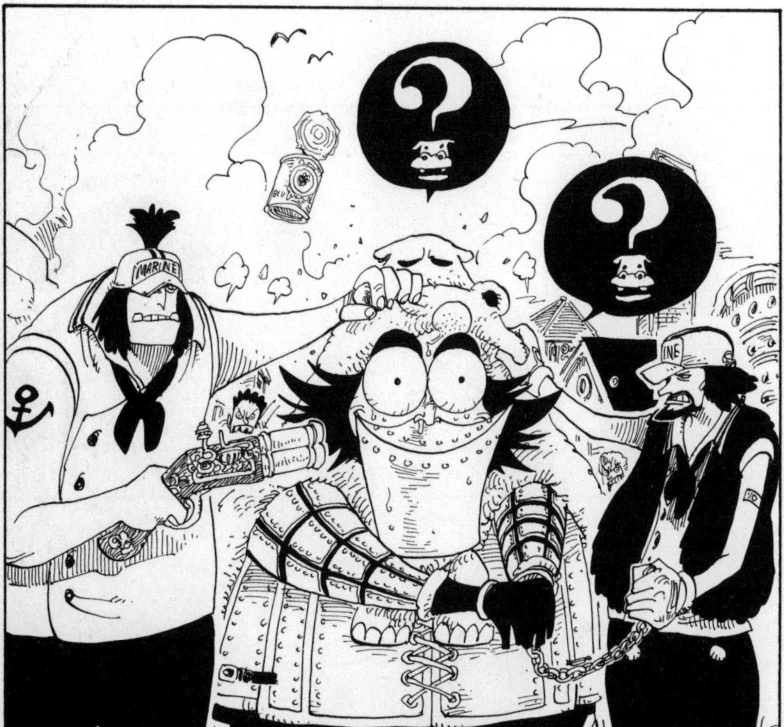
MARINE

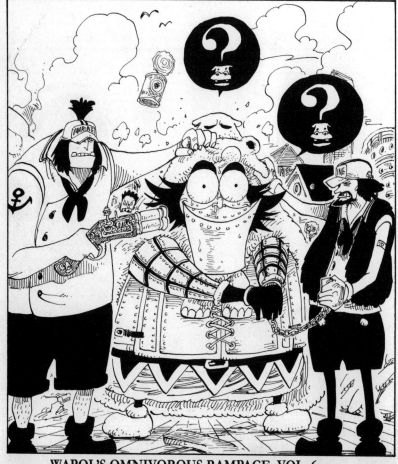

WAPOL'S OMNIVOROUS RAMPAGE, VOL. 6:
"I, KING WAPOL, AM CAPTURED"

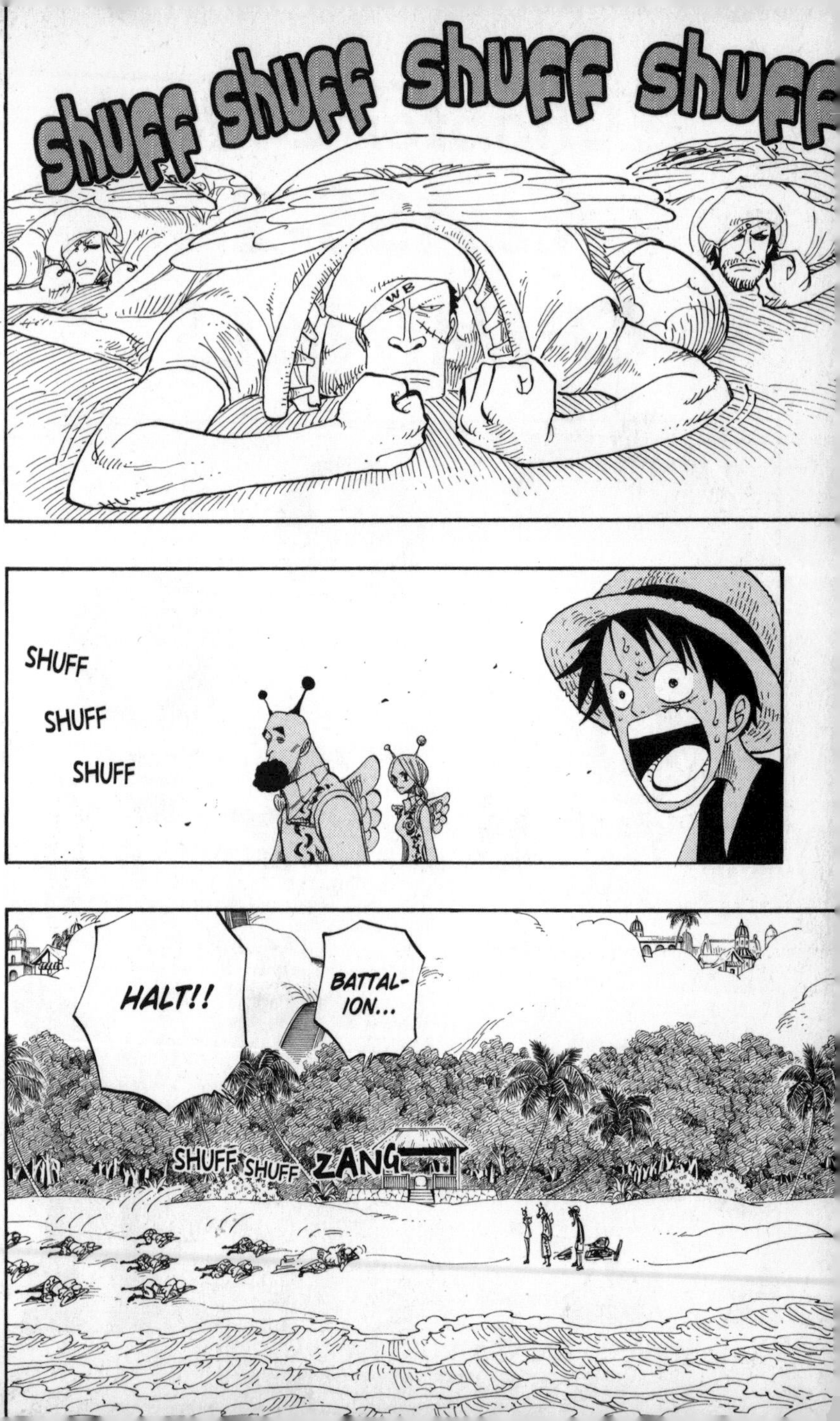
SHUFF SHUFF SHUFF SHUFF
SHUFF
SHUFF
SHUFF
BATTAL-
ION...
HALT!!
ZANG
SHUFF
SHUFF

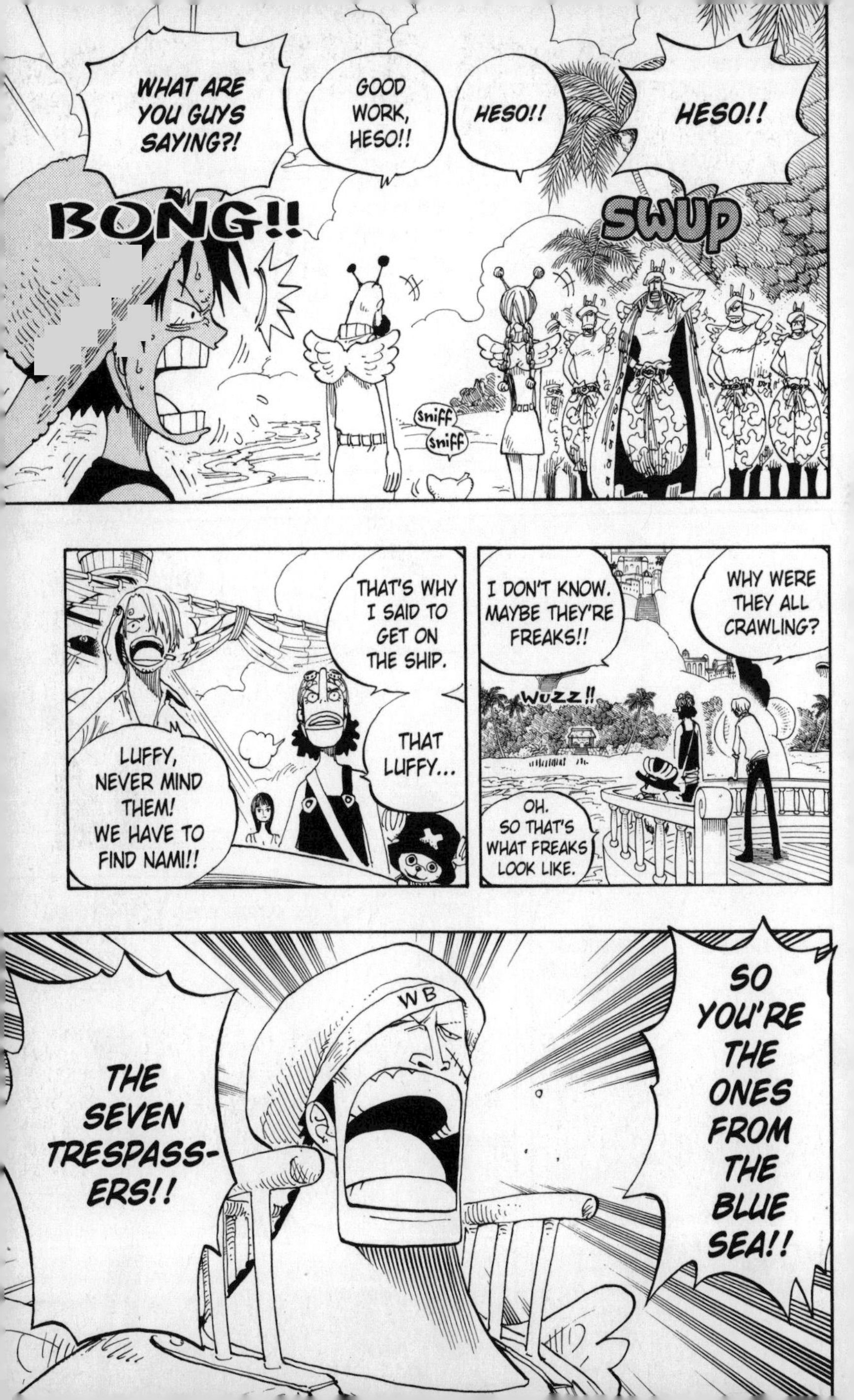
HESO!!
SWUP
HESO!!
GOOD WORK, HESO!!
WHAT ARE YOU GUYS SAYING?!
BONG!!
sniff sniff
WHY WERE THEY ALL CRAWLING?
I DON'T KNOW. MAYBE THEY'RE FREAKS!!
WUZZ!!
OH. SO THAT'S WHAT FREAKS LOOK LIKE.
THAT'S WHY I SAID TO GET ON THE SHIP.
THAT LUFFY...
LUFFY, NEVER MIND THEM! WE HAVE TO FIND NAMI!!
SO YOU'RE THE ONES FROM THE BLUE SEA!!
WB
THE SEVEN TRESPASSERS!!

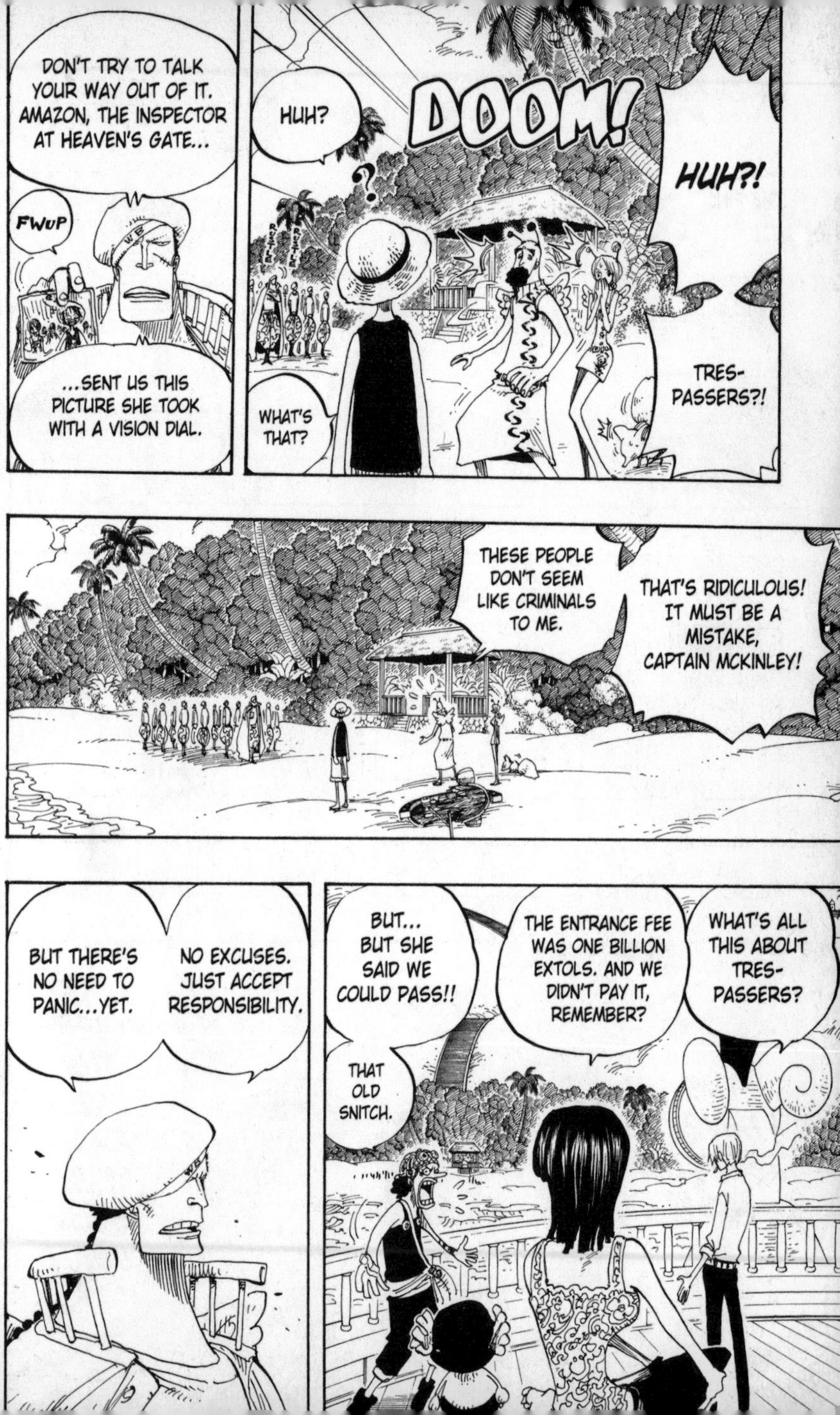
DOOM!
HUH?!
HUH?
RUSTLE
RUSTLE
TRES-PASSERS?!
WHAT'S THAT?
DON'T TRY TO TALK YOUR WAY OUT OF IT. AMAZON, THE INSPECTOR AT HEAVEN'S GATE...
FWUP
...SENT US THIS PICTURE SHE TOOK WITH A VISION DIAL.
THAT'S RIDICULOUS! IT MUST BE A MISTAKE, CAPTAIN MCKINLEY!
THESE PEOPLE DON'T SEEM LIKE CRIMINALS TO ME.
WHAT'S ALL THIS ABOUT TRES-PASSERS?
THE ENTRANCE FEE WAS ONE BILLION EXTOLS. AND WE DIDN'T PAY IT, REMEMBER?
BUT... BUT SHE SAID WE COULD PASS!!
THAT OLD SNITCH.
NO EXCUSES. JUST ACCEPT RESPONSIBILITY.
BUT THERE'S NO NEED TO PANIC...YET.

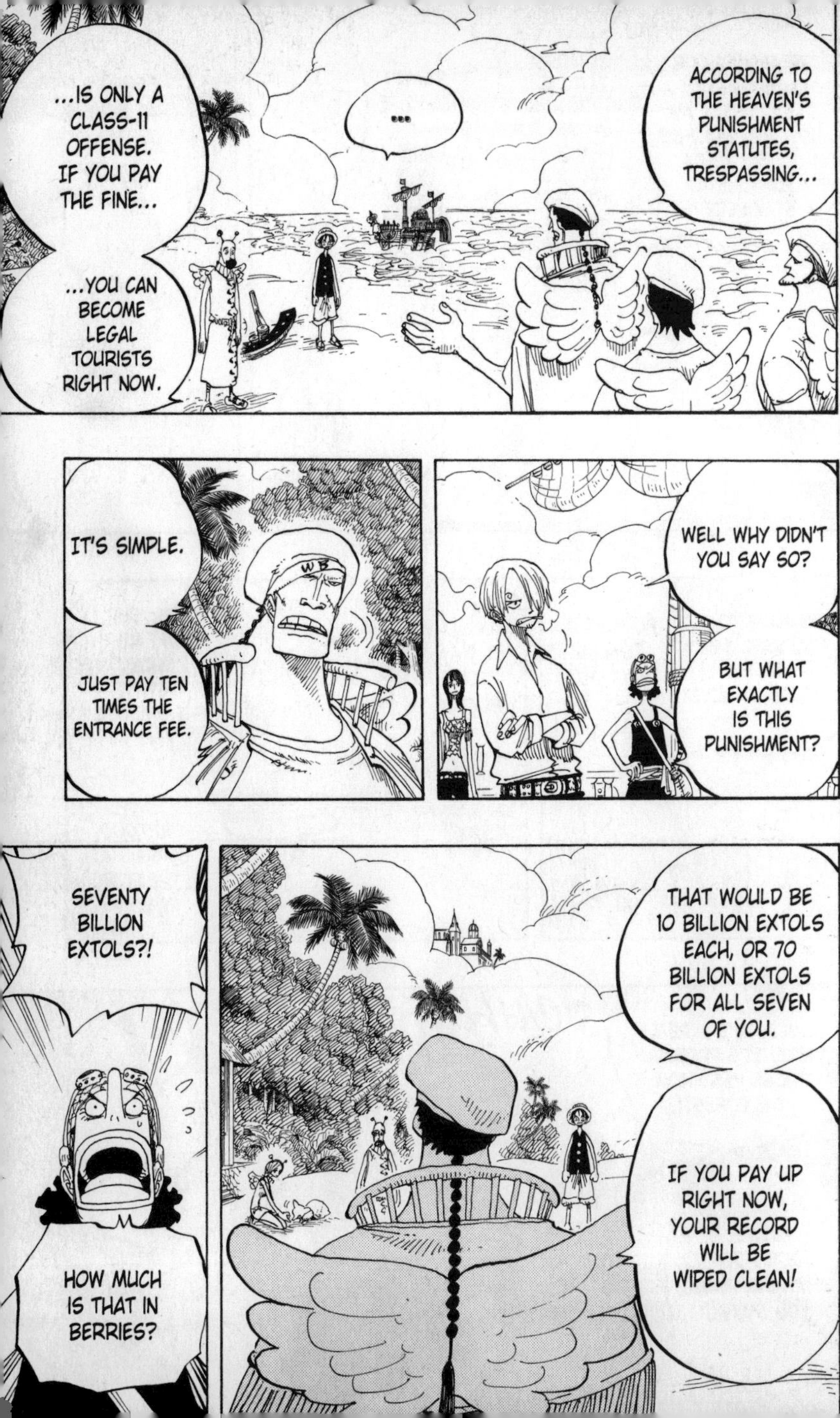
ACCORDING TO THE HEAVEN'S PUNISHMENT STATUTES, TRESPASSING...
...
...IS ONLY A CLASS-11 OFFENSE. IF YOU PAY THE FINE...
...YOU CAN BECOME LEGAL TOURISTS RIGHT NOW.
WELL WHY DIDN'T YOU SAY SO?
BUT WHAT EXACTLY IS THIS PUNISHMENT?
IT'S SIMPLE.
JUST PAY TEN TIMES THE ENTRANCE FEE.
THAT WOULD BE 10 BILLION EXTOLS EACH, OR 70 BILLION EXTOLS FOR ALL SEVEN OF YOU.
IF YOU PAY UP RIGHT NOW, YOUR RECORD WILL BE WIPED CLEAN!
SEVENTY BILLION EXTOLS?!
HOW MUCH IS THAT IN BERRIES?

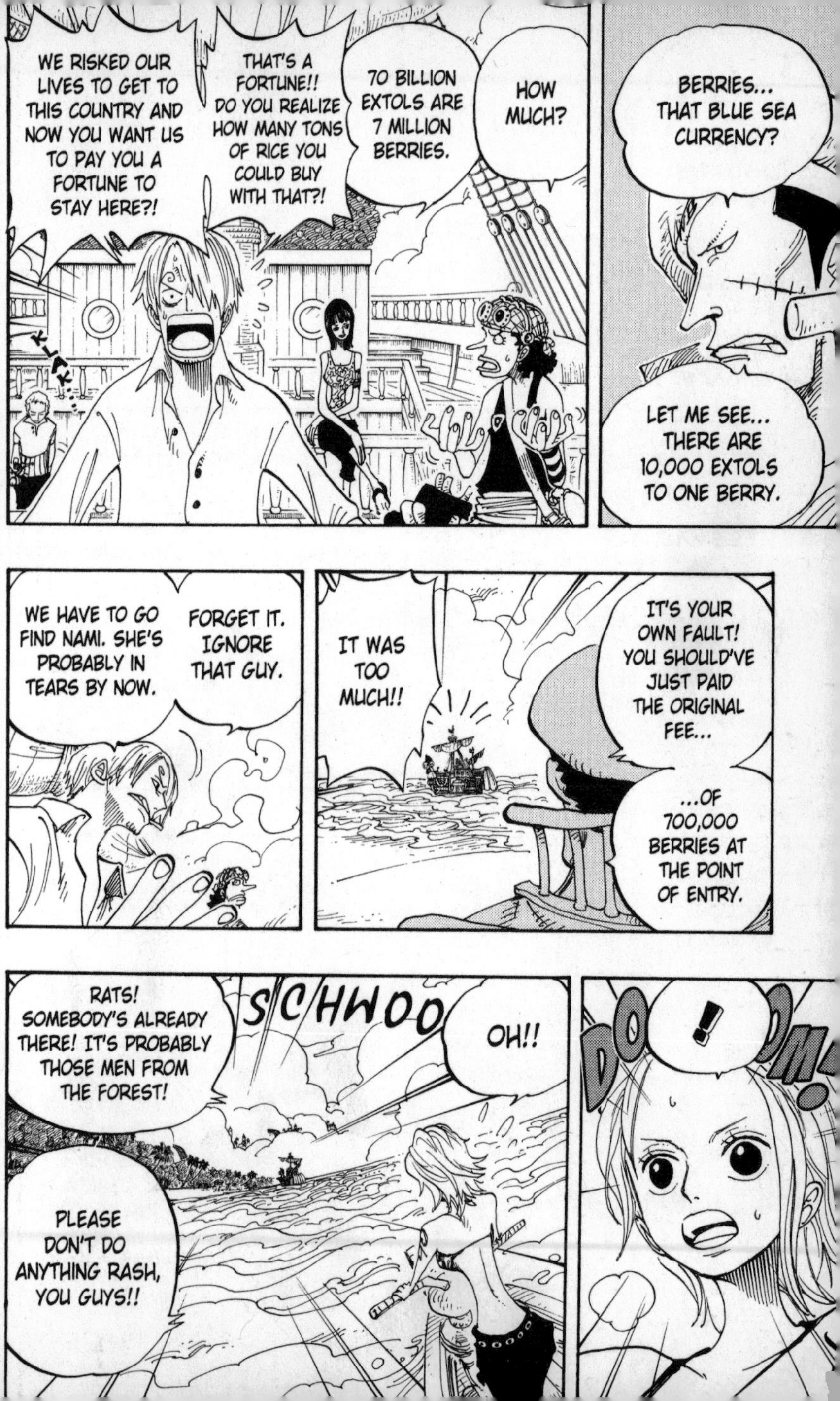
BERRIES... THAT BLUE SEA CURRENCY?
LET ME SEE... THERE ARE 10,000 EXTOLS TO ONE BERRY.
HOW MUCH?
70 BILLION EXTOLS ARE 7 MILLION BERRIES.
THAT'S A FORTUNE!! DO YOU REALIZE HOW MANY TONS OF RICE YOU COULD BUY WITH THAT?!
WE RISKED OUR LIVES TO GET TO THIS COUNTRY AND NOW YOU WANT US TO PAY YOU A FORTUNE TO STAY HERE?!
KLAK
IT'S YOUR OWN FAULT! YOU SHOULD'VE JUST PAID THE ORIGINAL FEE...
...OF 700,000 BERRIES AT THE POINT OF ENTRY.
IT WAS TOO MUCH!!
FORGET IT. IGNORE THAT GUY.
WE HAVE TO GO FIND NAMI. SHE'S PROBABLY IN TEARS BY NOW.
DOOM
!
OH!!
SCHWOO
RATS! SOMEBODY'S ALREADY THERE! IT'S PROBABLY THOSE MEN FROM THE FOREST!
PLEASE DON'T DO ANYTHING RASH, YOU GUYS!!

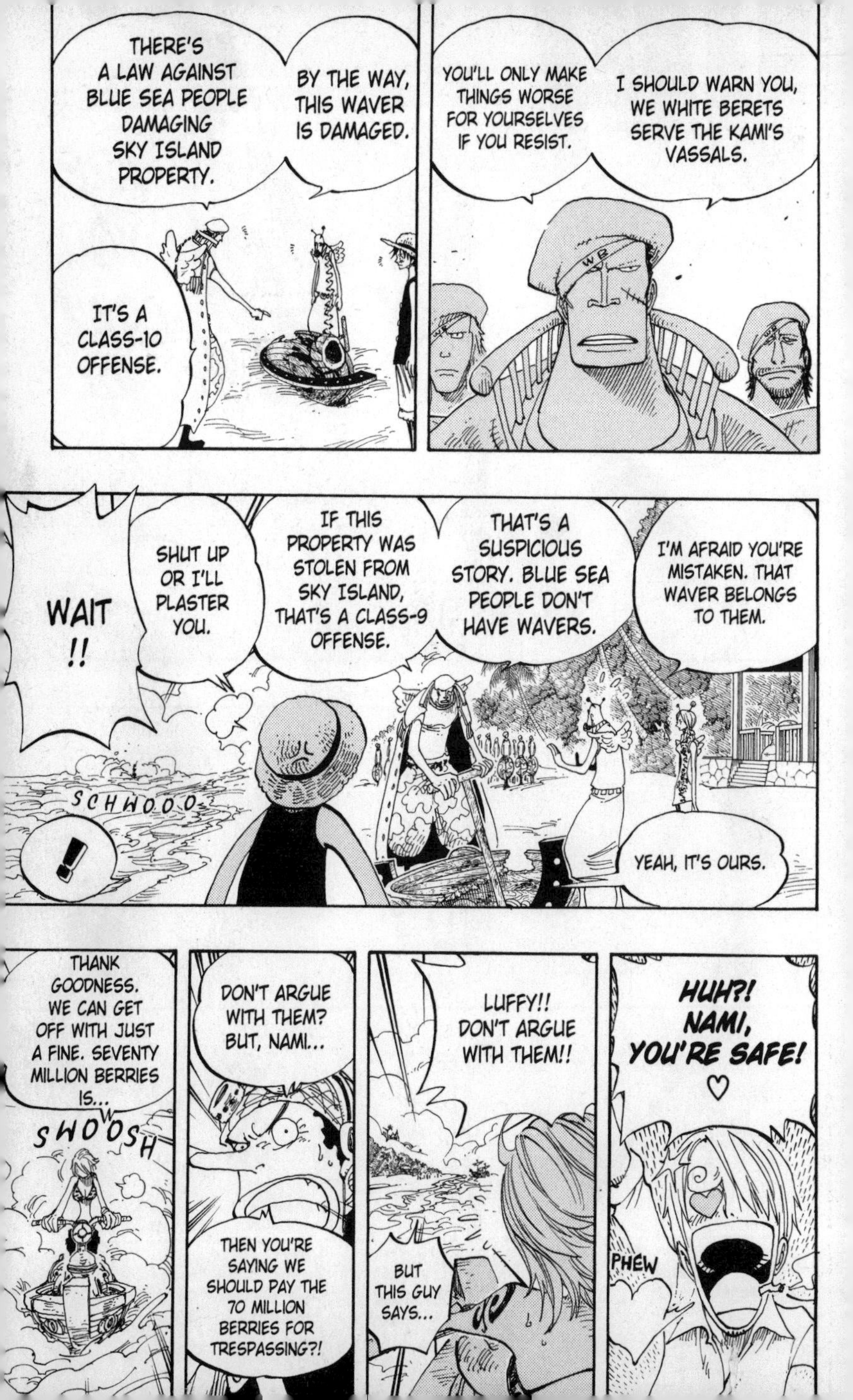
I SHOULD WARN YOU, WE WHITE BERETS SERVE THE KAMI'S VASSALS.
YOU'LL ONLY MAKE THINGS WORSE FOR YOURSELVES IF YOU RESIST.
BY THE WAY, THIS WAVER IS DAMAGED.
THERE'S A LAW AGAINST BLUE SEA PEOPLE DAMAGING SKY ISLAND PROPERTY.
IT'S A CLASS-10 OFFENSE.
I'M AFRAID YOU'RE MISTAKEN. THAT WAVER BELONGS TO THEM.
THAT'S A SUSPICIOUS STORY. BLUE SEA PEOPLE DON'T HAVE WAVERS.
IF THIS PROPERTY WAS STOLEN FROM SKY ISLAND, THAT'S A CLASS-9 OFFENSE.
SHUT UP OR I'LL PLASTER YOU.
WAIT !!
YEAH, IT'S OURS.
SCHWOOO
!
HUH?! NAMI, YOU'RE SAFE! ♥
PHEW
LUFFY!! DON'T ARGUE WITH THEM!!
BUT THIS GUY SAYS...
DON'T ARGUE WITH THEM? BUT, NAMI...
THEN YOU'RE SAYING WE SHOULD PAY THE 70 MILLION BERRIES FOR TRESPASSING?!
THANK GOODNESS. WE CAN GET OFF WITH JUST A FINE. SEVENTY MILLION BERRIES IS...
SWOOSH

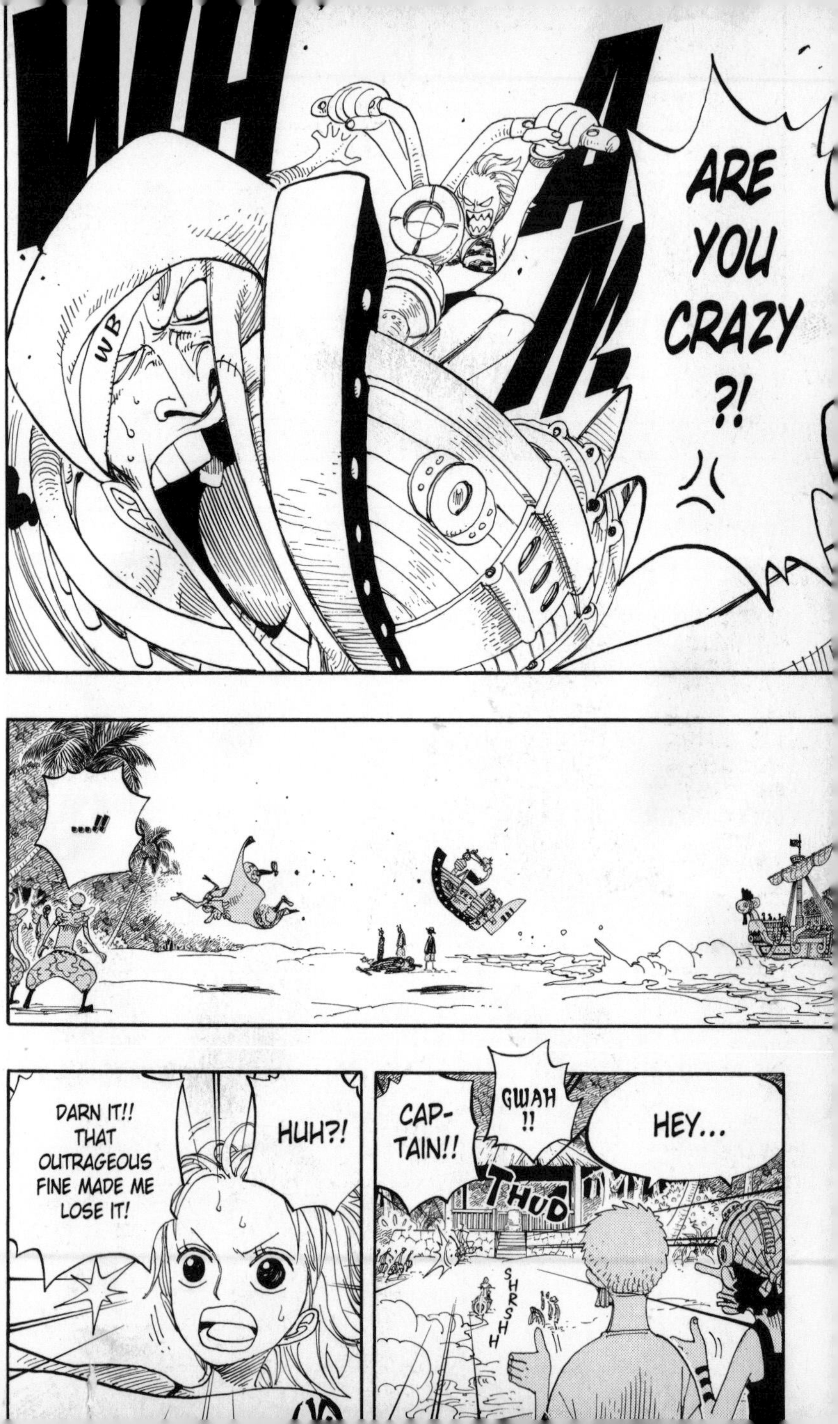
ARE YOU CRAZY ?!
WHAM
...!!
HEY...
GWAH !!
CAP-TAIN!!
THUD
SHRSHH
HUH?!
DARN IT!! THAT OUTRAGEOUS FINE MADE ME LOSE IT!

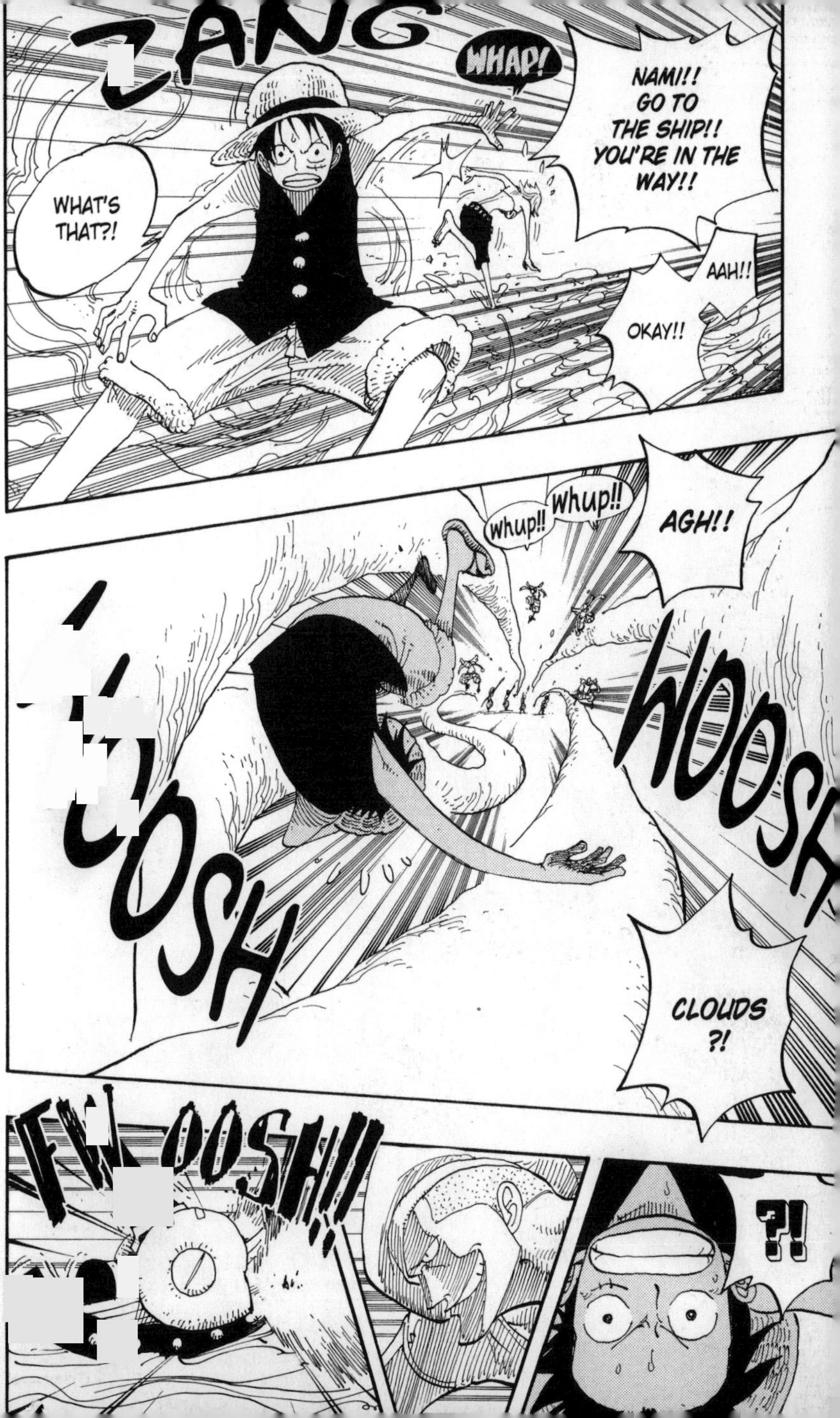
NAMI!! GO TO THE SHIP!! YOU'RE IN THE WAY!!
WHAP!
AAH!!
OKAY!!
ZANG
WHAT'S THAT?!
AGH!!
Whup!!
whup!!
WOOSH
CLOUDS ?!
?!
FW OOSH!!

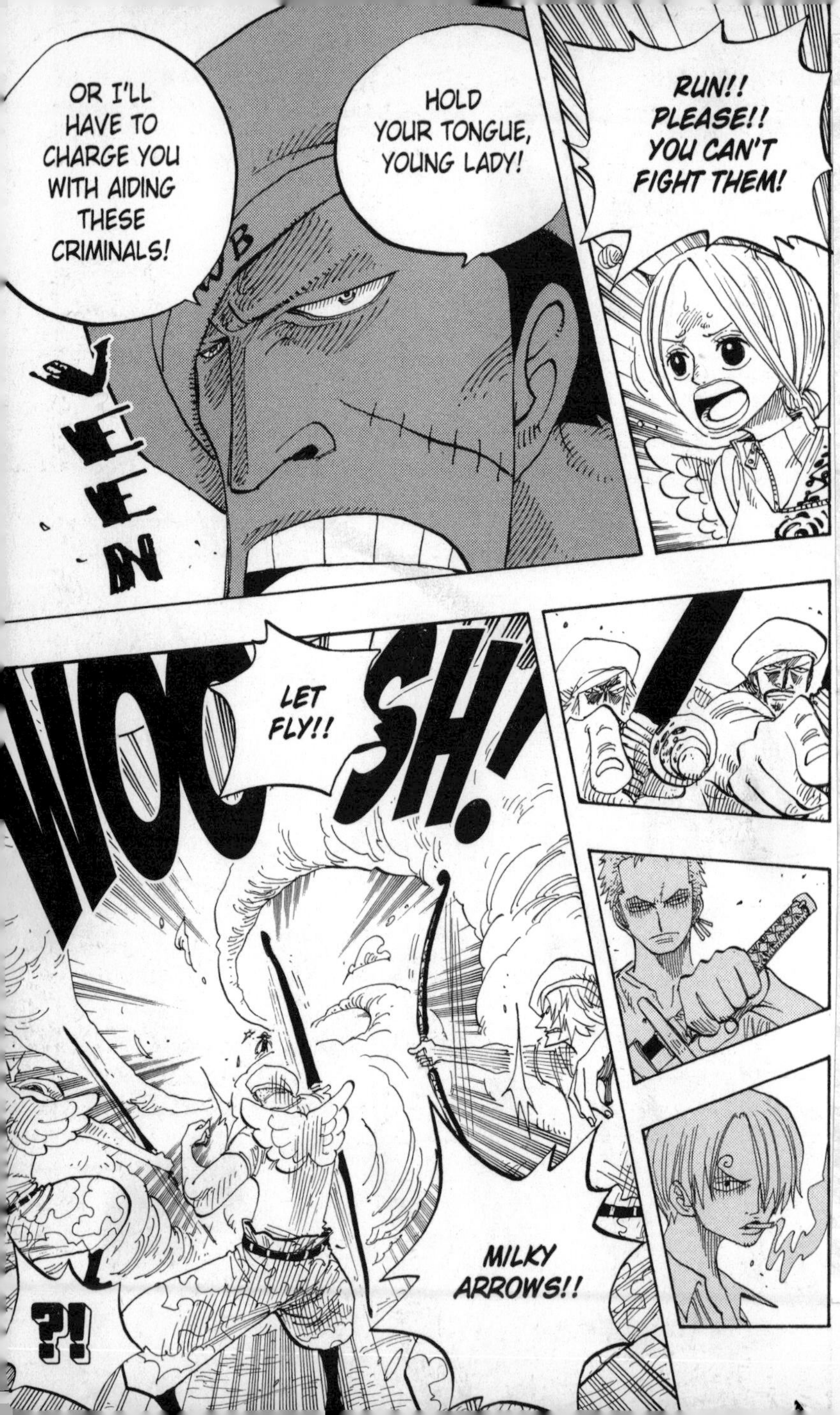
RUN!! PLEASE!! YOU CAN'T FIGHT THEM!
HOLD YOUR TONGUE, YOUNG LADY!
OR I'LL HAVE TO CHARGE YOU WITH AIDING THESE CRIMINALS!
VEEN
LET FLY!!
WOOSH!
MILKY ARROWS!!
?!

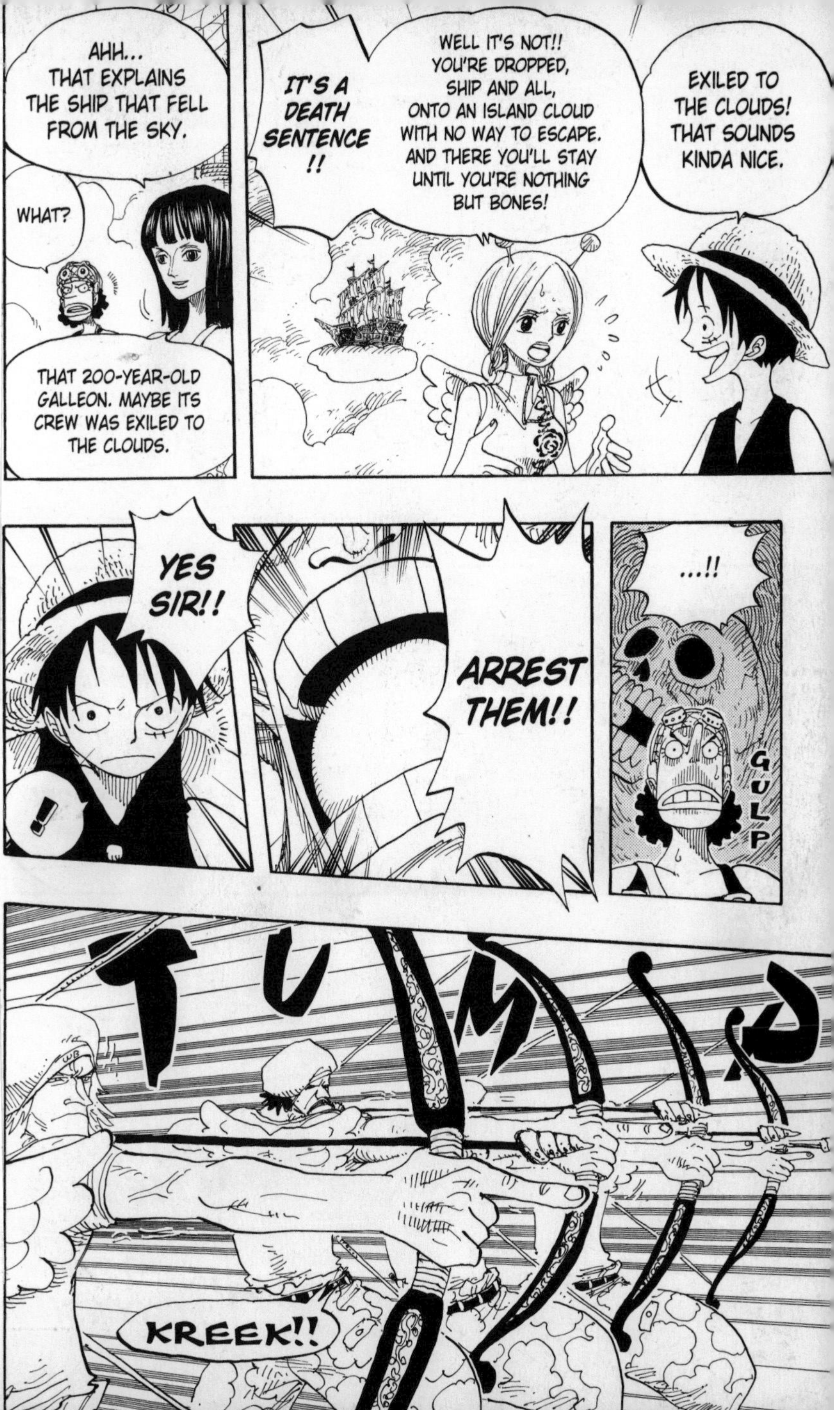
EXILED TO THE CLOUDS! THAT SOUNDS KINDA NICE.
WELL IT'S NOT!! YOU'RE DROPPED, SHIP AND ALL, ONTO AN ISLAND CLOUD WITH NO WAY TO ESCAPE. AND THERE YOU'LL STAY UNTIL YOU'RE NOTHING BUT BONES!
IT'S A DEATH SENTENCE!!
AHH... THAT EXPLAINS THE SHIP THAT FELL FROM THE SKY.
WHAT?
THAT 200-YEAR-OLD GALLEON. MAYBE ITS CREW WAS EXILED TO THE CLOUDS.
...!!
GULP
ARREST THEM!!
YES SIR!!
!
KREEK!!

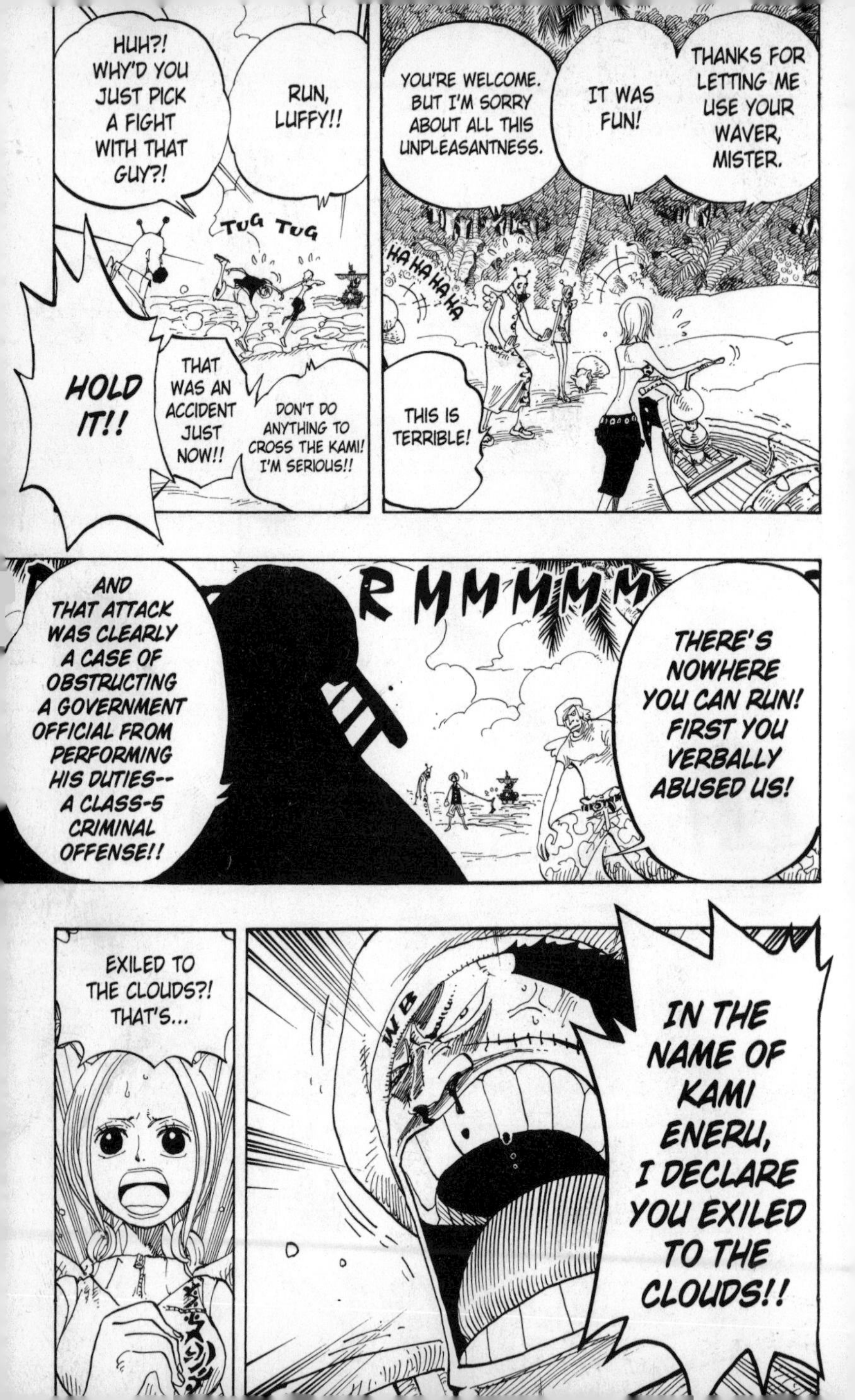
THANKS FOR LETTING ME USE YOUR WAVER, MISTER.
IT WAS FUN!
YOU'RE WELCOME. BUT I'M SORRY ABOUT ALL THIS UNPLEASANTNESS.
HA HA HA HA
THIS IS TERRIBLE!
RUN, LUFFY!!
HUH?! WHY'D YOU JUST PICK A FIGHT WITH THAT GUY?!
TUG TUG
DON'T DO ANYTHING TO CROSS THE KAMI! I'M SERIOUS!!
THAT WAS AN ACCIDENT JUST NOW!!
HOLD IT!!
RMMMMM
THERE'S NOWHERE YOU CAN RUN! FIRST YOU VERBALLY ABUSED US!
AND THAT ATTACK WAS CLEARLY A CASE OF OBSTRUCTING A GOVERNMENT OFFICIAL FROM PERFORMING HIS DUTIES-- A CLASS-5 CRIMINAL OFFENSE!!
IN THE NAME OF KAMI ENERU, I DECLARE YOU EXILED TO THE CLOUDS!!
EXILED TO THE CLOUDS?! THAT'S...

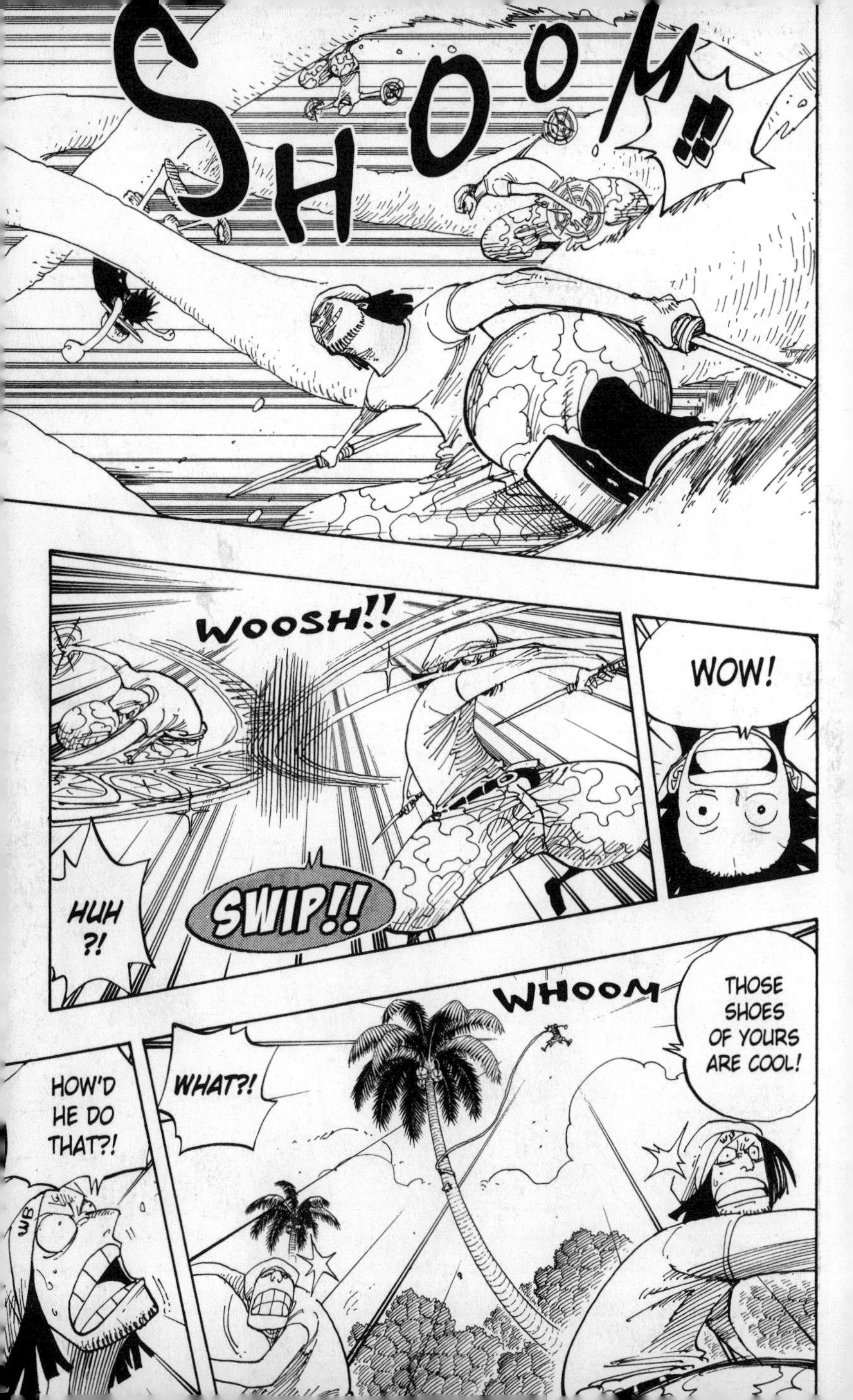
SHOOM!!
WOW!
WOOSH!!
SWIP!!
HUH ?!
THOSE SHOES OF YOURS ARE COOL!
WHOOM
WHAT?!
HOW'D HE DO THAT?!

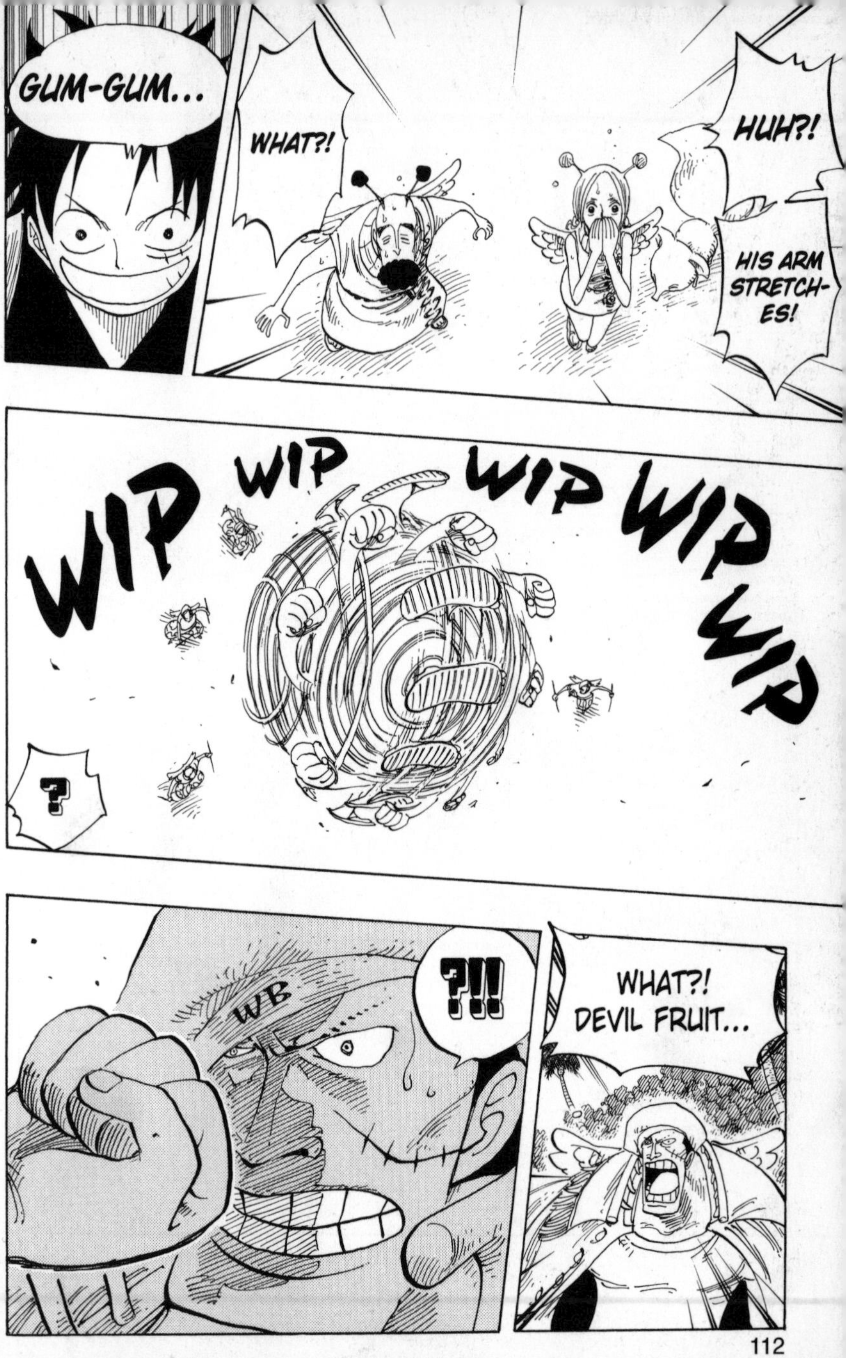
HUH?!
HIS ARM STRETCH-ES!
WHAT?!
GUM-GUM...
WIP WIP WIP WIP WIP WIP
?
WHAT?! DEVIL FRUIT...
?!!

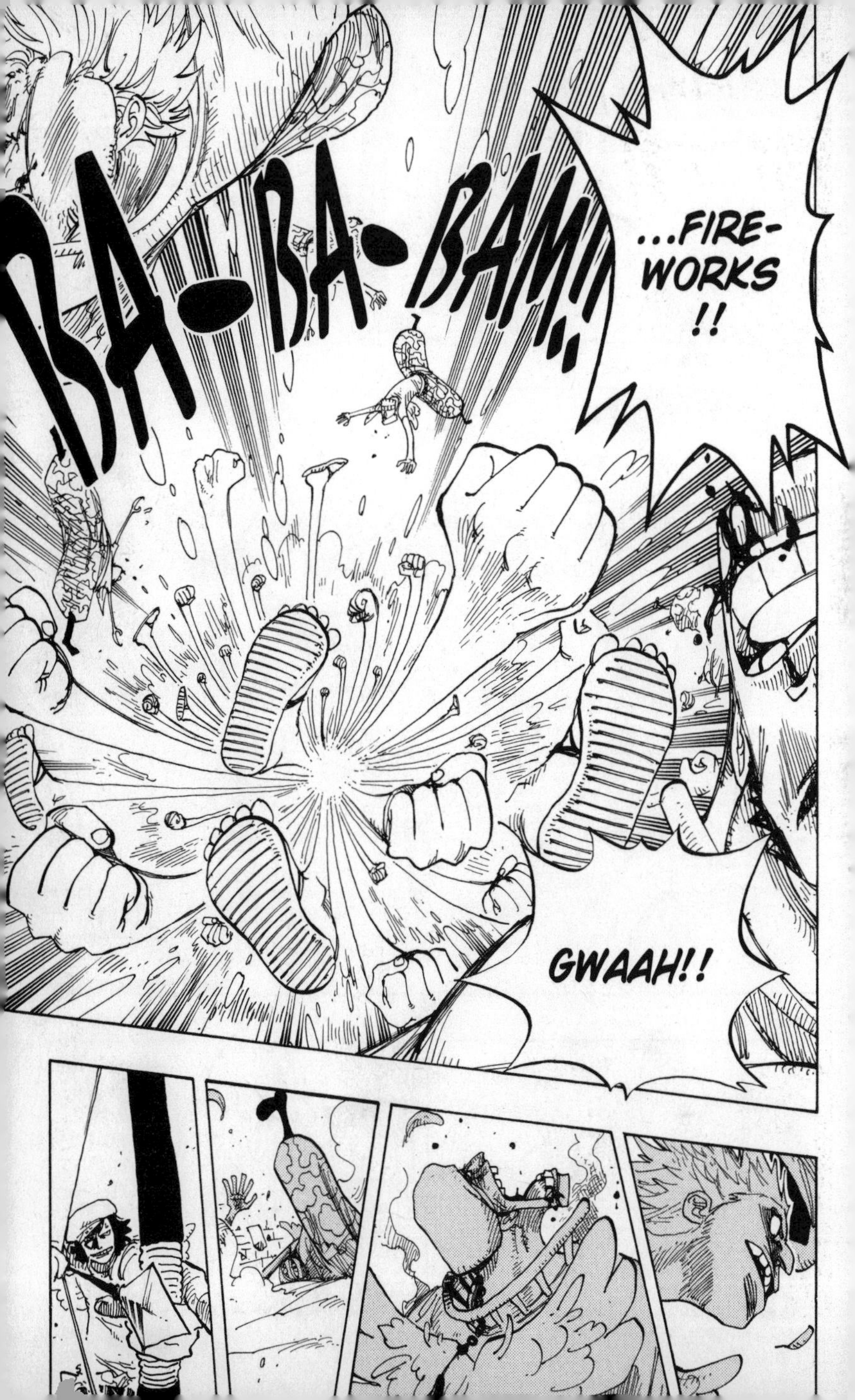
...FIRE-WORKS!!
BA-BA-BAM!!
GWAAH!!

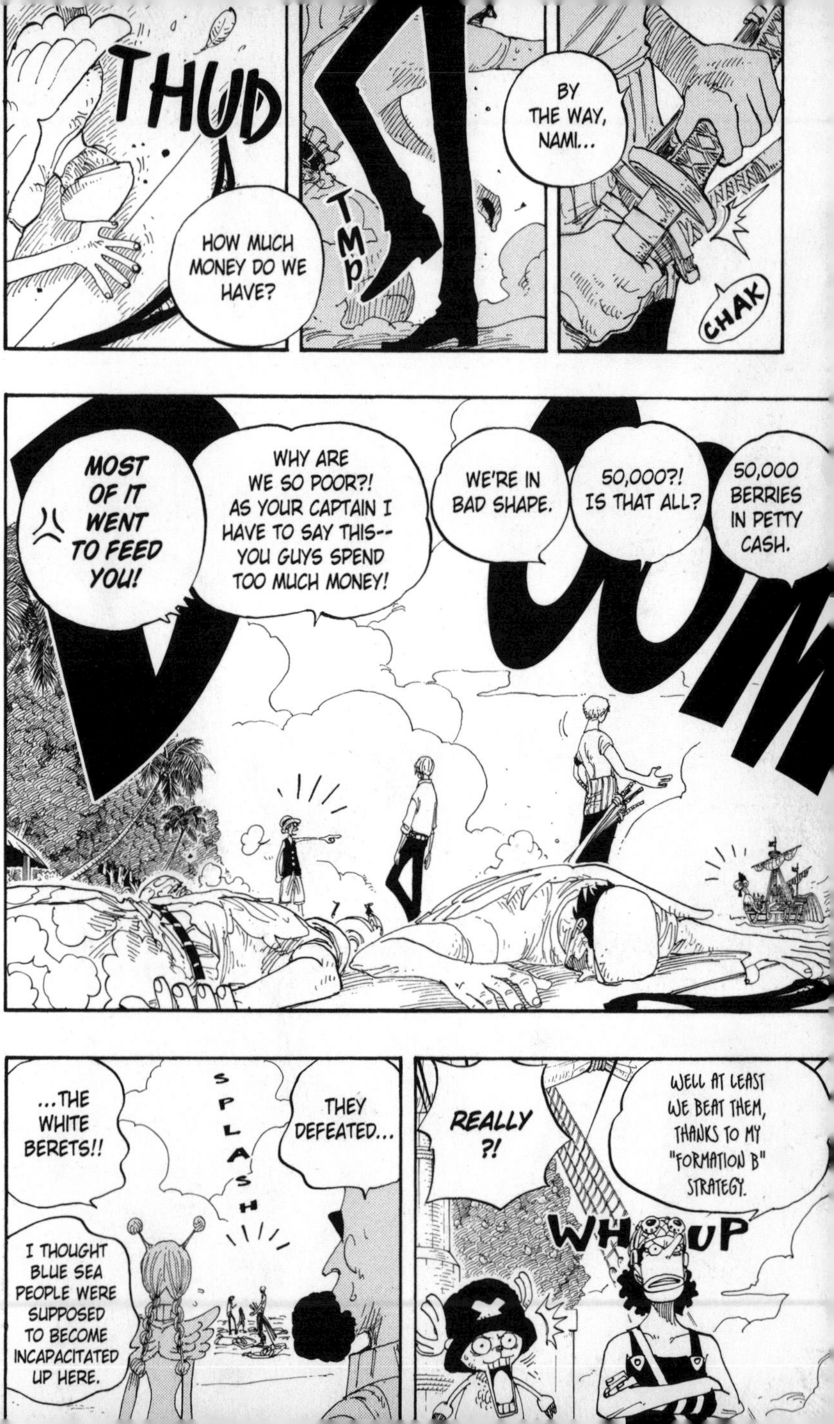
BY THE WAY, NAMI...
CHAK
TMP
THUD
HOW MUCH MONEY DO WE HAVE?
50,000 BERRIES IN PETTY CASH.
50,000?! IS THAT ALL?
WE'RE IN BAD SHAPE.
WHY ARE WE SO POOR?! AS YOUR CAPTAIN I HAVE TO SAY THIS-- YOU GUYS SPEND TOO MUCH MONEY!
MOST OF IT WENT TO FEED YOU!
WELL AT LEAST WE BEAT THEM, THANKS TO MY "FORMATION B" STRATEGY.
REALLY ?!
WHUP
THEY DEFEATED...
...THE WHITE BERETS!!
SPLASH
I THOUGHT BLUE SEA PEOPLE WERE SUPPOSED TO BECOME INCAPACITATED UP HERE.

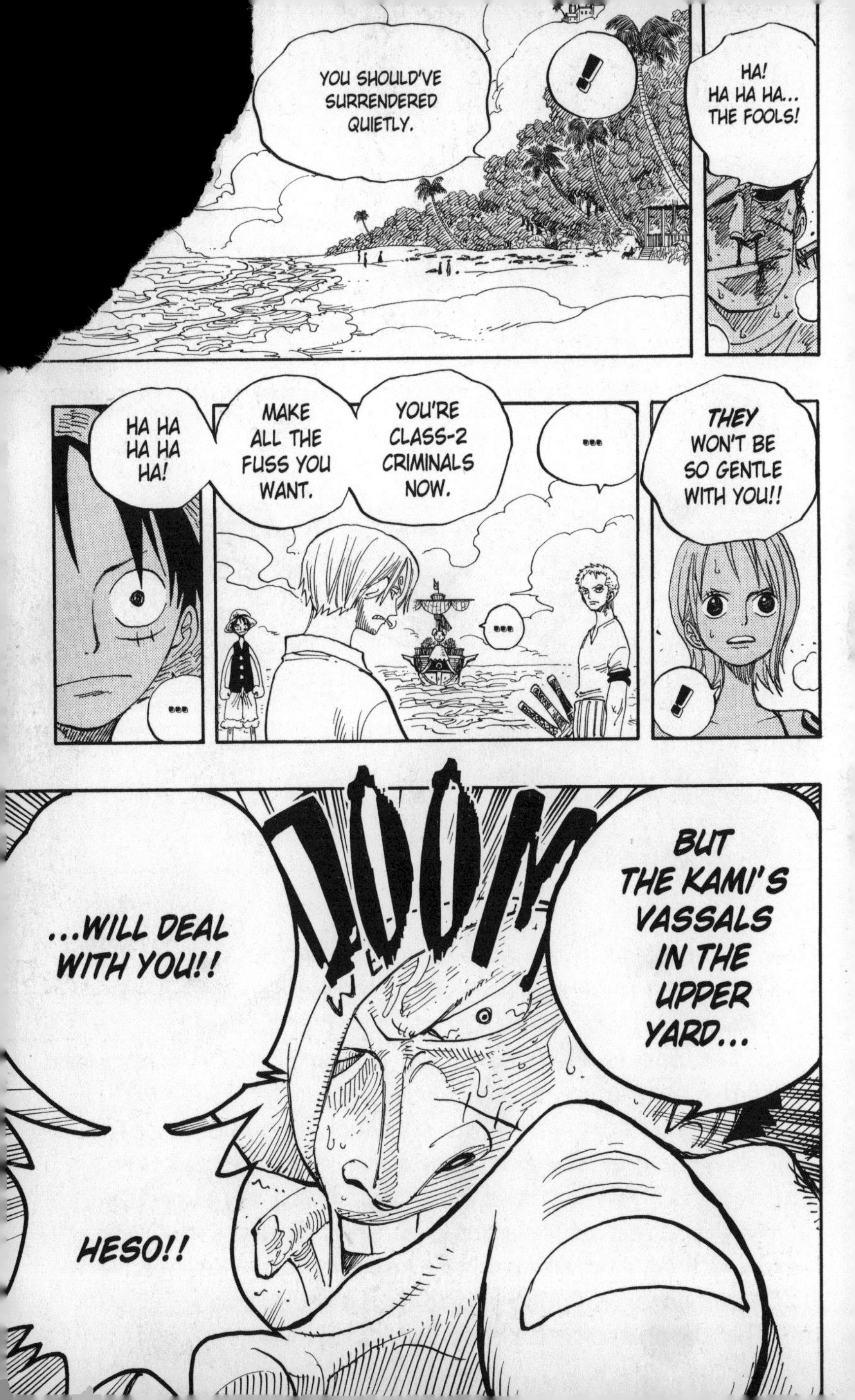
HA! HA HA HA... THE FOOLS!
!
YOU SHOULD'VE SURRENDERED QUIETLY.
THEY WON'T BE SO GENTLE WITH YOU!!
!
...
YOU'RE CLASS-2 CRIMINALS NOW.
MAKE ALL THE FUSS YOU WANT.
...
HA HA HA HA HA!
...
BUT THE KAMI'S VASSALS IN THE UPPER YARD...
DOOM
...WILL DEAL WITH YOU!!
HESO!!

The Bad Stuff Cor[redacted]

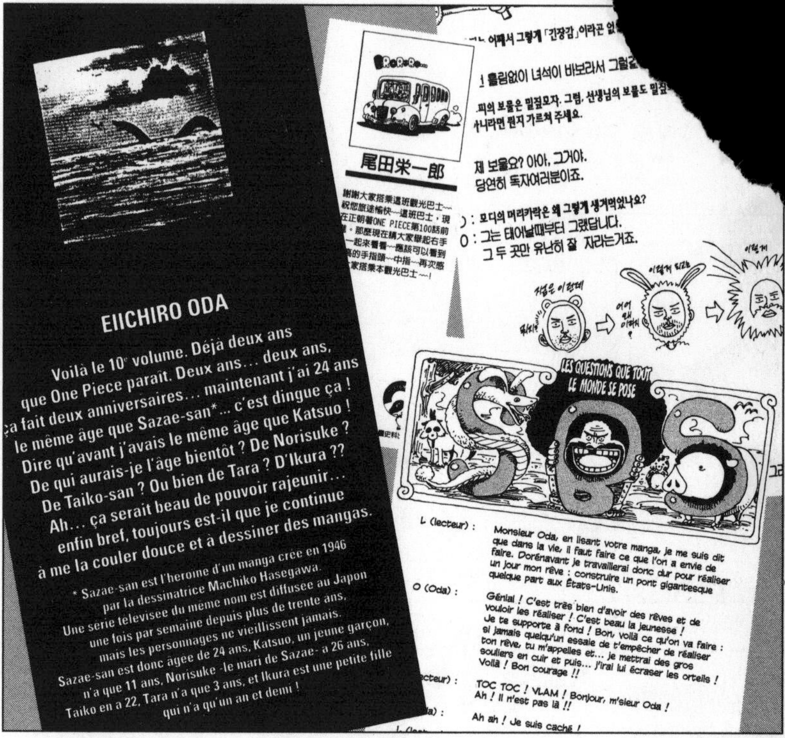
EIICHIRO ODA

Voilà le 10e volume. Déjà deux ans que One Piece paraît. Deux ans… deux ans, ça fait deux anniversaires… maintenant j'ai 24 ans le même âge que Sazae-san*… c'est dingue ça ! Dire qu'avant j'avais le même âge que Katsuo ! De qui aurais-je l'âge bientôt ? De Norisuke ? De Taiko-san ? Ou bien de Tara ? D'Ikura ?? Ah… ça serait beau de pouvoir rajeunir… enfin bref, toujours est-il que je continue à me la couler douce et à dessiner des mangas.

* Sazae-san est l'héroïne d'un manga créé en 1946 par la dessinatrice Machiko Hasegawa. Une série télévisée du même nom est diffusée au Japon une fois par semaine depuis plus de trente ans, mais les personnages ne vieillissent jamais. Sazae-san est donc âgée de 24 ans, Katsuo, un jeune garçon, n'a que 11 ans, Norisuke -le mari de Sazae- a 26 ans, Taiko en a 22, Tara n'a que 3 ans, et Ikura est une petite fille qui n'a qu'un an et demi !

尾田栄一郎

謝謝大家搭乘這班觀光巴士~~ 祝您旅途愉快~~這班巴士，現在正朝著ONE PIECE第100話前進。那麼現在請大家舉起右手一起來看看~~應該可以看到你的手指頭~~中指~~再次感謝大家搭乘本觀光巴士~~!

…어째서 그렇게「긴장감」이라곤 없…
…! 틀림없이 녀석이 바보라서 그럴…
…피의 보물은 밀짚모자. 그럼, 선생님의 보물도 밀짚…
…니라면 편지 가르쳐 주세요.

제 보물요? 아아, 그거야.
당연히 독자여러분이죠.

…: 모디의 머리카락은 왜 그렇게 생겨먹었나요?
O : 그는 태어날때부터 그랬답니다.
그 두 곳만 유난히 잘 자라는거죠.

LES QUESTIONS QUE TOUT LE MONDE SE POSE

SBS

L (lecteur) : Monsieur Oda, en lisant votre manga, je me suis dit que dans la vie, il faut faire ce que l'on a envie de faire. Dorénavant je travaillerai donc dur pour réaliser un jour mon rêve : construire un pont gigantesque quelque part aux États-Unis.

O (Oda) : Génial ! C'est très bien d'avoir des rêves et de vouloir les réaliser ! C'est beau la jeunesse ! Je te supporte à fond ! Bon, voilà ce qu'on va faire : si jamais quelqu'un essaie de t'empêcher de réaliser ton rêve, tu m'appelles et… je mettrai des gros souliers en cuir et puis… j'irai lui écraser les orteils ! Voilà ! Bon courage !!

…ecteur) : TOC TOC ! VLAM ! Bonjour, m'sieur Oda ! Ah ! Il n'est pas là !!

…a) : Ah ah ! Je suis caché !

O: ⬆ To the left is an author's page from volume 10 in French. In it I mention that I'm the same age as Sazae-san. But the French don't know who Sazae-san is, of course, so an explanation is included in the paragraph below.

Thank you for going to so much trouble. I'll refrain from making unnecessary comments hereafter. (I'm lying.) And to the right, much to my surprise, they've even translated the SBS Question Corner. Oh no! All our silly banter has crossed the oceans. The children of the world must be saying, "The Japanese are so stupid."

It's okay they're our friends too.

Chapter 243:
TRIAL

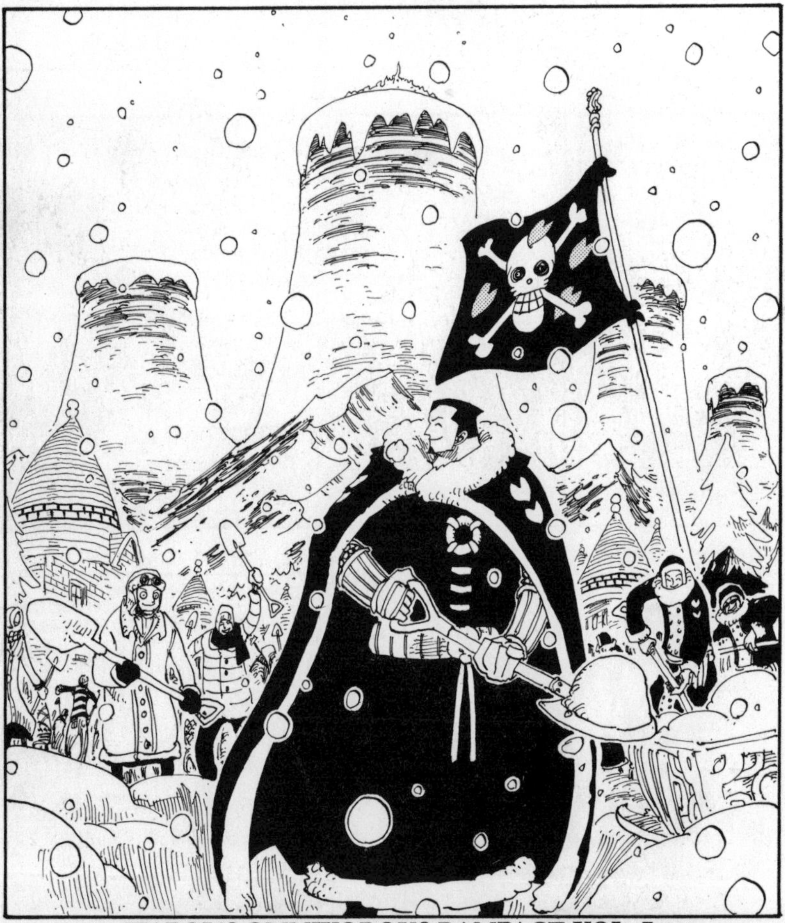

WAPOL'S OMNIVOROUS RAMPAGE VOL. 7:
"KING DALTON OF THE CHERRY BLOSSOM KINGDOM"

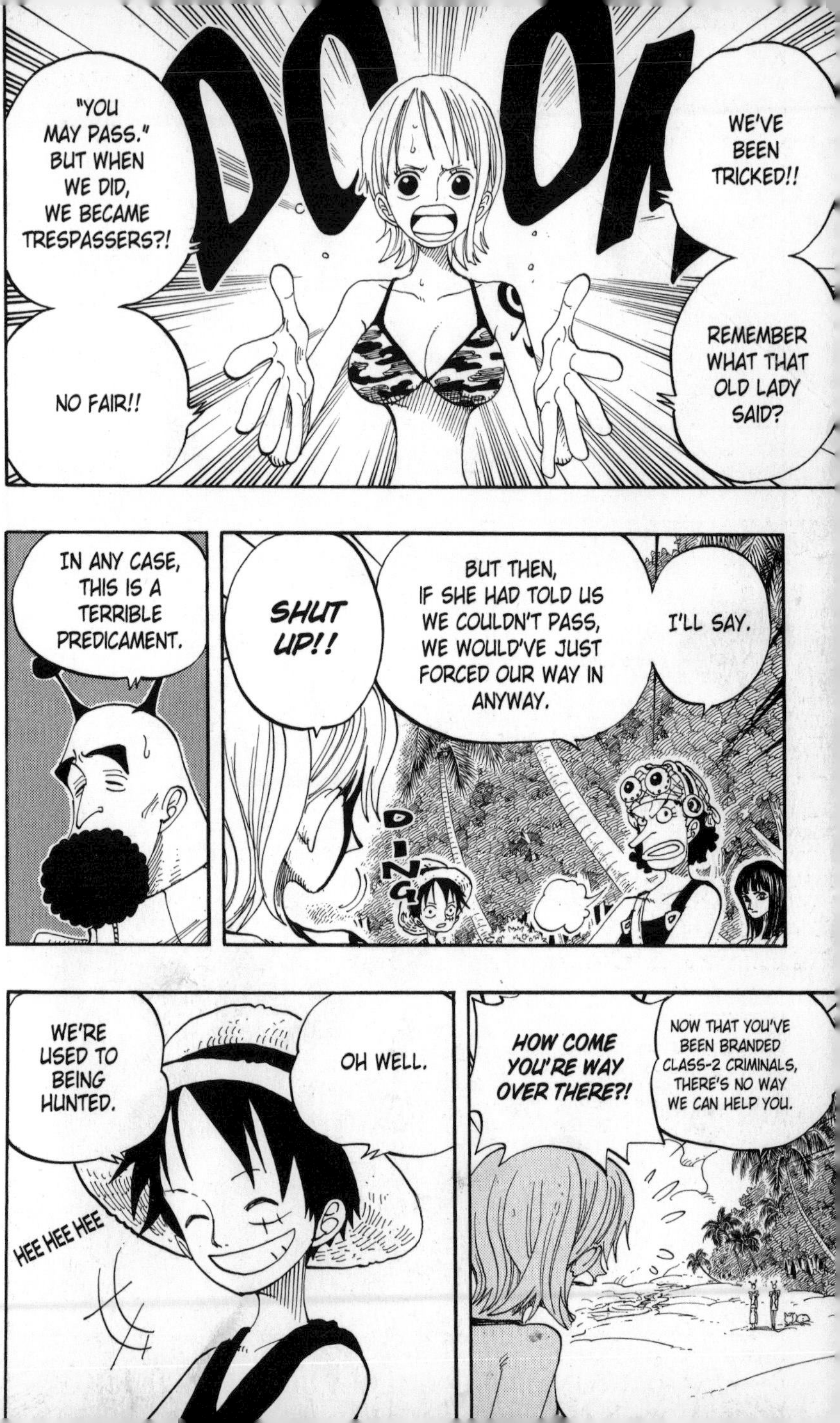
WE'VE BEEN TRICKED!!
REMEMBER WHAT THAT OLD LADY SAID?
"YOU MAY PASS." BUT WHEN WE DID, WE BECAME TRESPASSERS?!
NO FAIR!!
I'LL SAY.
BUT THEN, IF SHE HAD TOLD US WE COULDN'T PASS, WE WOULD'VE JUST FORCED OUR WAY IN ANYWAY.
SHUT UP!!
DING
IN ANY CASE, THIS IS A TERRIBLE PREDICAMENT.
NOW THAT YOU'VE BEEN BRANDED CLASS-2 CRIMINALS, THERE'S NO WAY WE CAN HELP YOU.
HOW COME YOU'RE WAY OVER THERE?!
OH WELL.
WE'RE USED TO BEING HUNTED.
HEE HEE HEE

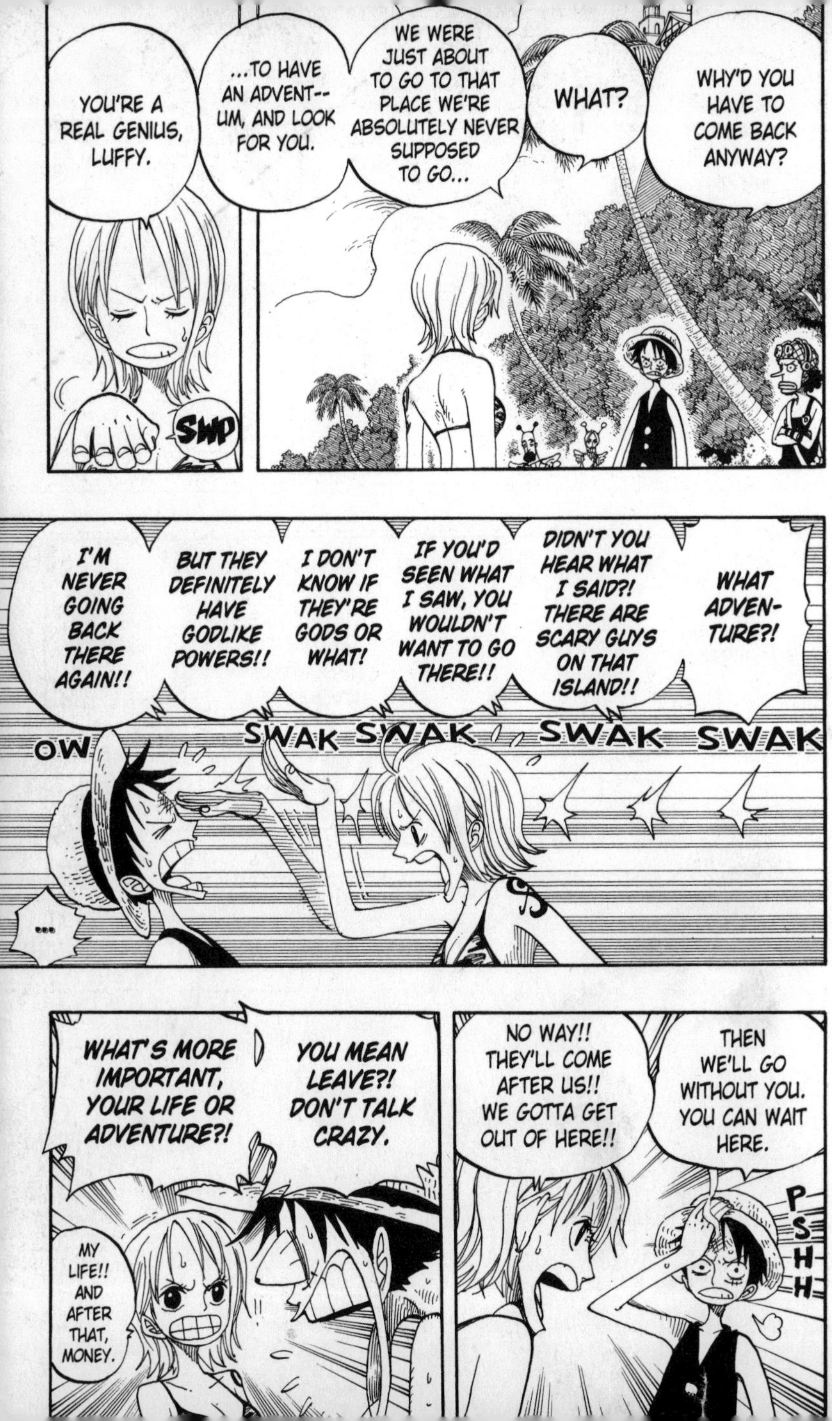
WHY'D YOU HAVE TO COME BACK ANYWAY?
WHAT?
WE WERE JUST ABOUT TO GO TO THAT PLACE WE'RE ABSOLUTELY NEVER SUPPOSED TO GO...
...TO HAVE AN ADVENT-- UM, AND LOOK FOR YOU.
YOU'RE A REAL GENIUS, LUFFY.
SWP
WHAT ADVEN-TURE?!
DIDN'T YOU HEAR WHAT I SAID?! THERE ARE SCARY GUYS ON THAT ISLAND!!
IF YOU'D SEEN WHAT I SAW, YOU WOULDN'T WANT TO GO THERE!!
I DON'T KNOW IF THEY'RE GODS OR WHAT!
BUT THEY DEFINITELY HAVE GODLIKE POWERS!!
I'M NEVER GOING BACK THERE AGAIN!!
SWAK
SWAK
SWAK
SWAK
OW
...
THEN WE'LL GO WITHOUT YOU. YOU CAN WAIT HERE.
NO WAY!! THEY'LL COME AFTER US!! WE GOTTA GET OUT OF HERE!!
PSHH
YOU MEAN LEAVE?! DON'T TALK CRAZY.
WHAT'S MORE IMPORTANT, YOUR LIFE OR ADVENTURE?!
MY LIFE!! AND AFTER THAT, MONEY.

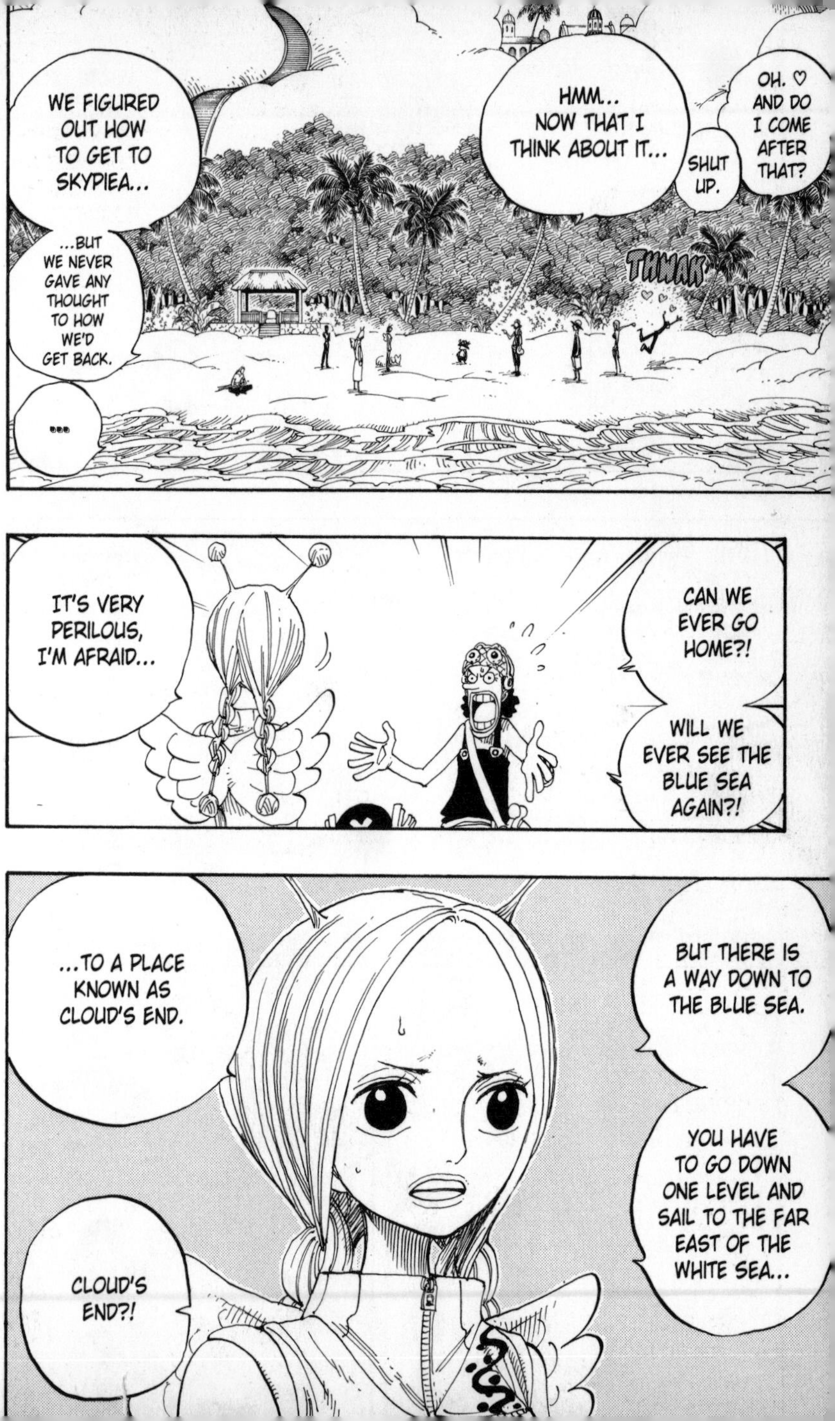
OH. ♡ AND DO I COME AFTER THAT?
SHUT UP.
THWAK
HMM... NOW THAT I THINK ABOUT IT...
WE FIGURED OUT HOW TO GET TO SKYPIEA...
...BUT WE NEVER GAVE ANY THOUGHT TO HOW WE'D GET BACK.
...
CAN WE EVER GO HOME?!
WILL WE EVER SEE THE BLUE SEA AGAIN?!
IT'S VERY PERILOUS, I'M AFRAID...
BUT THERE IS A WAY DOWN TO THE BLUE SEA.
YOU HAVE TO GO DOWN ONE LEVEL AND SAIL TO THE FAR EAST OF THE WHITE SEA...
...TO A PLACE KNOWN AS CLOUD'S END.
CLOUD'S END?!

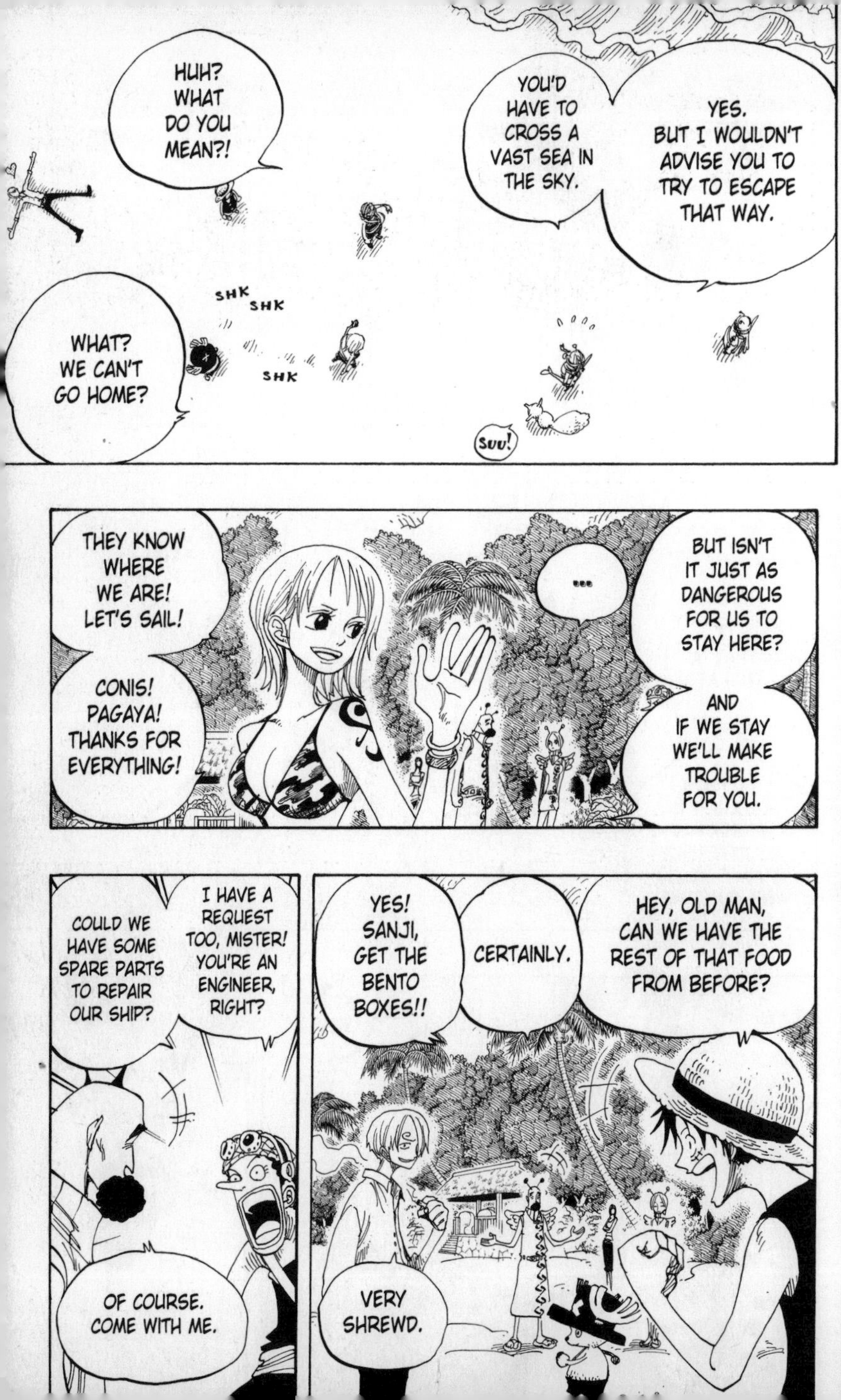
YES. BUT I WOULDN'T ADVISE YOU TO TRY TO ESCAPE THAT WAY.
YOU'D HAVE TO CROSS A VAST SEA IN THE SKY.
HUH? WHAT DO YOU MEAN?!
SHK SHK
SHK
SUU!
WHAT? WE CAN'T GO HOME?
BUT ISN'T IT JUST AS DANGEROUS FOR US TO STAY HERE?
...
AND IF WE STAY WE'LL MAKE TROUBLE FOR YOU.
THEY KNOW WHERE WE ARE! LET'S SAIL!
CONIS! PAGAYA! THANKS FOR EVERYTHING!
HEY, OLD MAN, CAN WE HAVE THE REST OF THAT FOOD FROM BEFORE?
CERTAINLY.
YES! SANJI, GET THE BENTO BOXES!!
VERY SHREWD.
I HAVE A REQUEST TOO, MISTER! YOU'RE AN ENGINEER, RIGHT?
COULD WE HAVE SOME SPARE PARTS TO REPAIR OUR SHIP?
OF COURSE. COME WITH ME.

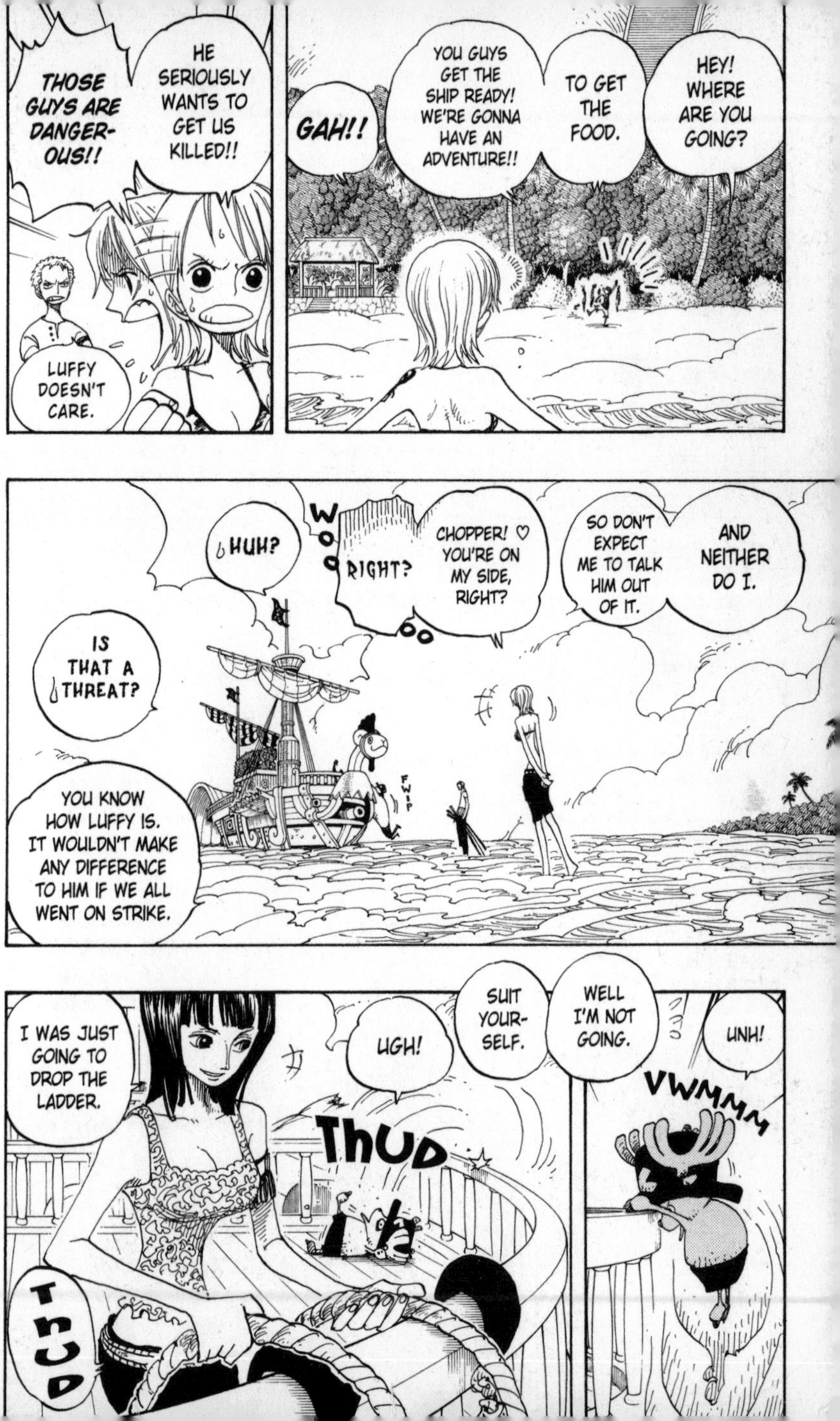
HEY! WHERE ARE YOU GOING?
TO GET THE FOOD.
YOU GUYS GET THE SHIP READY! WE'RE GONNA HAVE AN ADVENTURE!!
GAH!!
HE SERIOUSLY WANTS TO GET US KILLED!!
THOSE GUYS ARE DANGER-OUS!!
LUFFY DOESN'T CARE.
AND NEITHER DO I.
SO DON'T EXPECT ME TO TALK HIM OUT OF IT.
CHOPPER! ♡ YOU'RE ON MY SIDE, RIGHT?
WOOO
RIGHT?
HUH?
IS THAT A THREAT?
FWIP
YOU KNOW HOW LUFFY IS. IT WOULDN'T MAKE ANY DIFFERENCE TO HIM IF WE ALL WENT ON STRIKE.
UNH!
VWMMM
WELL I'M NOT GOING.
SUIT YOURSELF.
UGH!
THUD
I WAS JUST GOING TO DROP THE LADDER.
THUD

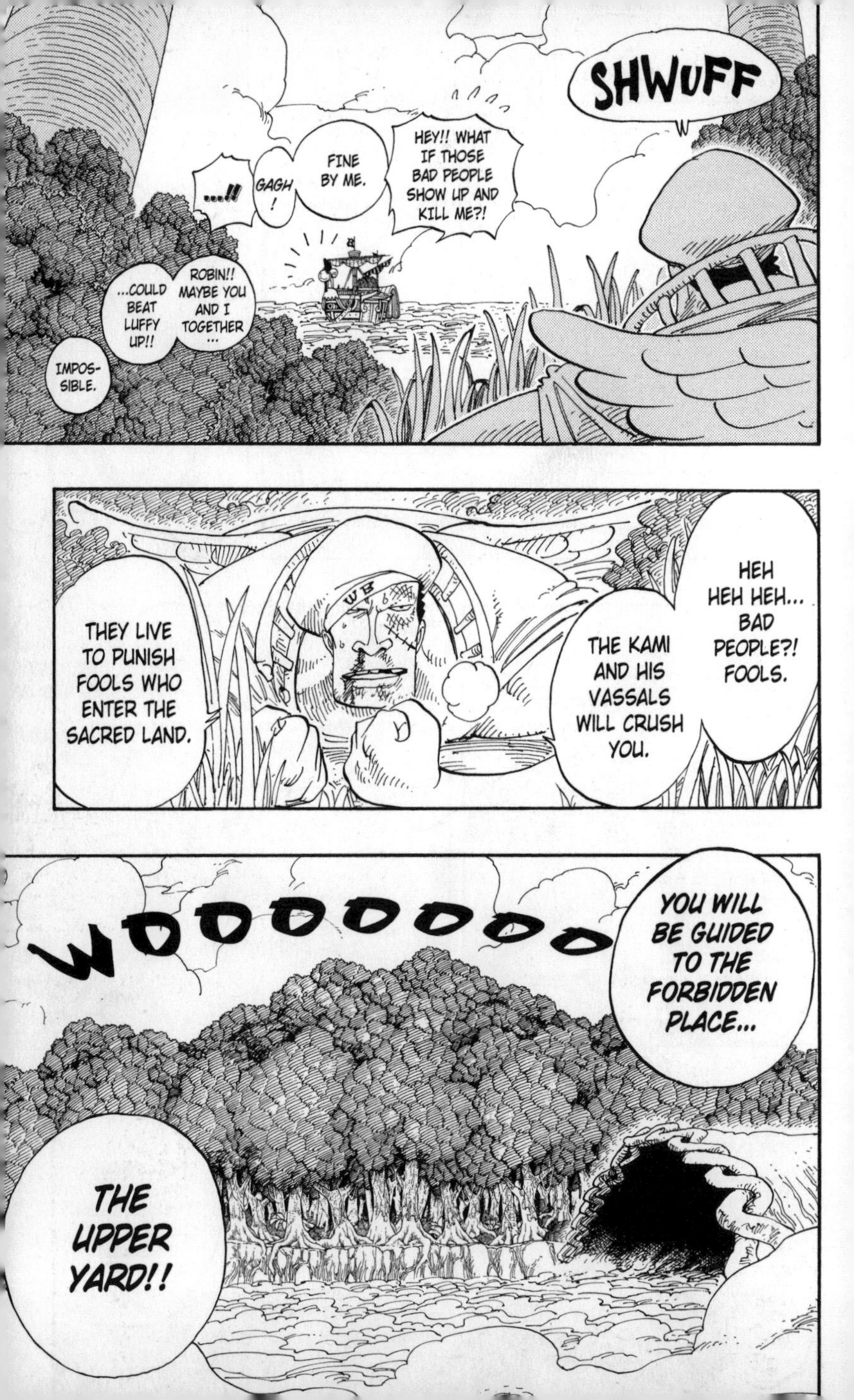
SHWUFF
HEY!! WHAT IF THOSE BAD PEOPLE SHOW UP AND KILL ME?!
FINE BY ME.
GAGH!
...!!
ROBIN!! MAYBE YOU AND I TOGETHER...
...COULD BEAT LUFFY UP!!
IMPOSSIBLE.
HEH HEH HEH... BAD PEOPLE?! FOOLS.
THE KAMI AND HIS VASSALS WILL CRUSH YOU.
THEY LIVE TO PUNISH FOOLS WHO ENTER THE SACRED LAND.
YOU WILL BE GUIDED TO THE FORBIDDEN PLACE...
WOOOOOOO
THE UPPER YARD!!

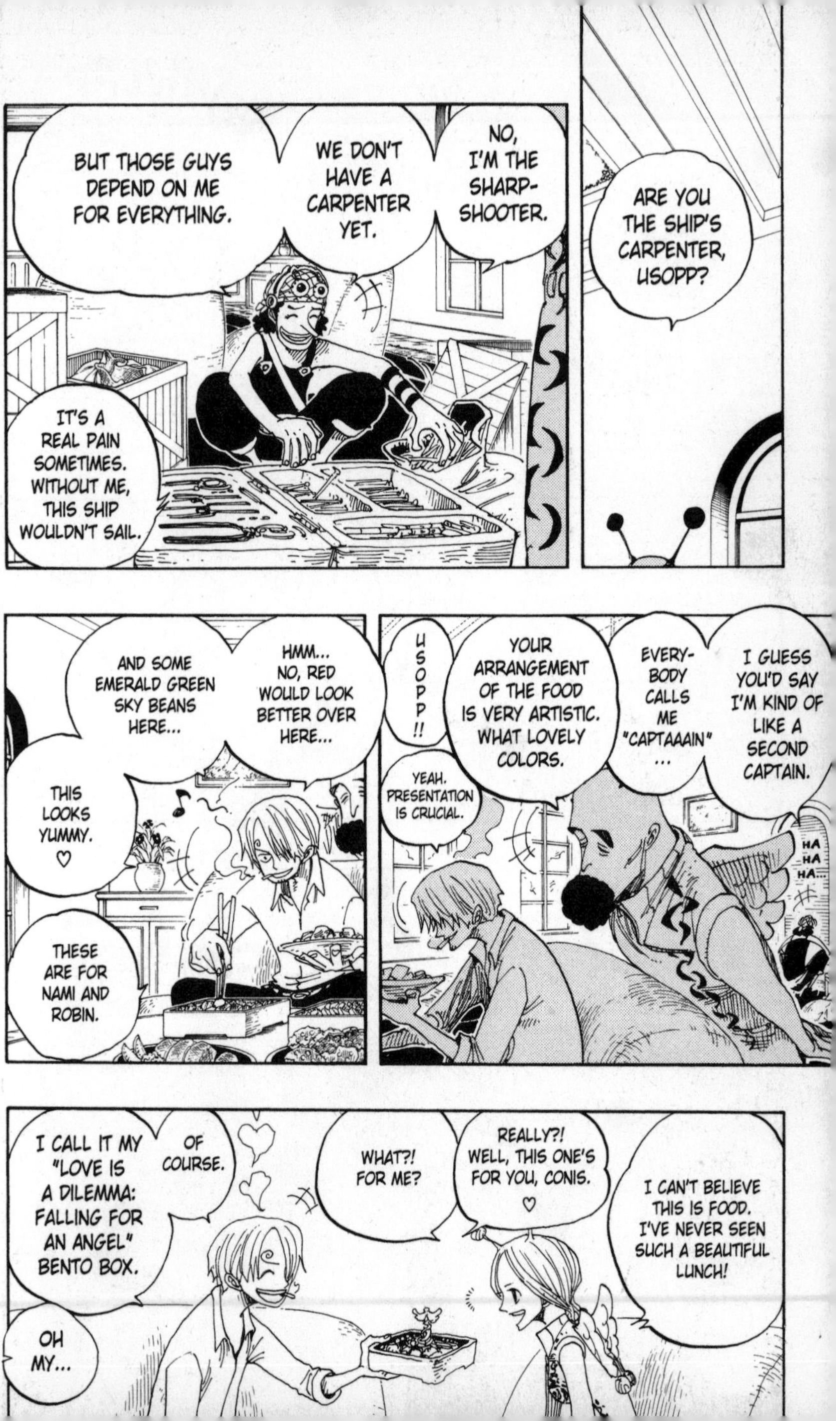
ARE YOU THE SHIP'S CARPENTER, USOPP?
NO, I'M THE SHARP-SHOOTER.
WE DON'T HAVE A CARPENTER YET.
BUT THOSE GUYS DEPEND ON ME FOR EVERYTHING.
IT'S A REAL PAIN SOMETIMES. WITHOUT ME, THIS SHIP WOULDN'T SAIL.
I GUESS YOU'D SAY I'M KIND OF LIKE A SECOND CAPTAIN.
EVERY-BODY CALLS ME "CAPTAAAIN" ...
YOUR ARRANGEMENT OF THE FOOD IS VERY ARTISTIC. WHAT LOVELY COLORS.
USOPP!!
YEAH. PRESENTATION IS CRUCIAL.
HA HA HA...
HMM... NO, RED WOULD LOOK BETTER OVER HERE...
AND SOME EMERALD GREEN SKY BEANS HERE...
THIS LOOKS YUMMY. ♡
THESE ARE FOR NAMI AND ROBIN.
I CAN'T BELIEVE THIS IS FOOD. I'VE NEVER SEEN SUCH A BEAUTIFUL LUNCH!
REALLY?! WELL, THIS ONE'S FOR YOU, CONIS. ♡
WHAT?! FOR ME?
OF COURSE.
I CALL IT MY "LOVE IS A DILEMMA: FALLING FOR AN ANGEL" BENTO BOX.
OH MY...

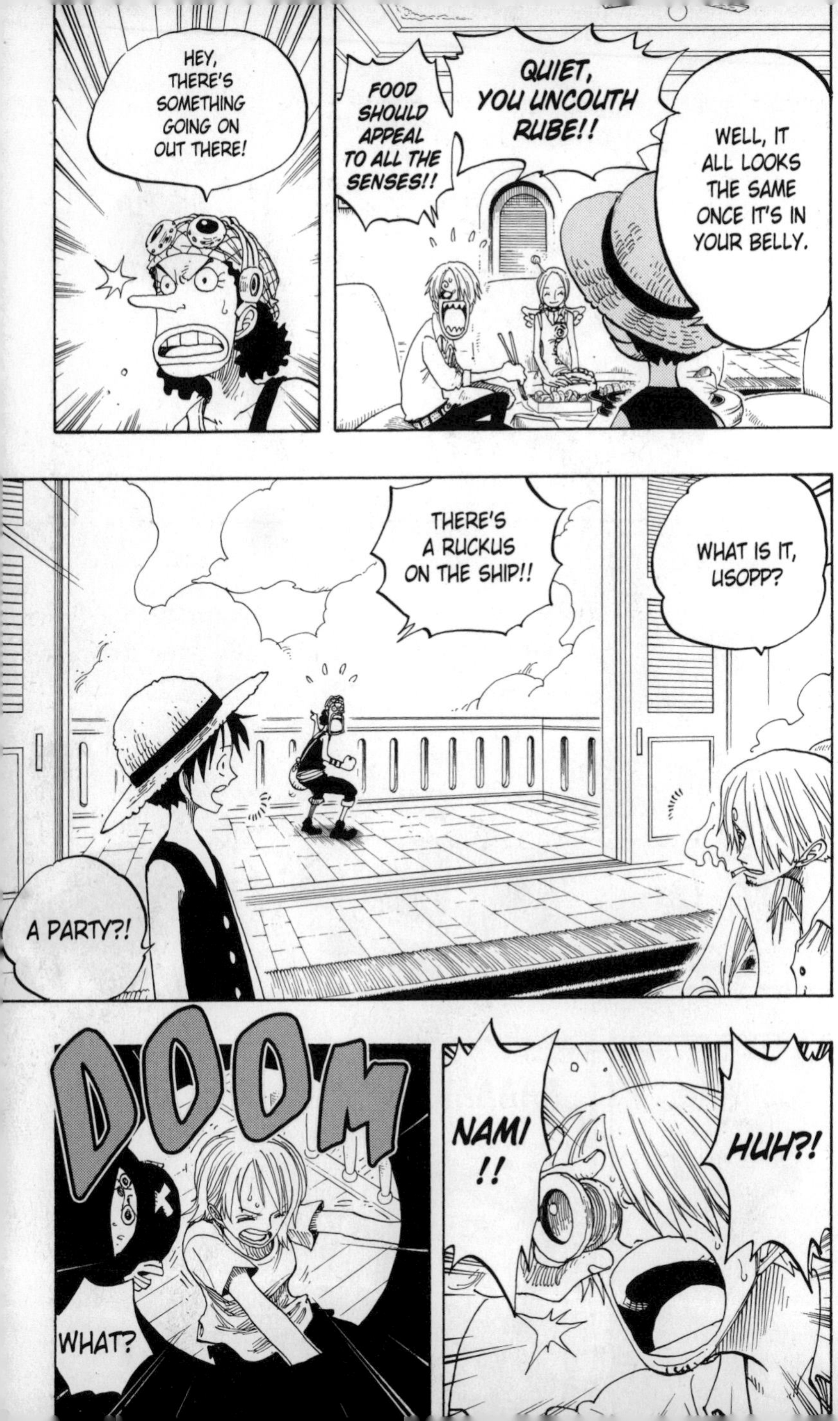
WELL, IT ALL LOOKS THE SAME ONCE IT'S IN YOUR BELLY.
QUIET, YOU UNCOUTH RUBE!!
FOOD SHOULD APPEAL TO ALL THE SENSES!!
HEY, THERE'S SOMETHING GOING ON OUT THERE!
WHAT IS IT, USOPP?
THERE'S A RUCKUS ON THE SHIP!!
A PARTY?!
HUH?!
NAMI !!
DOOM
WHAT?

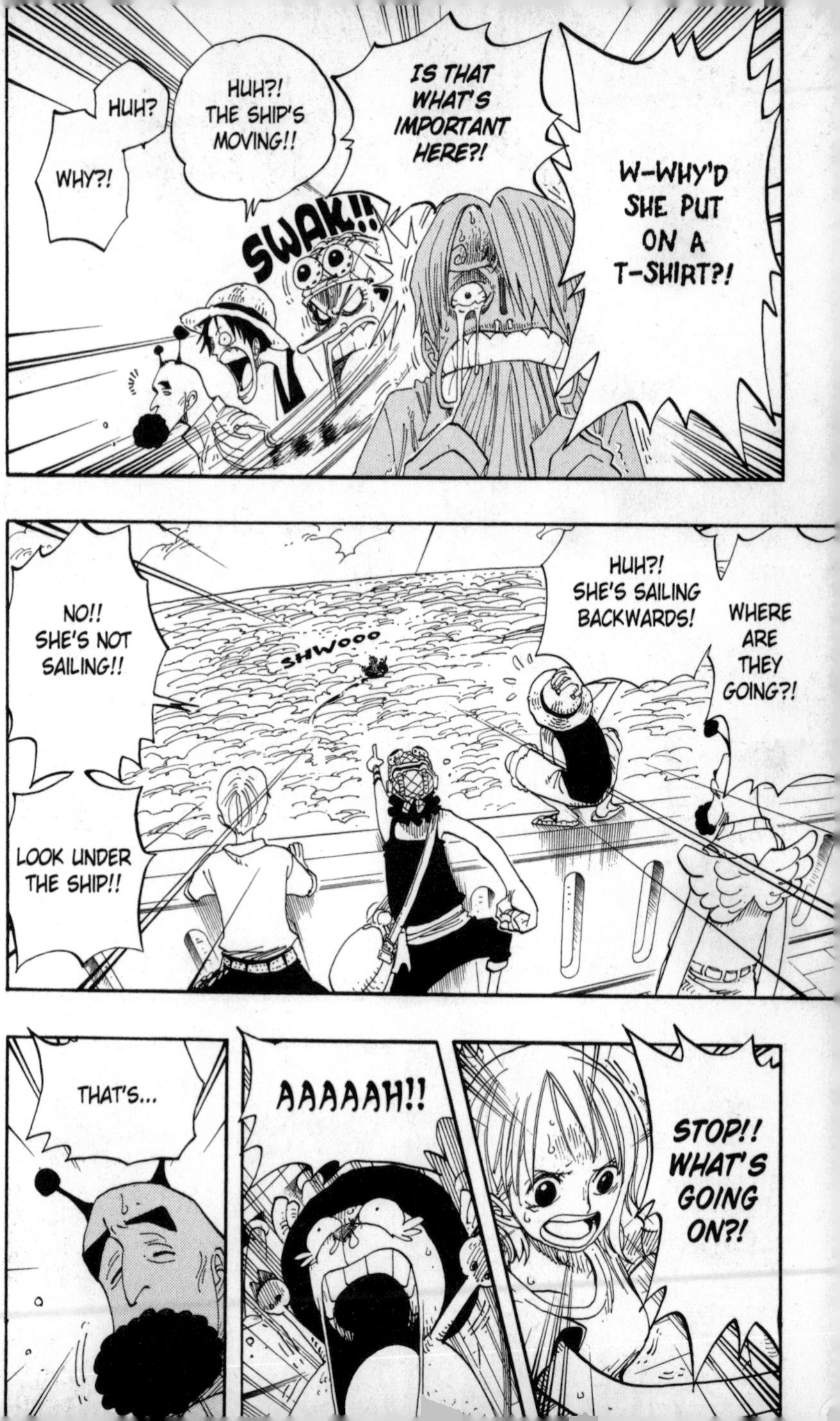
W-WHY'D SHE PUT ON A T-SHIRT?!
IS THAT WHAT'S IMPORTANT HERE?!
SWAK!!
HUH?! THE SHIP'S MOVING!!
HUH?
WHY?!
WHERE ARE THEY GOING?!
HUH?! SHE'S SAILING BACKWARDS!
SHWOOO
NO!! SHE'S NOT SAILING!!
LOOK UNDER THE SHIP!!
STOP!! WHAT'S GOING ON?!
AAAAAH!!
THAT'S...

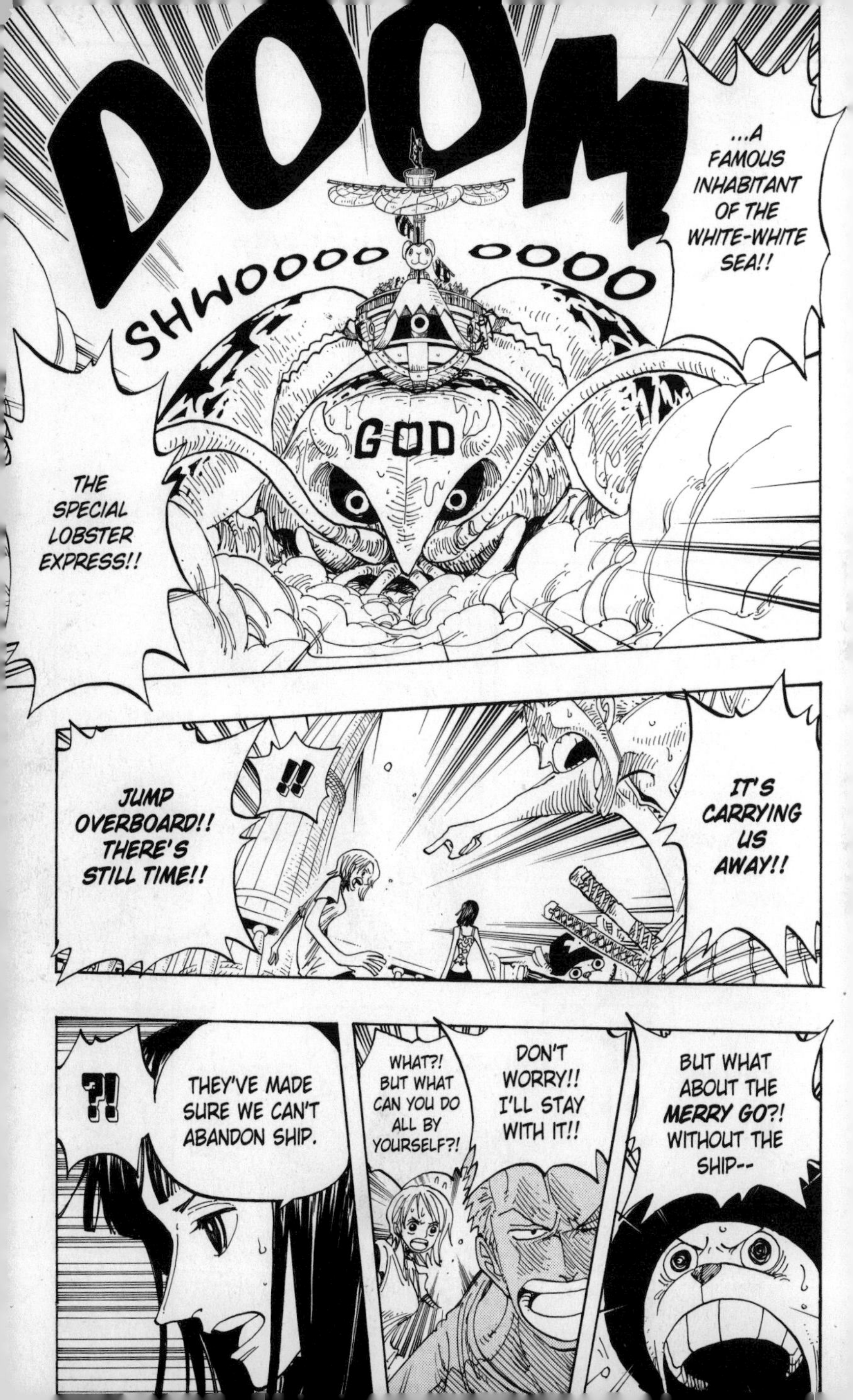
DOOM
SHWOOOO OOOO
...A FAMOUS INHABITANT OF THE WHITE-WHITE SEA!!
GOD
THE SPECIAL LOBSTER EXPRESS!!
IT'S CARRYING US AWAY!!
!!
JUMP OVERBOARD!! THERE'S STILL TIME!!
BUT WHAT ABOUT THE *MERRY GO*?! WITHOUT THE SHIP--
DON'T WORRY!! I'LL STAY WITH IT!!
WHAT?! BUT WHAT CAN YOU DO ALL BY YOURSELF?!
?!
THEY'VE MADE SURE WE CAN'T ABANDON SHIP.

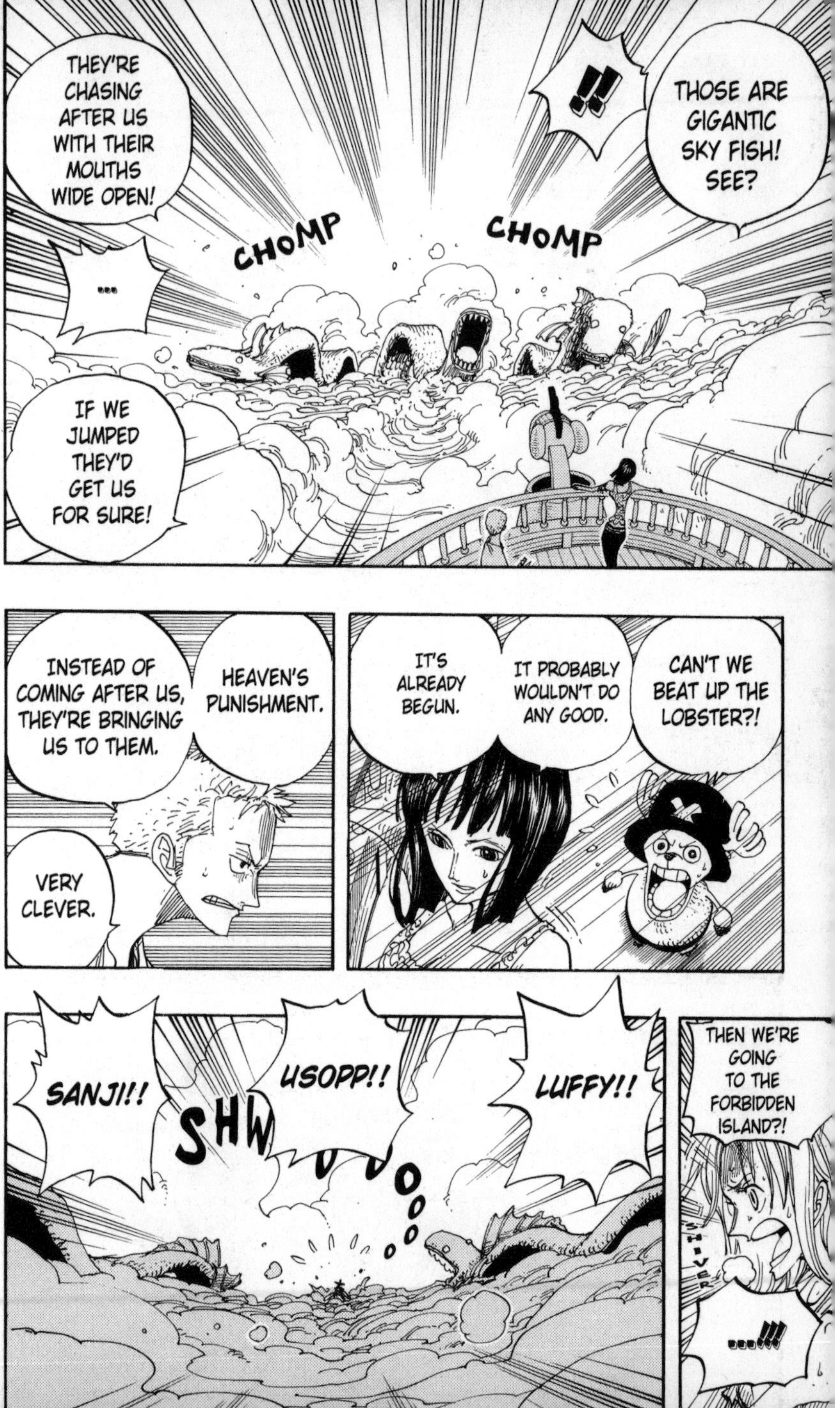
THOSE ARE GIGANTIC SKY FISH! SEE?
!!
THEY'RE CHASING AFTER US WITH THEIR MOUTHS WIDE OPEN!
CHOMP
CHOMP
...
IF WE JUMPED THEY'D GET US FOR SURE!
CAN'T WE BEAT UP THE LOBSTER?!
IT PROBABLY WOULDN'T DO ANY GOOD.
IT'S ALREADY BEGUN.
HEAVEN'S PUNISHMENT.
INSTEAD OF COMING AFTER US, THEY'RE BRINGING US TO THEM.
VERY CLEVER.
THEN WE'RE GOING TO THE FORBIDDEN ISLAND?!
SHIVER
...!!!
LUFFY!!
USOPP!!
SANJI!!
SHWOOOOOO

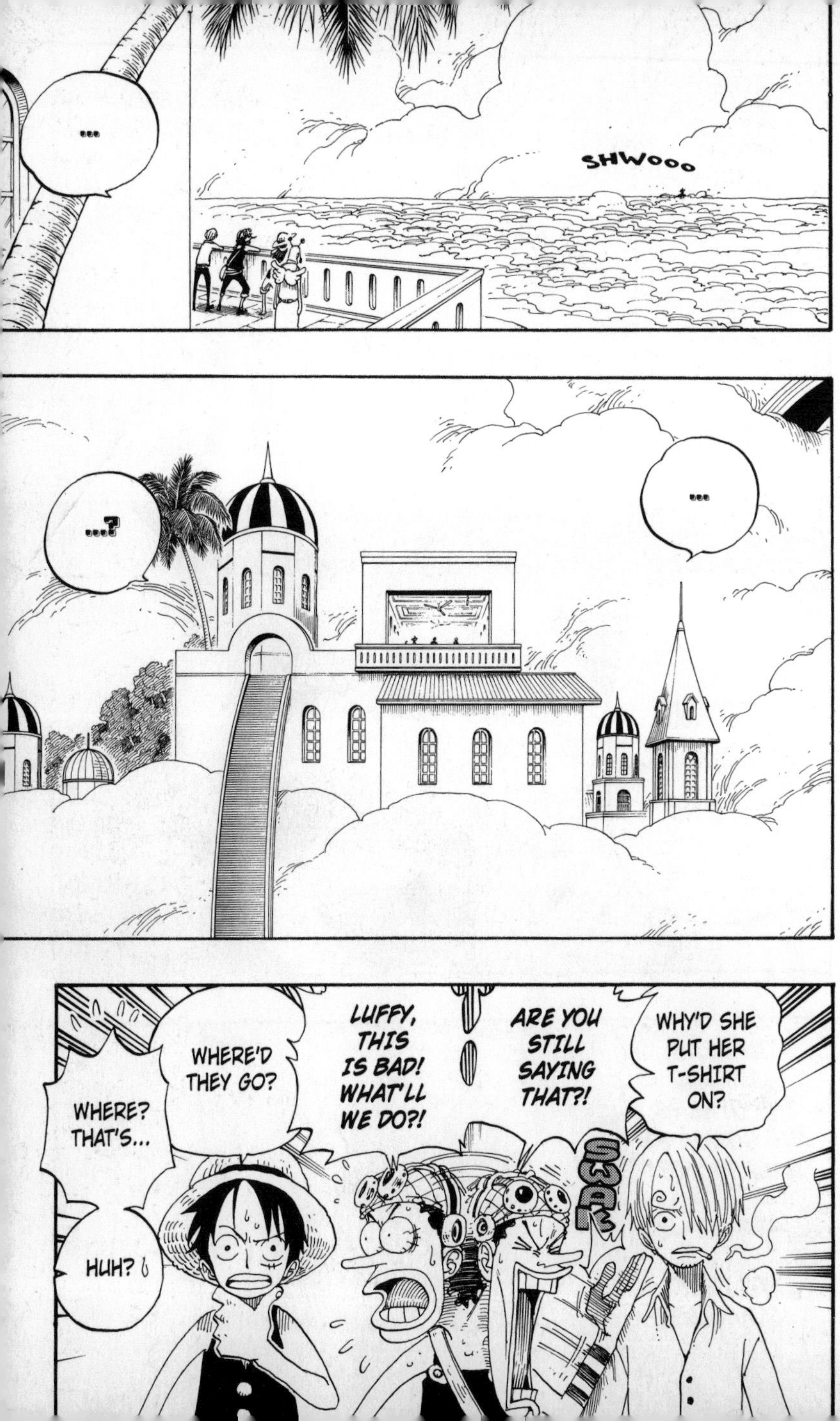
SHWOOO
...
...
...?
WHY'D SHE PUT HER T-SHIRT ON?
SWAK
ARE YOU STILL SAYING THAT?!
LUFFY, THIS IS BAD! WHAT'LL WE DO?!
WHERE'D THEY GO?
WHERE? THAT'S...
HUH?

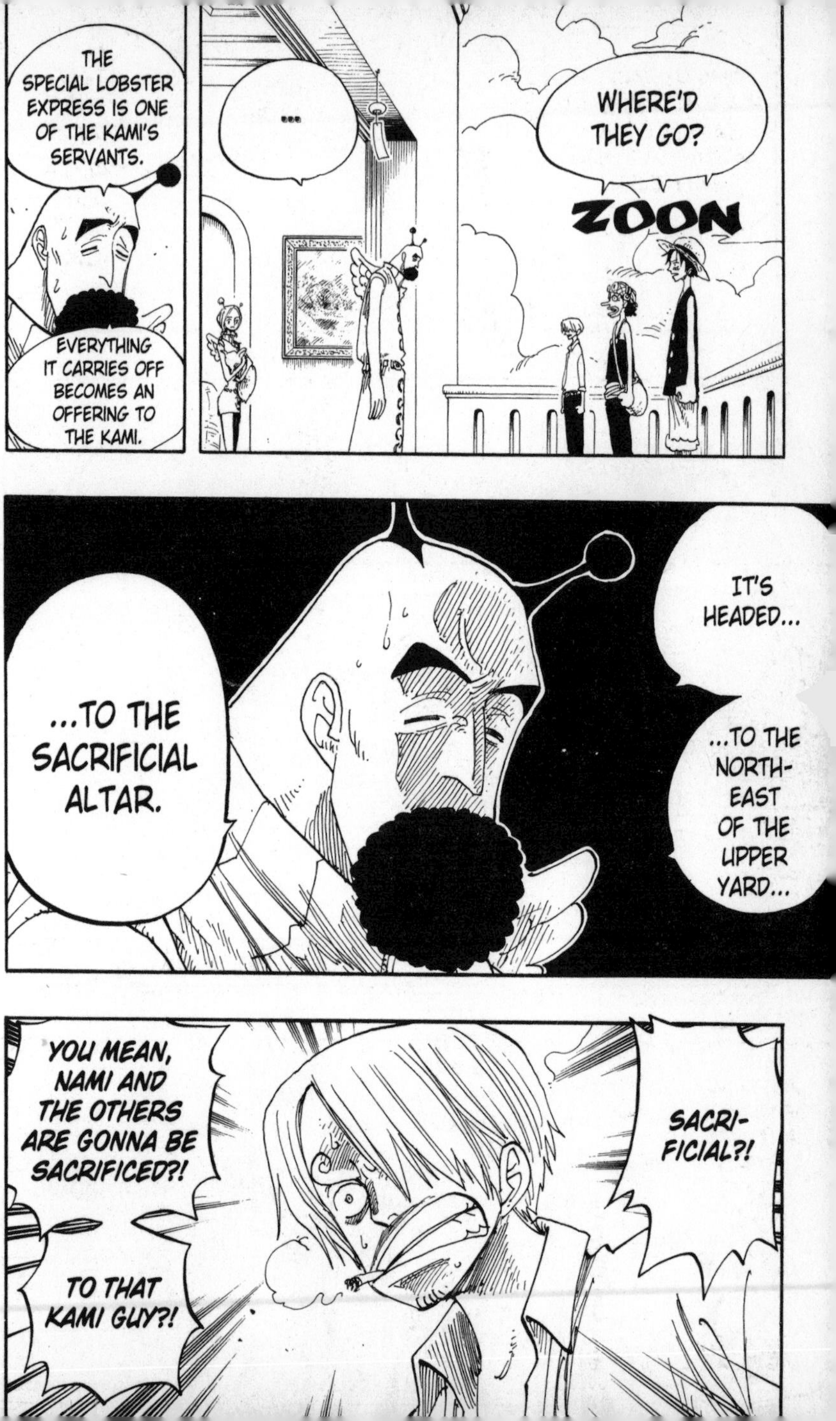
WHERE'D THEY GO?
ZOON
...
THE SPECIAL LOBSTER EXPRESS IS ONE OF THE KAMI'S SERVANTS.
EVERYTHING IT CARRIES OFF BECOMES AN OFFERING TO THE KAMI.
IT'S HEADED...
...TO THE NORTH-EAST OF THE UPPER YARD...
...TO THE SACRIFICIAL ALTAR.
SACRI-FICIAL?!
YOU MEAN, NAMI AND THE OTHERS ARE GONNA BE SACRIFICED?!
TO THAT KAMI GUY?!

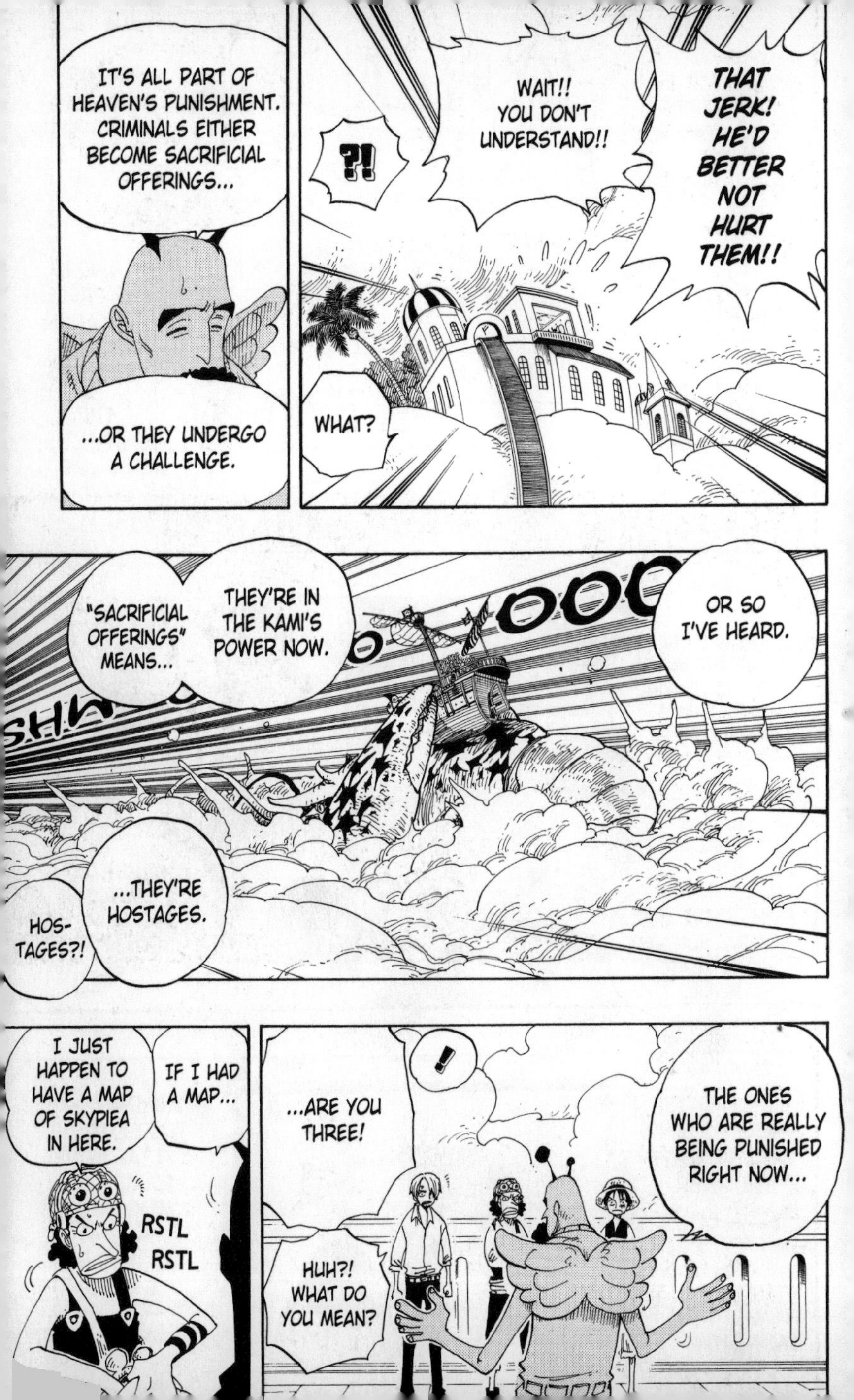
THAT JERK! HE'D BETTER NOT HURT THEM!!
WAIT!! YOU DON'T UNDERSTAND!!
?!
WHAT?
IT'S ALL PART OF HEAVEN'S PUNISHMENT. CRIMINALS EITHER BECOME SACRIFICIAL OFFERINGS...
...OR THEY UNDERGO A CHALLENGE.
OR SO I'VE HEARD.
THEY'RE IN THE KAMI'S POWER NOW.
"SACRIFICIAL OFFERINGS" MEANS...
...THEY'RE HOSTAGES.
HOS-TAGES?!
THE ONES WHO ARE REALLY BEING PUNISHED RIGHT NOW...
!
...ARE YOU THREE!
HUH?! WHAT DO YOU MEAN?
IF I HAD A MAP...
I JUST HAPPEN TO HAVE A MAP OF SKYPIEA IN HERE.
RSTL RSTL

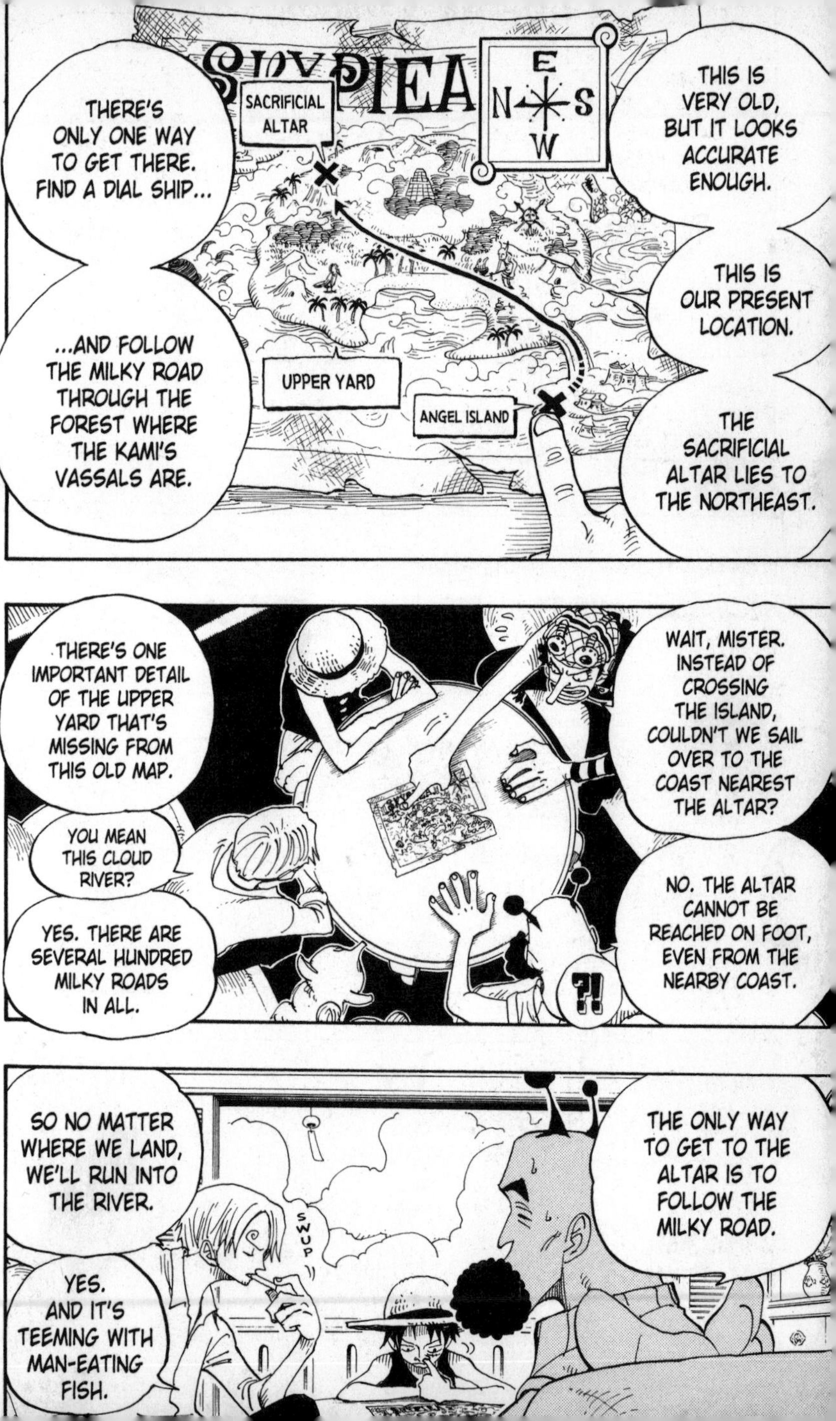
THIS IS VERY OLD, BUT IT LOOKS ACCURATE ENOUGH.
E
N
S
W
SACRIFICIAL ALTAR
UPPER YARD
ANGEL ISLAND
THIS IS OUR PRESENT LOCATION.
THE SACRIFICIAL ALTAR LIES TO THE NORTHEAST.
THERE'S ONLY ONE WAY TO GET THERE. FIND A DIAL SHIP...
...AND FOLLOW THE MILKY ROAD THROUGH THE FOREST WHERE THE KAMI'S VASSALS ARE.
WAIT, MISTER. INSTEAD OF CROSSING THE ISLAND, COULDN'T WE SAIL OVER TO THE COAST NEAREST THE ALTAR?
NO. THE ALTAR CANNOT BE REACHED ON FOOT, EVEN FROM THE NEARBY COAST.
?!
THERE'S ONE IMPORTANT DETAIL OF THE UPPER YARD THAT'S MISSING FROM THIS OLD MAP.
YOU MEAN THIS CLOUD RIVER?
YES. THERE ARE SEVERAL HUNDRED MILKY ROADS IN ALL.
THE ONLY WAY TO GET TO THE ALTAR IS TO FOLLOW THE MILKY ROAD.
SWUP
SO NO MATTER WHERE WE LAND, WE'LL RUN INTO THE RIVER.
YES. AND IT'S TEEMING WITH MAN-EATING FISH.

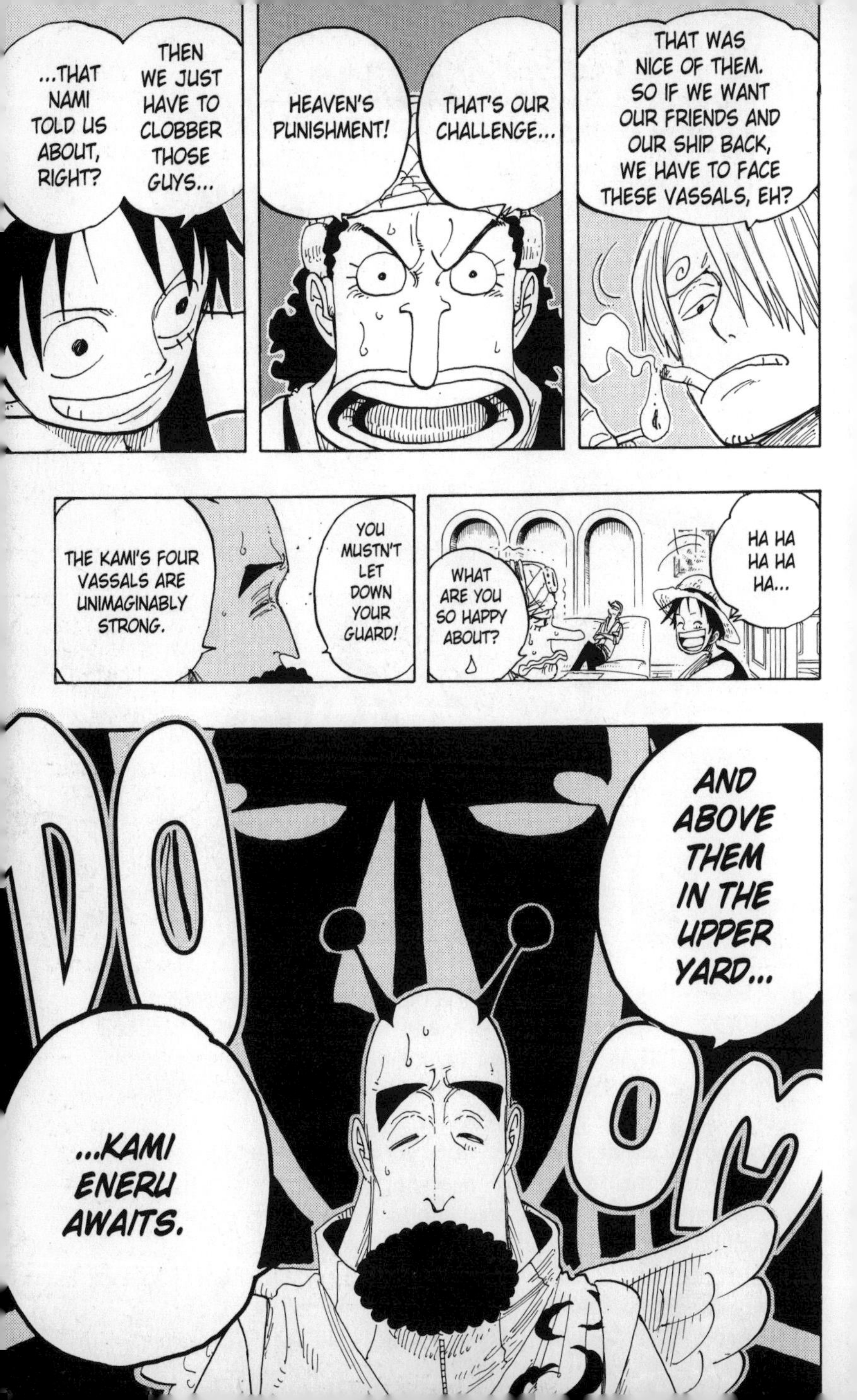
THAT WAS NICE OF THEM. SO IF WE WANT OUR FRIENDS AND OUR SHIP BACK, WE HAVE TO FACE THESE VASSALS, EH?
THAT'S OUR CHALLENGE...
HEAVEN'S PUNISHMENT!
THEN WE JUST HAVE TO CLOBBER THOSE GUYS...
...THAT NAMI TOLD US ABOUT, RIGHT?
HA HA HA HA HA...
WHAT ARE YOU SO HAPPY ABOUT?
YOU MUSTN'T LET DOWN YOUR GUARD!
THE KAMI'S FOUR VASSALS ARE UNIMAGINABLY STRONG.
AND ABOVE THEM IN THE UPPER YARD...
...KAMI ENERU AWAITS.
DOOM

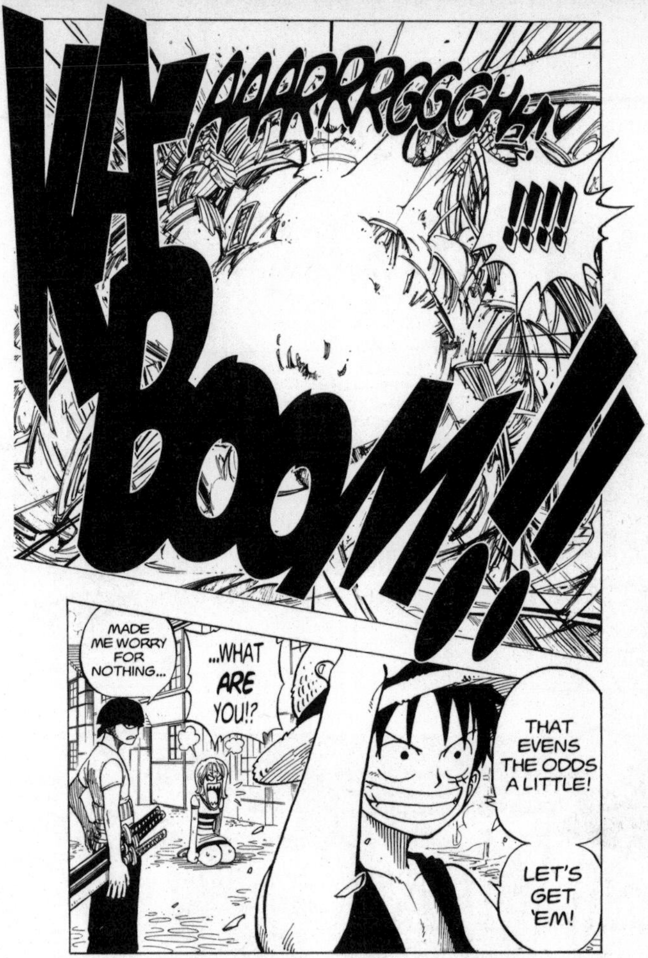
AAARRGGGH!!!!
KA-BOOM!!
THAT EVENS THE ODDS A LITTLE!
LET'S GET 'EM!
...WHAT ARE YOU!?
MADE ME WORRY FOR NOTHING...

O: Hmm... This is the American version. In November of 2002 *SHONEN JUMP* made its debut in the United States. It has attracted quite a lot of interest. DragonBall, Sand Land, Shaman King, Naruto, Yu-Gi-Oh! and One Piece are all published in it.
Wow, I wonder what's gonna happen? Manga like One Piece are being read in many countries now. The global expansion is getting more and more interesting.
But I'll just keep doing what I've been doing.
Well, this concludes the Special SBS Question Corner International Investigation Committee section.
Please look forward to all the ~~stupid~~ fun Question Corners in the next volume. See you then!

Chapter 244:
S.O.S.

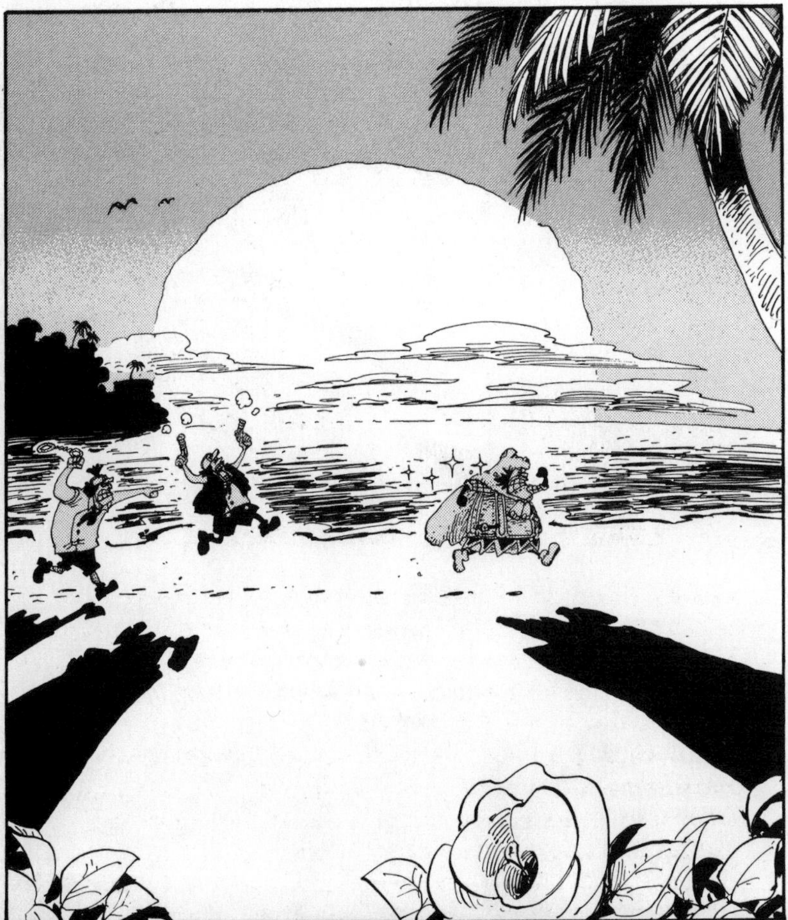

WAPOL'S OMNIVOROUS RAMPAGE VOL. 8:
"MY GREAT TEARFUL ESCAPE"

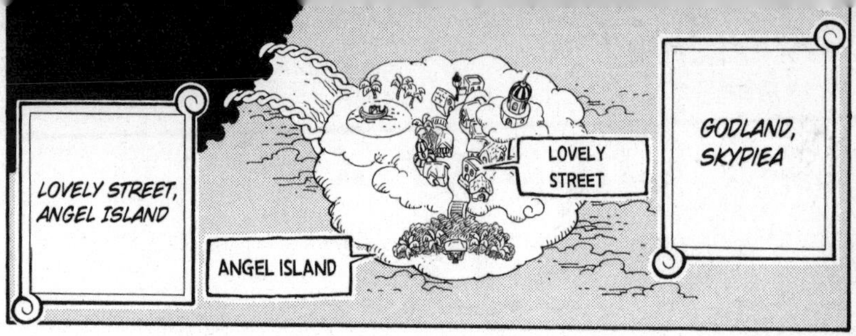
GODLAND, SKYPIEA
LOVELY STREET
ANGEL ISLAND
LOVELY STREET, ANGEL ISLAND

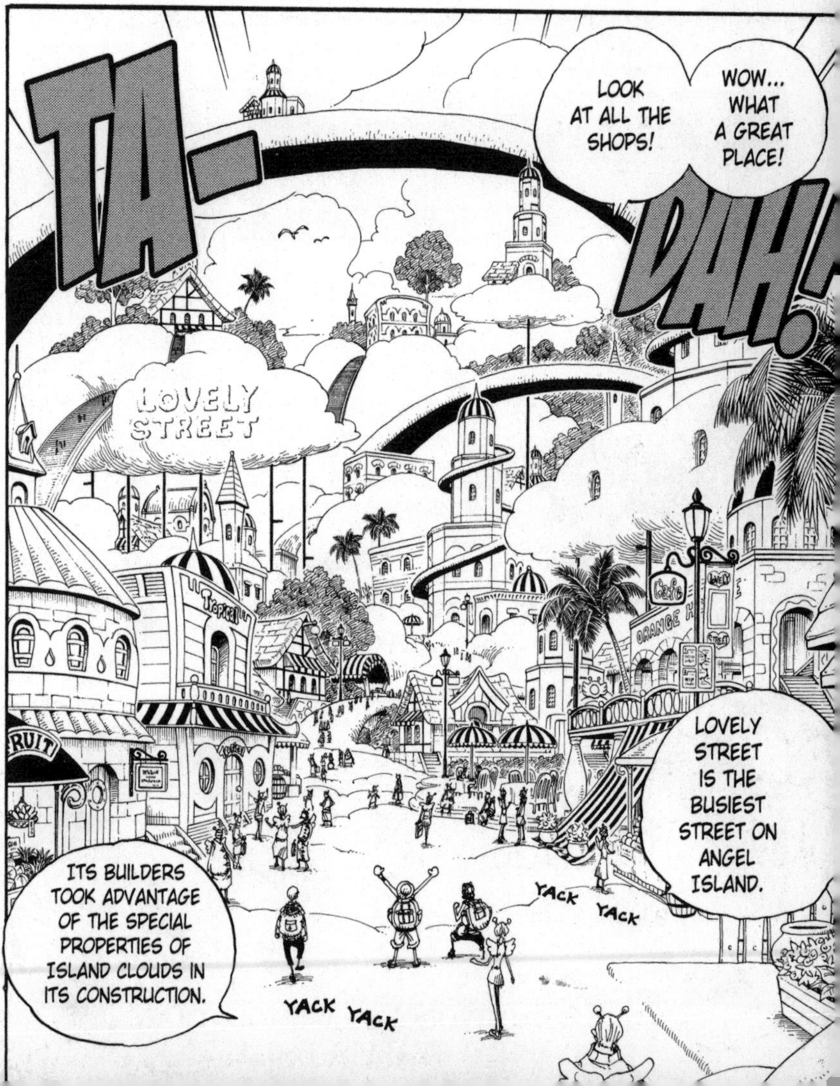
TA-DAH!!
WOW... WHAT A GREAT PLACE!
LOOK AT ALL THE SHOPS!
LOVELY STREET
Tropical
Cafe
FRUIT
LOVELY STREET IS THE BUSIEST STREET ON ANGEL ISLAND.
YACK YACK
ITS BUILDERS TOOK ADVANTAGE OF THE SPECIAL PROPERTIES OF ISLAND CLOUDS IN ITS CONSTRUCTION.
YACK YACK

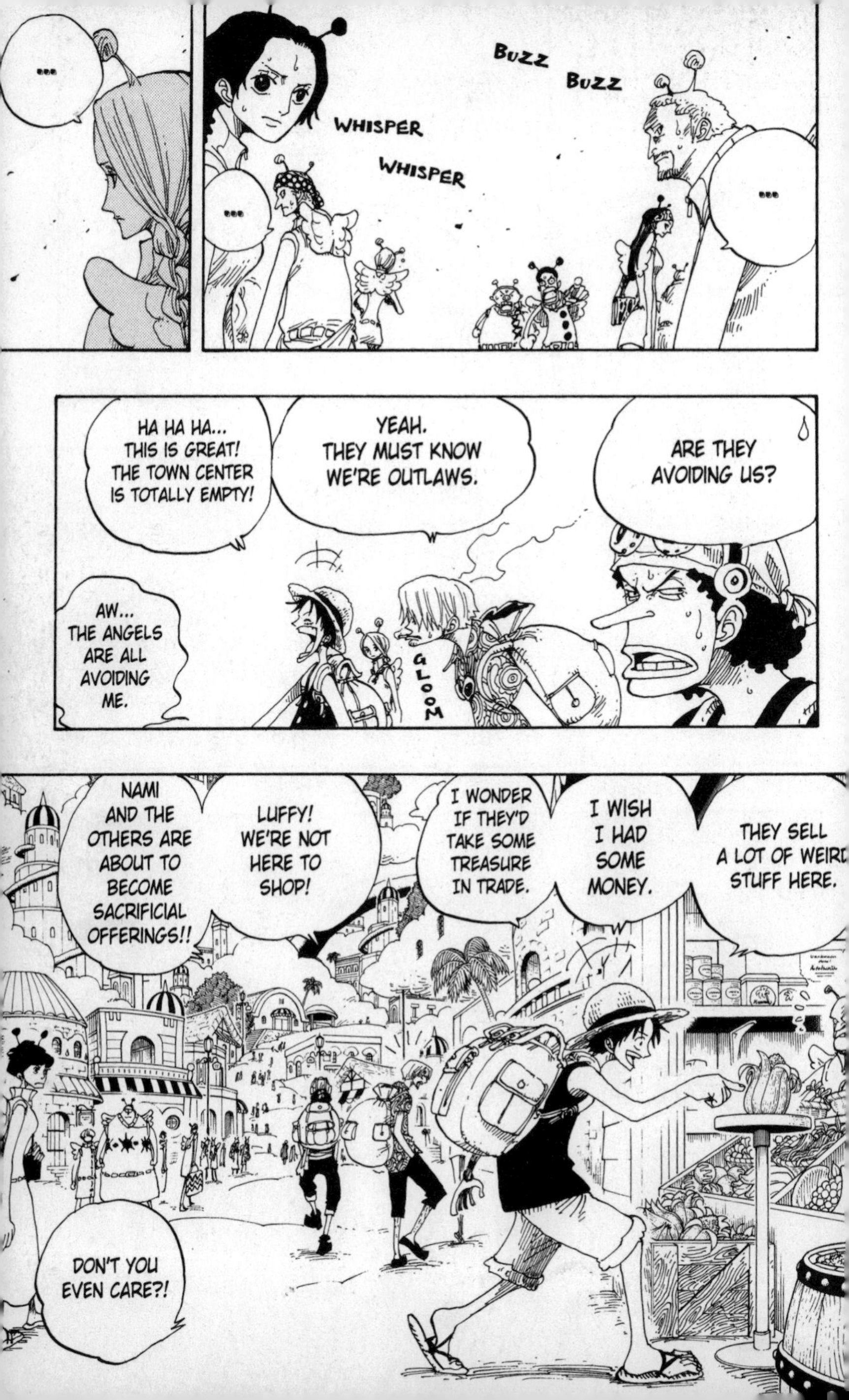
BUZZ
BUZZ
WHISPER
WHISPER
...
...
...
ARE THEY AVOIDING US?
YEAH. THEY MUST KNOW WE'RE OUTLAWS.
HA HA HA... THIS IS GREAT! THE TOWN CENTER IS TOTALLY EMPTY!
GLOOM
AW... THE ANGELS ARE ALL AVOIDING ME.
THEY SELL A LOT OF WEIRD STUFF HERE.
I WISH I HAD SOME MONEY.
I WONDER IF THEY'D TAKE SOME TREASURE IN TRADE.
LUFFY! WE'RE NOT HERE TO SHOP!
NAMI AND THE OTHERS ARE ABOUT TO BECOME SACRIFICIAL OFFERINGS!!
DON'T YOU EVEN CARE?!

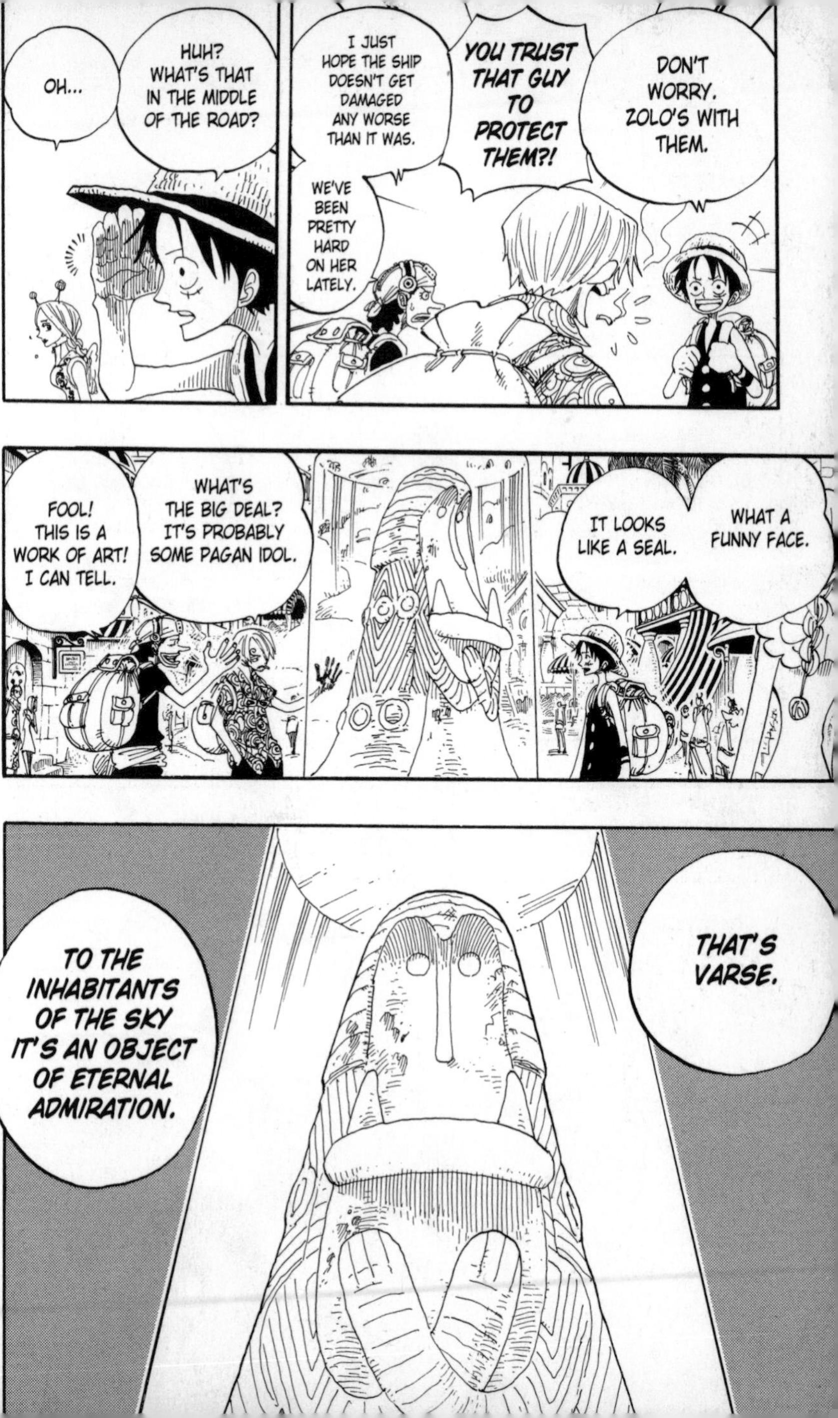
DON'T WORRY. ZOLO'S WITH THEM.
YOU TRUST THAT GUY TO PROTECT THEM?!
I JUST HOPE THE SHIP DOESN'T GET DAMAGED ANY WORSE THAN IT WAS.
WE'VE BEEN PRETTY HARD ON HER LATELY.
HUH? WHAT'S THAT IN THE MIDDLE OF THE ROAD?
OH...
WHAT A FUNNY FACE.
IT LOOKS LIKE A SEAL.
WHAT'S THE BIG DEAL? IT'S PROBABLY SOME PAGAN IDOL.
FOOL! THIS IS A WORK OF ART! I CAN TELL.
THAT'S VARSE.
TO THE INHABITANTS OF THE SKY IT'S AN OBJECT OF ETERNAL ADMIRATION.

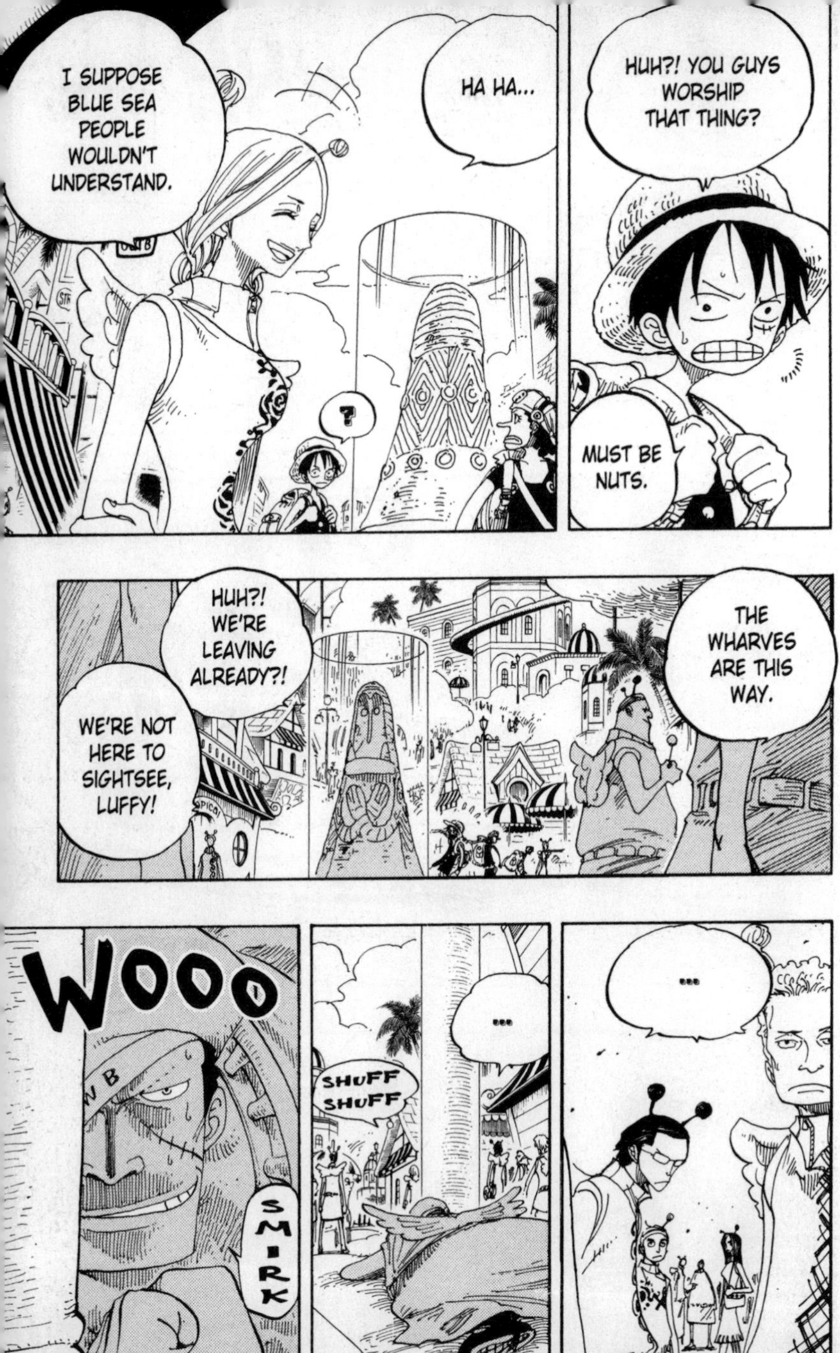
HUH?! YOU GUYS WORSHIP THAT THING?
MUST BE NUTS.
HA HA...
I SUPPOSE BLUE SEA PEOPLE WOULDN'T UNDERSTAND.
?
THE WHARVES ARE THIS WAY.
HUH?! WE'RE LEAVING ALREADY?!
WE'RE NOT HERE TO SIGHTSEE, LUFFY!
...
...
SHUFF SHUFF
WOOO
SMIRK

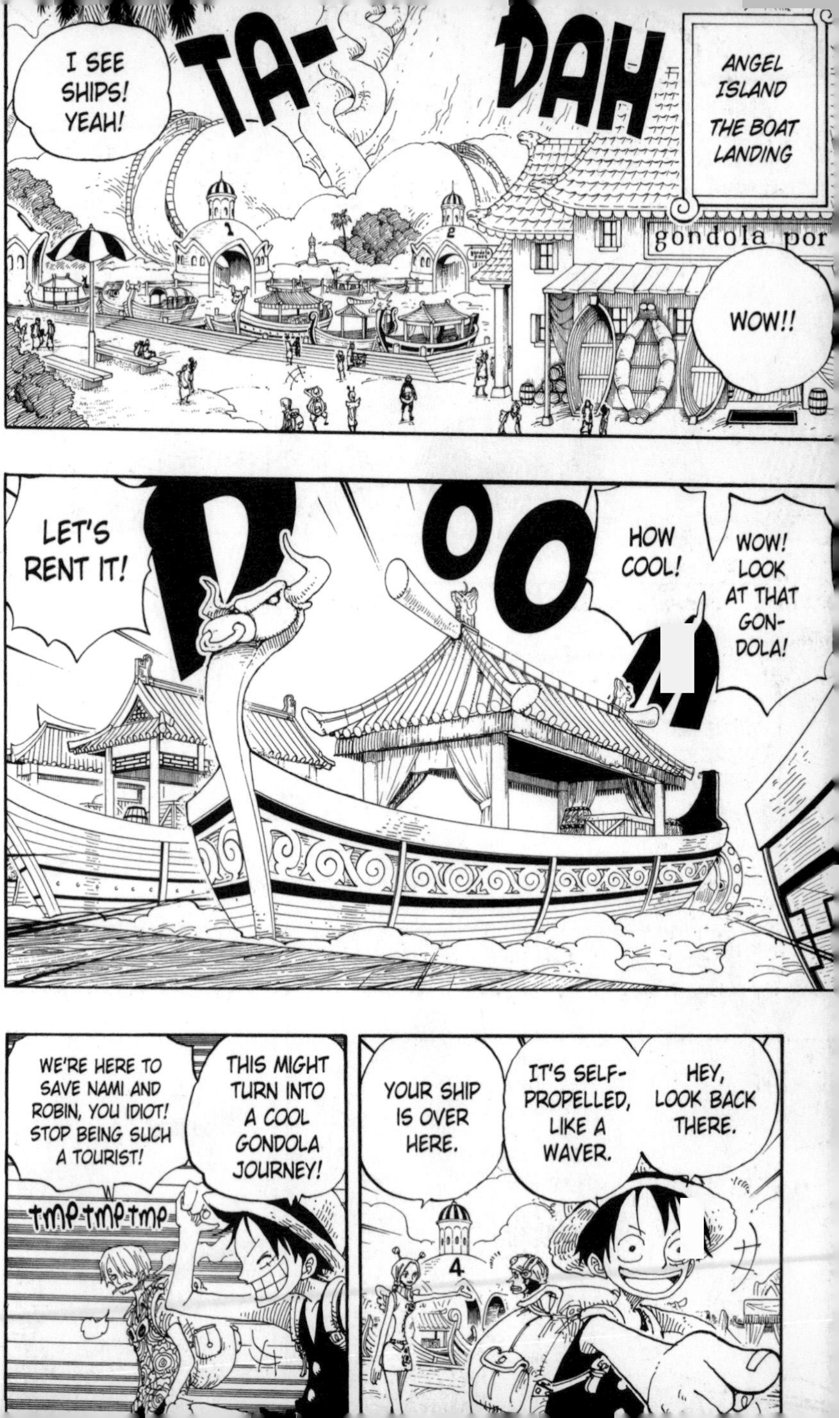
ANGEL ISLAND THE BOAT LANDING
TA- DAH
gondola por
WOW!!
I SEE SHIPS! YEAH!
WOW! LOOK AT THAT GON- DOLA!
HOW COOL!
LET'S RENT IT!
HEY, LOOK BACK THERE.
IT'S SELF- PROPELLED, LIKE A WAVER.
YOUR SHIP IS OVER HERE.
4
THIS MIGHT TURN INTO A COOL GONDOLA JOURNEY!
WE'RE HERE TO SAVE NAMI AND ROBIN, YOU IDIOT! STOP BEING SUCH A TOURIST!
TMP TMP TMP

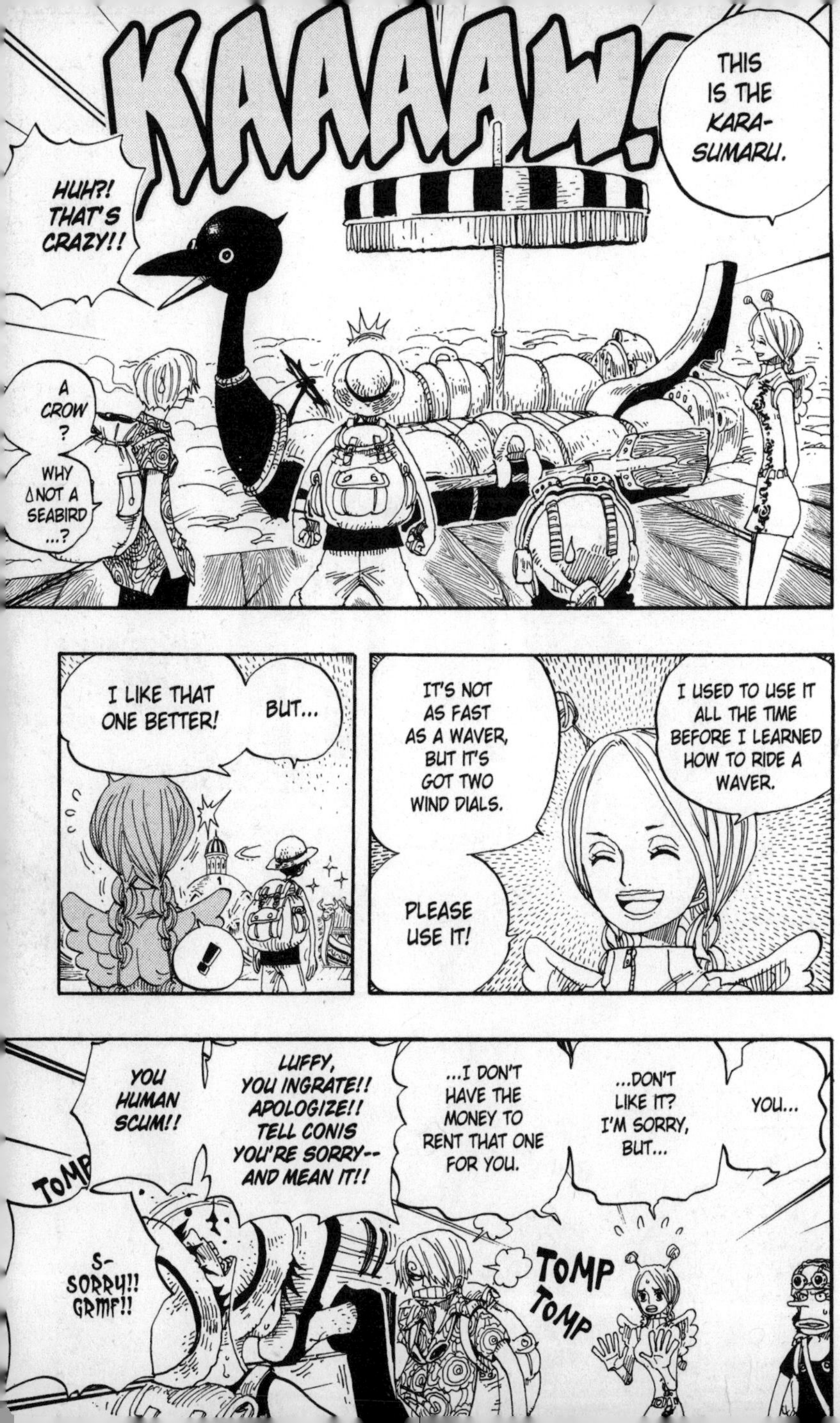
THIS IS THE KARA-SUMARU.
KAAAAW!
HUH?! THAT'S CRAZY!!
A CROW?
WHY NOT A SEABIRD...?
I USED TO USE IT ALL THE TIME BEFORE I LEARNED HOW TO RIDE A WAVER.
IT'S NOT AS FAST AS A WAVER, BUT IT'S GOT TWO WIND DIALS.
PLEASE USE IT!
BUT...
I LIKE THAT ONE BETTER!
!
YOU...
...DON'T LIKE IT? I'M SORRY, BUT...
...I DON'T HAVE THE MONEY TO RENT THAT ONE FOR YOU.
TOMP
TOMP
LUFFY, YOU INGRATE!! APOLOGIZE!! TELL CONIS YOU'RE SORRY-- AND MEAN IT!!
YOU HUMAN SCUM!!
TOMP
S-SORRY!! GRMF!!

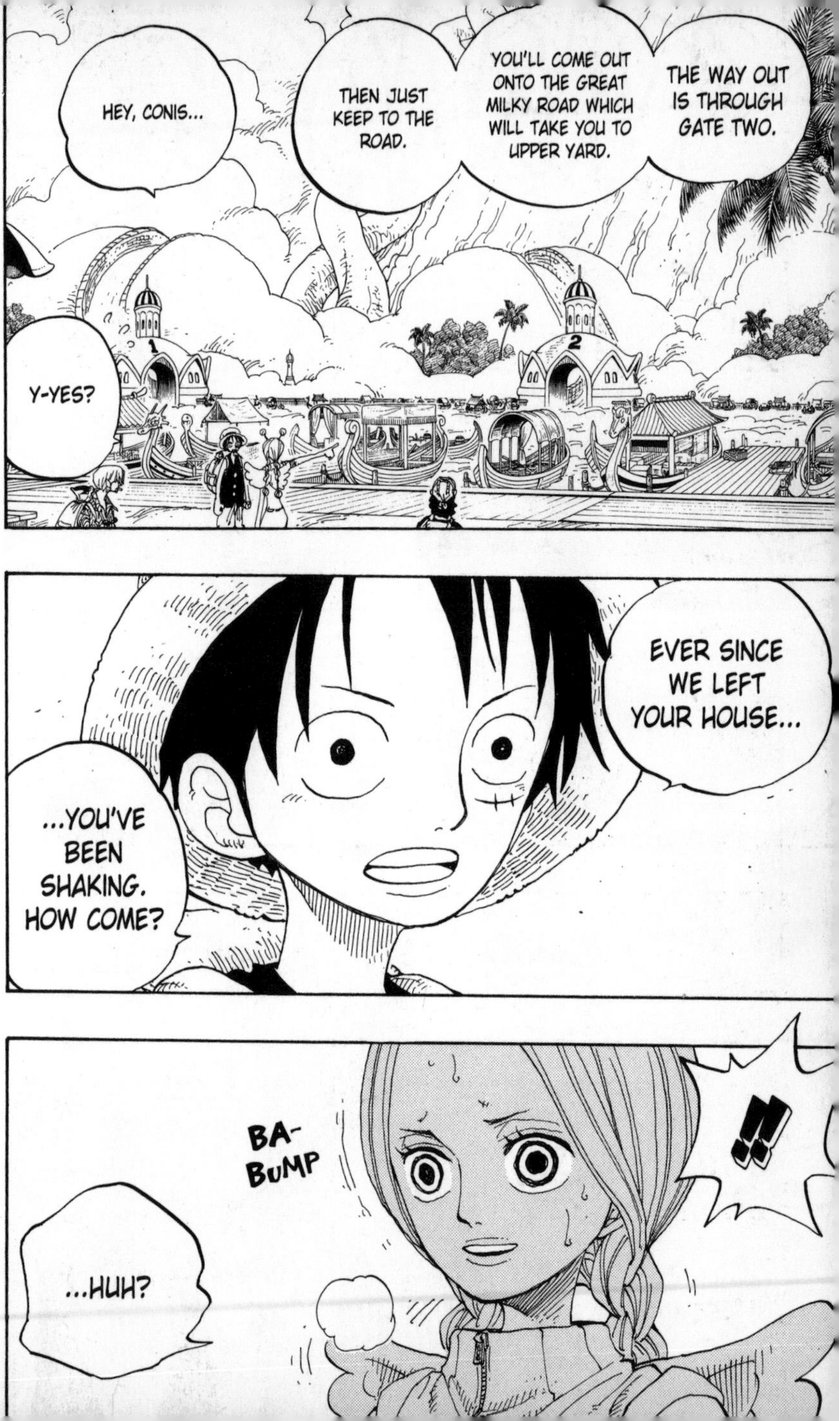
THE WAY OUT IS THROUGH GATE TWO.
YOU'LL COME OUT ONTO THE GREAT MILKY ROAD WHICH WILL TAKE YOU TO UPPER YARD.
THEN JUST KEEP TO THE ROAD.
HEY, CONIS...
Y-YES?
EVER SINCE WE LEFT YOUR HOUSE...
...YOU'VE BEEN SHAKING. HOW COME?
!!
BA-BUMP
...HUH?

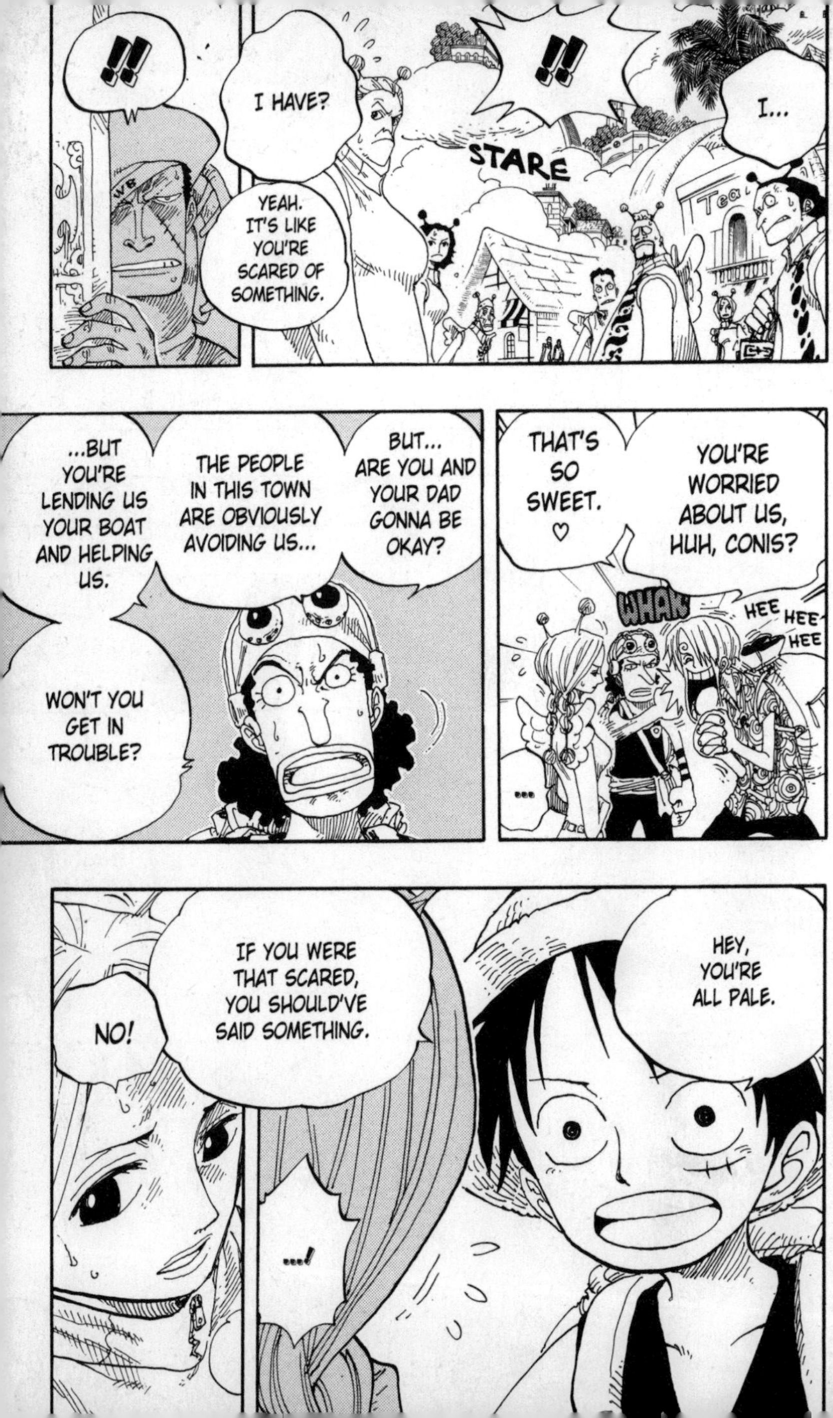
I...
!!
STARE
I HAVE?
YEAH. IT'S LIKE YOU'RE SCARED OF SOMETHING.
!!
YOU'RE WORRIED ABOUT US, HUH, CONIS?
THAT'S SO SWEET. ♡
WHAK
HEE HEE HEE
...
BUT... ARE YOU AND YOUR DAD GONNA BE OKAY?
THE PEOPLE IN THIS TOWN ARE OBVIOUSLY AVOIDING US...
...BUT YOU'RE LENDING US YOUR BOAT AND HELPING US.
WON'T YOU GET IN TROUBLE?
HEY, YOU'RE ALL PALE.
IF YOU WERE THAT SCARED, YOU SHOULD'VE SAID SOMETHING.
...!
NO!

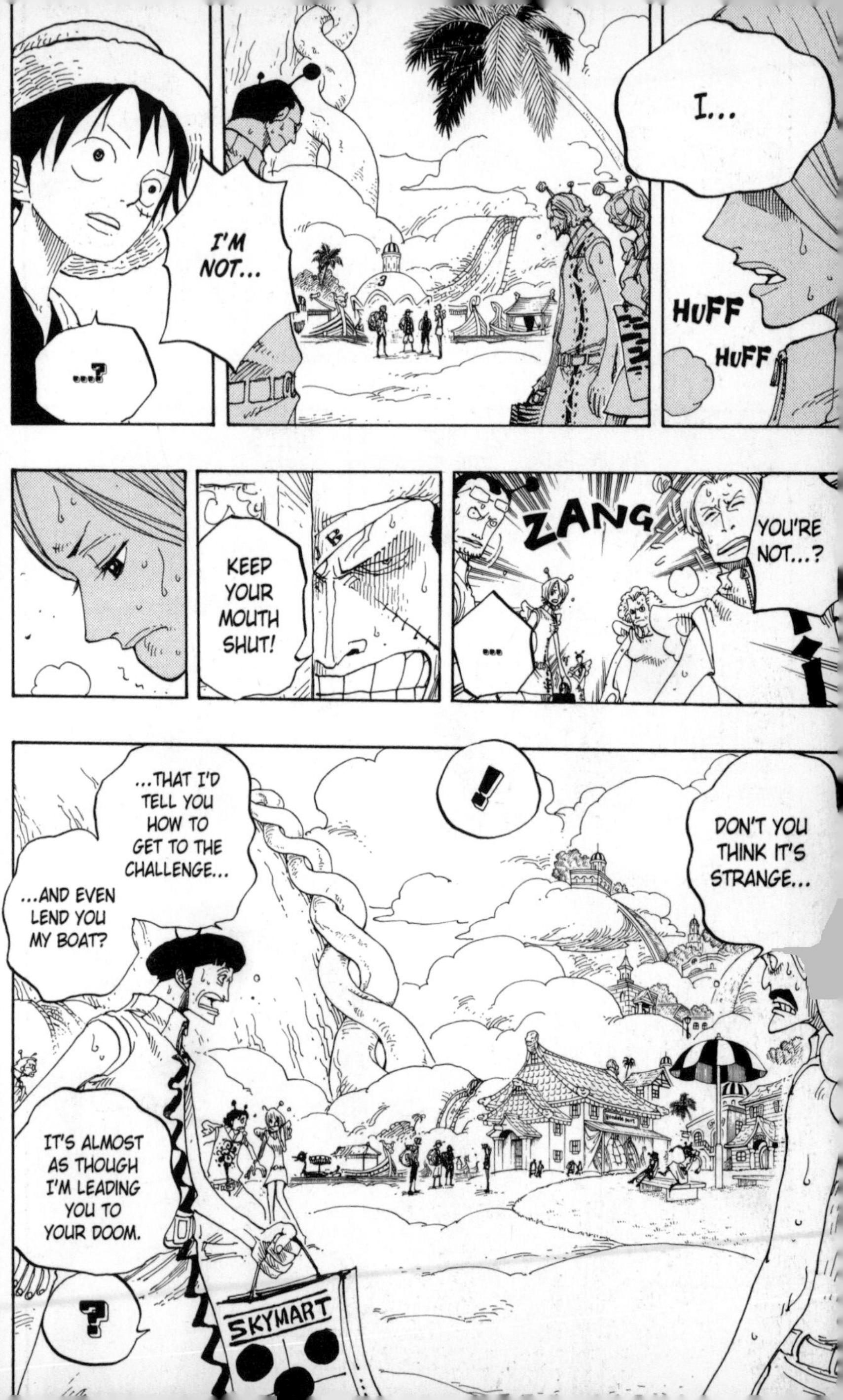
I...
HUFF
HUFF
I'M NOT...
...?
YOU'RE NOT...?
ZANG
...
KEEP YOUR MOUTH SHUT!
!
DON'T YOU THINK IT'S STRANGE...
...THAT I'D TELL YOU HOW TO GET TO THE CHALLENGE...
...AND EVEN LEND YOU MY BOAT?
IT'S ALMOST AS THOUGH I'M LEADING YOU TO YOUR DOOM.
?
SKYMART

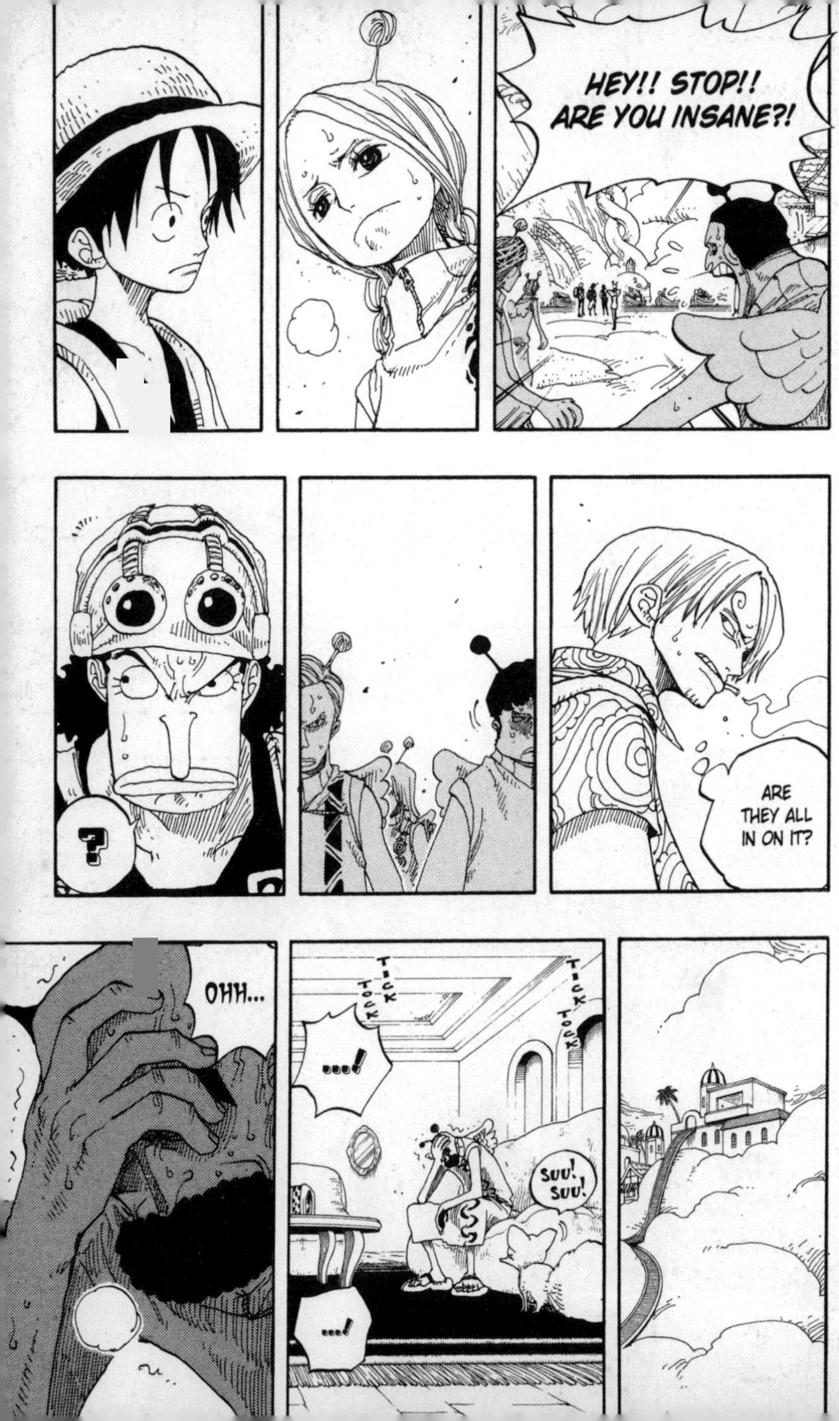
HEY!! STOP!! ARE YOU INSANE?!
ARE THEY ALL IN ON IT?
?
TICK TOCK
TICK TOCK
...!
SUU! SUU!
...!
OHH...

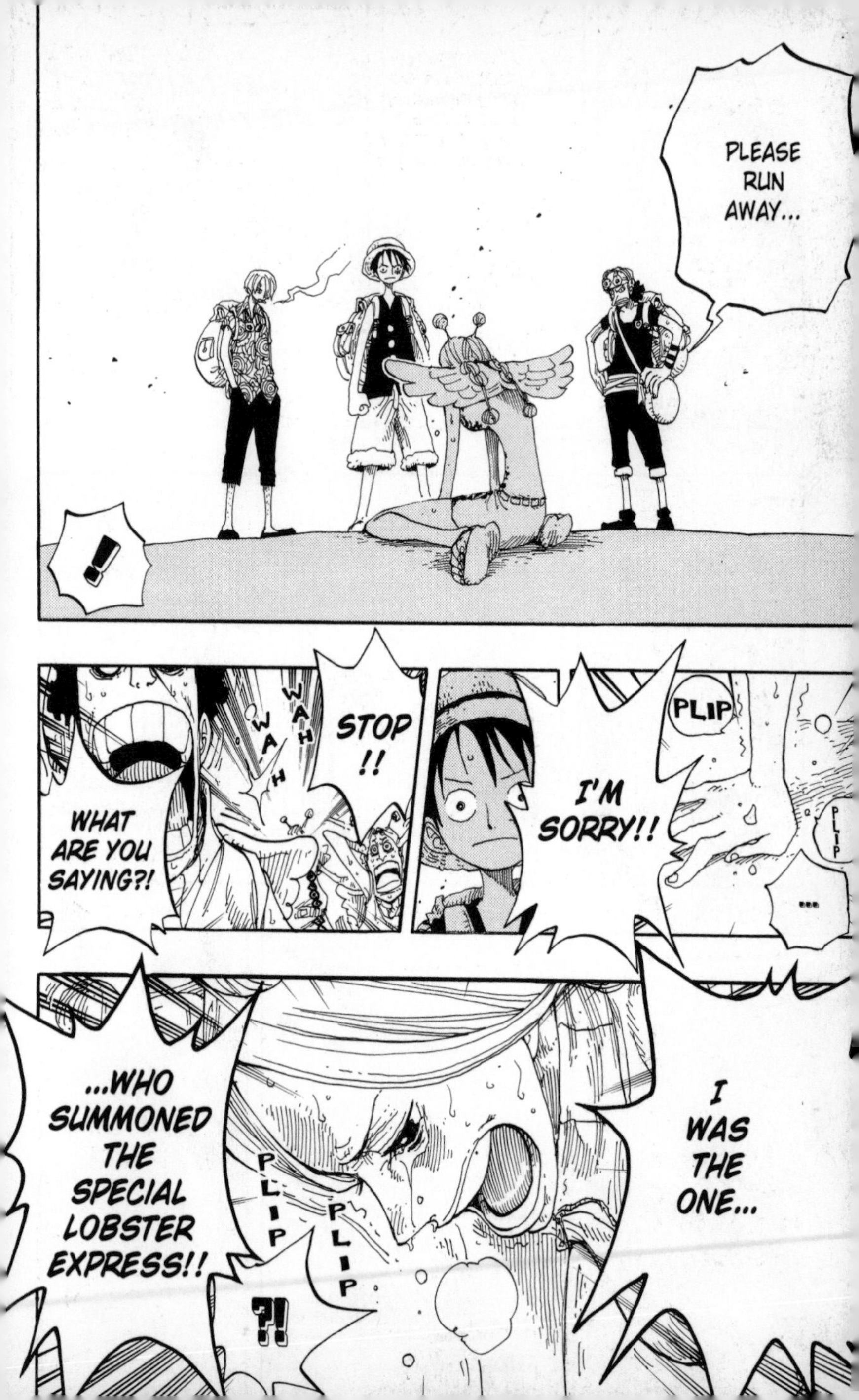
PLEASE RUN AWAY...
!
PLIP
I'M SORRY!!
PLIP
...
STOP!!
WAH WAH
WHAT ARE YOU SAYING?!
I WAS THE ONE...
PLIP
PLIP
...WHO SUMMONED THE SPECIAL LOBSTER EXPRESS!!
?!

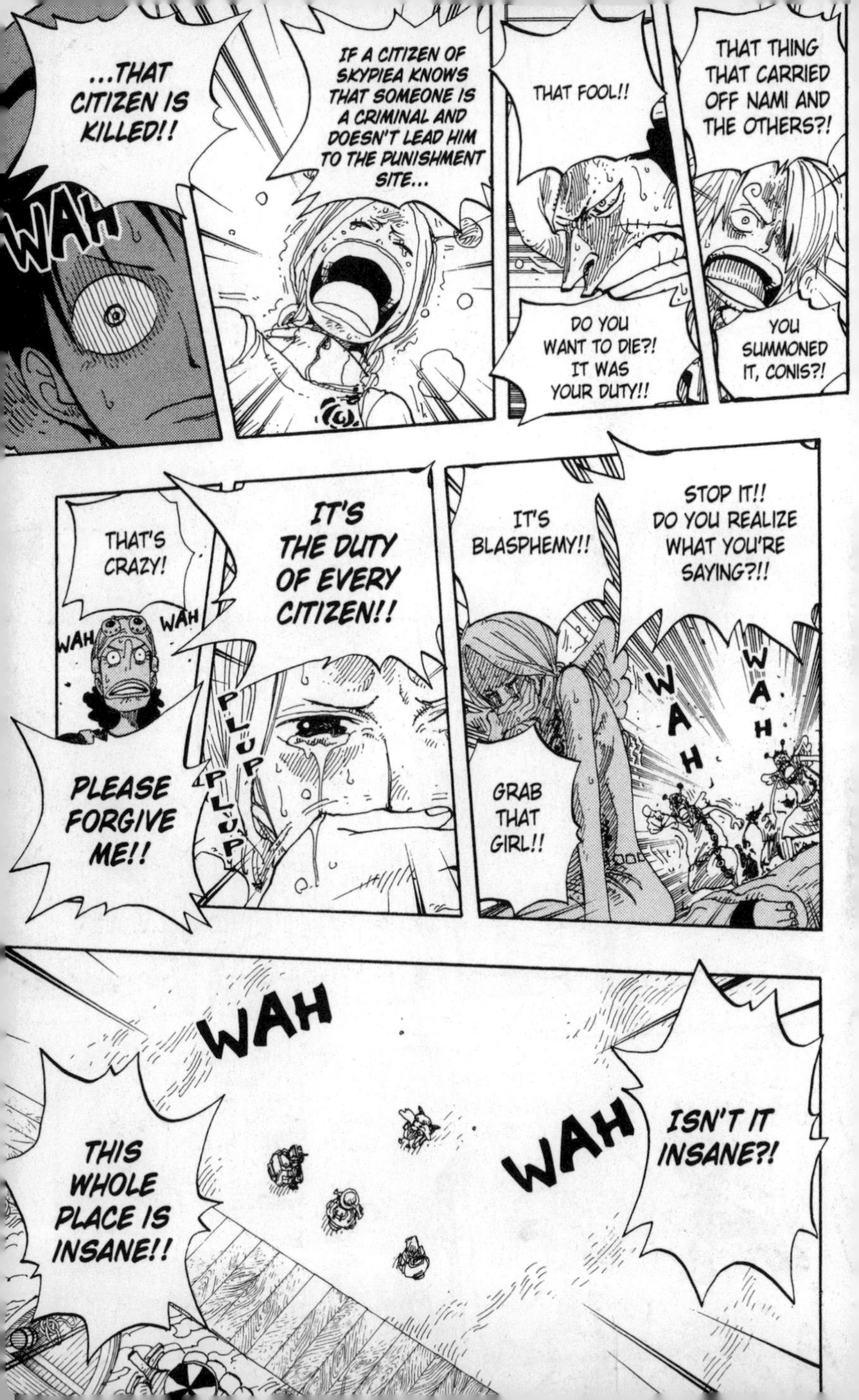
THAT THING THAT CARRIED OFF NAMI AND THE OTHERS?!
YOU SUMMONED IT, CONIS?!
THAT FOOL!!
DO YOU WANT TO DIE?! IT WAS YOUR DUTY!!
IF A CITIZEN OF SKYPIEA KNOWS THAT SOMEONE IS A CRIMINAL AND DOESN'T LEAD HIM TO THE PUNISHMENT SITE...
...THAT CITIZEN IS KILLED!!
WAH
STOP IT!! DO YOU REALIZE WHAT YOU'RE SAYING?!!
IT'S BLASPHEMY!!
WAH
WAH
GRAB THAT GIRL!!
IT'S THE DUTY OF EVERY CITIZEN!!
PLUP
PLUP
PLEASE FORGIVE ME!!
THAT'S CRAZY!
WAH
WAH
ISN'T IT INSANE?!
WAH
WAH
THIS WHOLE PLACE IS INSANE!!

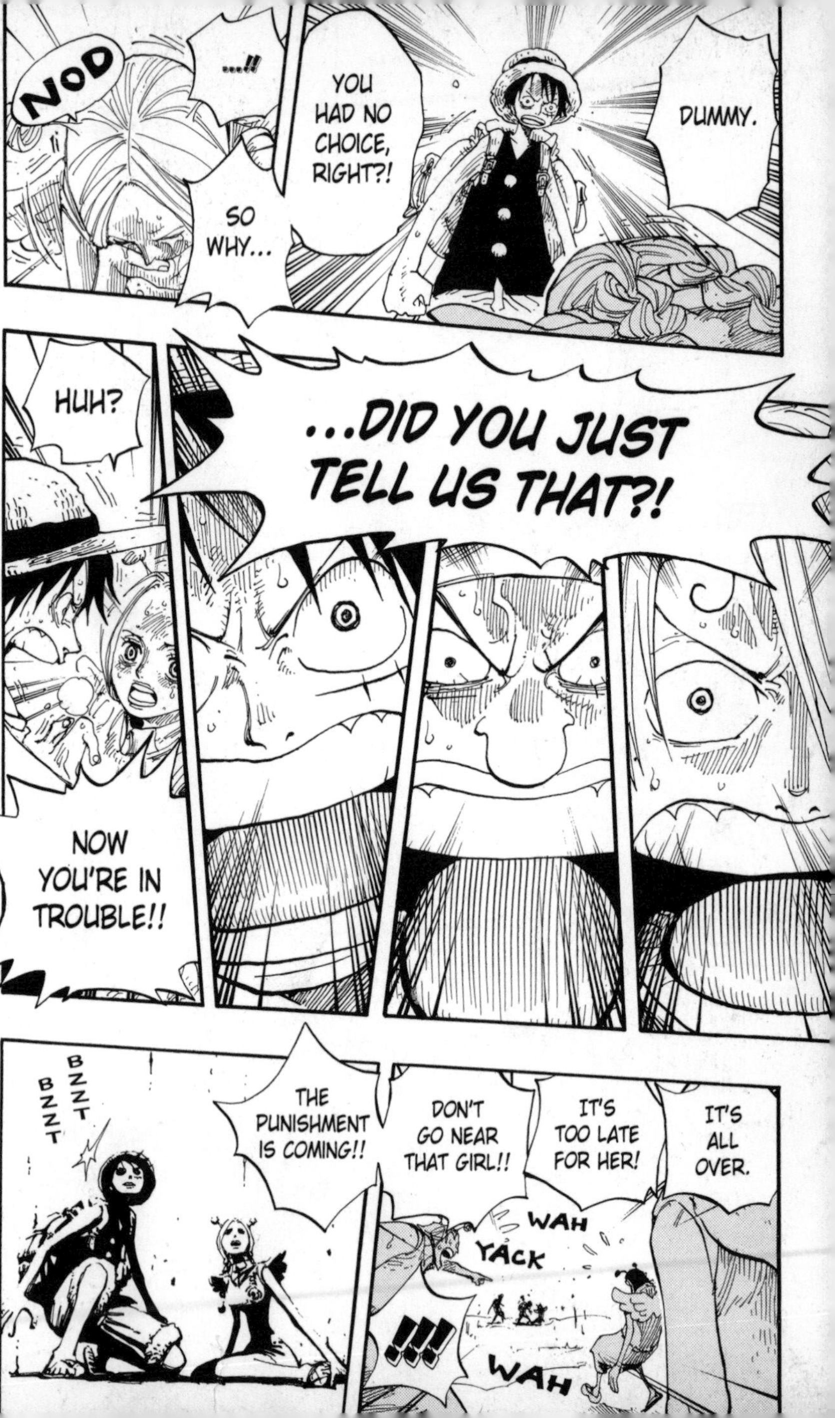
DUMMY.
YOU HAD NO CHOICE, RIGHT?!
SO WHY...
...!!
NOD
...DID YOU JUST TELL US THAT?!
HUH?
NOW YOU'RE IN TROUBLE!!
IT'S ALL OVER.
IT'S TOO LATE FOR HER!
DON'T GO NEAR THAT GIRL!!
THE PUNISHMENT IS COMING!!
WAH
YACK
!!!
WAH
BZZT
BZZT

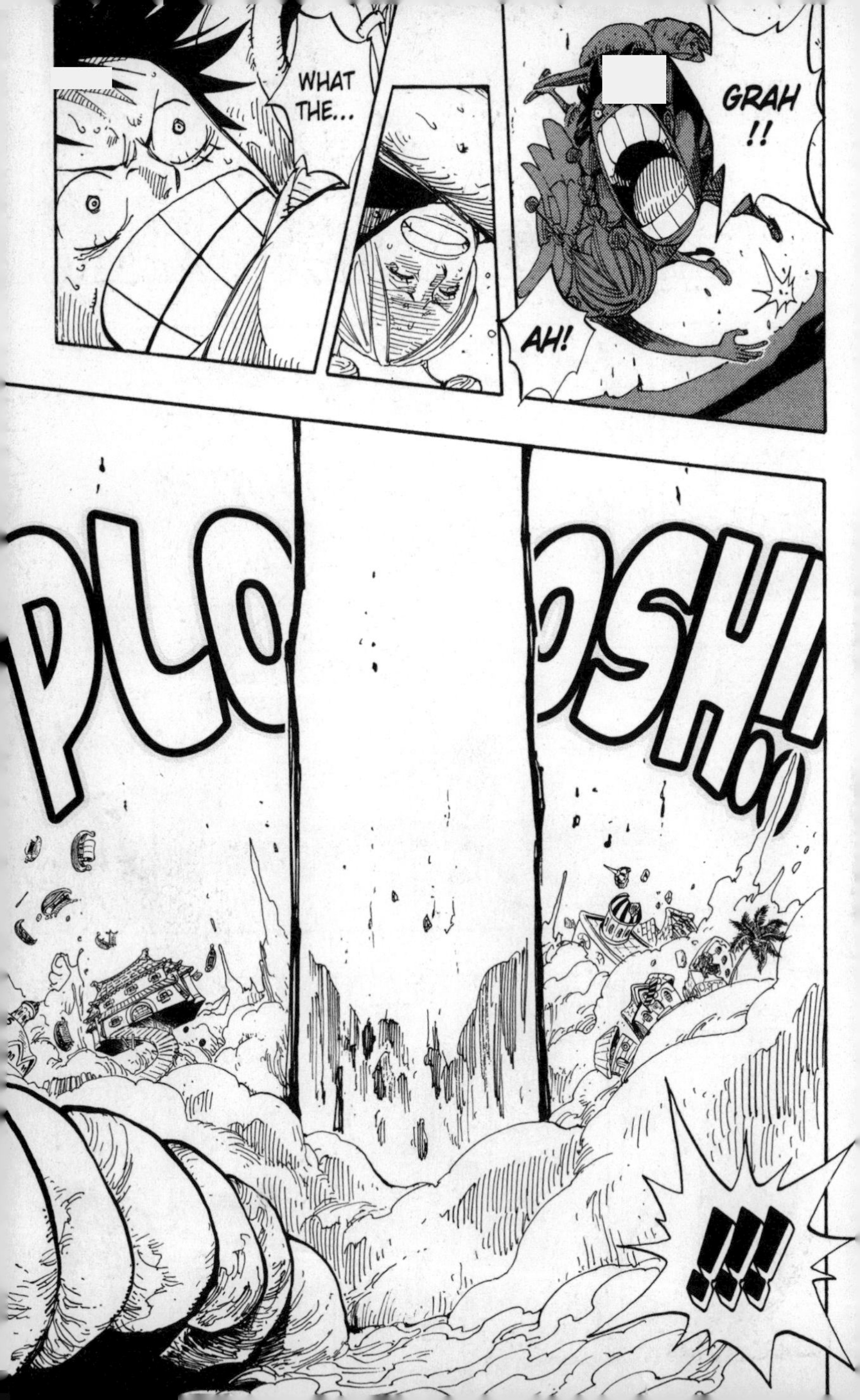
GRAH!!
AH!
WHAT THE...
PLOOSH!!
!!!

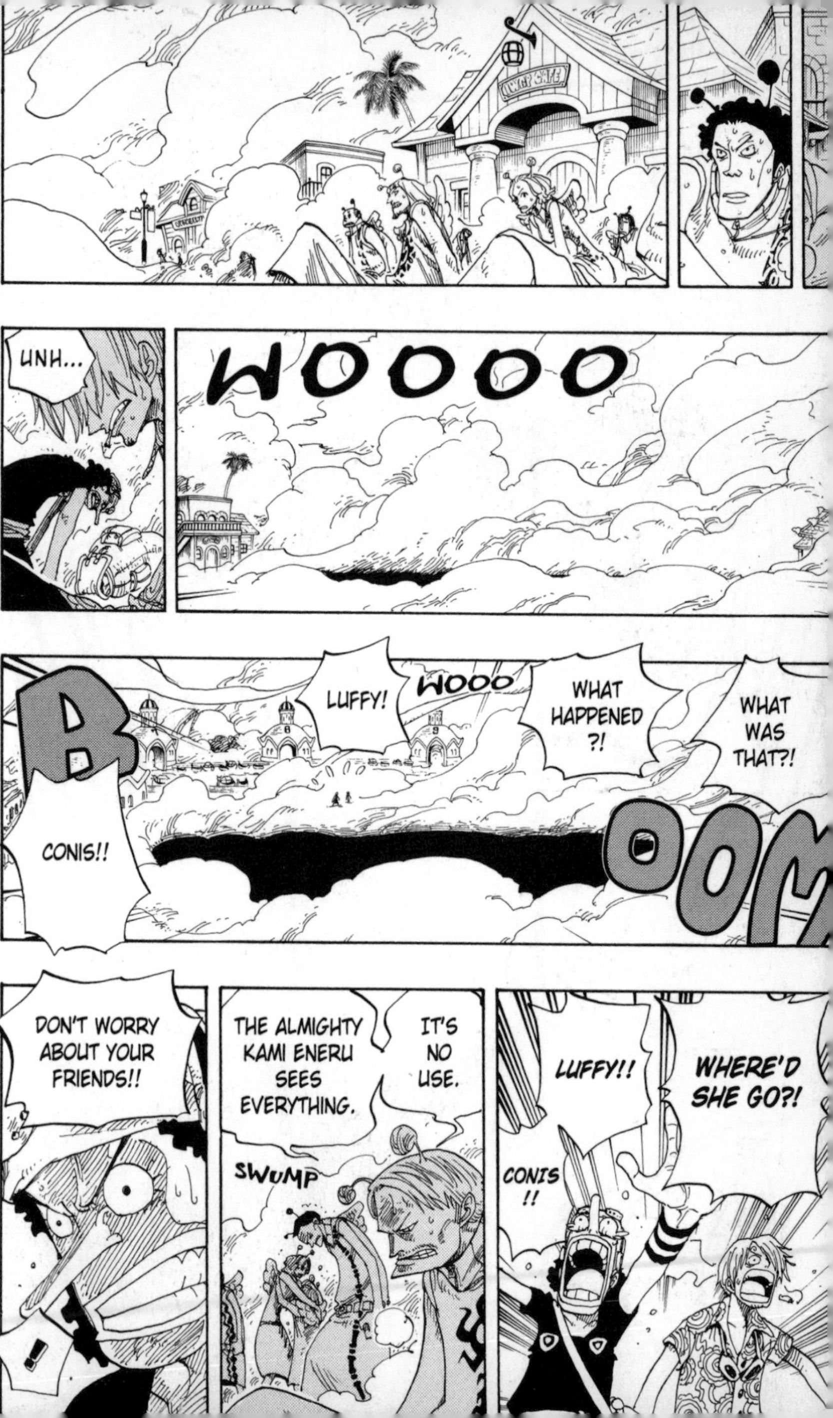
WOOOO
UNH...
WHAT WAS THAT?!
WHAT HAPPENED?!
WOOO
LUFFY!
B
OOM
CONIS!!
WHERE'D SHE GO?!
LUFFY!!
CONIS!!
IT'S NO USE.
THE ALMIGHTY KAMI ENERU SEES EVERYTHING.
SWUMP
DON'T WORRY ABOUT YOUR FRIENDS!!
!

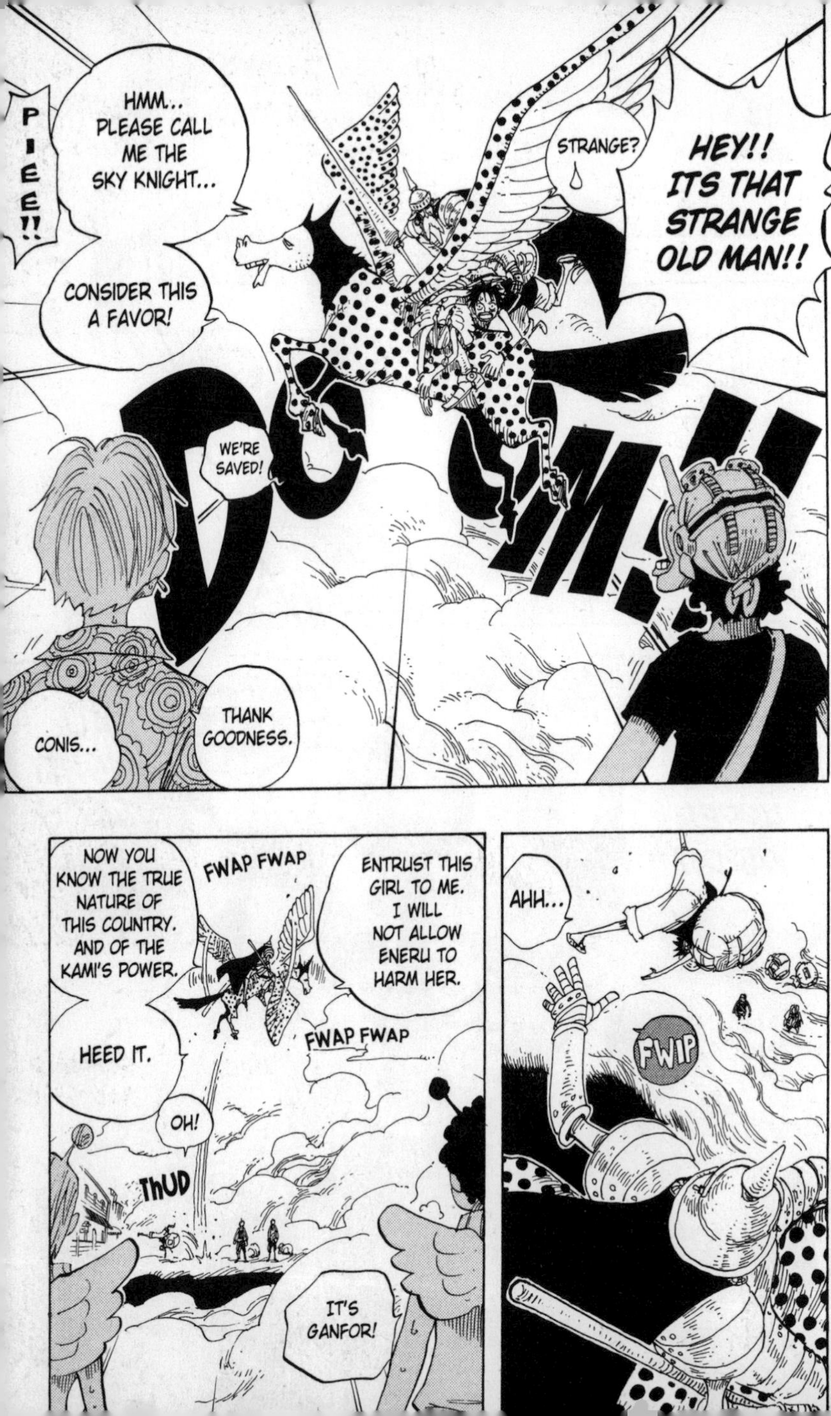

HEY!! ITS THAT STRANGE OLD MAN!!
STRANGE?
PIEE!!
HMM... PLEASE CALL ME THE SKY KNIGHT...
CONSIDER THIS A FAVOR!
DOOM!!
WE'RE SAVED!
THANK GOODNESS.
CONIS...
AHH...
FWIP
ENTRUST THIS GIRL TO ME. I WILL NOT ALLOW ENERU TO HARM HER.
FWAP FWAP
NOW YOU KNOW THE TRUE NATURE OF THIS COUNTRY. AND OF THE KAMI'S POWER.
HEED IT.
FWAP FWAP
OH!
THUD
IT'S GANFOR!

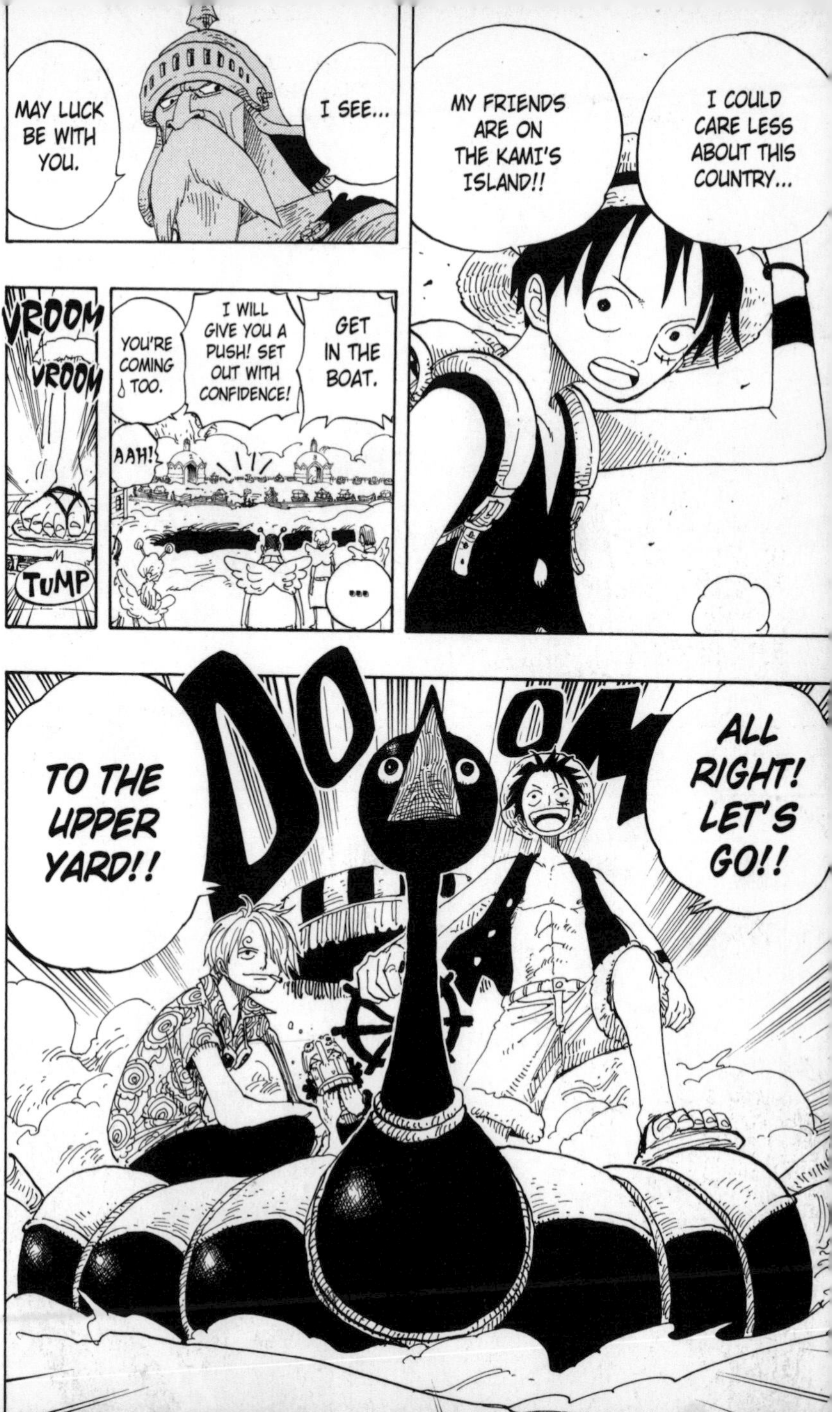

I COULD CARE LESS ABOUT THIS COUNTRY...
MY FRIENDS ARE ON THE KAMI'S ISLAND!!
I SEE...
MAY LUCK BE WITH YOU.
GET IN THE BOAT.
I WILL GIVE YOU A PUSH! SET OUT WITH CONFIDENCE!
YOU'RE COMING TOO.
AAH!!
...
VROOM
VROOM
TUMP
ALL RIGHT! LET'S GO!!
DOOM
TO THE UPPER YARD!!

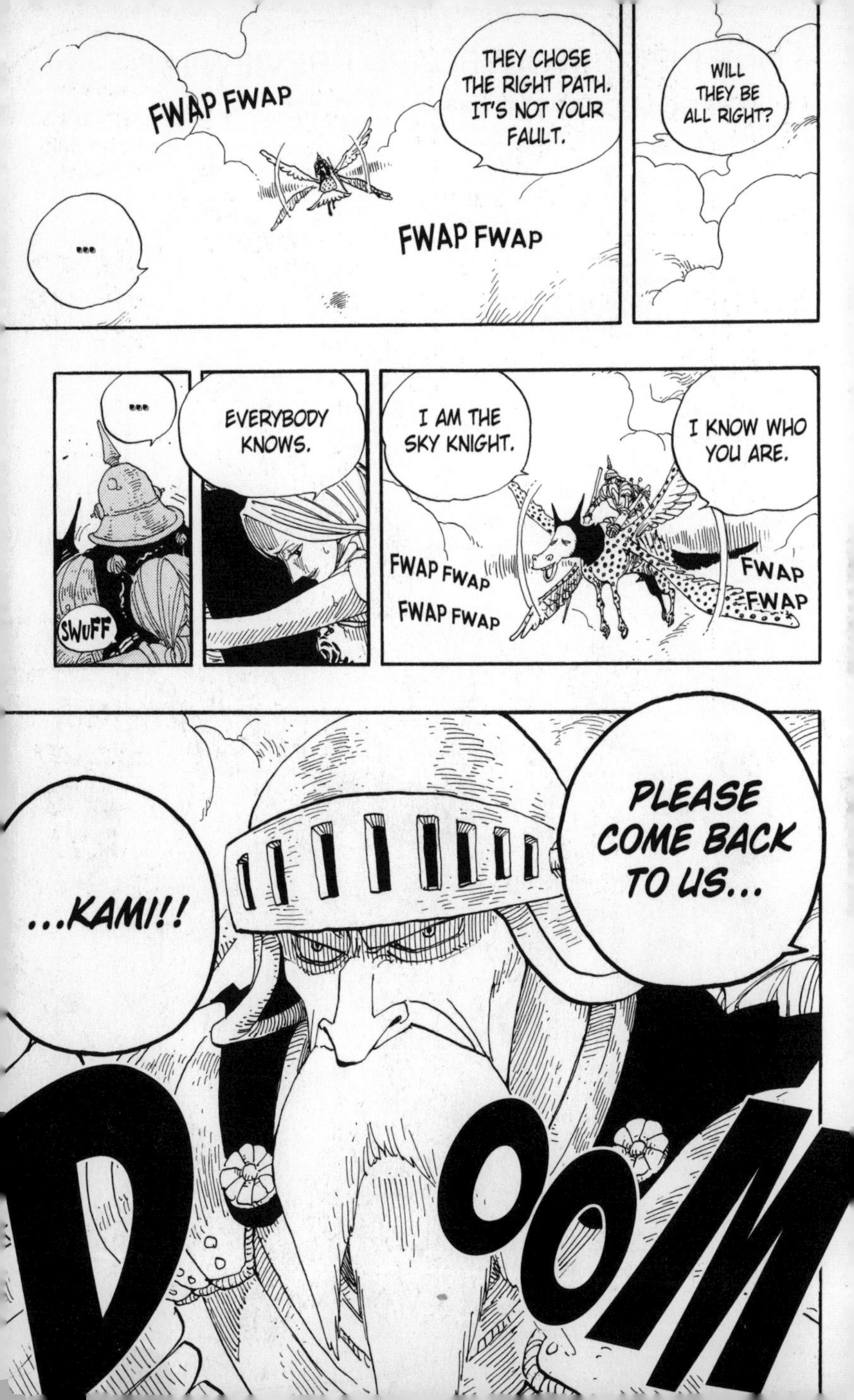
WILL THEY BE ALL RIGHT?
THEY CHOSE THE RIGHT PATH. IT'S NOT YOUR FAULT.
FWAP FWAP
FWAP FWAP
...
I KNOW WHO YOU ARE.
FWAP FWAP
I AM THE SKY KNIGHT.
FWAP FWAP
FWAP FWAP
EVERYBODY KNOWS.
...
SWUFF
PLEASE COME BACK TO US...
...KAMI!!
DOOM

ONE PIECE STORYBOARD PREVIEW!! #20

(FROM CHAPTER 247: BALL CHALLENGE)

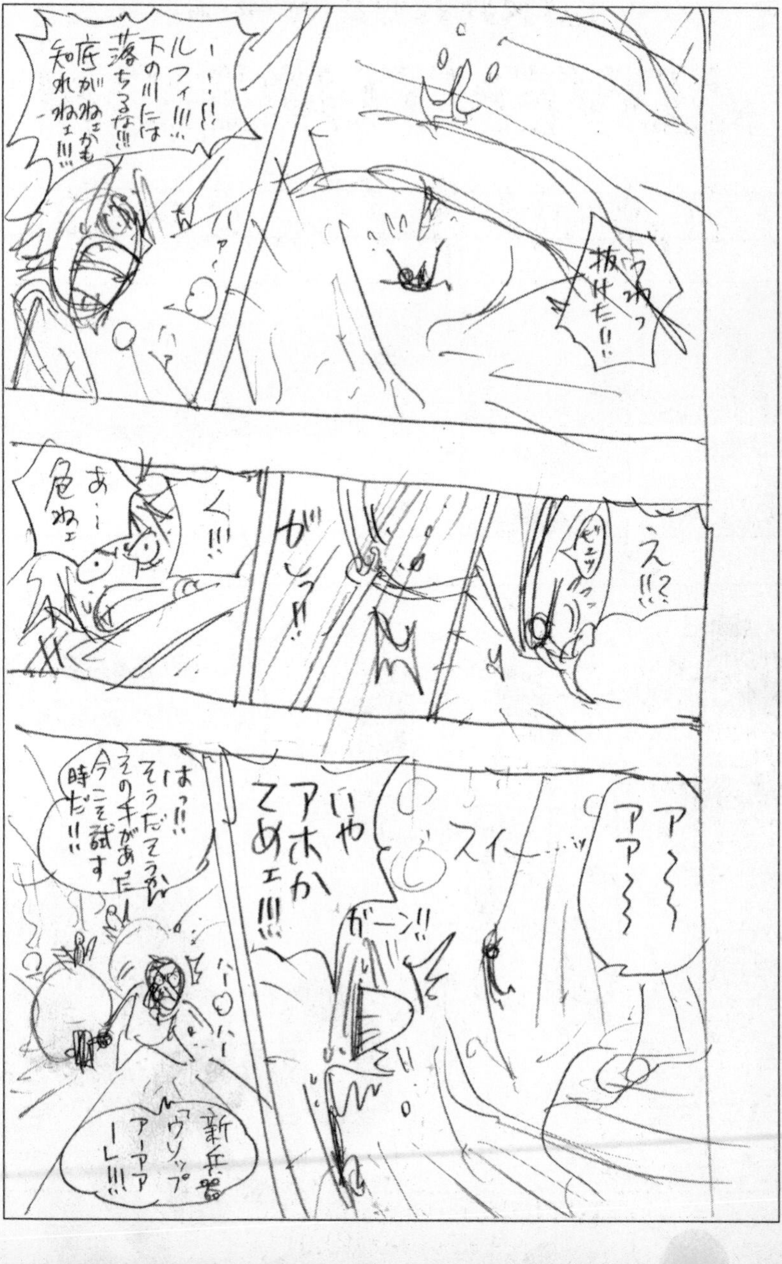
うわっ
抜けた!!
ルフィ!!! 下の川には落ちるな!!! 底がねェかも知れねェ!!!
え!!?
がしっ!!
く!!
あ…危ねェ
アァ〜〜
アァ〜〜
スイ〜…ッ
いやアホかてめェ!!!
ガーン!!
はっ!! そうだそうか その手があった!! 今こそ試す時だ!!
新兵器「ウソップアーアアーレ!!!」

Chapter 245:
ADVENTURE ON KAMI'S ISLAND

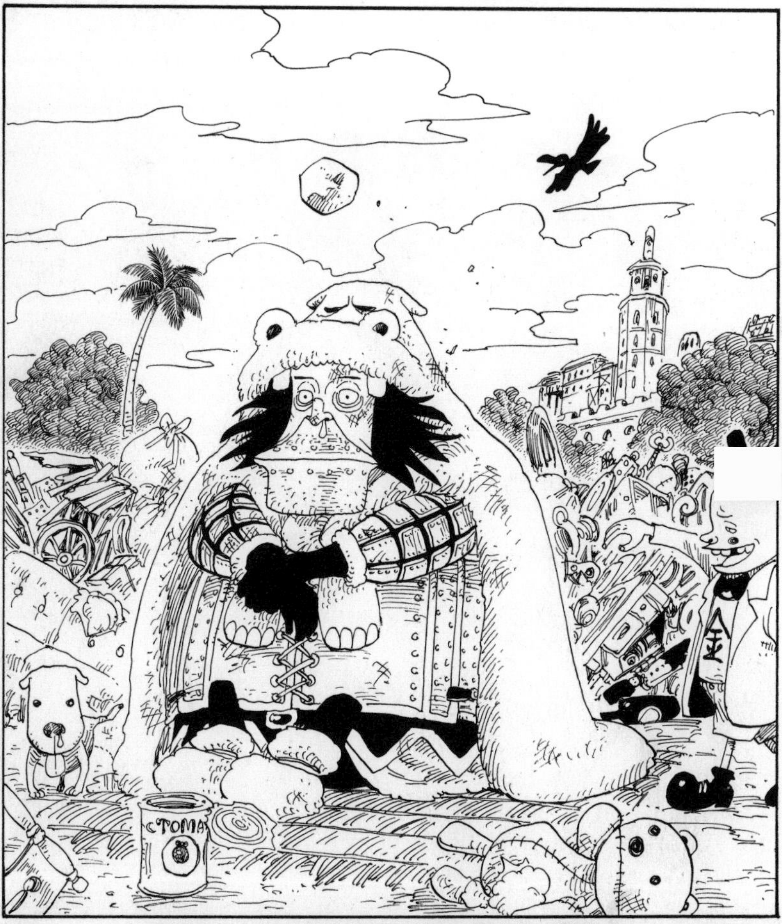
TOMA

WAPOL'S OMNIVOROUS RAMPAGE, VOL. 9:
"A KING NO MORE"

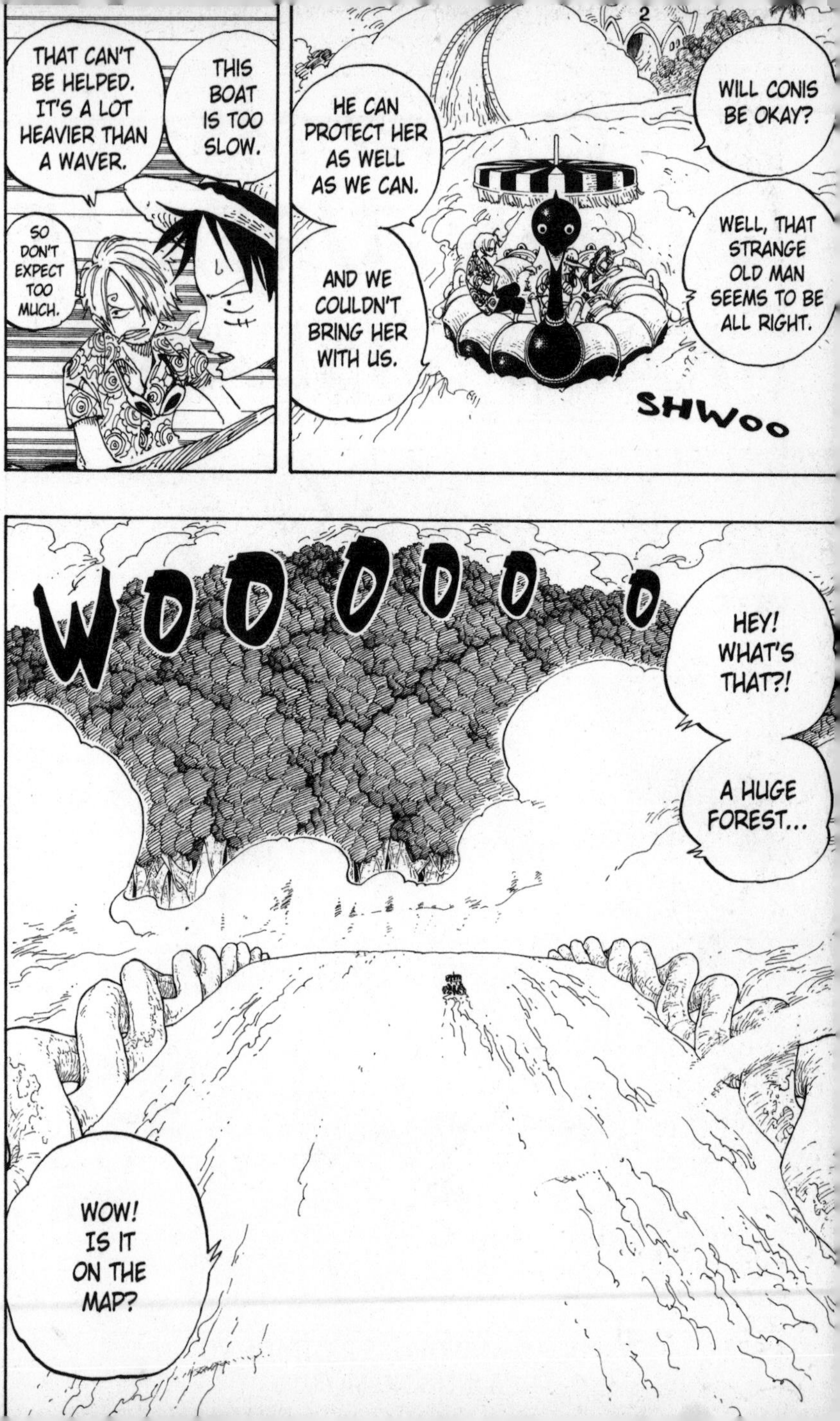
WILL CONIS BE OKAY?
WELL, THAT STRANGE OLD MAN SEEMS TO BE ALL RIGHT.
HE CAN PROTECT HER AS WELL AS WE CAN.
AND WE COULDN'T BRING HER WITH US.
SHWOO
THIS BOAT IS TOO SLOW.
THAT CAN'T BE HELPED. IT'S A LOT HEAVIER THAN A WAVER.
SO DON'T EXPECT TOO MUCH.
HEY! WHAT'S THAT?!
A HUGE FOREST...
WOOOOOO
WOW! IS IT ON THE MAP?

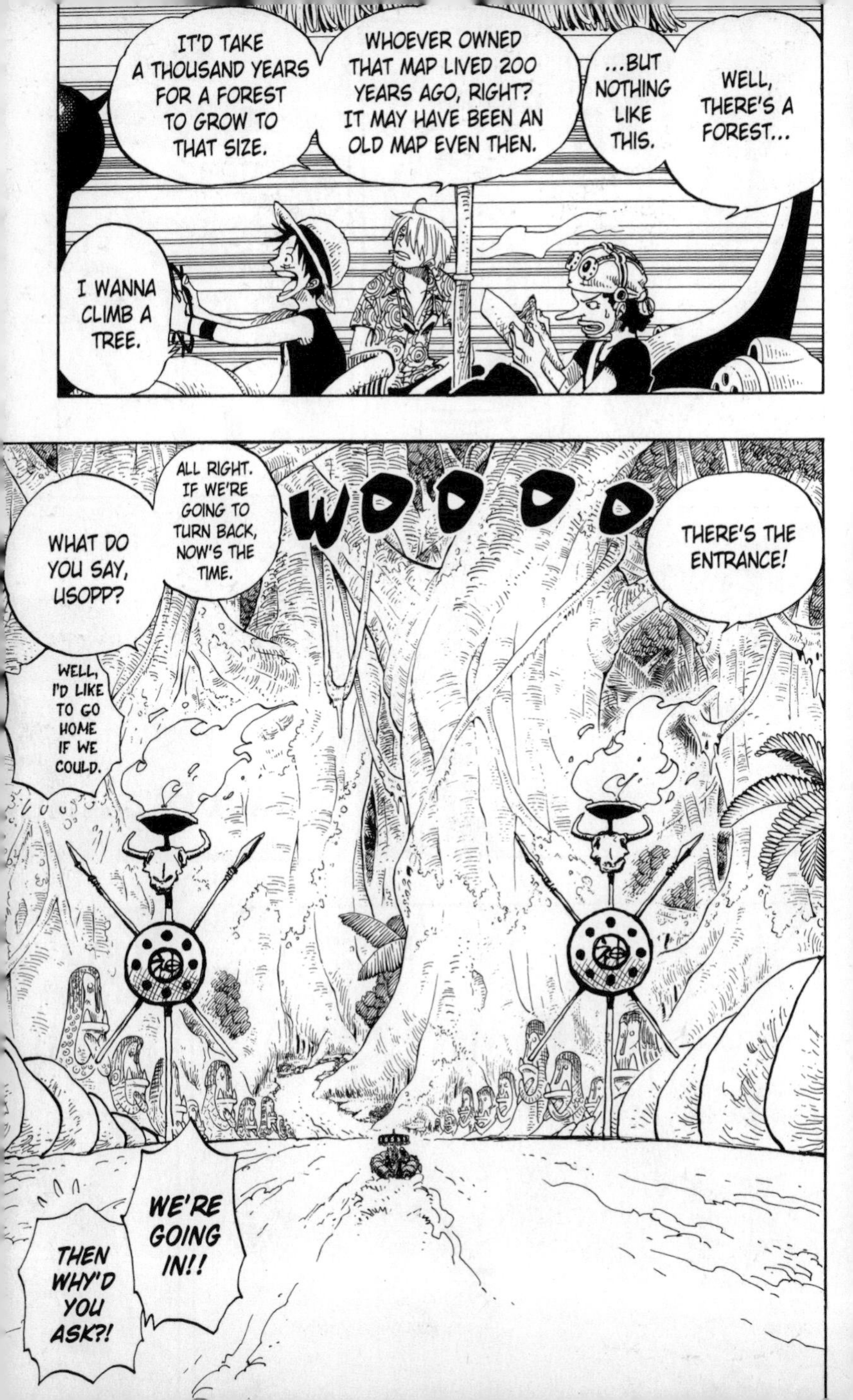
WELL, THERE'S A FOREST...
...BUT NOTHING LIKE THIS.
WHOEVER OWNED THAT MAP LIVED 200 YEARS AGO, RIGHT? IT MAY HAVE BEEN AN OLD MAP EVEN THEN.
IT'D TAKE A THOUSAND YEARS FOR A FOREST TO GROW TO THAT SIZE.
I WANNA CLIMB A TREE.
THERE'S THE ENTRANCE!
WOOOD
ALL RIGHT. IF WE'RE GOING TO TURN BACK, NOW'S THE TIME.
WHAT DO YOU SAY, USOPP?
WELL, I'D LIKE TO GO HOME IF WE COULD.
WE'RE GOING IN!!
THEN WHY'D YOU ASK?!

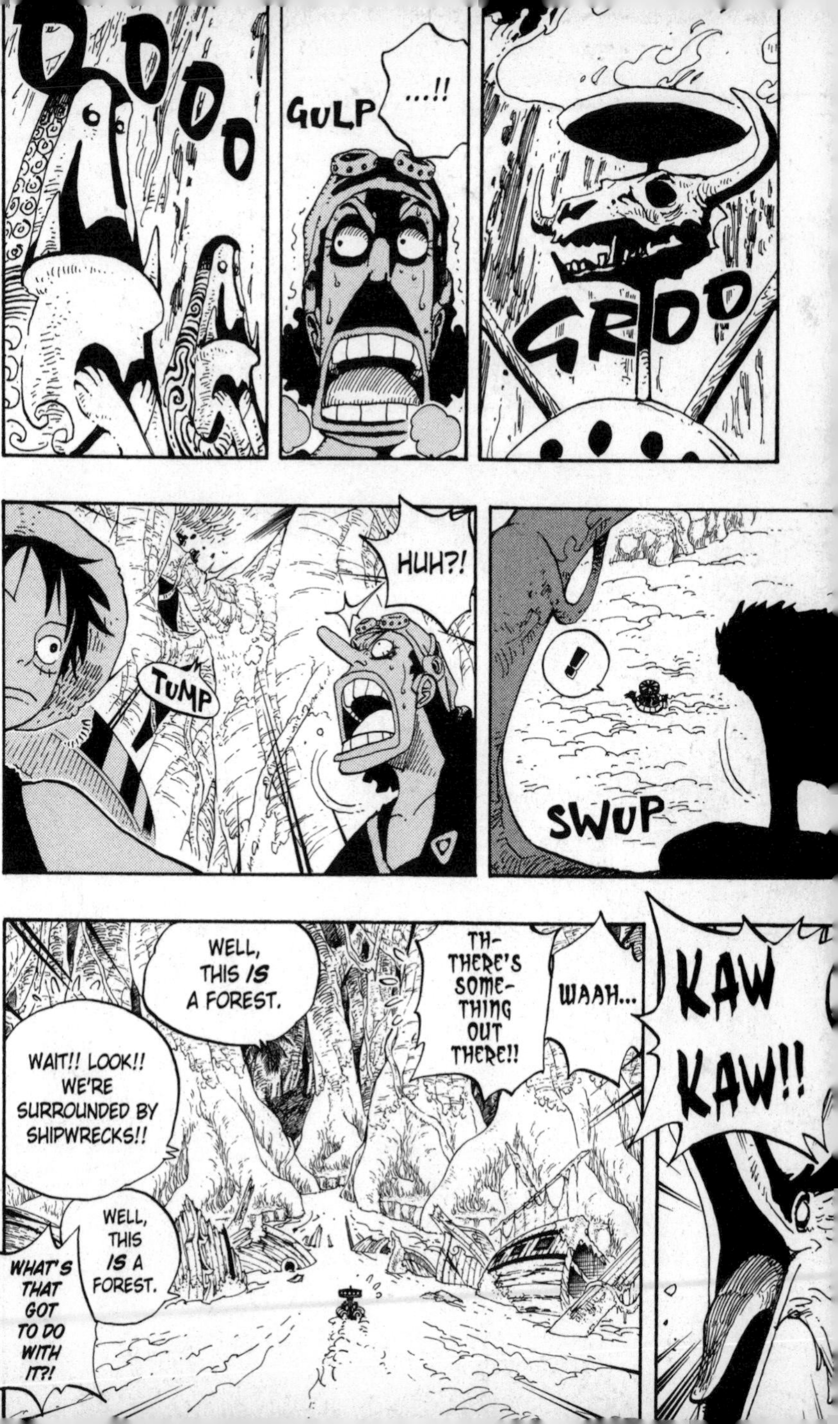
GRDD
...!!
GULP
DDDDD
!
SWUP
HUH?!
TUMP
KAW KAW!!
WAAH...
TH-THERE'S SOME-THING OUT THERE!!
WELL, THIS *IS* A FOREST.
WAIT!! LOOK!! WE'RE SURROUNDED BY SHIPWRECKS!!
WELL, THIS *IS* A FOREST.
WHAT'S THAT GOT TO DO WITH IT?!

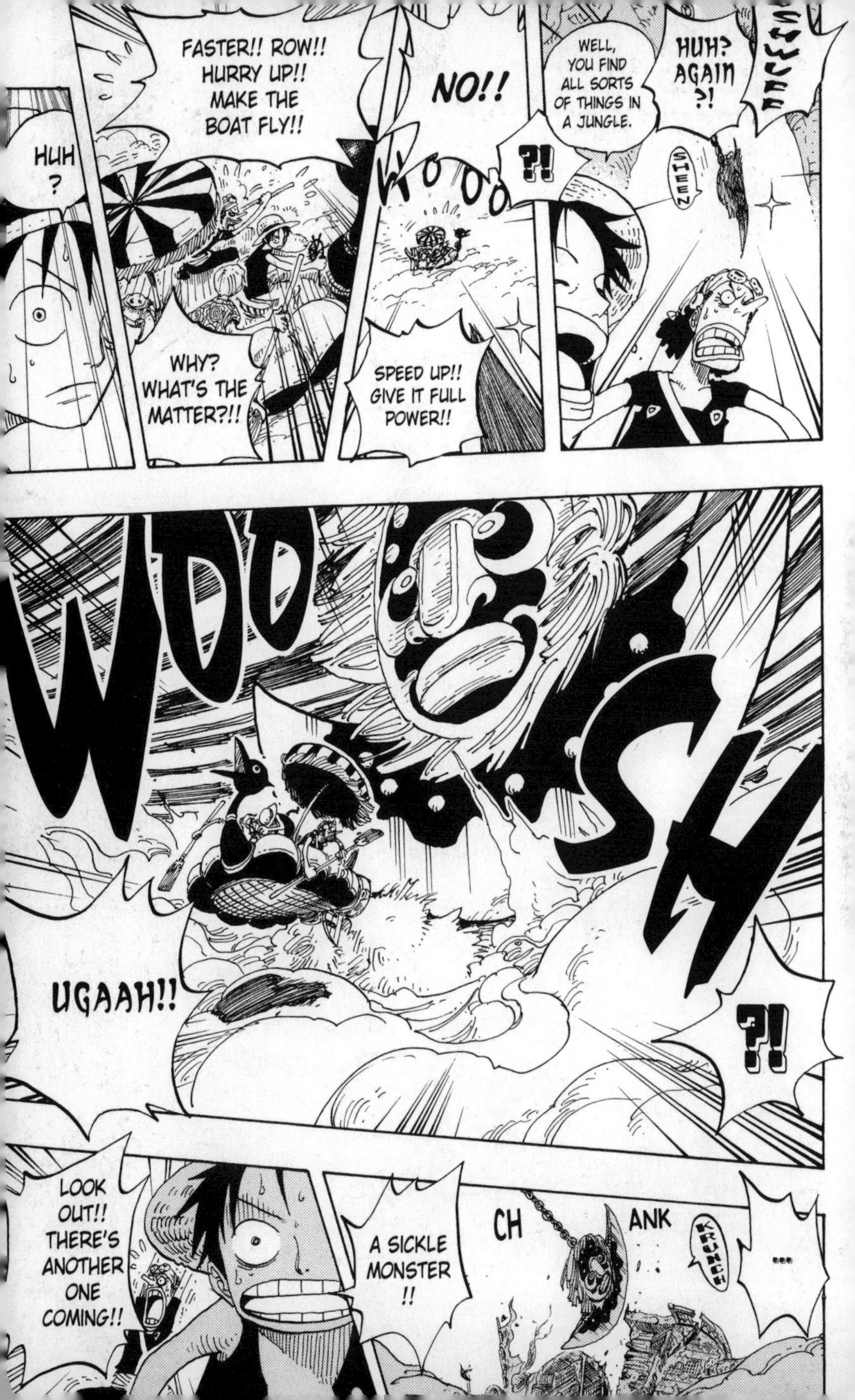
SHWUFF
HUH? AGAIN ?!
SHEEN
WELL, YOU FIND ALL SORTS OF THINGS IN A JUNGLE.
?!
NO!!
WOOO
SPEED UP!! GIVE IT FULL POWER!!
FASTER!! ROW!! HURRY UP!! MAKE THE BOAT FLY!!
WHY? WHAT'S THE MATTER?!!
HUH ?
?!
WOOOSH
UGAAH!!
...
KRUNCH
CH ANK
A SICKLE MONSTER !!
LOOK OUT!! THERE'S ANOTHER ONE COMING!!

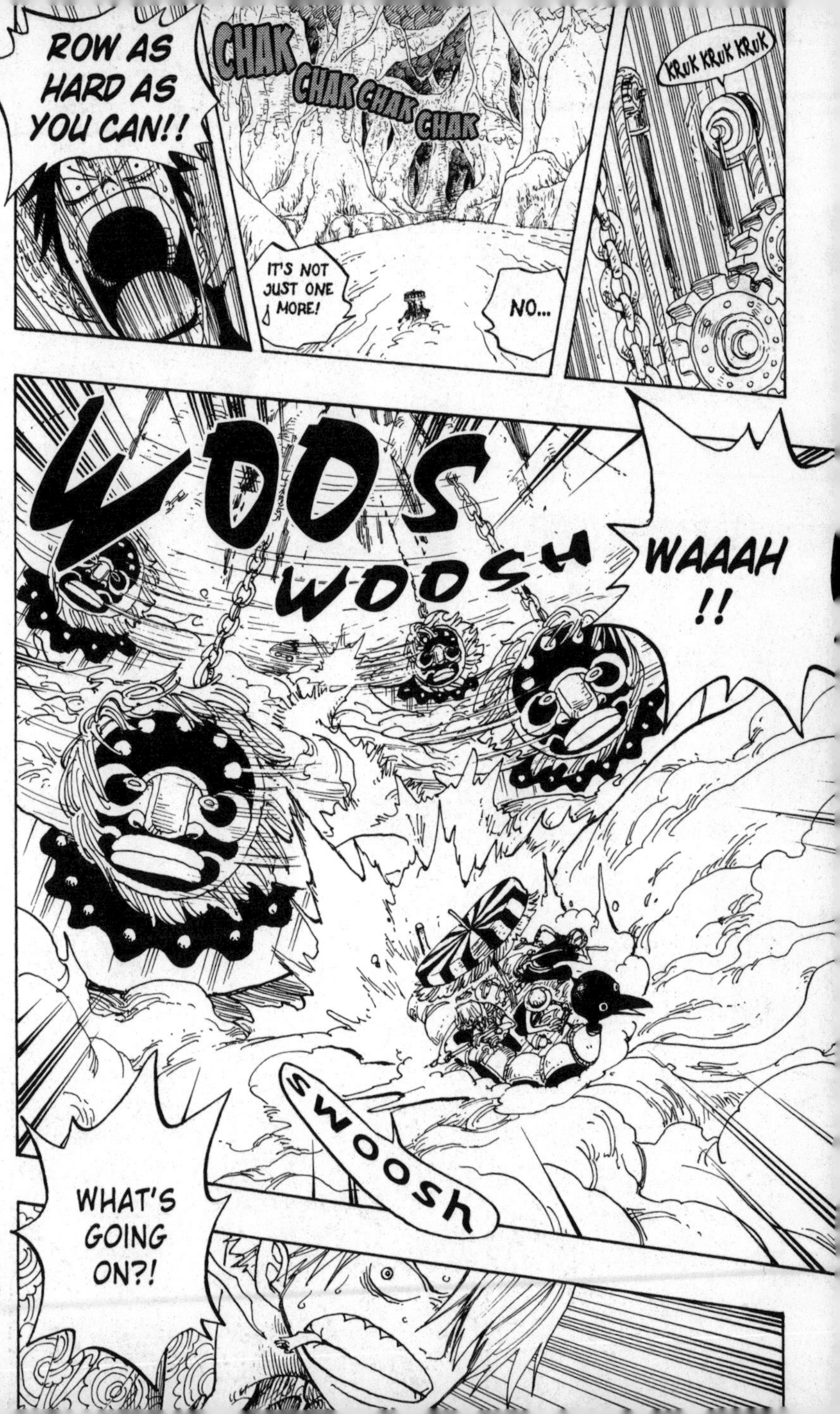
KRUK KRUK KRUK
CHAK CHAK CHAK CHAK
NO...
IT'S NOT JUST ONE MORE!
ROW AS HARD AS YOU CAN!!
WAAAH !!
WOOS WOOSH
SWOOSH
WHAT'S GOING ON?!

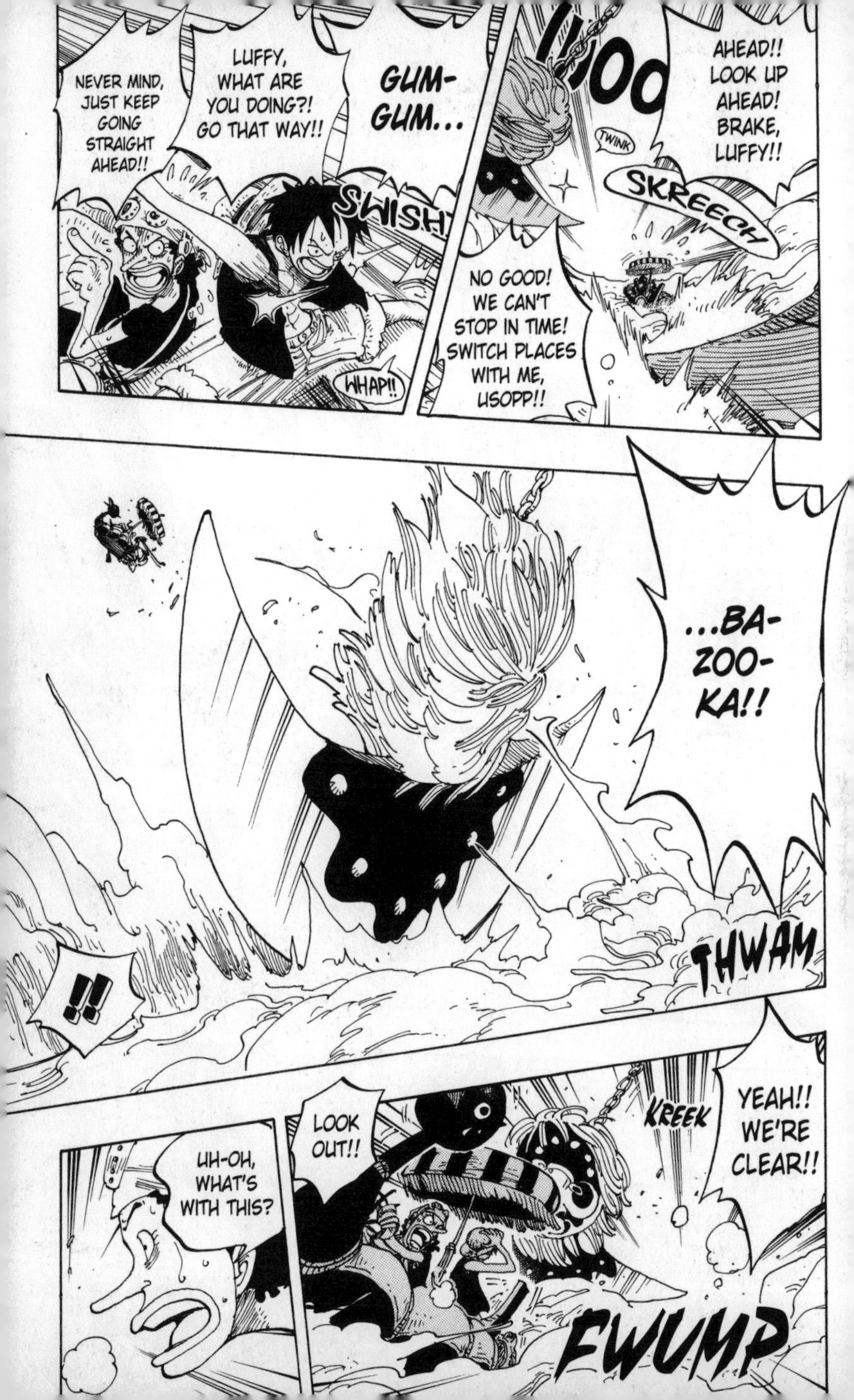
WOO
AHEAD!! LOOK UP AHEAD! BRAKE, LUFFY!!
TWINK
SKREEECH
NO GOOD! WE CAN'T STOP IN TIME! SWITCH PLACES WITH ME, USOPP!!
GUM-GUM...
LUFFY, WHAT ARE YOU DOING?! GO THAT WAY!!
NEVER MIND, JUST KEEP GOING STRAIGHT AHEAD!!
SWISH
WHAP!!
...BA-ZOO-KA!!
THWAM
!!
YEAH!! WE'RE CLEAR!!
KREEK
LOOK OUT!!
FWUMP
UH-OH, WHAT'S WITH THIS?

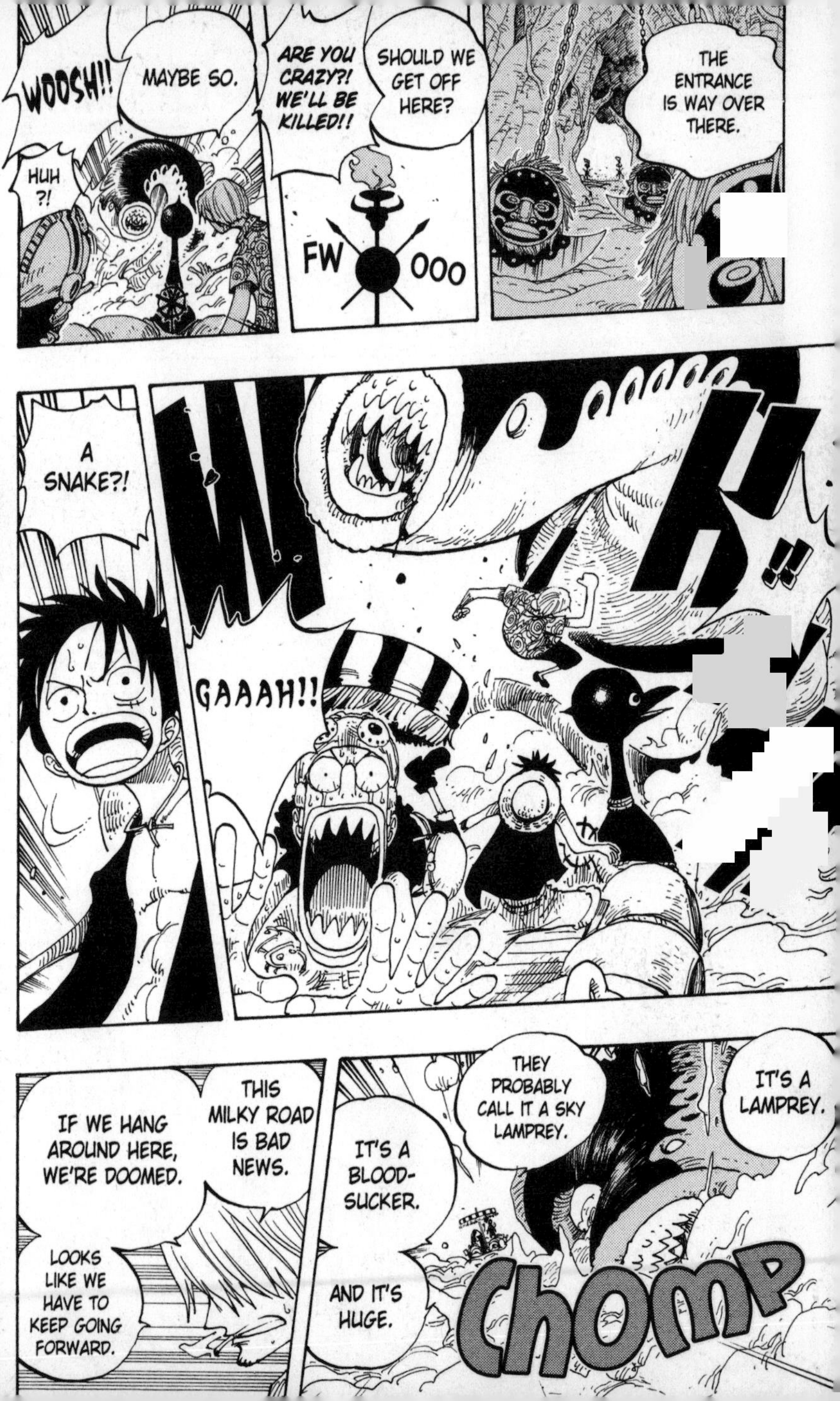
THE ENTRANCE IS WAY OVER THERE.
SHOULD WE GET OFF HERE?
ARE YOU CRAZY?! WE'LL BE KILLED!!
FW OOO
MAYBE SO.
WOOSH!!
HUH ?!
GAAAH!!
A SNAKE?!
IT'S A LAMPREY.
THEY PROBABLY CALL IT A SKY LAMPREY.
IT'S A BLOOD-SUCKER.
AND IT'S HUGE.
CHOMP
THIS MILKY ROAD IS BAD NEWS.
IF WE HANG AROUND HERE, WE'RE DOOMED.
LOOKS LIKE WE HAVE TO KEEP GOING FORWARD.

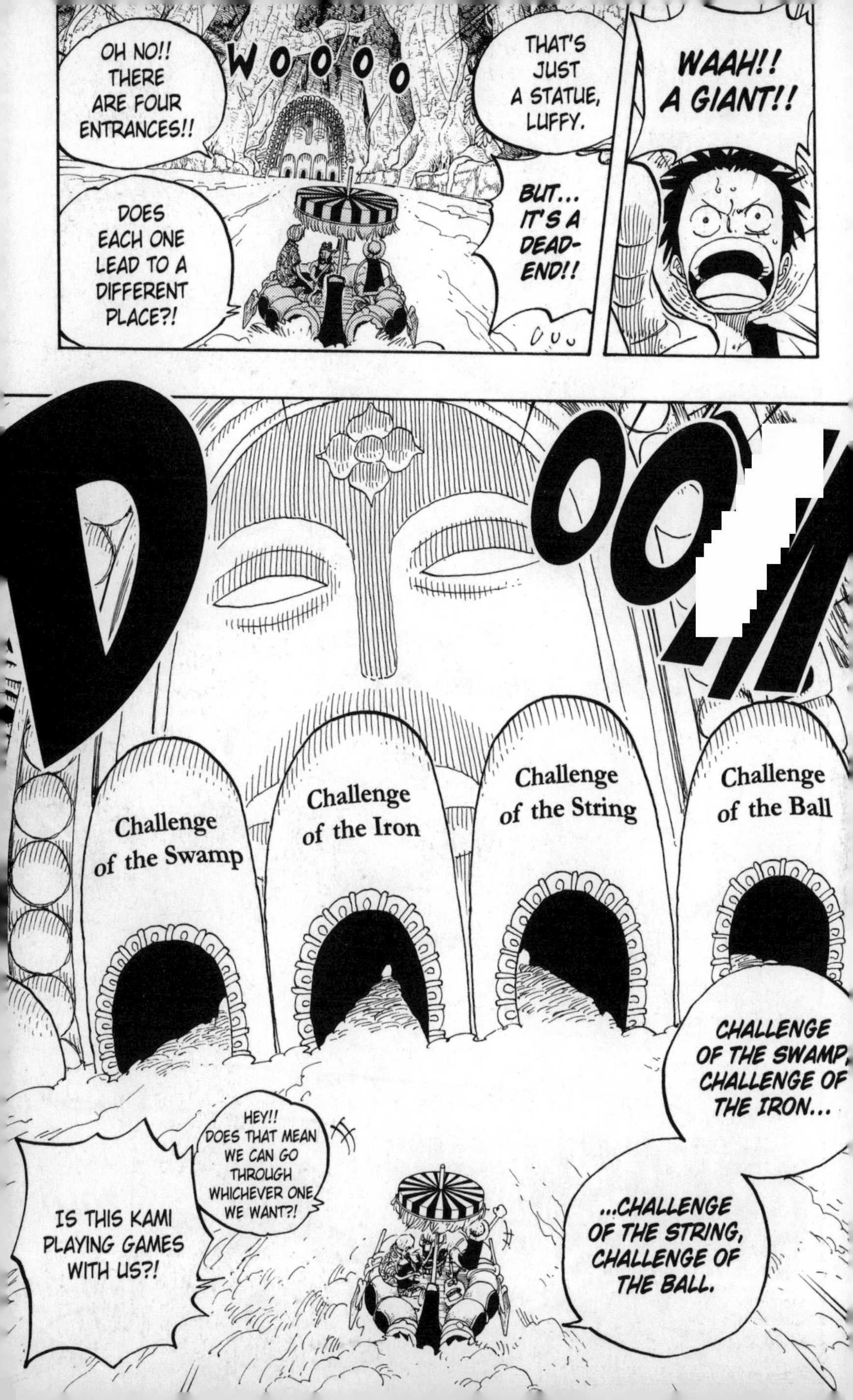
WAAH!! A GIANT!!
THAT'S JUST A STATUE, LUFFY.
BUT... IT'S A DEAD-END!!
WOOOO
OH NO!! THERE ARE FOUR ENTRANCES!!
DOES EACH ONE LEAD TO A DIFFERENT PLACE?!
DOOM
Challenge of the Ball
Challenge of the String
Challenge of the Iron
Challenge of the Swamp
CHALLENGE OF THE SWAMP, CHALLENGE OF THE IRON...
...CHALLENGE OF THE STRING, CHALLENGE OF THE BALL.
HEY!! DOES THAT MEAN WE CAN GO THROUGH WHICHEVER ONE WE WANT?!
IS THIS KAMI PLAYING GAMES WITH US?!

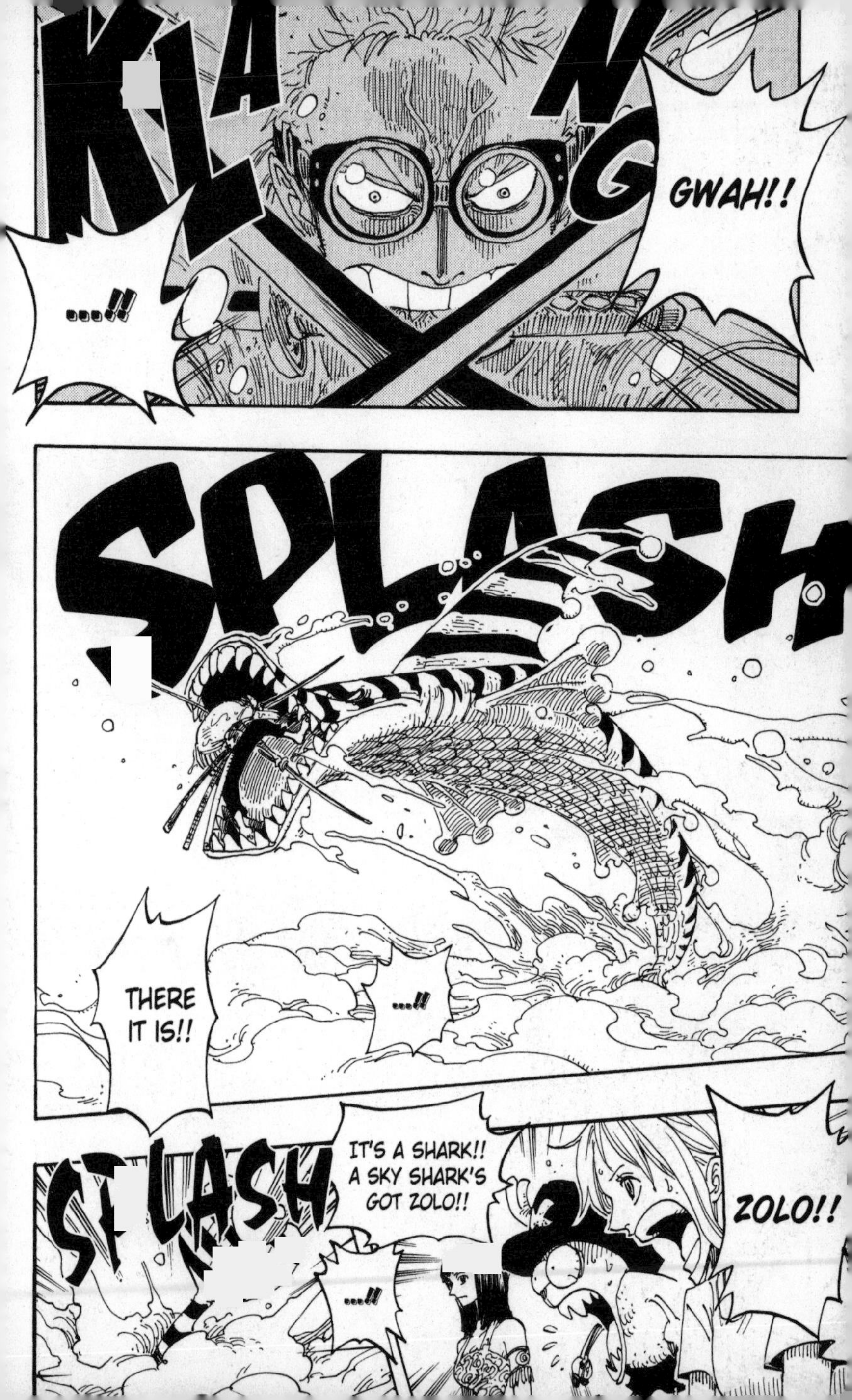
KLANG
GWAH!!
...!!
SPLASH
...!!
THERE IT IS!!
ZOLO!!
IT'S A SHARK!! A SKY SHARK'S GOT ZOLO!!
...!!
SPLASH

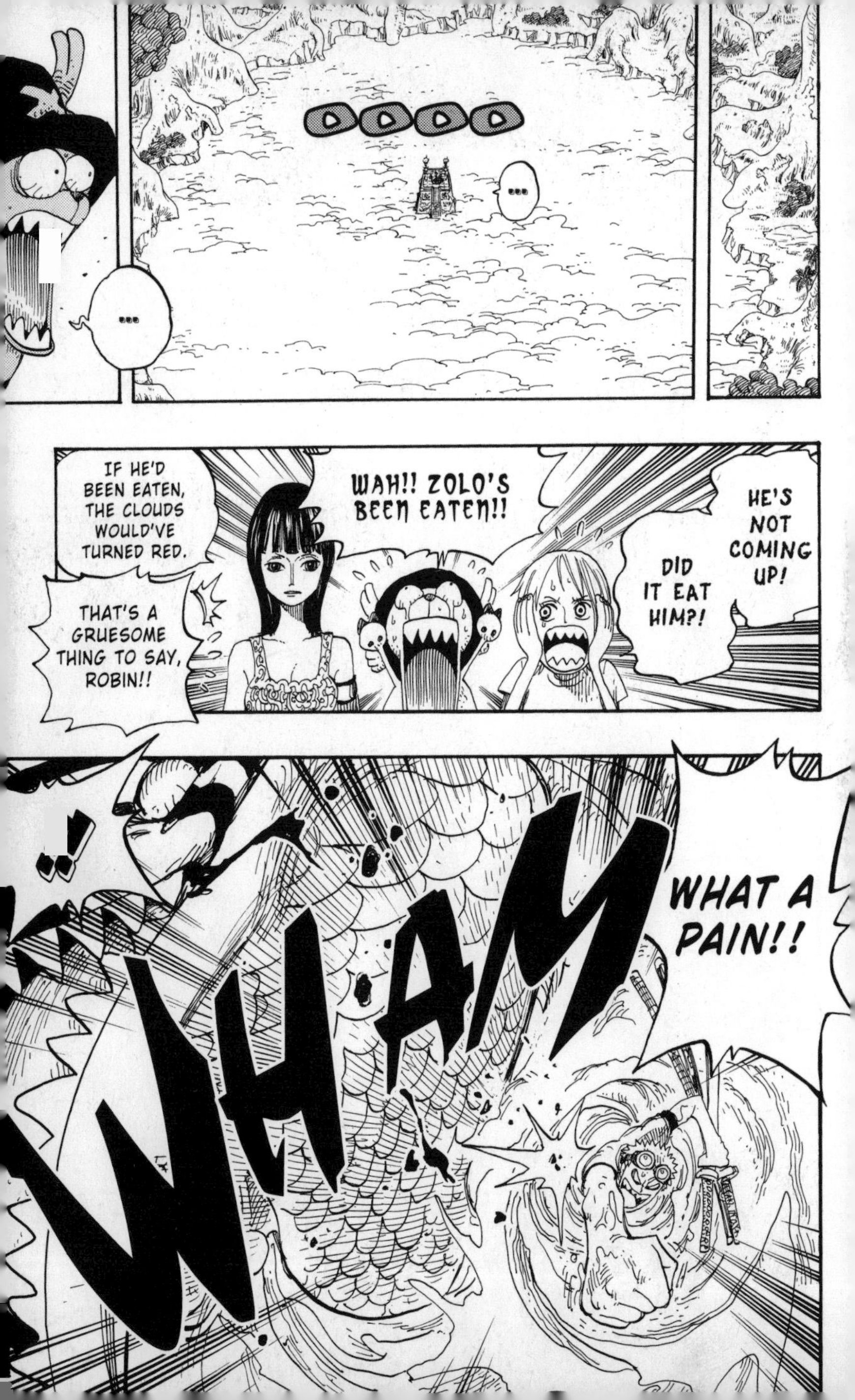
...
...
HE'S NOT COMING UP!
DID IT EAT HIM?!
WAH!! ZOLO'S BEEN EATEN!!
IF HE'D BEEN EATEN, THE CLOUDS WOULD'VE TURNED RED.
THAT'S A GRUESOME THING TO SAY, ROBIN!!
WHAT A PAIN!!
WHAM
!!

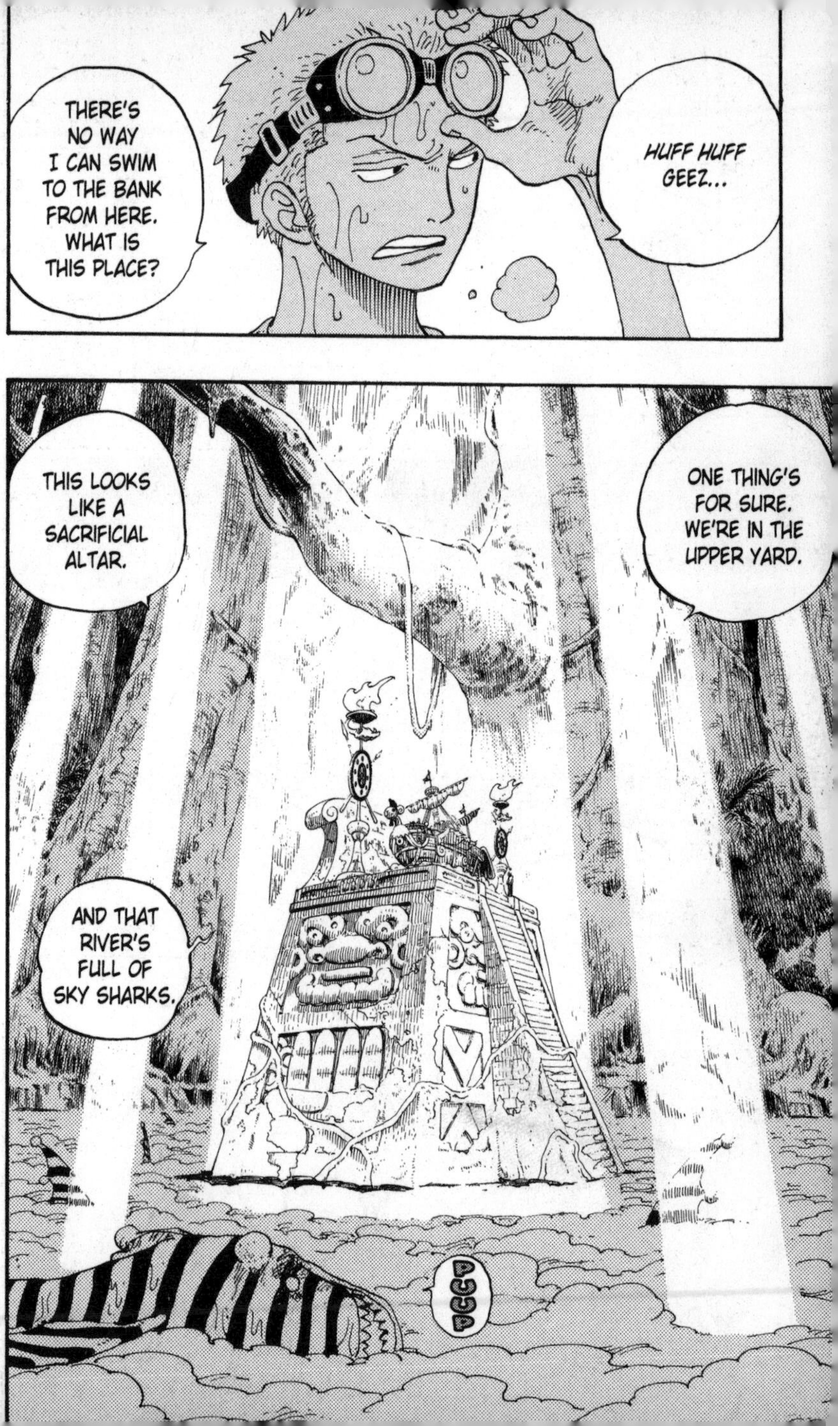
HUFF HUFF GEEZ...
THERE'S NO WAY I CAN SWIM TO THE BANK FROM HERE. WHAT IS THIS PLACE?
ONE THING'S FOR SURE. WE'RE IN THE UPPER YARD.
THIS LOOKS LIKE A SACRIFICIAL ALTAR.
AND THAT RIVER'S FULL OF SKY SHARKS.

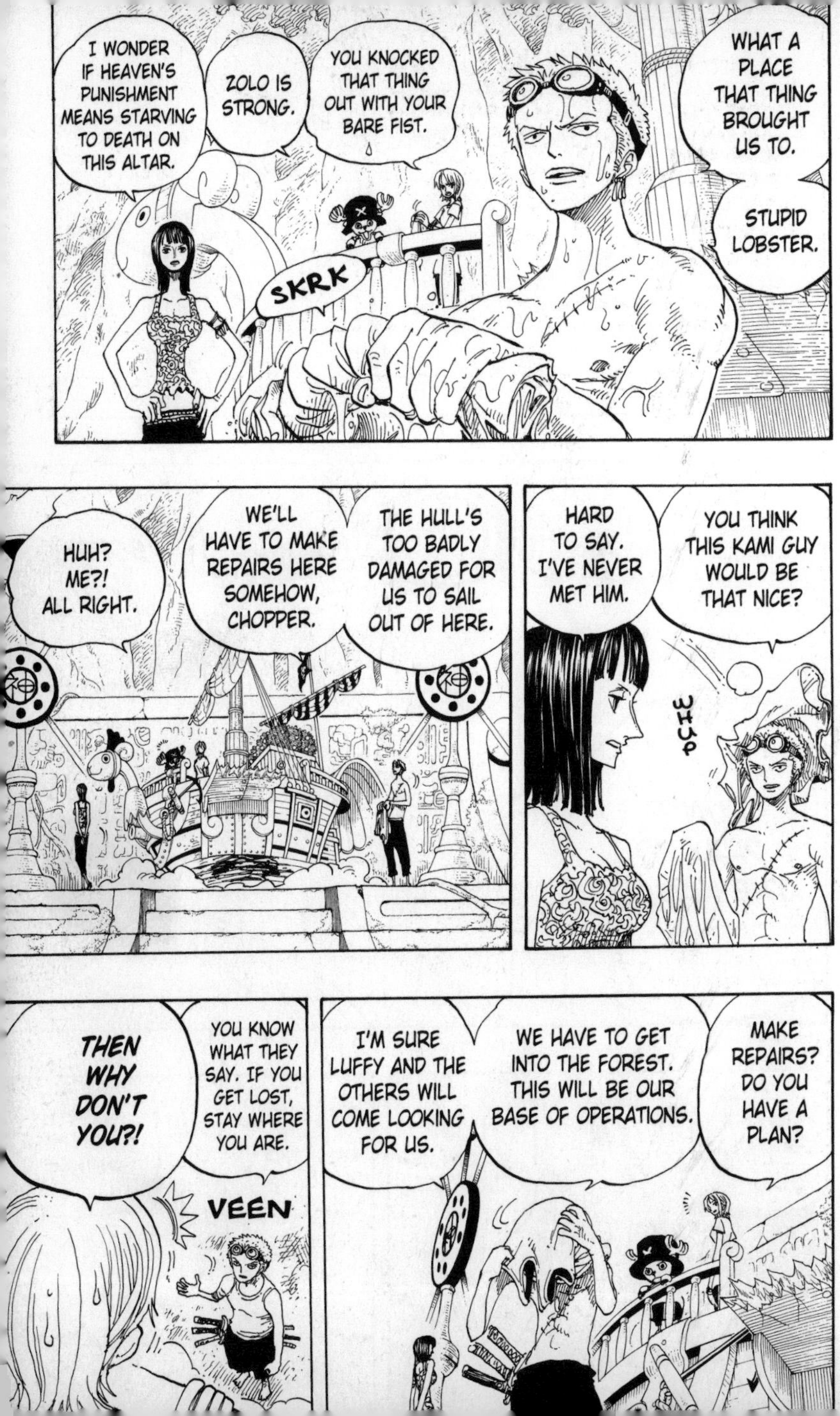
WHAT A PLACE THAT THING BROUGHT US TO.
STUPID LOBSTER.
YOU KNOCKED THAT THING OUT WITH YOUR BARE FIST.
ZOLO IS STRONG.
I WONDER IF HEAVEN'S PUNISHMENT MEANS STARVING TO DEATH ON THIS ALTAR.
SKRK
YOU THINK THIS KAMI GUY WOULD BE THAT NICE?
HARD TO SAY. I'VE NEVER MET HIM.
WHUP
THE HULL'S TOO BADLY DAMAGED FOR US TO SAIL OUT OF HERE.
WE'LL HAVE TO MAKE REPAIRS HERE SOMEHOW, CHOPPER.
HUH? ME?! ALL RIGHT.
MAKE REPAIRS? DO YOU HAVE A PLAN?
WE HAVE TO GET INTO THE FOREST. THIS WILL BE OUR BASE OF OPERATIONS.
I'M SURE LUFFY AND THE OTHERS WILL COME LOOKING FOR US.
YOU KNOW WHAT THEY SAY. IF YOU GET LOST, STAY WHERE YOU ARE.
THEN WHY DON'T YOU?!
VEEN

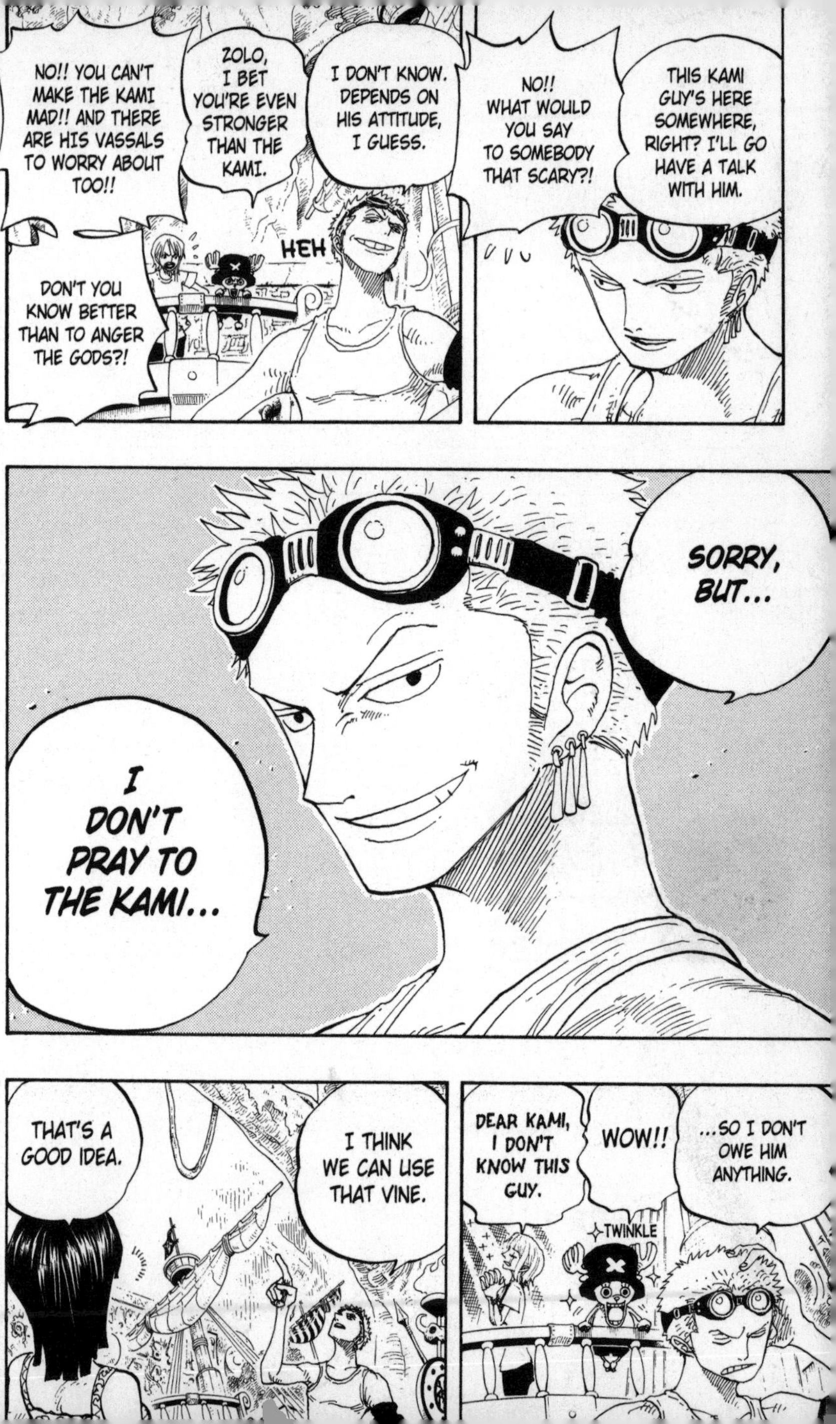
THIS KAMI GUY'S HERE SOMEWHERE, RIGHT? I'LL GO HAVE A TALK WITH HIM.
NO!! WHAT WOULD YOU SAY TO SOMEBODY THAT SCARY?!
I DON'T KNOW. DEPENDS ON HIS ATTITUDE, I GUESS.
ZOLO, I BET YOU'RE EVEN STRONGER THAN THE KAMI.
HEH
NO!! YOU CAN'T MAKE THE KAMI MAD!! AND THERE ARE HIS VASSALS TO WORRY ABOUT TOO!!
DON'T YOU KNOW BETTER THAN TO ANGER THE GODS?!
SORRY, BUT...
I DON'T PRAY TO THE KAMI...
...SO I DON'T OWE HIM ANYTHING.
WOW!!
TWINKLE
DEAR KAMI, I DON'T KNOW THIS GUY.
I THINK WE CAN USE THAT VINE.
THAT'S A GOOD IDEA.

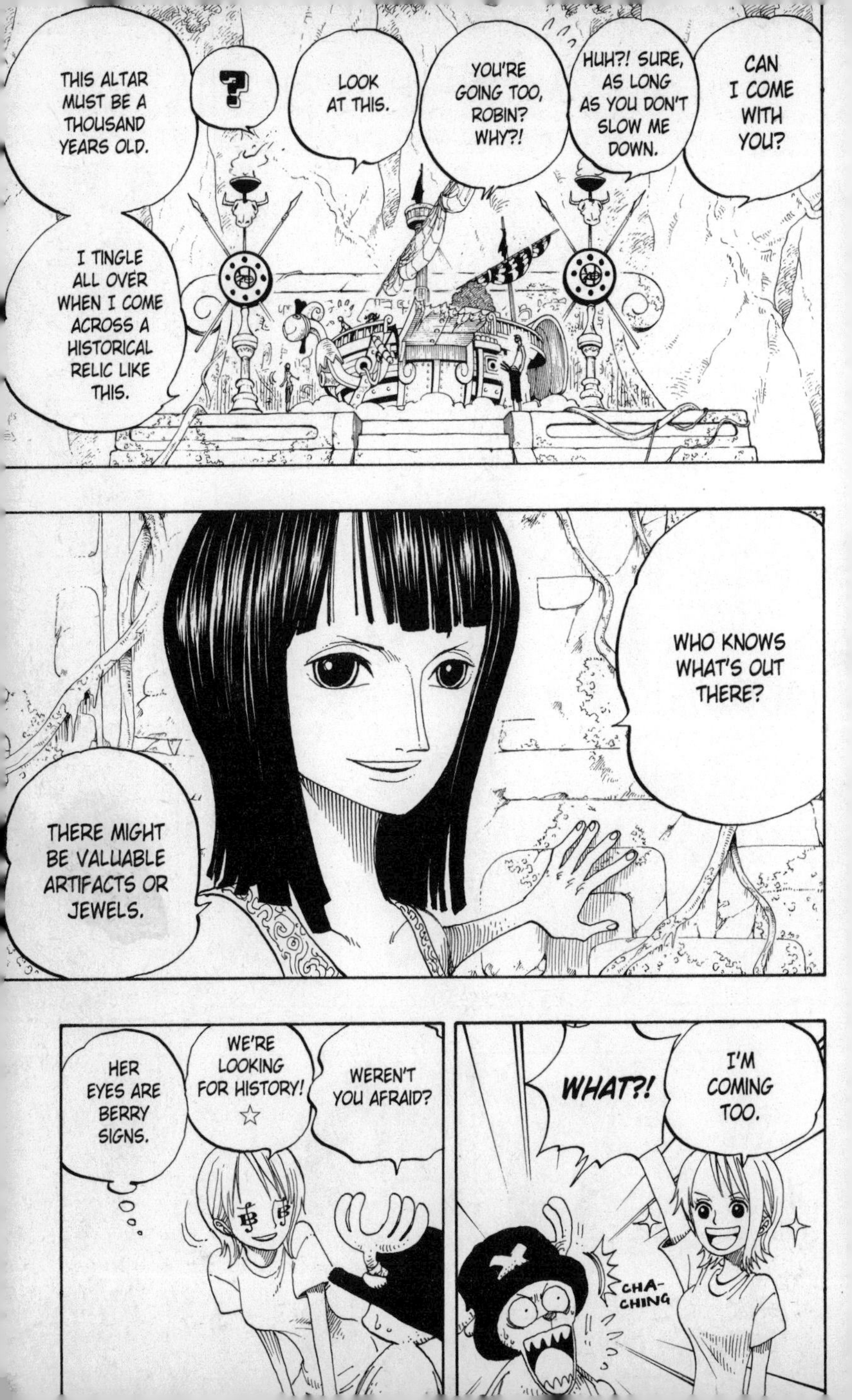
CAN I COME WITH YOU?
HUH?! SURE, AS LONG AS YOU DON'T SLOW ME DOWN.
YOU'RE GOING TOO, ROBIN? WHY?!
LOOK AT THIS.
?
THIS ALTAR MUST BE A THOUSAND YEARS OLD.
I TINGLE ALL OVER WHEN I COME ACROSS A HISTORICAL RELIC LIKE THIS.
WHO KNOWS WHAT'S OUT THERE?
THERE MIGHT BE VALUABLE ARTIFACTS OR JEWELS.
I'M COMING TOO.
WHAT?!
CHA-CHING
WEREN'T YOU AFRAID?
WE'RE LOOKING FOR HISTORY! ☆
HER EYES ARE BERRY SIGNS.

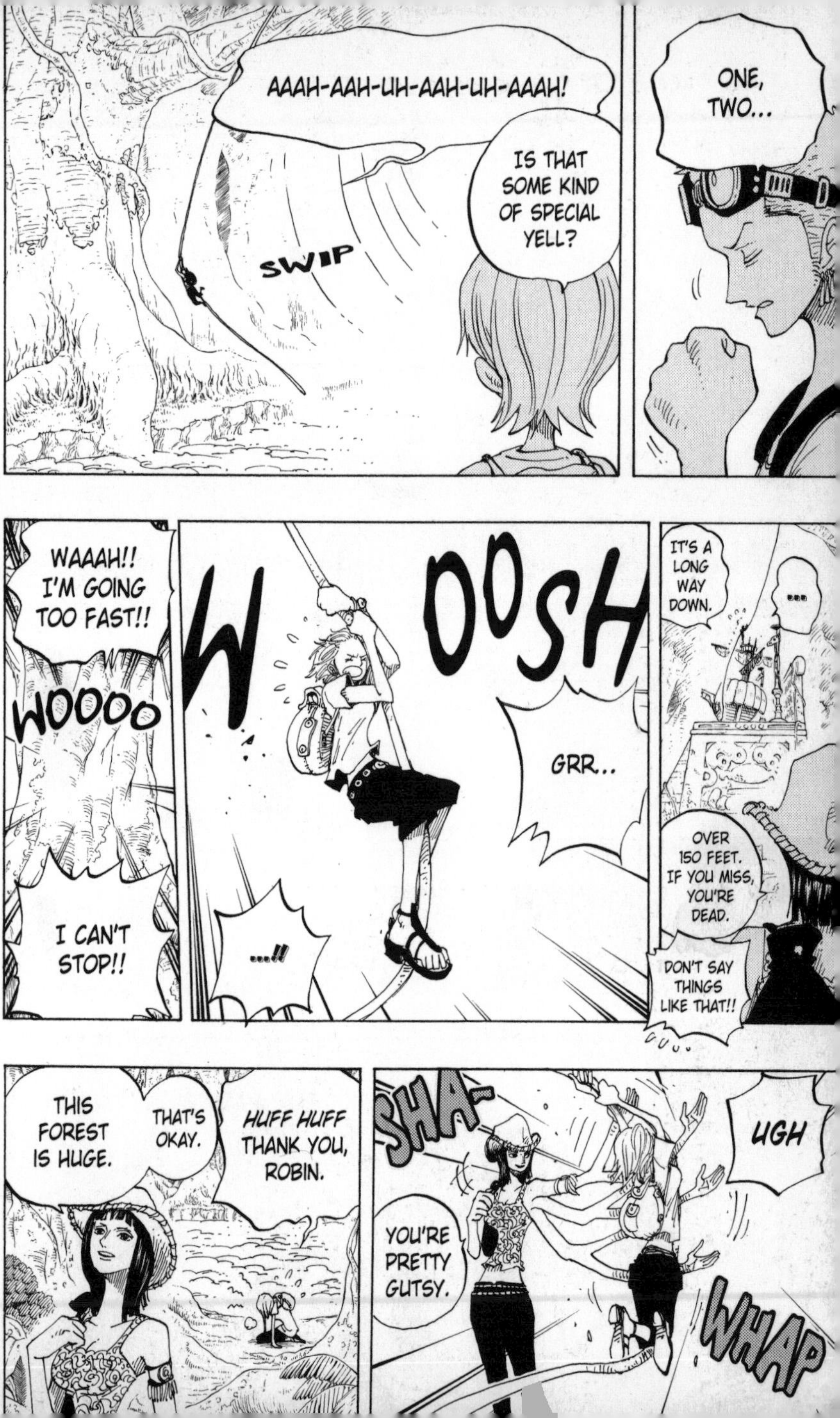
ONE, TWO...
AAAH-AAH-UH-AAH-UH-AAAH!
IS THAT SOME KIND OF SPECIAL YELL?
SWIP
IT'S A LONG WAY DOWN.
...
OVER 150 FEET. IF YOU MISS, YOU'RE DEAD.
DON'T SAY THINGS LIKE THAT!!
WOOSH
GRR...
...!!
WAAAH!! I'M GOING TOO FAST!!
WOOOO
I CAN'T STOP!!
UGH
SHA-
YOU'RE PRETTY GUTSY.
WHAP
HUFF HUFF THANK YOU, ROBIN.
THAT'S OKAY.
THIS FOREST IS HUGE.

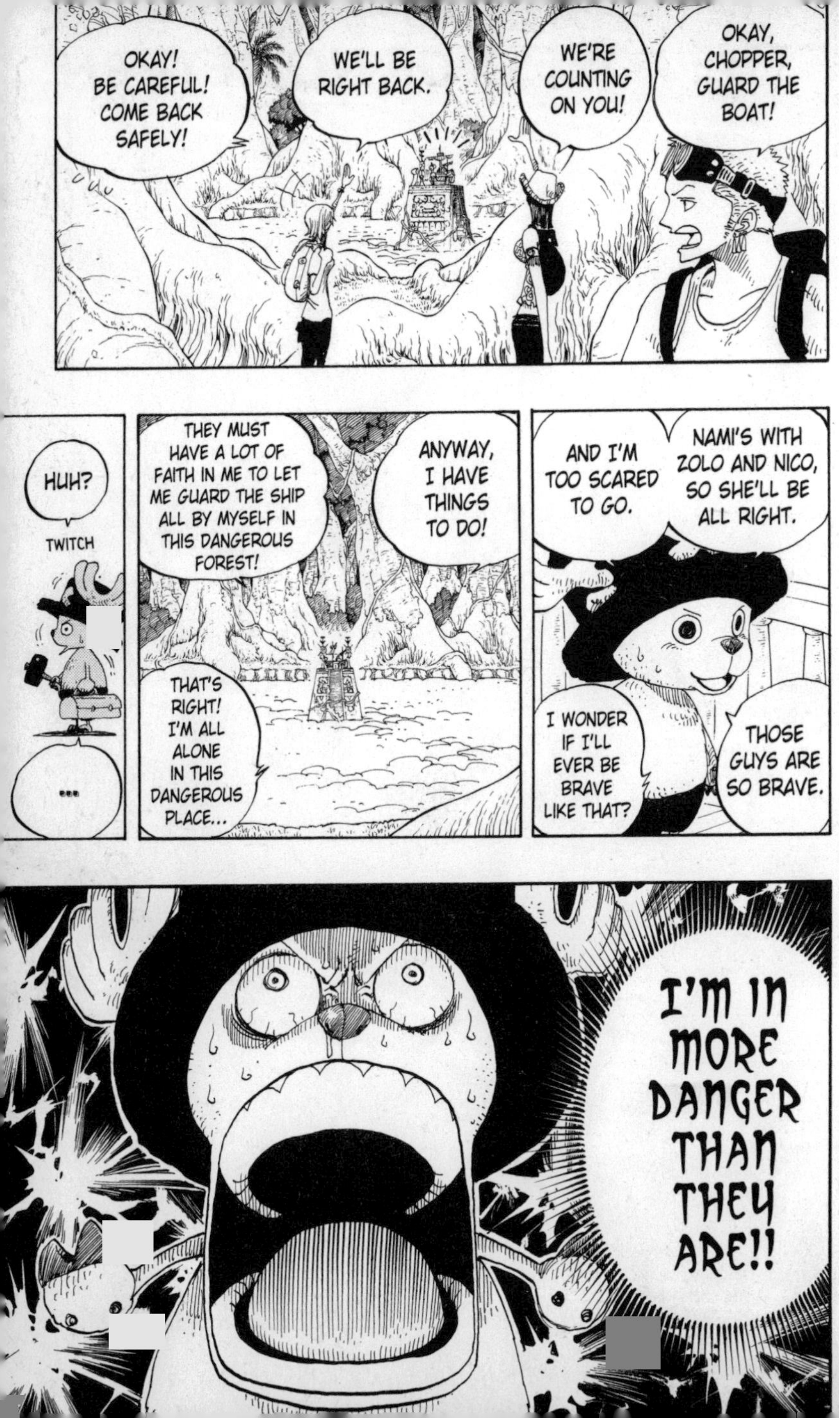
OKAY, CHOPPER, GUARD THE BOAT!
WE'RE COUNTING ON YOU!
WE'LL BE RIGHT BACK.
OKAY! BE CAREFUL! COME BACK SAFELY!
NAMI'S WITH ZOLO AND NICO, SO SHE'LL BE ALL RIGHT.
AND I'M TOO SCARED TO GO.
THOSE GUYS ARE SO BRAVE.
I WONDER IF I'LL EVER BE BRAVE LIKE THAT?
ANYWAY, I HAVE THINGS TO DO!
THEY MUST HAVE A LOT OF FAITH IN ME TO LET ME GUARD THE SHIP ALL BY MYSELF IN THIS DANGEROUS FOREST!
THAT'S RIGHT! I'M ALL ALONE IN THIS DANGEROUS PLACE...
HUH?
TWITCH
...
I'M IN MORE DANGER THAN THEY ARE!!

OF THE FOREST OF NO RETURN

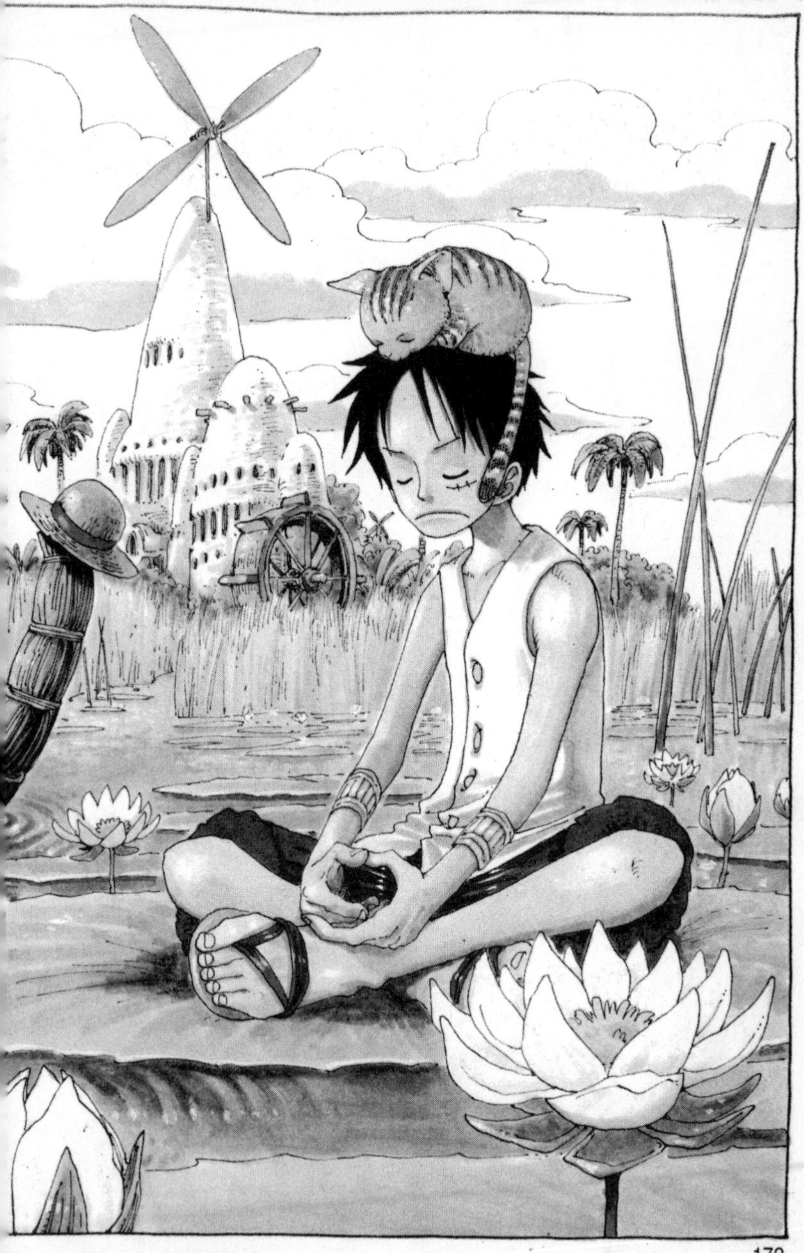

Chapter 246: SATORI, VASSAL

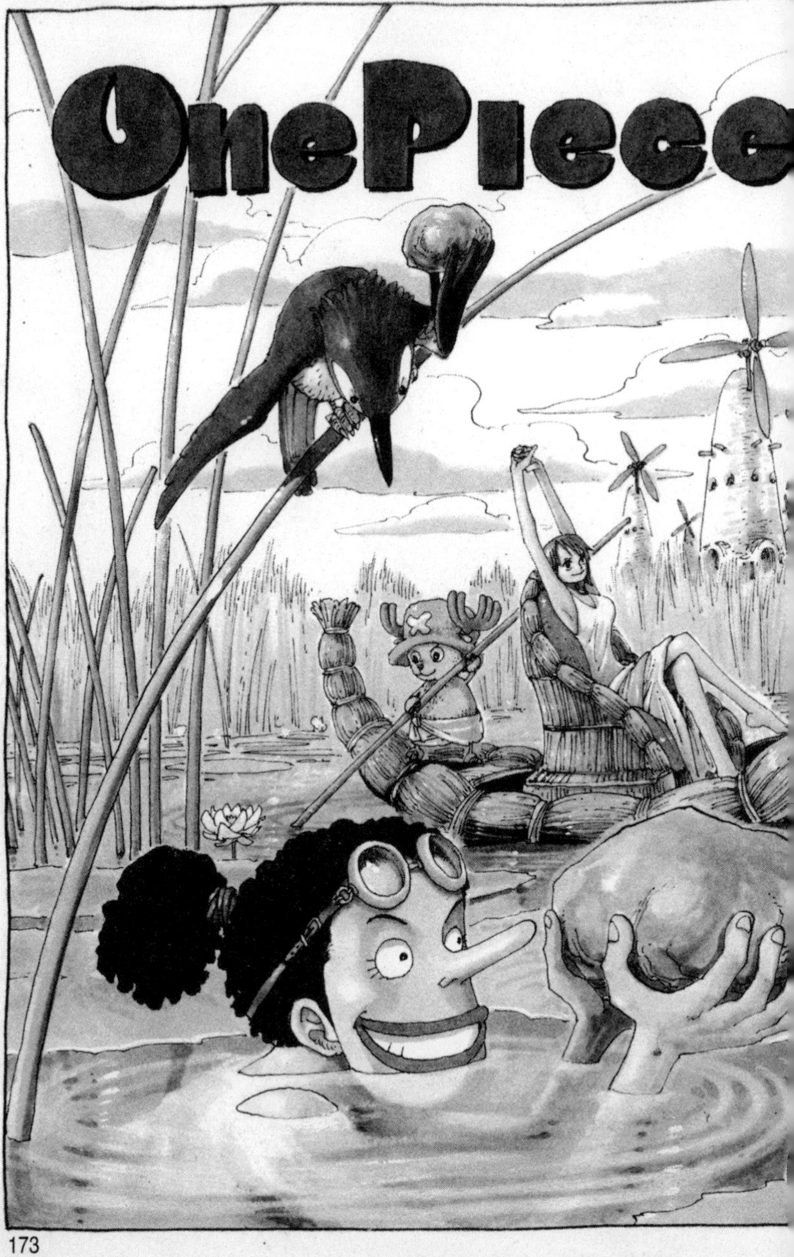
One Piece

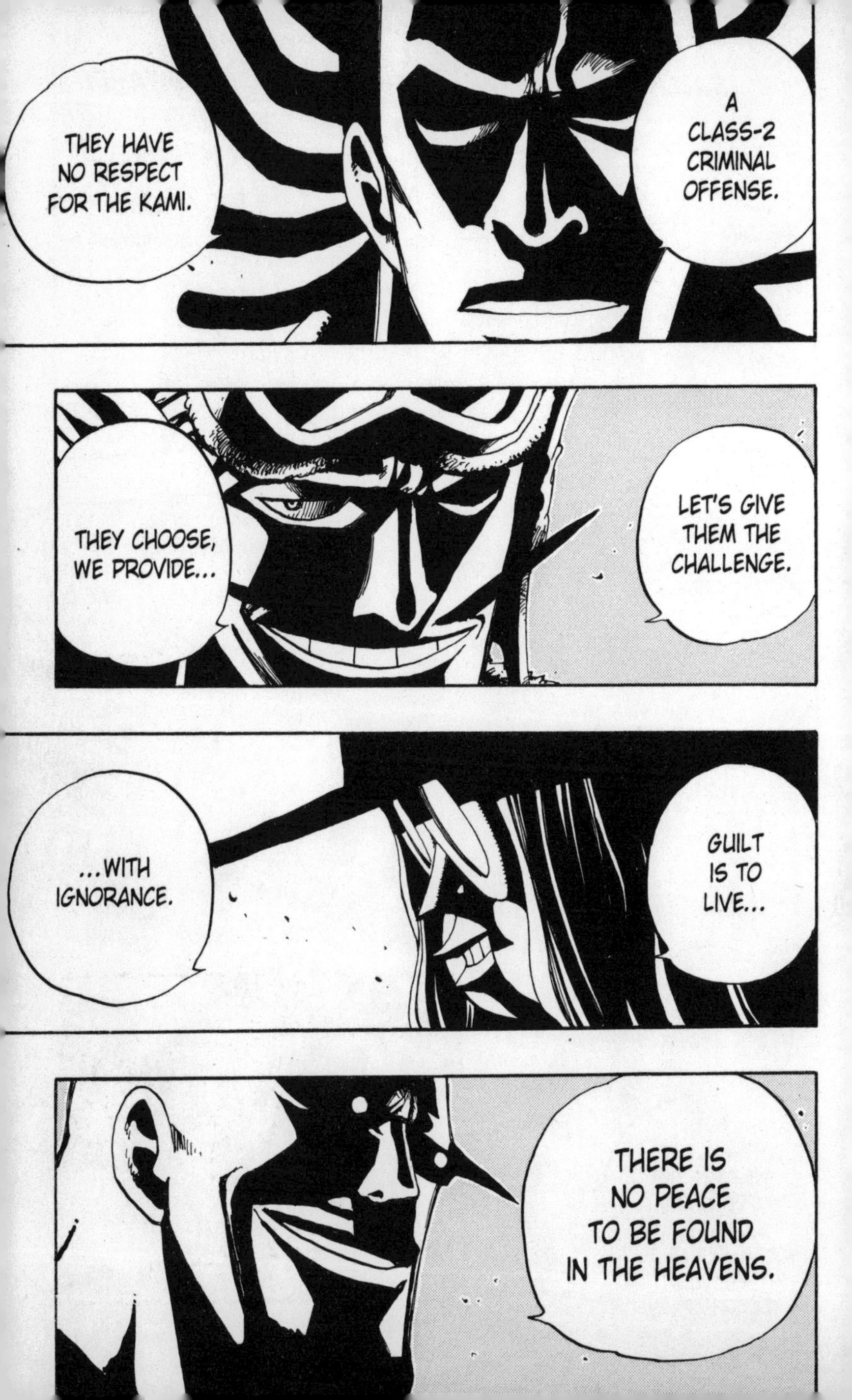
A CLASS-2 CRIMINAL OFFENSE.
THEY HAVE NO RESPECT FOR THE KAMI.
LET'S GIVE THEM THE CHALLENGE.
THEY CHOOSE, WE PROVIDE...
GUILT IS TO LIVE...
...WITH IGNORANCE.
THERE IS NO PEACE TO BE FOUND IN THE HEAVENS.

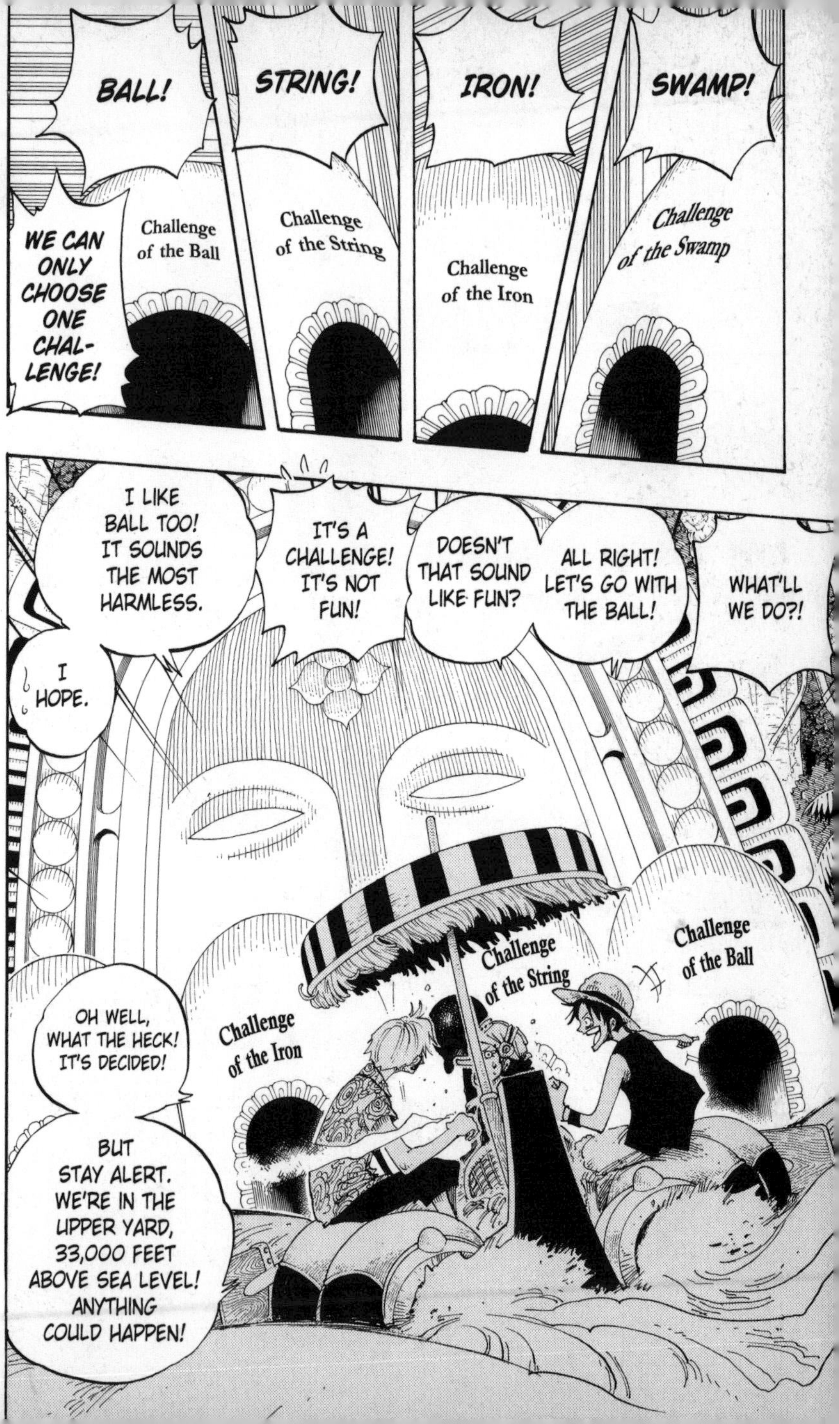
SWAMP!
Challenge of the Swamp
IRON!
Challenge of the Iron
STRING!
Challenge of the String
BALL!
Challenge of the Ball
WE CAN ONLY CHOOSE ONE CHALLENGE!
WHAT'LL WE DO?!
ALL RIGHT! LET'S GO WITH THE BALL!
DOESN'T THAT SOUND LIKE FUN?
IT'S A CHALLENGE! IT'S NOT FUN!
I LIKE BALL TOO! IT SOUNDS THE MOST HARMLESS.
I HOPE.
Challenge of the Ball
Challenge of the String
Challenge of the Iron
OH WELL, WHAT THE HECK! IT'S DECIDED!
BUT STAY ALERT. WE'RE IN THE UPPER YARD, 33,000 FEET ABOVE SEA LEVEL! ANYTHING COULD HAPPEN!

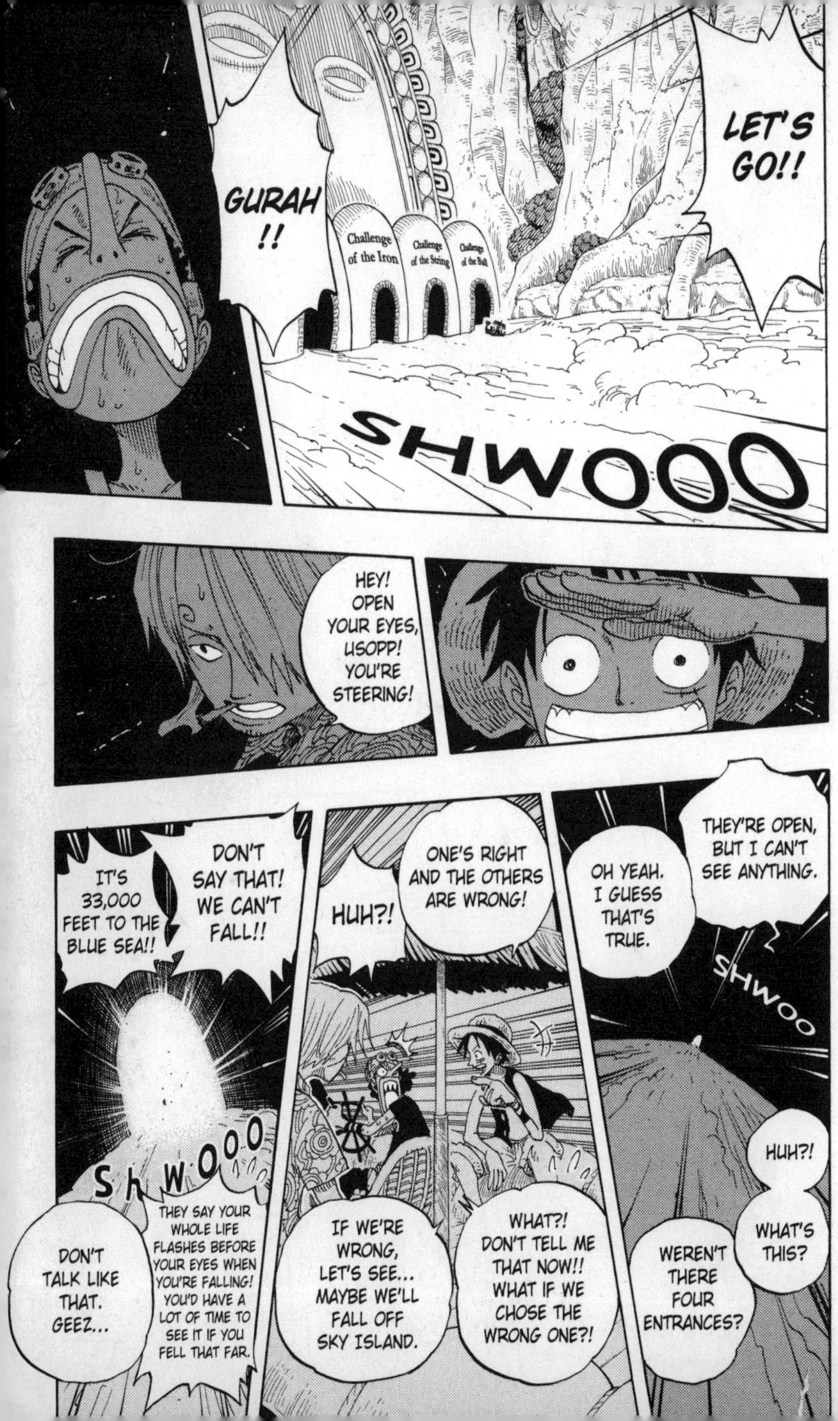
LET'S GO!!
Challenge of the Ball
Challenge of the String
Challenge of the Iron
GURAH !!
SHWOOO
HEY! OPEN YOUR EYES, USOPP! YOU'RE STEERING!
THEY'RE OPEN, BUT I CAN'T SEE ANYTHING.
OH YEAH. I GUESS THAT'S TRUE.
SHWOO
HUH?!
WHAT'S THIS?
WEREN'T THERE FOUR ENTRANCES?
ONE'S RIGHT AND THE OTHERS ARE WRONG!
HUH?!
WHAT?! DON'T TELL ME THAT NOW!! WHAT IF WE CHOSE THE WRONG ONE?!
IF WE'RE WRONG, LET'S SEE... MAYBE WE'LL FALL OFF SKY ISLAND.
DON'T SAY THAT! WE CAN'T FALL!!
IT'S 33,000 FEET TO THE BLUE SEA!!
SHWOOO
THEY SAY YOUR WHOLE LIFE FLASHES BEFORE YOUR EYES WHEN YOU'RE FALLING! YOU'D HAVE A LOT OF TIME TO SEE IT IF YOU FELL THAT FAR.
DON'T TALK LIKE THAT. GEEZ...

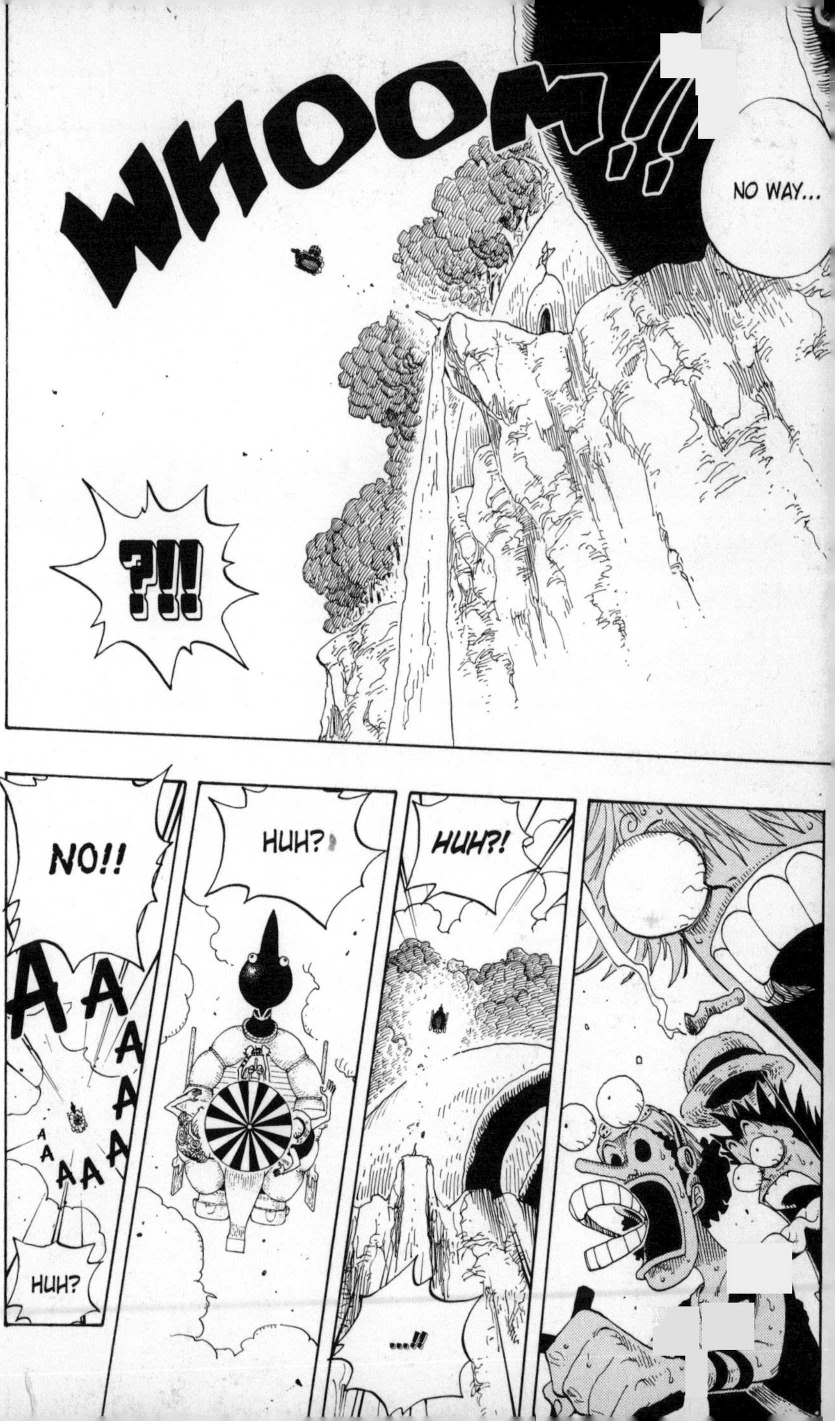

WHOOM!!
NO WAY...
?!!
HUH?!
...!!
HUH?
NO!!
AAAAAAAAAA
HUH?

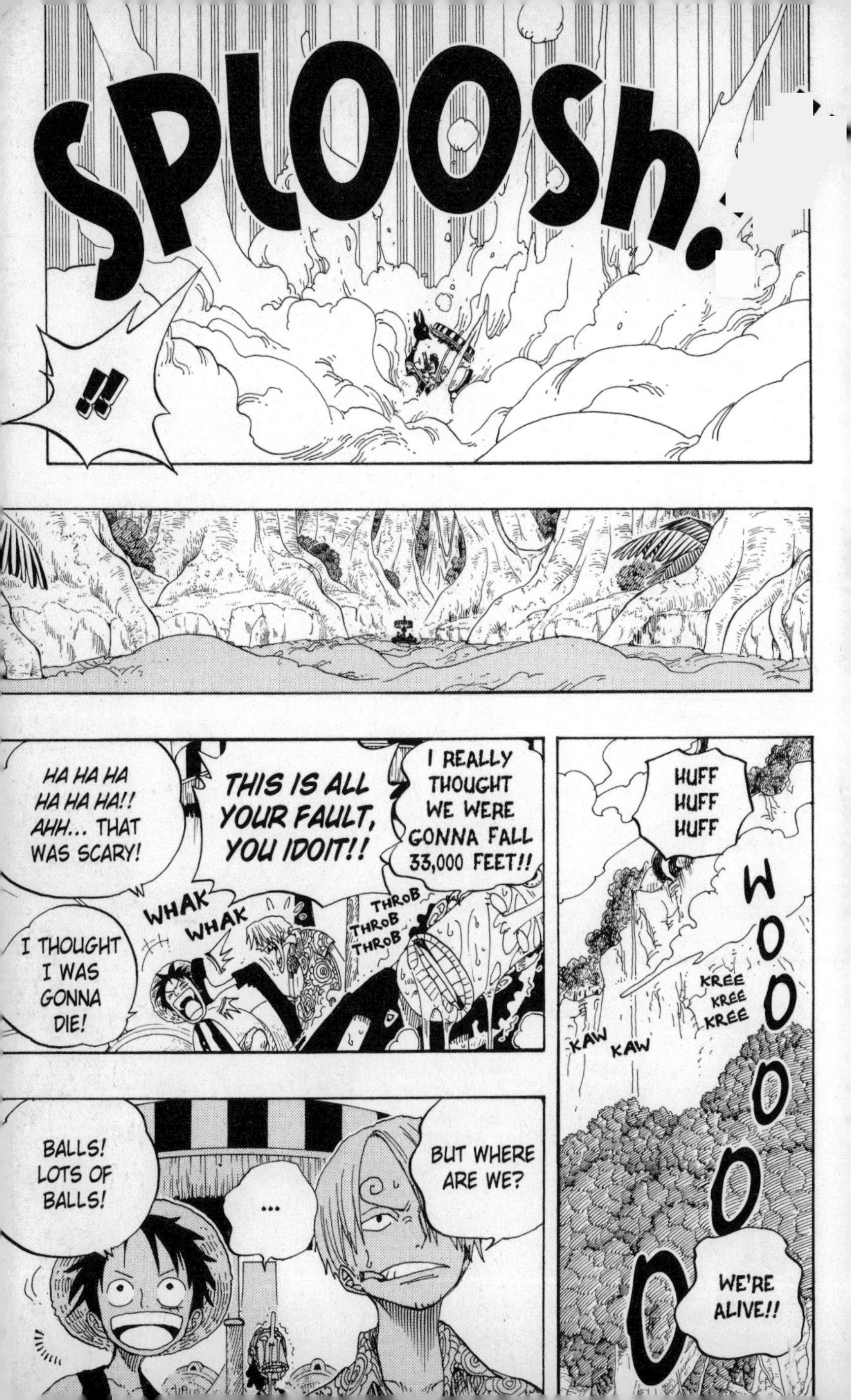
SPLOOSH!!
!!
HUFF HUFF HUFF
WOOOOOO
KREE KREE KREE
KAW KAW
WE'RE ALIVE!!
I REALLY THOUGHT WE WERE GONNA FALL 33,000 FEET!!
THIS IS ALL YOUR FAULT, YOU IDOIT!!
HA HA HA HA HA HA!! AHH... THAT WAS SCARY!
THROB THROB THROB
WHAK WHAK
I THOUGHT I WAS GONNA DIE!
BUT WHERE ARE WE?
...
BALLS! LOTS OF BALLS!

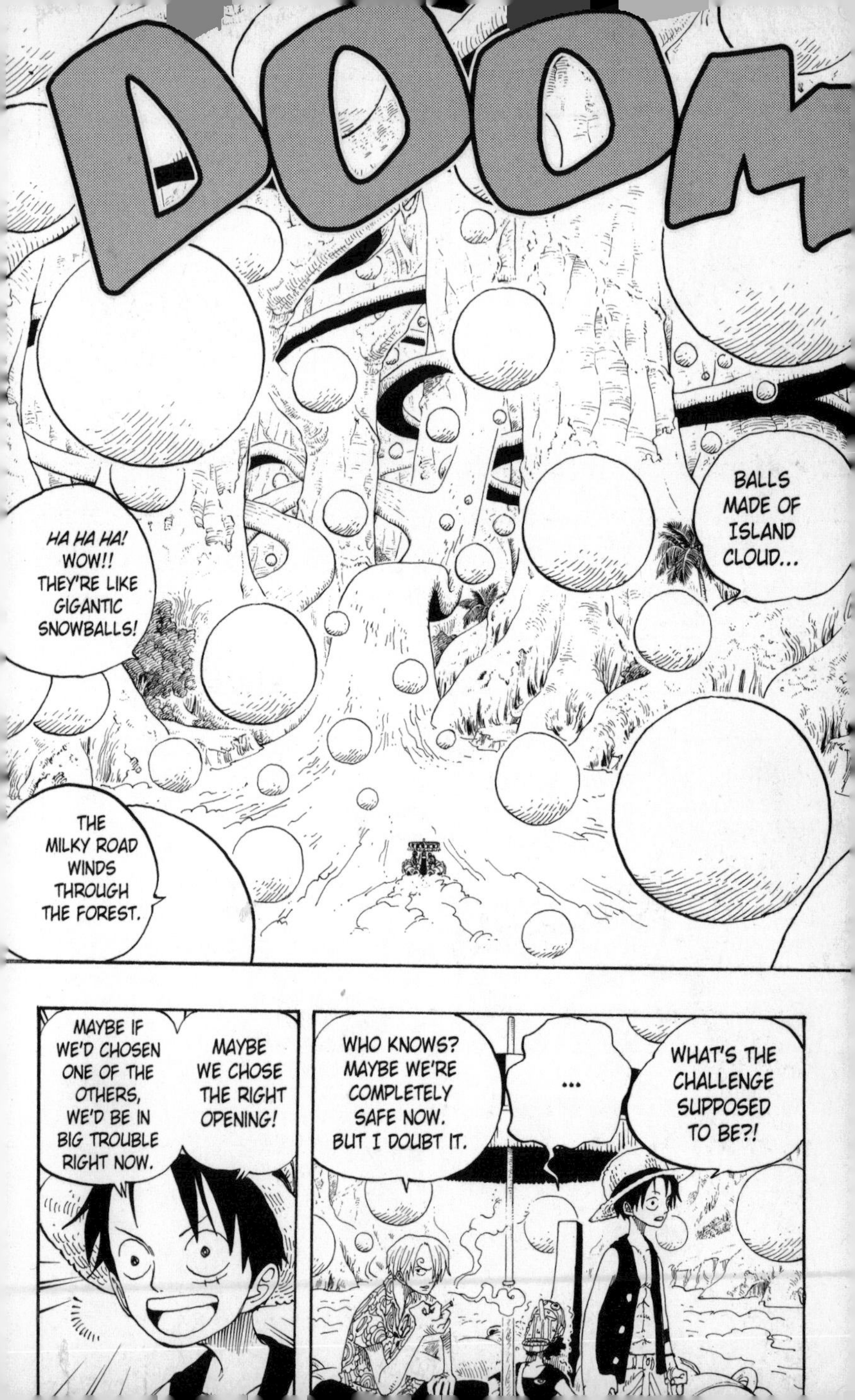
DOOM
BALLS MADE OF ISLAND CLOUD...
HA HA HA! WOW!! THEY'RE LIKE GIGANTIC SNOWBALLS!
THE MILKY ROAD WINDS THROUGH THE FOREST.
WHAT'S THE CHALLENGE SUPPOSED TO BE?!
...
WHO KNOWS? MAYBE WE'RE COMPLETELY SAFE NOW. BUT I DOUBT IT.
MAYBE WE CHOSE THE RIGHT OPENING!
MAYBE IF WE'D CHOSEN ONE OF THE OTHERS, WE'D BE IN BIG TROUBLE RIGHT NOW.

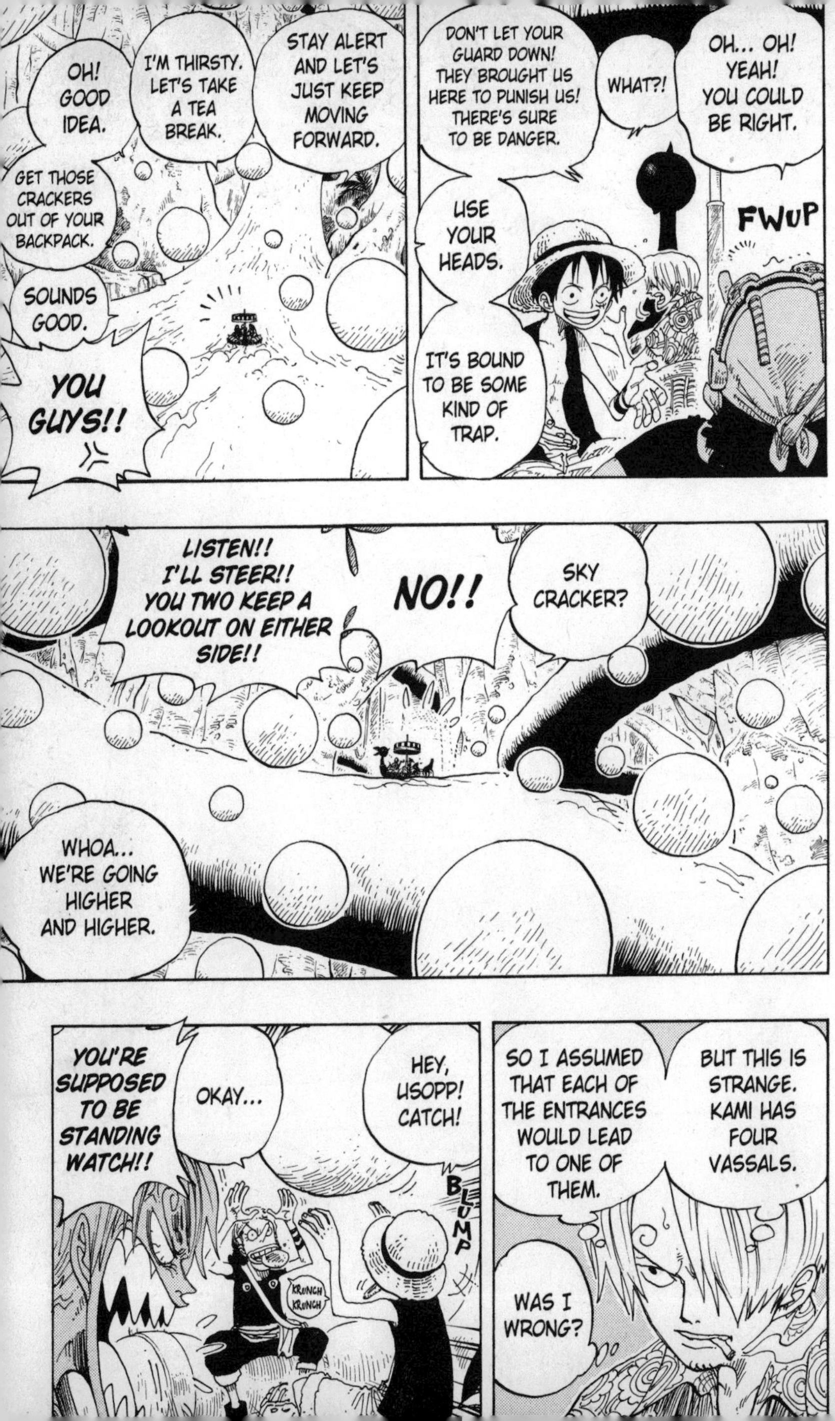
OH... OH! YEAH! YOU COULD BE RIGHT.
WHAT?!
DON'T LET YOUR GUARD DOWN! THEY BROUGHT US HERE TO PUNISH US! THERE'S SURE TO BE DANGER.
FWUP
USE YOUR HEADS.
IT'S BOUND TO BE SOME KIND OF TRAP.
STAY ALERT AND LET'S JUST KEEP MOVING FORWARD.
I'M THIRSTY. LET'S TAKE A TEA BREAK.
OH! GOOD IDEA.
GET THOSE CRACKERS OUT OF YOUR BACKPACK.
SOUNDS GOOD.
YOU GUYS!!
SKY CRACKER?
NO!!
LISTEN!! I'LL STEER!! YOU TWO KEEP A LOOKOUT ON EITHER SIDE!!
WHOA... WE'RE GOING HIGHER AND HIGHER.
BUT THIS IS STRANGE. KAMI HAS FOUR VASSALS.
SO I ASSUMED THAT EACH OF THE ENTRANCES WOULD LEAD TO ONE OF THEM.
WAS I WRONG?
HEY, USOPP! CATCH!
BLUMP
OKAY...
YOU'RE SUPPOSED TO BE STANDING WATCH!!
KRUNCH KRUNCH

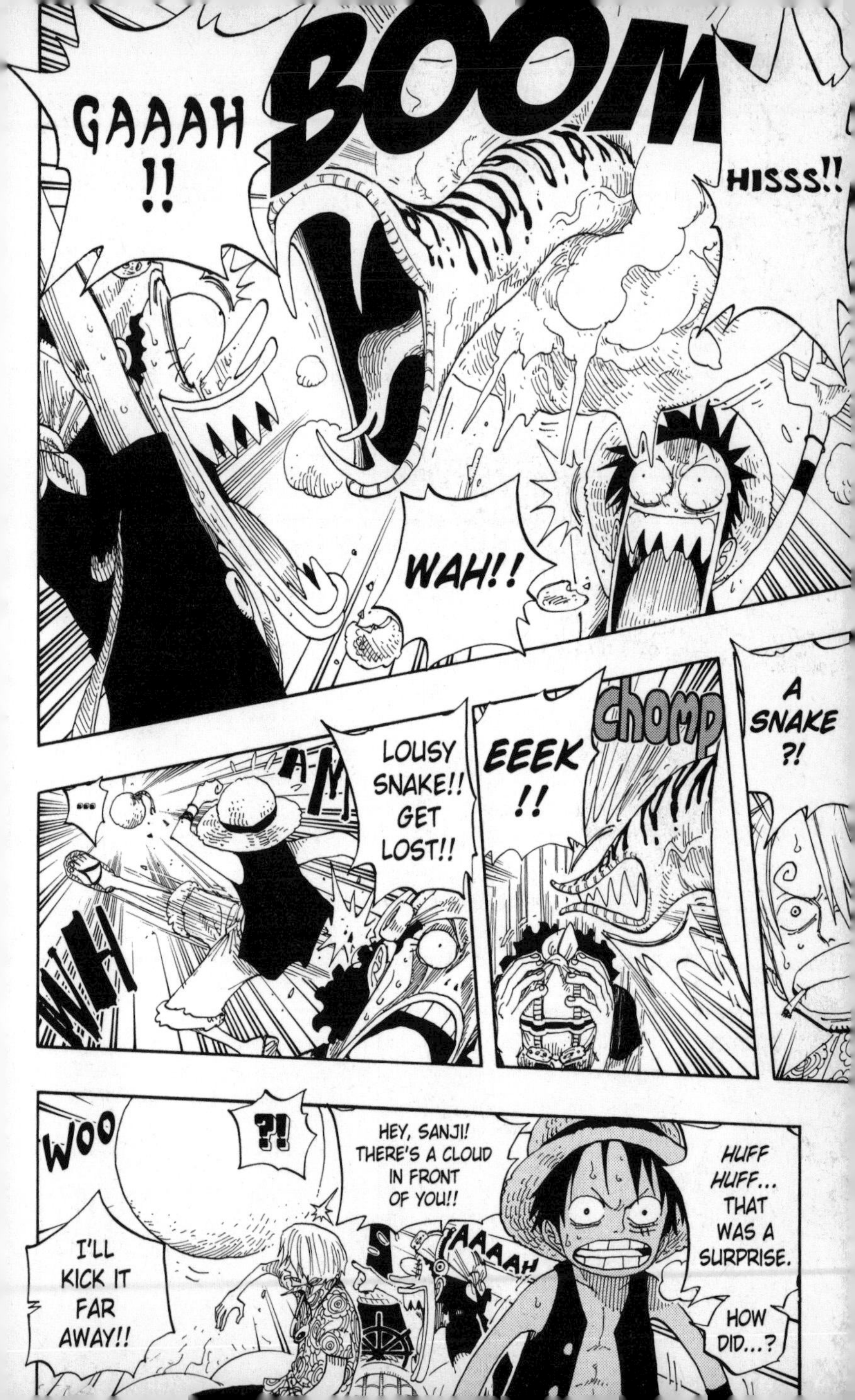
BOOM
HISSS!!
GAAAH !!
WAH!!
A SNAKE ?!
CHOMP
EEEK !!
LOUSY SNAKE!! GET LOST!!
...
HUFF HUFF... THAT WAS A SURPRISE.
HOW DID...?
HEY, SANJI! THERE'S A CLOUD IN FRONT OF YOU!!
?!
AAAAAH
WOO
I'LL KICK IT FAR AWAY!!

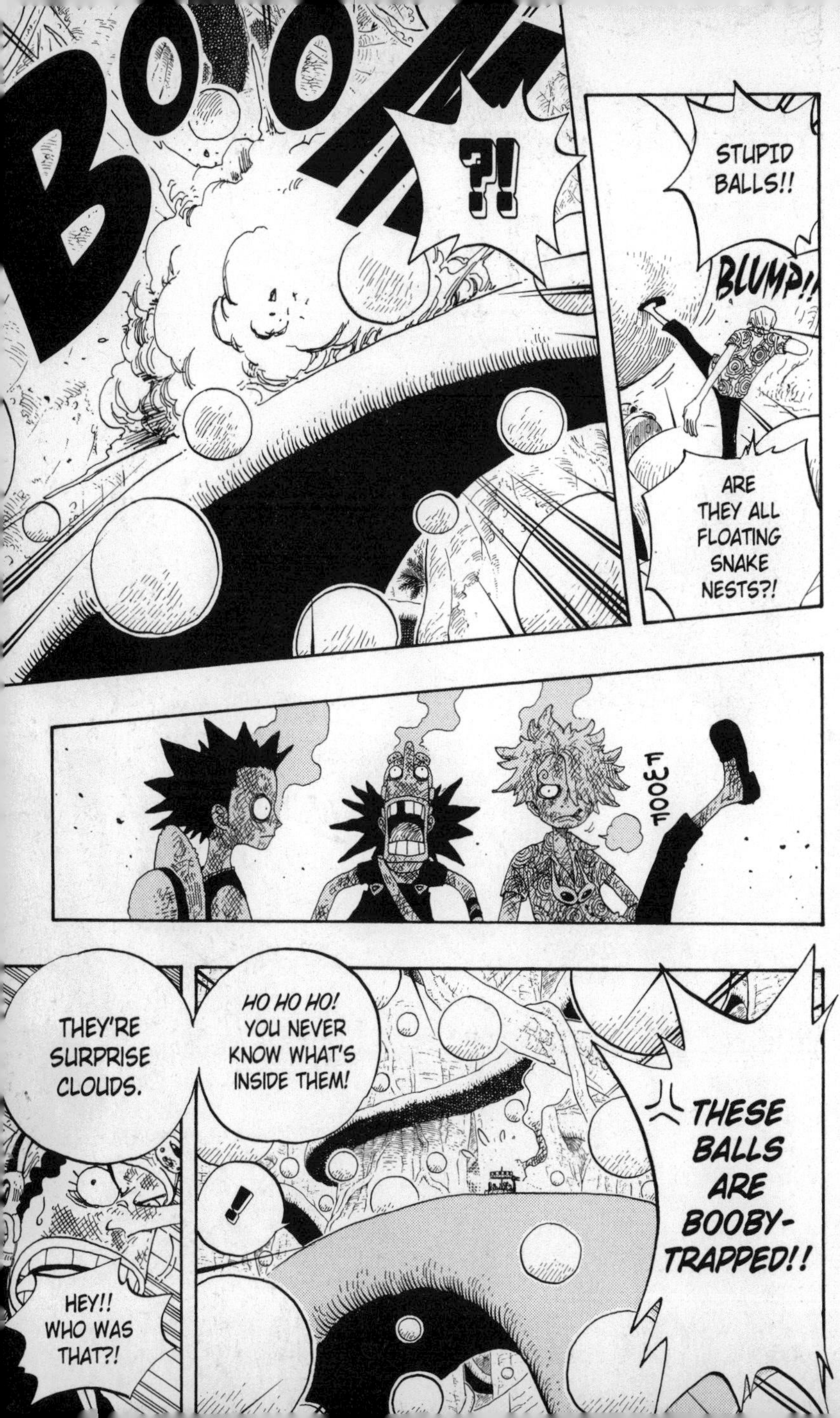
STUPID BALLS!!
BLUMP!!
ARE THEY ALL FLOATING SNAKE NESTS?!
BOOM
?!
FWOOF
THESE BALLS ARE BOOBY-TRAPPED!!
!
HO HO HO! YOU NEVER KNOW WHAT'S INSIDE THEM!
THEY'RE SURPRISE CLOUDS.
HEY!! WHO WAS THAT?!

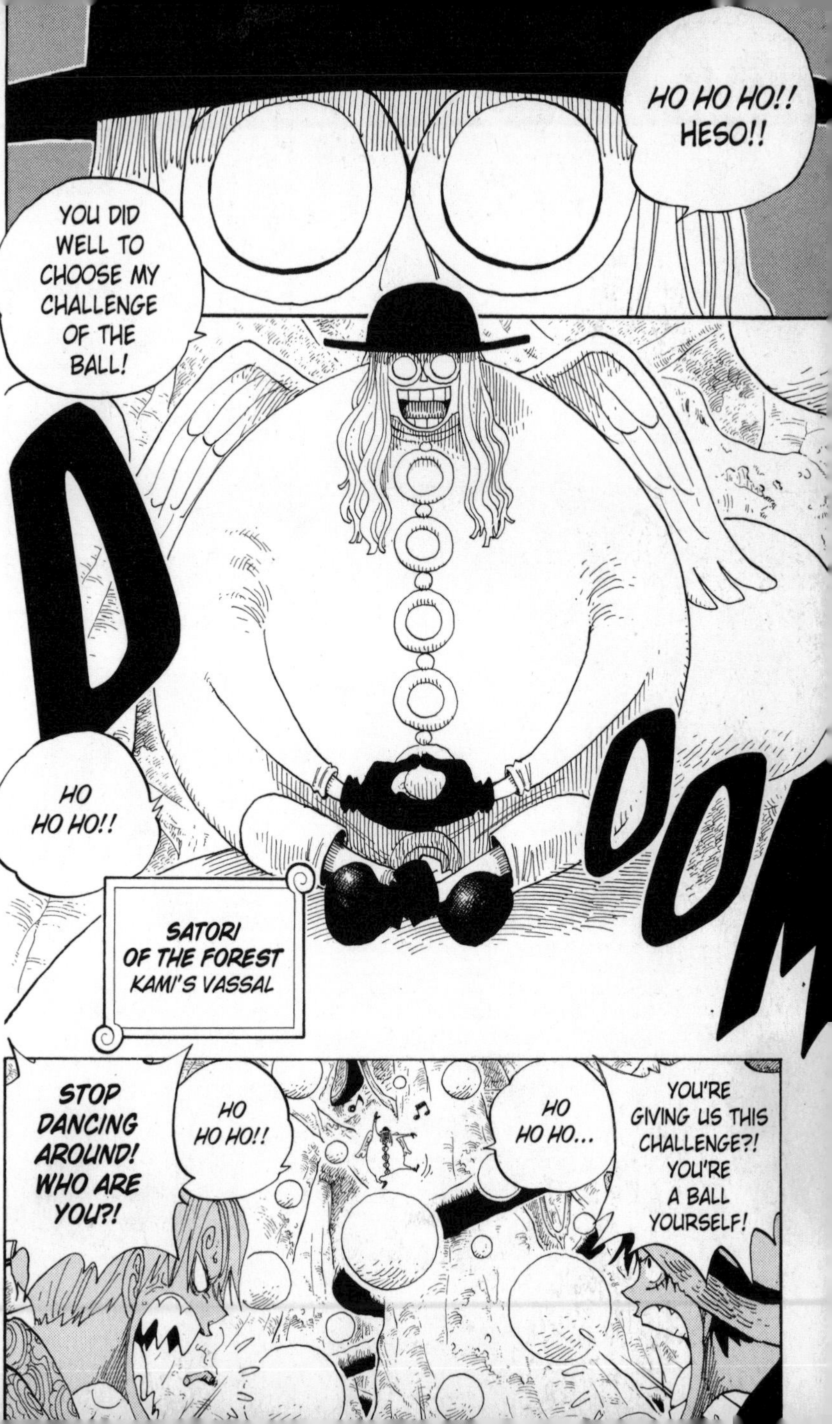
HO HO HO!! HESO!!
YOU DID WELL TO CHOOSE MY CHALLENGE OF THE BALL!
DOOM
HO HO HO!!
SATORI OF THE FOREST KAMI'S VASSAL
YOU'RE GIVING US THIS CHALLENGE?! YOU'RE A BALL YOURSELF!
HO HO HO...
HO HO HO!!
STOP DANCING AROUND! WHO ARE YOU?!

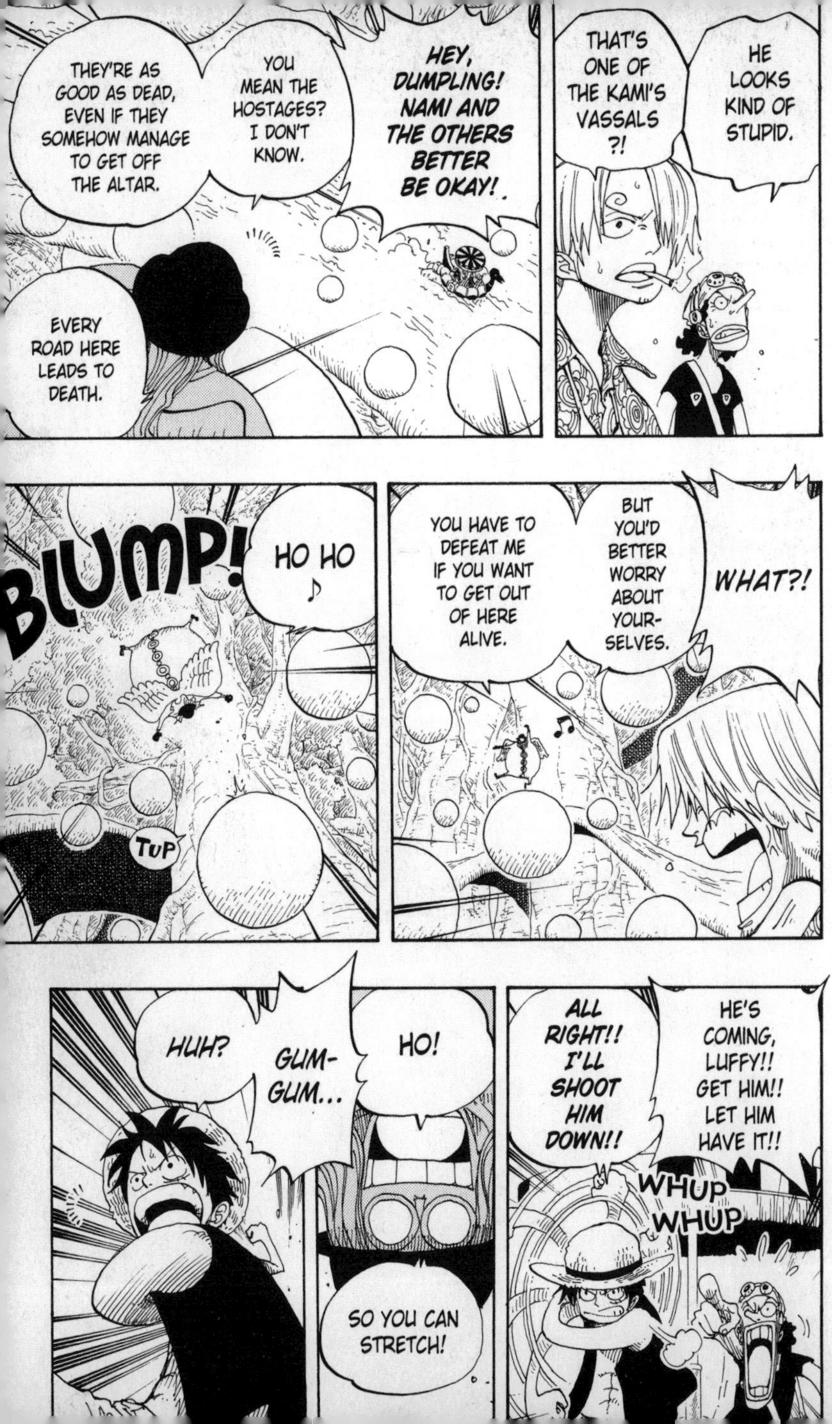
HE LOOKS KIND OF STUPID.
THAT'S ONE OF THE KAMI'S VASSALS?!
HEY, DUMPLING! NAMI AND THE OTHERS BETTER BE OKAY!
YOU MEAN THE HOSTAGES? I DON'T KNOW.
THEY'RE AS GOOD AS DEAD, EVEN IF THEY SOMEHOW MANAGE TO GET OFF THE ALTAR.
EVERY ROAD HERE LEADS TO DEATH.
WHAT?!
BUT YOU'D BETTER WORRY ABOUT YOURSELVES.
YOU HAVE TO DEFEAT ME IF YOU WANT TO GET OUT OF HERE ALIVE.
HO HO ♪
BLUMP!
TUP
HE'S COMING, LUFFY!! GET HIM!! LET HIM HAVE IT!!
ALL RIGHT!! I'LL SHOOT HIM DOWN!!
WHUP WHUP
HO!
SO YOU CAN STRETCH!
GUM-GUM...
HUH?

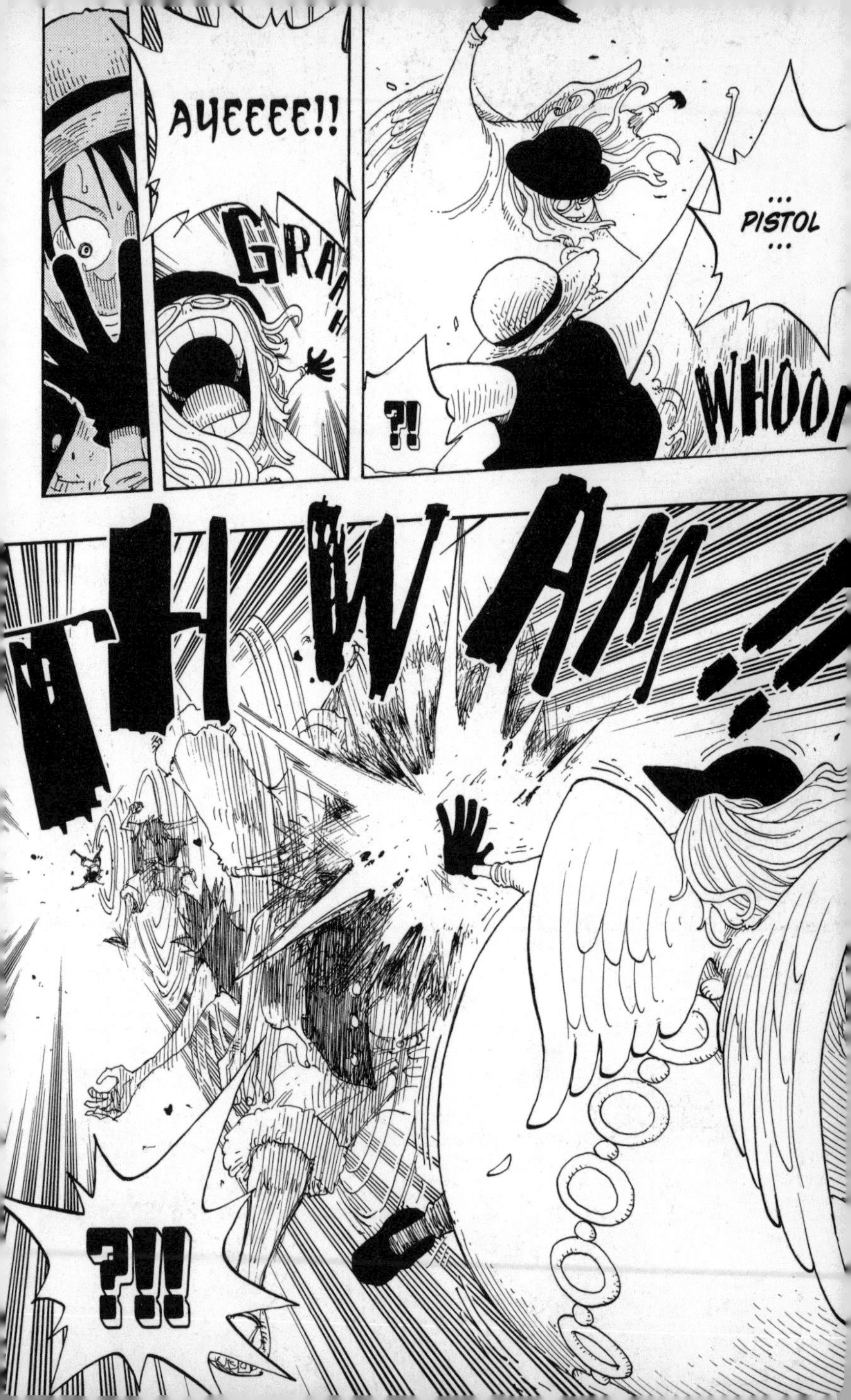

... PISTOL ...
WHOO
?!
AYEEEE!!
GRAAH
THWAM!!
?!!

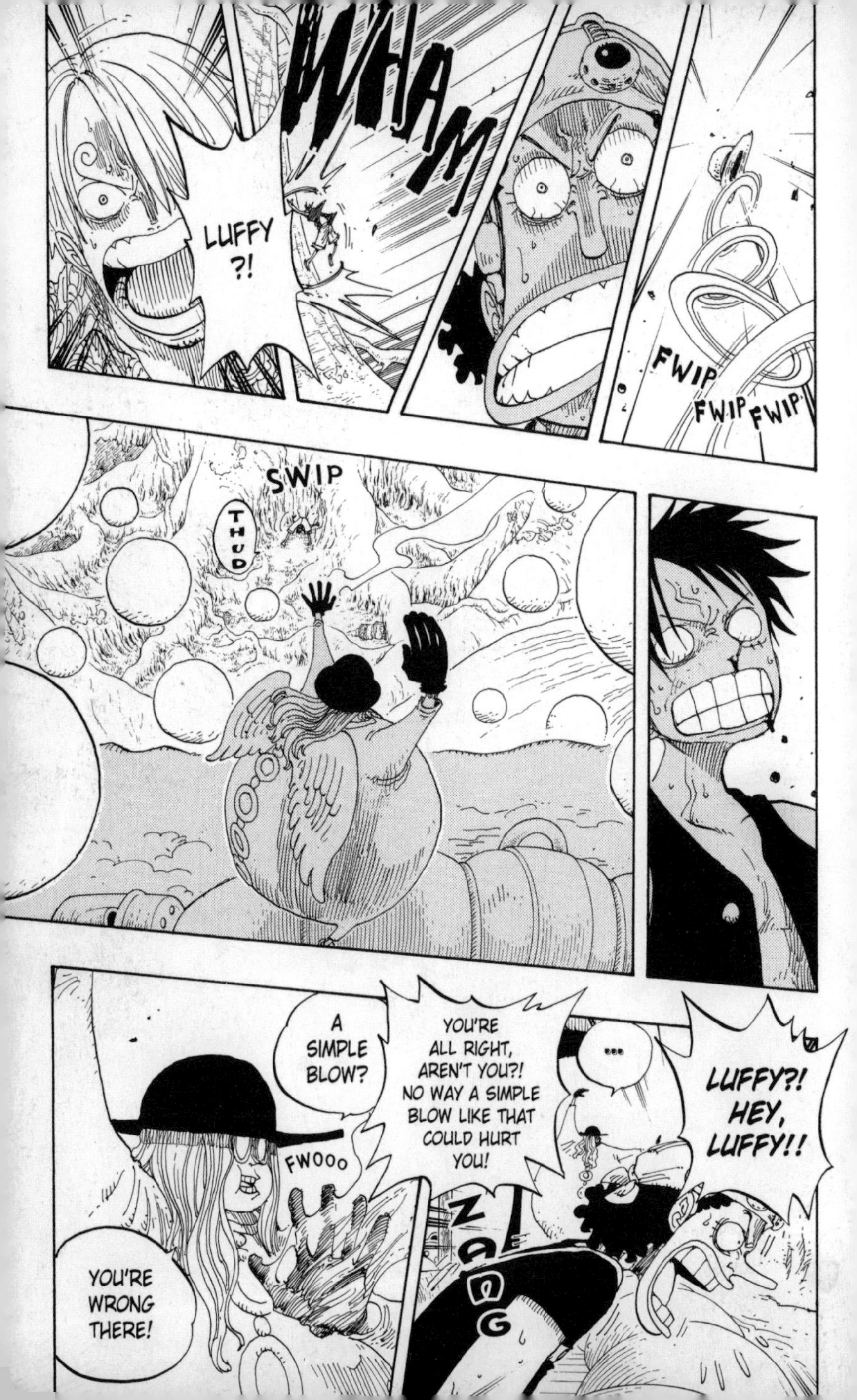
FWIP
FWIP
FWIP
WHAM
LUFFY ?!
SWIP
THUD
LUFFY?! HEY, LUFFY!!
...
YOU'RE ALL RIGHT, AREN'T YOU?! NO WAY A SIMPLE BLOW LIKE THAT COULD HURT YOU!
A SIMPLE BLOW?
ZING
FWOOO
YOU'RE WRONG THERE!

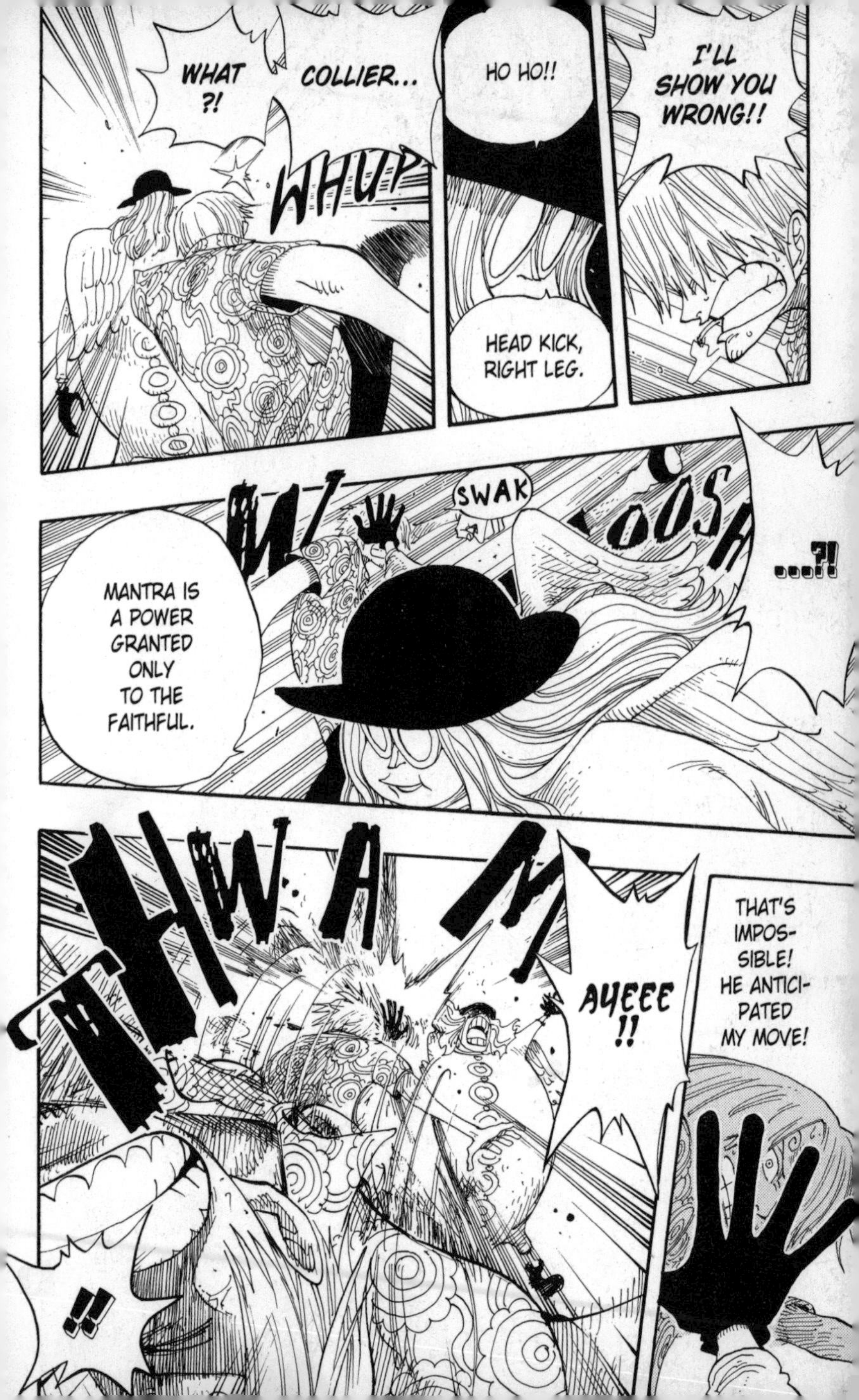
I'LL SHOW YOU WRONG!!
HO HO!!
HEAD KICK, RIGHT LEG.
COLLIER...
WHAT ?!
WHUP
...?!
WOOSH
SWAK
MANTRA IS A POWER GRANTED ONLY TO THE FAITHFUL.
THAT'S IMPOS-SIBLE! HE ANTICI-PATED MY MOVE!
AYEEE !!
THWAM
!!

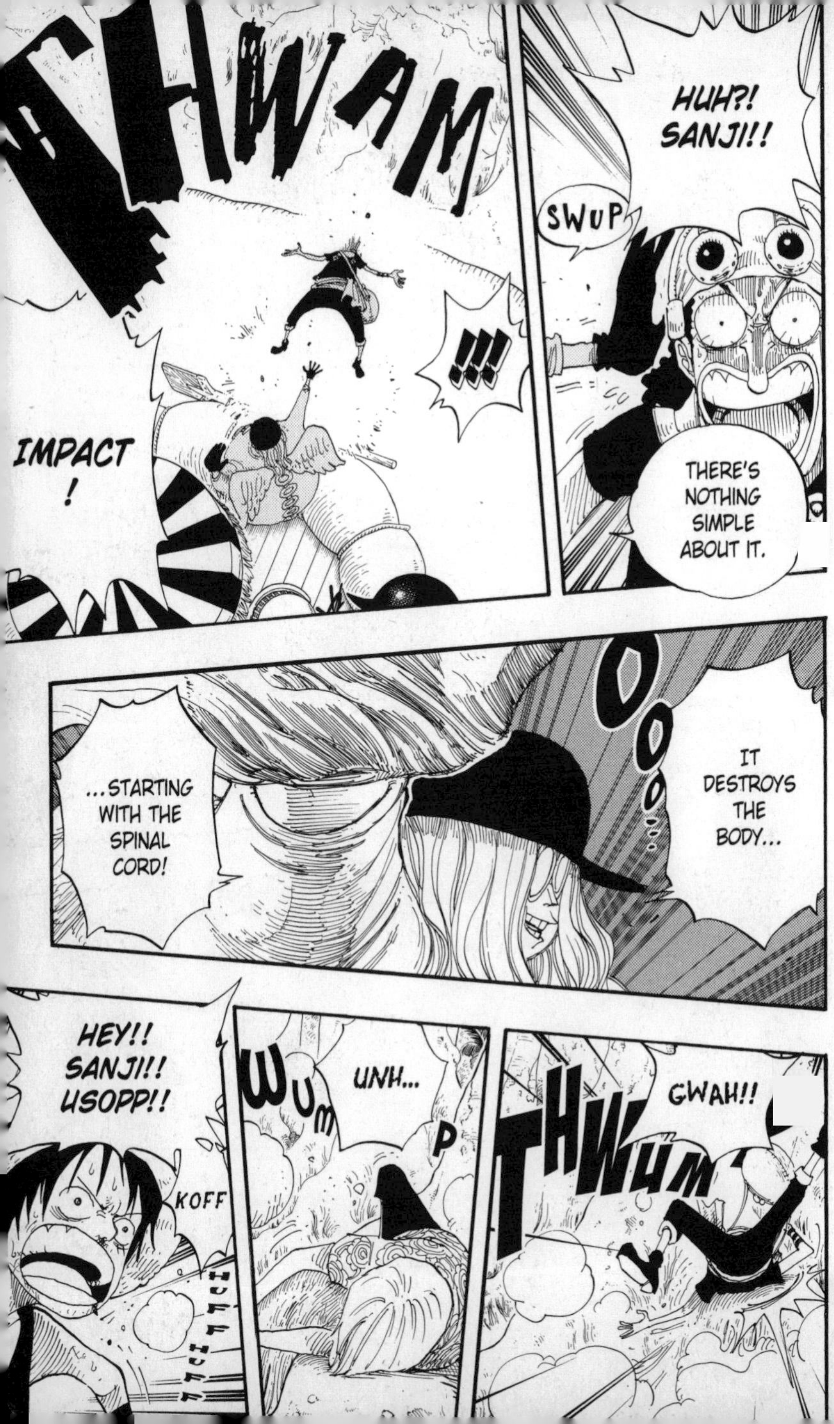
HUH?! SANJI!!
SWUP
THERE'S NOTHING SIMPLE ABOUT IT.
THWAM
!!!
IMPACT!
IT DESTROYS THE BODY...
...STARTING WITH THE SPINAL CORD!
GWAH!!
THWUMP
UNH...
WUMP
HEY!! SANJI!! USOPP!!
KOFF
HUFF HUFF

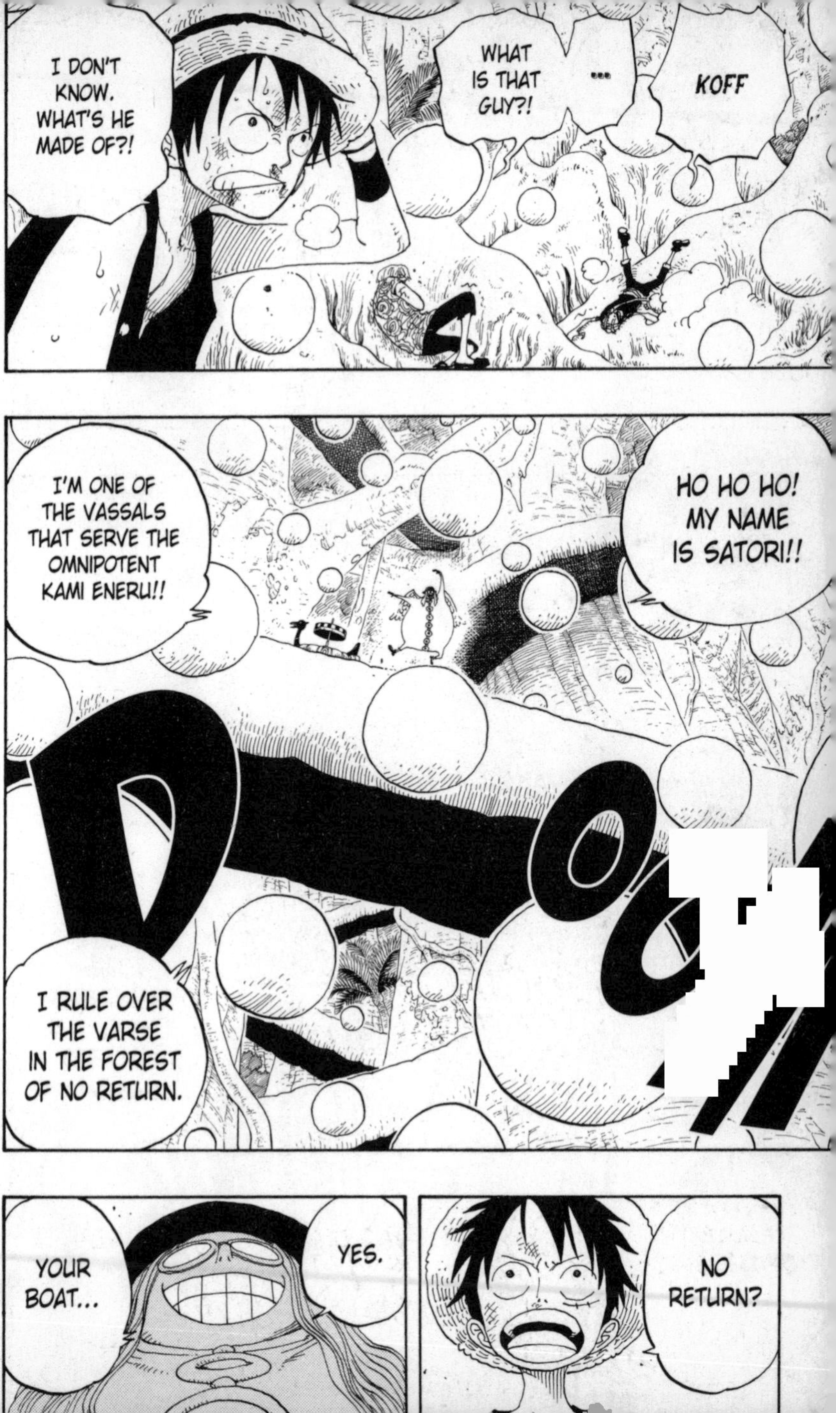
KOFF
...
WHAT IS THAT GUY?!
I DON'T KNOW. WHAT'S HE MADE OF?!
HO HO HO! MY NAME IS SATORI!!
I'M ONE OF THE VASSALS THAT SERVE THE OMNIPOTENT KAMI ENERU!!
I RULE OVER THE VARSE IN THE FOREST OF NO RETURN.
NO RETURN?
YES.
YOUR BOAT...

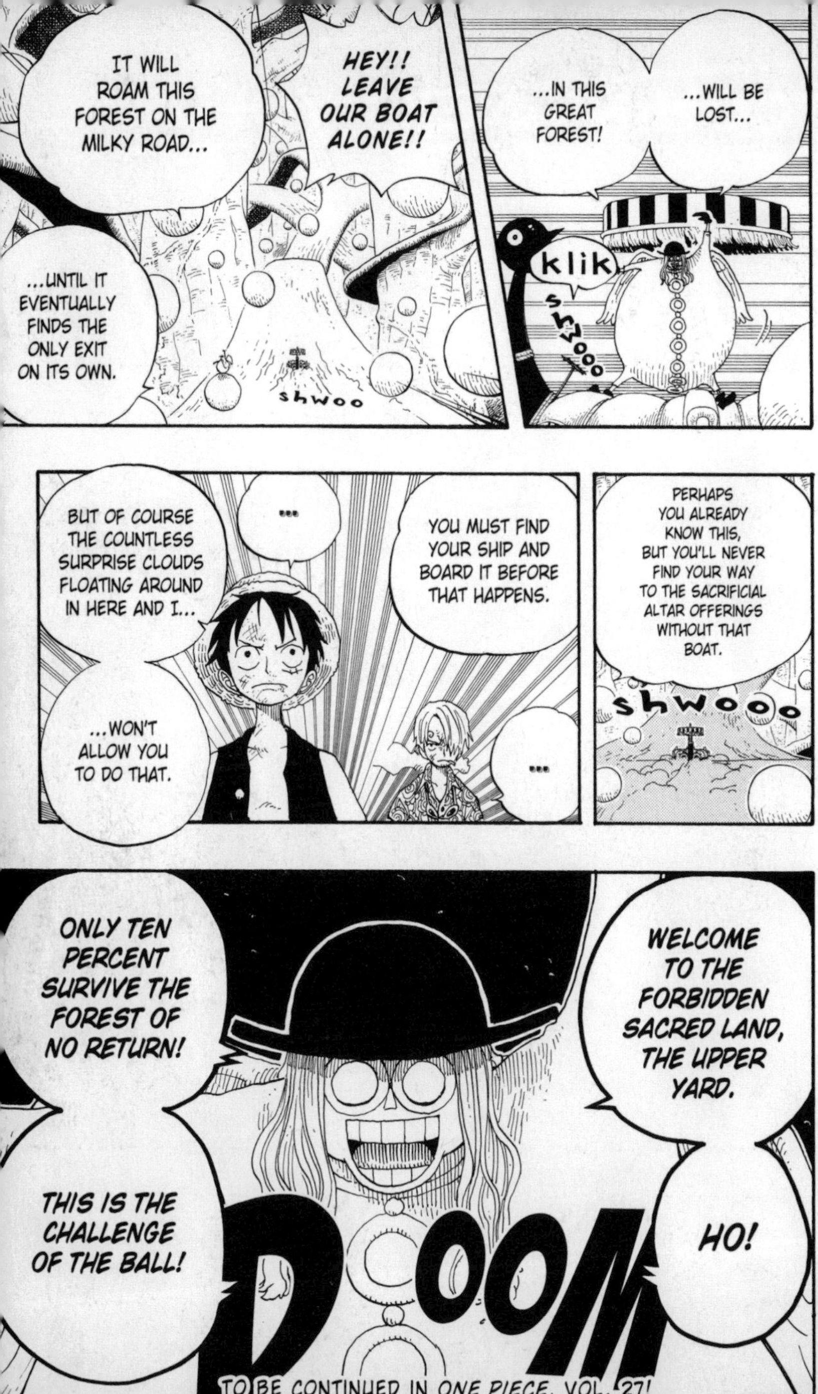
...WILL BE LOST...
...IN THIS GREAT FOREST!
klik
shwooo
HEY!! LEAVE OUR BOAT ALONE!!
IT WILL ROAM THIS FOREST ON THE MILKY ROAD...
...UNTIL IT EVENTUALLY FINDS THE ONLY EXIT ON ITS OWN.
shwoo
PERHAPS YOU ALREADY KNOW THIS, BUT YOU'LL NEVER FIND YOUR WAY TO THE SACRIFICIAL ALTAR OFFERINGS WITHOUT THAT BOAT.
shwooo
YOU MUST FIND YOUR SHIP AND BOARD IT BEFORE THAT HAPPENS.
...
...
BUT OF COURSE THE COUNTLESS SURPRISE CLOUDS FLOATING AROUND IN HERE AND I...
...WON'T ALLOW YOU TO DO THAT.
WELCOME TO THE FORBIDDEN SACRED LAND, THE UPPER YARD.
HO!
ONLY TEN PERCENT SURVIVE THE FOREST OF NO RETURN!
THIS IS THE CHALLENGE OF THE BALL!
DOOM

TO BE CONTINUED IN ONE PIECE, VOL. 27!

COMING NEXT VOLUME:

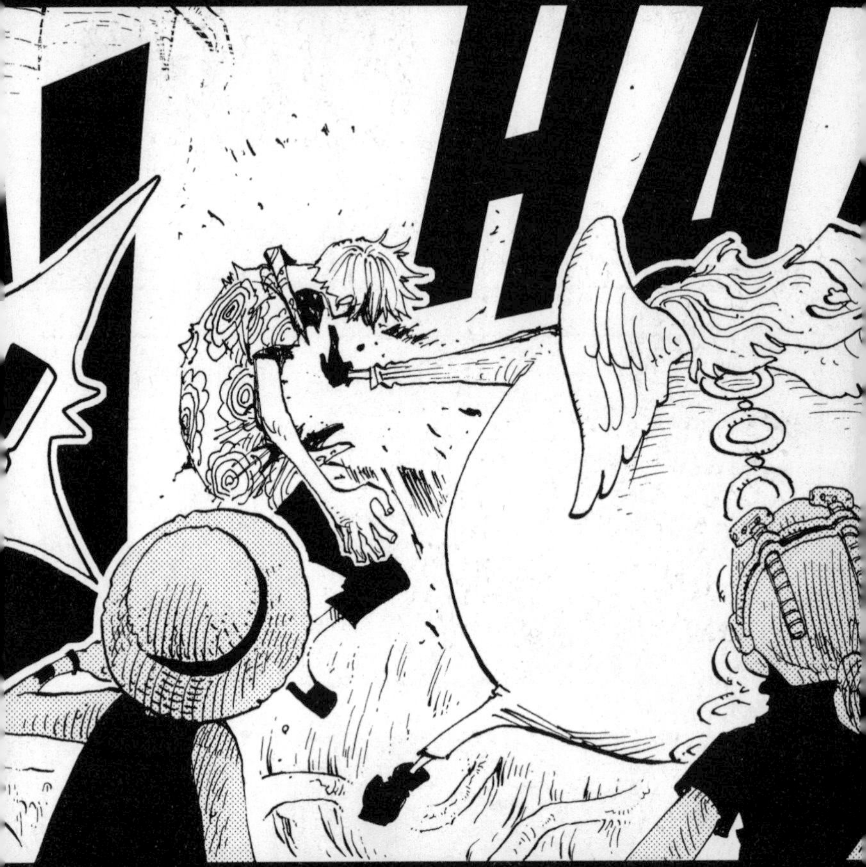

The Straw Hats have been branded criminals for entering Skypiea without paying the toll! Their only chance for a way out is a series of challenges given to them by the Kami's vassals. Meanwhile, Nami makes an important discovery about the island. Is there treasure hidden on Skypiea?!

ON SALE NOW!

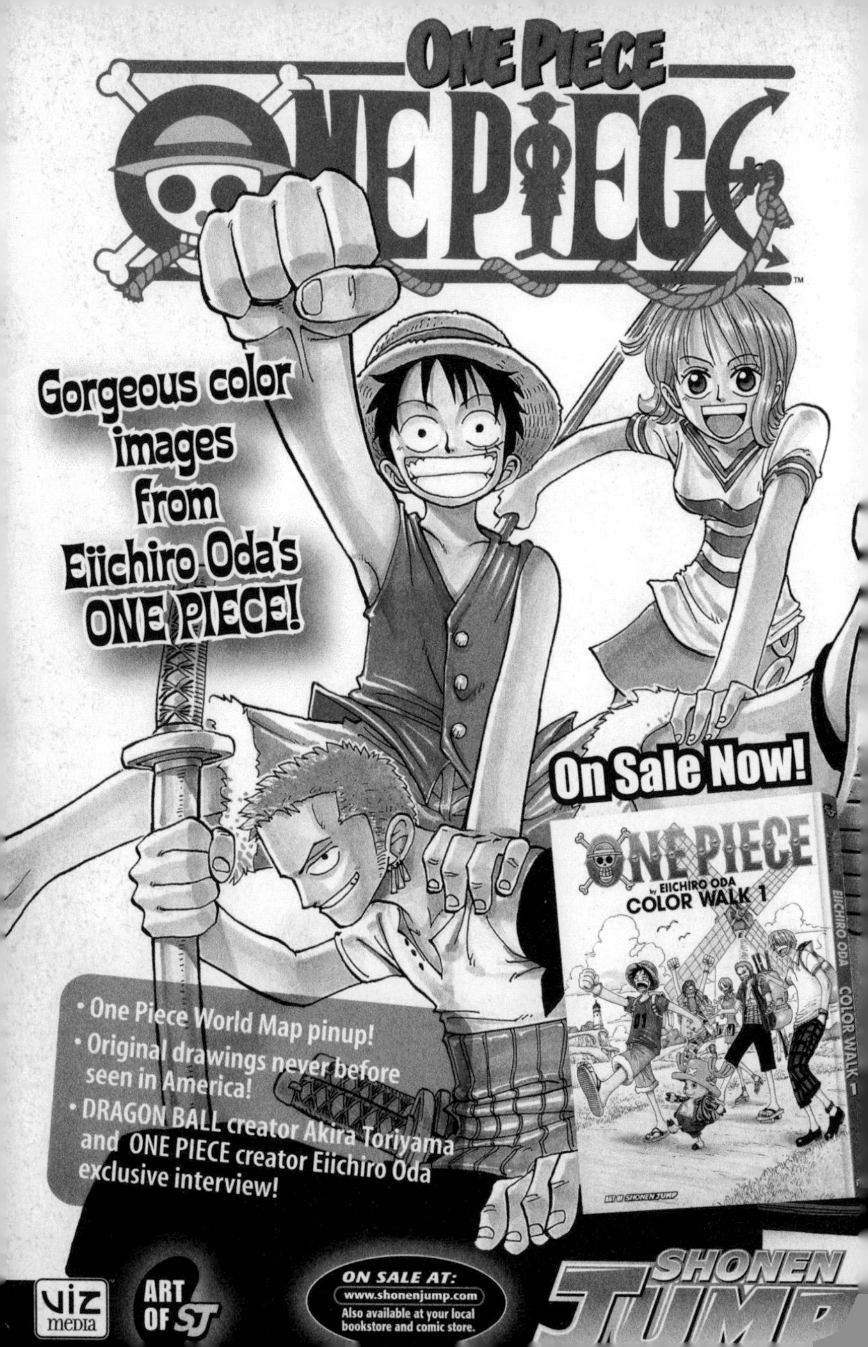

ONE PIECE
ONE PIECE
Gorgeous color images from Eiichiro Oda's ONE PIECE!
On Sale Now!
ONE PIECE
by EIICHIRO ODA
COLOR WALK 1
EIICHIRO ODA
COLOR WALK 1
• One Piece World Map pinup!
• Original drawings never before seen in America!
• DRAGON BALL creator Akira Toriyama and ONE PIECE creator Eiichiro Oda exclusive interview!
viz media
ART OF SJ
ON SALE AT:
www.shonenjump.com
Also available at your local bookstore and comic store.
SHONEN JUMP

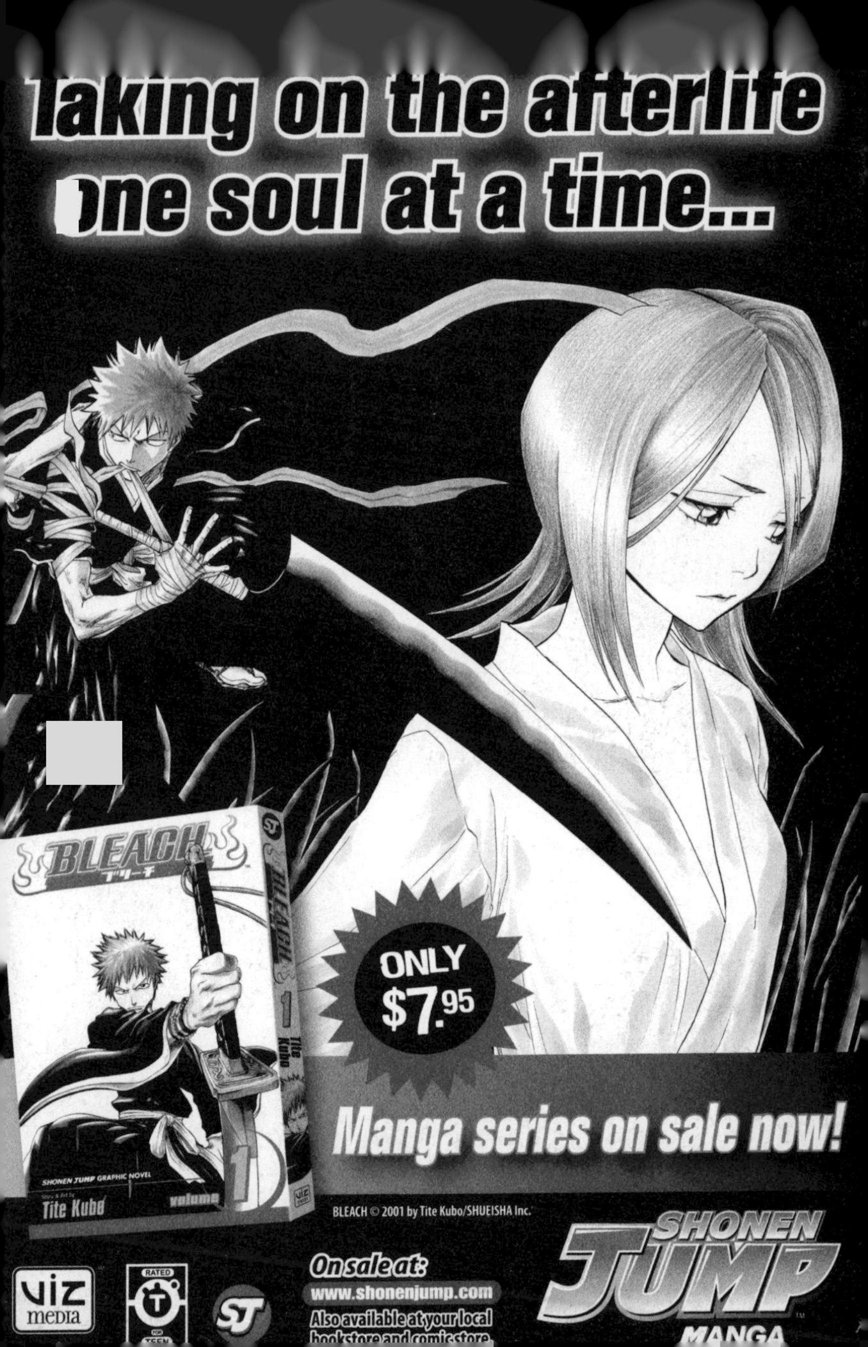
Taking on the afterlife one soul at a time...
BLEACH
ブリーチ
SHONEN JUMP GRAPHIC NOVEL
Tite Kubo
volume 1
ONLY $7.95
Manga series on sale now!
BLEACH © 2001 by Tite Kubo/SHUEISHA Inc.
On sale at:
www.shonenjump.com
Also available at your local bookstore and comic store.
viz media
RATED T FOR TEEN
SJ
SHONEN JUMP MANGA

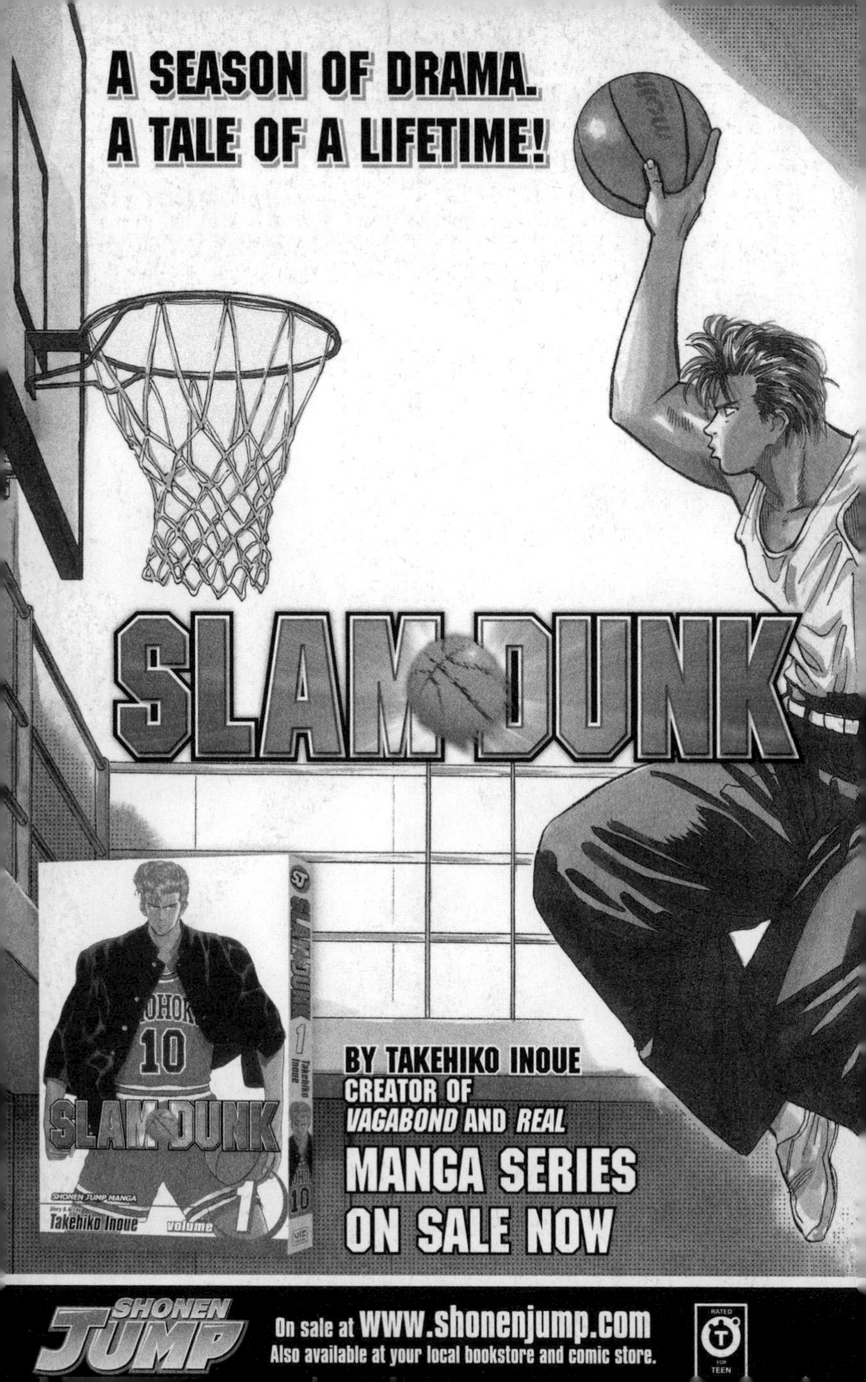
A SEASON OF DRAMA.
A TALE OF A LIFETIME!
SLAM DUNK
SLAM DUNK
SHONEN JUMP MANGA
Takehiko Inoue
volume 1
BY TAKEHIKO INOUE
CREATOR OF
VAGABOND AND REAL
MANGA SERIES
ON SALE NOW
SHONEN JUMP
On sale at WWW.shonenjump.com
Also available at your local bookstore and comic store.
RATED T FOR TEEN